1991

For Re-
Conte, enjoy our
friendship

Vicky

*Diana's Hunt*
*Caccia di Diana*

University of Pennsylvania Press
MIDDLE AGES SERIES
*Edited by Edward Peters*
Henry Charles Lea Professor
of Medieval History
University of Pennsylvania


A complete listing of the books in this series
appears at the back of this volume

# *DIANA'S HUNT*
# *CACCIA DI DIANA*
## Boccaccio's First Fiction

Edited and Translated by
ANTHONY K. CASSELL and
VICTORIA KIRKHAM

*upp*

UNIVERSITY OF PENNSYLVANIA PRESS
*Philadelphia*

Permission to reprint portions of Victoria Kirkham's article "Numerology and Allegory in Boccaccio's *Caccia di Diana*," which appeared in *Traditio* 34 (1978): 303–329, is granted by Fordham University Press, Copyright © 1978 by Fordham University.

Copyright © 1991 by the University of Pennsylvania Press
All rights reserved
Printed in the United States of America

Library of Congress Cataloging-in-Publication Data

Boccaccio, Giovanni, 1313–1375.
  [Caccia di Diana. English]
  Diana's hunt: Caccia di Diana: Boccaccio's first fiction /
edited and translated by Anthony K. Cassell and Victoria Kirkham.
    p.   cm. — (Middle Ages series)
  Translation of: Caccia di Diana.
  Includes bibliographical references and index.
  ISBN 0-8122-8219-1
  1. Boccaccio, Giovanni, 1313–1375. Caccia di Diana.  I. Cassell, Anthony K. (Anthony Kimber), 1941– .  II. Kirkham, Victoria. III. Title.  IV. Series.
PQ4275.C3E5  1991
853'.1—dc20                                             90-45815
                                                                CIP

*To our families*

# CONTENTS

Illustrations ix
Editors' Preface xi
Acknowledgments xiii
Abbreviations xv

Introduction 1
  1  The Background 3
  2  Poetic Structure 22
  3  The Allegorical Stag 39
  Notes to the Introduction 69

*Caccia di Diana. Diana's Hunt* 97
  Commentary to the Poem 152
  Glossary of the Huntresses 196
  Appendix: *Ternario* and *Ballata* with English Translation 220

Bibliography of Works Consulted 229
Index 247

# ILLUSTRATIONS

1. Stags consuming snakes. Pseudo-Oppian, *Cynegetica,* Greek, ca. A.D. 200. Venice, Biblioteca Nazionale Marciana, MS. Gr. Z. 479, fol. 27 v.   41

2. Stag nosing serpent from a crack in the earth. Latin *Physiologus,* Rheims, ninth century. Bern, Burgerbibliothek, MS. 318, fol. 17 r.   42

3. Triumph of the Cross. San Clemente, Rome. Apse mosaic, twelfth century.   45

4. Triumph of the Cross. San Clemente, Rome. Apse mosaic, detail: stag drawing forth serpent beneath an acanthus; stags drinking from the four rivers of Paradise.   46

5. Stags confronted at the rivers of Paradise. San Giovanni in Laterano, Rome. Detail from apse mosaic, thirteenth century.   47

6. Stags drinking from the rivers of Paradise. Baptistry of San Giovanni in Fonte, Naples, lunette mosaic, ca. 400.   48

7. Francesco di Giorgio Martini (attributed): Diana, Venus, and huntress-nymphs. Sienese *cassone,* fifteenth century. Museo Stibbert, Florence.   60

8. Stag and doe among animals and birds at the Fountain of Life. Gospels of Saint-Médard de Soissons. Carolingian, ninth century. Paris, Bibliothèque Nationale, MS. lat. 8850, fol. 6 v.   64

9. The Marriage of Adam and Eve. Bartholomaeus Anglicus, *De proprietatibus rerum,* trans. Jean Corbechon, *Des Proprietez des choses.* Fitzwilliam Museum, MS. 251, fol. 16.   65

# EDITORS' PREFACE

This project began during a conversation between two old friends over coffee one morning the day after a Dante Society Council meeting in Cambridge (Massachusetts) late in 1982. We discovered that we both wished Boccaccio's first work were available in English for our teaching. To fill the need, Cassell had, in fact, begun translating it, and since Kirkham had recently published a long article on the poem, we decided to join forces.

The text of the *Caccia di Diana* in Vittore Branca's edition (Giovanni Boccaccio, *Tutte le opere*, vol. 1 [Milan: Mondadori, 1967]), used as a *texte de base*, was electronically scanned on KDEM and entered into WordPerfect at the University of Pennsylvania by Kirkham and edited, through a collation of all six extant manuscripts, by Cassell in Florence and Illinois. Both of us went over the translation of the work painstakingly several times, revising and polishing.

Incorporating some materials researched by Cassell, Kirkham researched and drafted the Introduction, the original nucleus of which was her article, "Numerology and Allegory in Boccaccio's *Caccia di Diana*," *Traditio* 34 (1978), 303–329. The Introduction was then revised stylistically by both collaborators, who interpolated further research, sources, and information. With animal and bestiary research compiled by Cassell, Kirkham drafted the Commentary, contributing most of the material on literary parallels in Boccaccio and on the stag as a baptismal emblem in art and literature. Both of us reviewed and expanded it, Cassell adding the philological notes on the manuscript tradition and on our preferred readings. The rest of the primary drafts, the texts and translations of the *Ternario* and *Ballata*, the Glossary of the Huntresses, and the Bibliography were prepared by Cassell and, once more, revised in the usual way. While Kirkham obtained the illustrations and permissions, Cassell smoothed—we hope!—the synthesis of our two voices, assembling the final manuscript.

We trust the result is seamless.

Champaign and Philadelphia, September 1989
Anthony K. Cassell and Victoria Kirkham

# ACKNOWLEDGMENTS

The editors would like to thank Vittore Branca for his advice and his kindness in permitting us to use his edition as a *texte de base* and for allowing us to adapt his notes on the huntresses for our Glossary. We would also like to acknowledge the generosity of those who have made possible the publication of this volume. Gratitude is due the Center for Italian Studies of the University of Pennsylvania, under the directorship of Robert E. A. Palmer, and the Ente Nazionale Giovanni Boccaccio, through its President, Francesco Mazzoni, for their contributions toward the production costs of this book.

In addition, some personal appreciations must be recorded.

★ ★ ★

Completion of this project was made possible on my part by a sabbatical leave as Fellow at the Harvard University Center for Italian Renaissance Studies. I thank in particular Maurizio Gavioli there for his good-natured patience in pandering to a chunky Bitnet correspondence between Florence and Champaign. In the electronic scanning of the Italian text, essential assistance came from the University of Pennsylvania: John A. Abercrombie, the Center for Computer Analysis of Texts, and the Center for Italian Studies then under the directorship of Malcolm Campbell. Other colleagues over the years, knowingly and not, have helped our project grow through collegial dialogue, especially David Anderson, Robert Hollander, Millicent Marcus, Janet Smarr, and Paul F. Watson. For support throughout, moral and material, I am especially grateful to the members of my family.

V. K.

★ ★ ★

I am deeply grateful for the help of my research assistant, David Larmour, now a colleague at Texas Tech, for his help in gathering and helping to complete the bibliography; my thanks also go to the Research board of the University of Illinois for providing funding for this assistance. I would also like to acknowledge a debt of gratitude, much overdue, to Dorothy Vinton of the University of Illinois Interlibrary system, and to James Gothard of the Language Laboratory in Urbana, for his patience in teaching me the arcana of electronic mail. To Janet Fitch go our thanks for both her tireless help and her professional editorial advice.

A. K. C.

# ABBREVIATIONS

| | |
|---|---|
| Am. vis. | *Amorosa visione* (Boccaccio) |
| Ameto | *Comedìa delle ninfe fiorentine (Ameto)* (Boccaccio) |
| AV | Authorized Version of the Bible (King James Bible) |
| Best. tosc., Il | *Il bestiario toscano* |
| Best. divin, Le | *Le Bestiaire divin* (Guillaume le Clerc) |
| Bestiary, The | Translation of pseudo-Hugh of Saint Victor's *De bestiis* by T. H. White |
| Clavis | *Clavis Melitonis* |
| De casibus | *De casibus virorum illustrium* (Boccaccio) |
| De mulieribus | *De mulieribus claris* (Boccaccio) |
| De sollert. an. | *De sollertia animalium* (Plutarch) |
| Dec. | *Decameron* (Boccaccio) |
| Decretum | *Decretum magistri Gratiani* (Gratian) |
| Elegia | *Elegia di madonna Fiammetta* (Boccaccio) |
| Esposizioni | *Esposizioni sopra la Comedìa di Dante* (Boccaccio) |
| Etym. | *Etymologiae* (Isidore of Seville) |
| Filoc. | *Filocolo* (Boccaccio) |
| Filostr. | *Filostrato* (Boccaccio) |
| Genealogie | *Genealogie deorum gentilium* (Boccaccio) |
| GSLI | *Giornale Storico della Letteratura Italiana* |
| HA | *Historia animalium* (Aelian and Aristotle) |
| Inf. | *Inferno* (Dante) |
| LBAR | *Le Bestiaire d'amour rimé* |
| LCL | Loeb Classical Library |
| LNR | *Liber naturae rerum* (Thomas of Cantimpré) |
| Met. | *Metamorphoses* (Ovid) |
| MLN | *Modern Language Notes* |
| Moralia | *Moralium libri sive expositio in librum Job* (Saint Gregory the Great) |
| Morals | *Morals on the Book of Job* (Saint Gregory the Great) |
| NEMLA | North-East Modern Language Association |
| NH | *Natural History* (Pliny) |
| Ninf. fies. | *Ninfale fiesolano* (Boccaccio) |
| Par. | *Paradiso* (Dante) |
| PG | *Patrologia Graeca* (Migne) |

| | |
|---|---|
| PL | *Patrologia Latina* (Migne) |
| *Purg.* | *Purgatorio* (Dante) |
| RSV | Revised Standard Version of the Bible |
| *Spec. nat.* | *Speculum naturale* (Vincent of Beauvais) |
| *ST* | *Summa Theologica* (Saint Thomas Aquinas) |
| *Stag* | *The Stag of Love* (Thiébaux) |
| *Tes.* | *Teseida delle nozze d'Emilia* (Boccaccio) |
| *Trattatello* | *Trattatello in laude di Dante* (Boccaccio) |
| *Tresors, Li* | *Li Livres dou Tresor* (Brunetto Latini) |
| *Wald. Phys.* | *Der waldensische Physiologus,* edited by A. Mayer |

All biblical citations are given in the Vulgate or Douay-Rheims versions unless otherwise indicated.

# Introduction

# 1
# THE BACKGROUND

## Dating and Subject Matter

*Diana's Hunt* is Giovanni Boccaccio's first work. A sylvan fantasy in terza rima, it has been dated by historical evidence and internal stylistic features to 1333–1334.[1] The author, then barely twenty, would have been about midway through a five-year course on canon law at the University of Naples. In truancy from a curriculum imposed by his father, he penned this imaginative tribute to the high-born ladies of the circles surrounding King Robert's court. His fiction makes them nymphs-for-a-day, convened to a hunt by the goddess Diana. At the end, surprisingly, the tutelar of chastity must yield to Venus, who descends from heaven and turns a great heap of slain beasts into handsome young men. By such startling reversals set in a woodland alive with bestiary and religious symbolism, the novice poet created a witty conundrum: although Diana loses, virtue wins; pagan divinities rule by turn, but we are in Christian allegorical territory.

The story is set in springtime, "that fair season when the new grasses reclothe each meadow, and the bright air smiles for the sweetness that moves the heavens." While the poem's solitary narrator (whose identity we do not know) is wondering how to shield himself from Love's bitter blows, a "gentle spirit" comes flying down and thrice summons the women whom Diana has elected her companions in Parthenope. Their names are called out one by one, but the last of the chosen, "that Lady whom Love honors more than any other for her lofty virtue," remains anonymous because, according to the narrator, "praise more sovereign would suit her name than I could here set forth."

Diana bathes with her newfound nymphs in a rivulet, divides them into four groups, and sends each party to hunt in a separate direction. The narrator notes one by one their venatic triumphs over such beasts as the roebuck, boar, lion, and unicorn. Then, just when it seems all has been said, more ladies with limers come rushing loudly into the woods. They too are Neapolitan noblewomen, again named seriatim, who energetically renew the chase, fanning out in teams toward the cardinal points, their bravest conquest a seven-member family of snakes.

At last, with noon approaching, Diana calls an end to the hunt and reassembles her followers. But "the Fair Lady, whose name is not spoken," now incites her companions to rebel against the goddess. Her authority rejected, Diana storms back up to heaven. On the advice of the Mystery Lady, the huntresses make a sacrificial fire of their kill and dedicate it to Venus, whom they solemnly invoke. Venus drops down on a little white cloud, announcing, "I am she from whom each one of you through her prayers awaits grace; and I promise you by the gods above that each one who is worthy to follow in my footsteps shall have what she asks." Love's avatar keeps her promise by transforming the burning beasts into happy young men. Naked, they leap from the flames, run through the meadow into a river, and resurface mantled in vermilion. Venus commands them to be wise and keep faith with their huntress-mistresses.

What follows this mass metamorphosis is an even more amazing turn of events. The narrator himself, who, we at last discover, has actually been a stag all along, undergoes the same wondrous transfiguration:

> And I saw myself offered to the Fair Lady, changed beyond doubt from a stag into a human being and a rational creature; and not unjustly, for nature never bestowed more worth or nobility than upon her, so chaste and pure.

The beauty and virtues of his Unnamed Lady are such that she seems to be an angelic creature from heaven, come to "extinguish" human vice and bring peace to the hearts of all troubled lovers. By serving her humbly, the narrator hopes to win "salvation" (Italian *salute*), the word that closes his remarks and the poem.

> It pleases me now to speak no further, because for a place more praiseworthy I reserve my words to praise more truthfully that beauty that her soul traces upon her, she through whom other women are honored and whom my heart ever contrives to serve. And I go back to contemplate in the green meadows that mercy and the other great virtue that adorns with beauty this Lady from whom I yet hope to have salvation.

## Boccaccio's Neapolitan Cultural Milieu

Boccaccio was in his early teens when he left Florence, the city of his childhood, to go live in Naples with his father, a businessman who transferred there as principal agent for the Bardi Bank and became "Counsellor and Chamberlain" to King Robert the Wise. Newly arrived, probably in 1327, for a sojourn that would stretch into twelve years, the adolescent had to work the counters, or *banchi,* as a money changer. Still, his father's privileged relationship with the monarch was to give him entrée to the court and prominent local families. Their names are memorialized in *Diana's Hunt,* a Who's Who in the Kingdom of Naples that rosters clans like the Caracciola, Sighinolfi, Barrile, Coppoli, Carafa, Brancaccia, and Aldimaresca.[2]

The city in that era was a capital of mixed cultures. At its court, the most brilliant on the European continent, an Angevin dynasty had ruled since 1266, and French was the official language. The nobility were a chivalric society, readers of romances imported from France and a public often visited by their own vernacular poets from north of the Alps. King Robert the Wise, who was acknowledged during his reign (1309–1343) as Italy's most powerful prince, followed his father and grandfather in a policy of close ties with the papacy, which was by then resident at Avignon, Robert's own city. High praise for that monarch came from the contemporary historian of Florence, Giovanni Villani, in whose estimation he is "the wisest of Christians for the last five hundred years, both in natural wisdom and learning, a very great master in theology and a consummate philosopher." This Second Solomon, as Boccaccio called him, was an amateur expert on medicine and became famous for the sermons he composed in Latin, of which 289 survive. Steeped in Aristotle, Averroës, and Scholastic thought, these pieces reflect a person of austere life, so much so that Dante rather sourly implied Robert should have stuck to kerystics instead of seeking the throne.[3]

Scholasticism flourished at the Dominican *Studium,* a center of intellectual activity whose establishment dated from 1269. Thomas Aquinas visited in 1272, and San Domenico Maggiore continued to be a seat of theology where his students taught. A university was founded at Naples by Emperor Frederick II (d. 1250); law, medicine, and the natural sciences, including the field of zoology in which Frederick himself practiced, held places of honor. Italy's most outstanding jurist, Cino da Pistoia, taught there alongside Luca da Penne, author of a major commentary on the Justinian Code. Luca's compilation, which reveals vast learning, is a profile in scholarship that Boccaccio emulated: some Greek classics in Latin translation; Plautus, Terence, Sallust, Cicero, Livy, Quintilian, Seneca, Suetonius, the two Plinys, Valerius Maximus; Saint Jerome, Augustine, Cassiodorus, Boethius, Isidore of Seville, Papias, Saint Bernard, Saint Thomas Aquinas, Egidius Romanus, Cino da Pistoia, Barbato da Sulmona, Francesco Petrarca.[4]

Boccaccio came to frequent one of the city's most celebrated cultural institutions, the royal library. Its holdings emphasized theology and medicine, classic and modern, works such as Gregory the Great's *Moralia in*

*Job,* writings by Augustine and Boethius, Aquinas's *Summa contra Gentiles,* Hippocrates, Galen, and texts from the Salerno school of medicine. Curator for many years was Paolo da Perugia, whose formative influence on his intellectual development, especially the *Genealogies of the Gentile Gods,* Boccaccio remembers fondly in the last book of that encyclopedia of allegorized myths:

> Advanced in years, of great and varied learning, he was long the librarian of the famous King Robert of Sicily and Jerusalem. If there was ever a man possessed of the curiosity of research he was the one. A word from his prince was sufficient to send him hunting through a dozen books of history, fable, or poetry.

Paolo, with great knowledge of Greek lore, had made a compendium of mythography called the *Collectiones,* but as Boccaccio's anecdote goes, the librarian's shrewish widow prevented its survival:

> to the very serious inconvenience of this book of mine [the *Genealogies*], I found that his saucy wife Biella, after his death, wilfully destroyed this and many other books of Paul's. . . . I am convinced that at the time when I knew him no one was his equal in studies of this sort.[5]

The young Boccaccio was not limited to French and Latin literature; he also had access to the latest works of his homeland. By around 1330, among the ever-growing number of Florentine merchants and bankers present in the bustling city, Tuscan literature began to eclipse the old-fashioned courtly fiction favored by the French aristocracy. Before 1323, two years after Dante's death (1321), the *Divine Comedy* reached Naples, ordered by one of the city's Florentines, or carried there by the preacher Agostino d'Ancona. Graziolo de' Bambaglioli, one of its earliest commentators, was in Naples between 1334 and 1335, and there are at least six extant manuscripts of the poem copied by various scribes and commentators illuminated in Naples during the Trecento.[6]

## Literary Background of *Diana's Hunt*

The plural cultures of its Neapolitan birthplace mingle in the poem. Despite its brevity, the *Hunt* vibrates with an amazing encyclopedic energy, reflecting the medieval passion for polyglot synthesis, a desire for ordered universal knowledge that promoted all manner of compendia and catalogs. Here, to give a list of women an artistic form, Boccaccio adapted from Dante a type of poetic form called a *sirventese,* then merged that inventory with a dictionary of animals, or bestiary. His narrative in

Tuscan, fusing Italian, Galloromance, and Latin literary traditions, displays a stylistic predilection for startling *contaminatio*—juxtaposition of material and ideas from many sources widely dissimilar in subject, medium, and manner. By conservative reckoning, the authorities on which the young writer relied range from Ovid's *Metamorphoses;* through Apuleius's *Golden Ass;* a panegyric by Claudian; Boethius's *On the Consolation of Philosophy;* the Bible; patristic exegeses of the Psalms; Gregory's *Moralia in Job;* Rabanus Maurus (works genuine and spurious); Isidore of Seville's *Etymologies;* Gratian's *Decretum;* poets of the *dolce stil novo;* Dante's *Vita nuova* and *Divine Comedy;* Petrarch's earliest lyrics; Latin, French, and Italian bestiaries; medieval hunt manuals and allegories; the Roman Catholic and Byzantine liturgies of baptism; and baptismal iconography in the visual arts.

## Poetry in Praise of Women

For purposes of *Diana's Hunt,* courtly Naples has reverted to a mythical "Parthenope," that Mediterranean promontory marked in antiquity by the name of the "virgin" whose tomb it kept.[7] This woodland, timeless as its immortal visitants, is a preserve posted for women only. Diana, fifty-nine Angevin nymphs, and Venus define a fantasy sphere where there rules, with civilizing force, the feminine power of chastity and love. The allegorical meanings layered in the confrontation between ladies and beasts will presently unfold.

But first, another question: why did Boccaccio choose for his literary debut a poem dominated by women?

The idea clearly came to him from a youthful work of Dante's, one now lost, but known from a reference in the sixth chapter of the *Vita nuova.* There Dante mentions an epistolary *sirventese,* written to praise the sixty most beautiful ladies of Florence, among whom his most blessed Beatrice held ninth position:

> There came to me a wish to record the name of that most gentle one and to accompany it with many ladies' names. . . . And I took the names of sixty of the most beautiful ladies in the city where my lady was placed by the Lord most high, and I composed a letter in the form of a *sirventese,* which I shall not write here; and I should not have mentioned it were it not to say what happened, marvelously, as I was composing it, that is, that the name of my lady would not suffer to stand on any number other than on nine, among the names of these women.[8]

The *sirventese,* a form that passed into Italy with the troubadours of Provence, could vary in versification as much as content, which was sometimes political, sometimes amorous. How, then, Dante would have devised his "letter" is hard to guess.[9] Nor can we say whether Boccaccio knew it directly. In any event, secondhand information from the *Vita nuova,* our sole record, would have been sufficient. To answer his Tuscan model, Boccaccio prepared a Neapolitan counterpart, honoring by name fifty-eight noble women of Naples. With the narrator's anonymous Mystery Lady and Diana herself, the ladies Boccaccio assembles for his hunt come to the same total as those lauded on Dante's list.

Under the rubric of poetry in praise of women, a heading that broadly defines the *Hunt,* other medieval gynotypical conventions come into play. Notwithstanding social custom, which made hunting a pastime for males or mixed company, Diana's bands, by literary tradition, formed self-sufficient female communities. As Boccaccio would have it, these nymphs in "venery" are also servants of Venus, who comes at their behest to gladden all hearts. Women very properly take charge where love is at issue, for on that subject they are the experts: from Andreas Capellanus's twelfth-century manual, *On the Art of Courtly Love,* to Boccaccio's own *Filocolo,* when love was debated had not women always been the arbiters? Did not Guido Cavalcanti and Dante, puzzling over love's nature, address themselves to feminine interlocutors? "Ladies who have understanding of love" are precisely the audience of privilege whom Dante invokes to extoll his "most blessed one" in the first canzone of the *Vita nuova.*[10]

So Boccaccio, in accordance with convention, looks to the ladies. Like Dante, he has a chosen love object, the huntress who "for the other women's welfare [*salute*] . . . went much like a guardian to the head of the group to guide them safely" (1.49–51). As the stag-narrator's mistress, she is distanced and kept anonymous by the rule of secrecy in courtly romance. The stag, who evidently has committed to memory passages in both prose and poetry from the *Vita nuova,* claims that her name must be suppressed because he is unworthy of speaking it.[11] Were Boccaccio to comment, he would adduce the custom of shielding milady's true identity with a *senhal,* or poetic sign. The sign behind which he chooses to screen his Mystery Lady in the *Hunt,* however, is not a false name, but a code number, a cipher that signals her symbolic character. Going by the qualities with which Boccaccio explicitly endows her, she can perform the same kind of miracles as Dante's Beatrice, who utterly dissipates evil, especially sensual thoughts in the men struck by her gaze: "When she goes walking, Love casts a frost into vile hearts from which their every thought freezes and perishes." Hers is a virtue contagious and irresistible, bringing salvation (*salute*) by guiding men to God.

In a wider sense, the power Dante attributes to Beatrice with his canzone in the nineteenth chapter of the *Vita nuova* applies to all the women in *Diana's Hunt*. The stag's mistress, with Medusan potential beneath her humanizing powers, has looks that kill unless they enkindle love: "Whoever gazes fixedly into her eyes becomes merciful or else must die" (18.29–30). Similarly, from the collective impact that the huntresses have on each creature they encounter, we can extrapolate the effect of any Angelic Lady on masculine admirers. Beatrice's eyes, like those of ancient forebearers and endless descendents in poetry, figuratively give forth "spirits kindled with love that strike the eyes of whoever then watches her, and passing inward, each one finds the heart." In witty parallel, the nymphs of Naples, armed with bows and arrows, actually shoot to death all the men/animals they find. Love's fatal glance is delightfully literalized and, through happy operation, at once murders and turns its targets into "something noble," that is, changes them from beasts who die to men who come alive.[12]

On one thematic level, then, *Diana's Hunt* capitalizes on a topos of the courtly and stilnovistic traditions, the ennobling power of women and love. It is a motif to which Boccaccio returned in later works—eventually, to the point of satirizing it. Those that repeat the pattern most obviously are the *Comedìa delle ninfe fiorentine,* or *Ameto,* which tells how seven nymphs "humanize" a young rustic; and, in sly mocking of a convention once so unquestioningly embraced, the first tale of the Fifth Day in the *Decameron:* "Cimone by loving becomes wise and kidnaps his lady Efigenia at sea."[13]

Diana's Neapolitan nymphs, authorized by literary tradition, are women who act aggressively to achieve their goals. The preponderance and power of women in this early poem set a standard that held, one way and another, throughout Boccaccio's writing career. Many novelle of the *Decameron,* dedicated to women and mostly narrated by women, rely on resourceful female protagonists. In the *Elegia di madonna Fiammetta (Amorous Fiammetta),* Boccaccio produced the first psychological romance with a female heroine; in his *Corbaccio* he explored the rhetoric of misogyny. Some thirty years after *Diana's Hunt,* he would compose the first collection ever of female biographies, *De mulieribus claris (Concerning Famous Women),* to immortalize the daughters of Eve whose deeds, blameworthy or laudable, deserve remembrance. That book, as an author's preface explains, required a female dedicatee. Fearing the offering too poor for Queen Giovanna of Naples, he selected Andrea Acciaiuoli, countess of Altavilla. Her given name, from the Greek *andres* (men), proclaims of itself, the scholar points out, her superiority to her sex.[14] But praise for her virile character masks Boccaccio's more practical motive for sending

Andrea his volume of women's lives: it was her brother, Niccolò Acciaiuoli, who had risen in the Angevin realm to become Grand Seneschal of Naples, who was in a position to help Boccaccio financially. Unfortunately, the support Boccaccio needed and hoped to receive in his later years from Niccolò was never forthcoming;[15] nevertheless, as a ploy to gain patronage, the dedication of *Concerning Famous Women* may tell us something about the ladies honored in his first work.

*Diana's Hunt,* we can assume, is dedicated to all whose names appear there. Not counting the stag's mistress, they are fifty-eight ladies of the Neapolitan aristocracy. Many are women otherwise lost to history. (What little is known of them we report in our Glossary.) Most are young, in their early teens, and still carry their patronymic. Of an age to marry, they may be humorously programmed for the poem as girls "hunting husbands" in the "virgin's territory," Parthenope.

At the same time, nomenclature suggests that Boccaccio had more in mind than a gallant tribute, sounded with nuptial overtones,[16] to the fairest damsels of the land. The budding poet clearly delights in caressing their names, whose forms and variants serve not only the wonderful pleasure of a medieval list, but resonate in themselves with euphony and rhythm. How quaintly they echo through the verses of the *Hunt* struck Francesco Torraca, who observed that "not less than nine are called Caterina. Three are the Vanellas, three the Zizzolas, three the Jacopas—Jacopa, Giacovella, Covella—three the Ceccas or Ceccolas, two the Beritas or Beritolas." But sheer joy in words, girlish names reeled off with paronomastic verve, is only one side of Boccaccio's play. In his strategy, the family and its cognomen count for just as much, if not more, than given names and sweet diminutives. It is no accident that the lady summoned at the start of the messenger's list—she who stands on number one, as Dante would have liked to put it—happens to be Zizzola Barrile. Although Zizzola eludes fuller identification, her surname is significant. Highly esteemed by both community and court, the Barrile (or Barrili) were blue bloods in the Capuan See, a neighborhood that boasted the rich cream of Neapolitan aristocracy. Giovanni Barrile, Captain General of Calabria and Chamberlain to King Robert, was one of those "citizens of probity" whose opinion the sovereign sought in 1332, before promulgating a law "against ribalds and heinous men who kidnap virgins under the pretense of marriage." In 1341 he would have represented his king at Petrarch's coronation as poet laureate on the Campidoglio, had he not fallen among thieves on the way to Rome. Like Petrarch, Boccaccio was a friend of Giovanni, a gentleman whose culture he compliments in his facetious dialect letter to Franceschino de' Bardi—"isso sape quant'a lu demone" (that fellow knows as much as the Devil)—and whom he calls more reverently, in honor of conversations they used to have about Virgil, "magni spiritus homo, Iohannes Barillus" (a man of great spirit) in the *Genealogie* XIV, 19. *Diana's Hunt* honors not only noblewomen of Naples but their kinsfolk as well, and thus, indirectly, the leading men of the Kingdom. The author aimed, in other words, to attract attention in glamorous social quarters, as he would again when, dreaming of a triumphal return to Naples from Florence in the early 1360s, he dedicated *Concerning Famous Women* to Niccolò Acciaiuoli's sister. He hoped for patronage beyond the ladies' power to give, but well within the political reach of their fathers.[17]

## Ovid, Claudian, Dante

A classic mythological rivalry between Diana and Venus propels the poem's dynamics, keyed most obviously to Ovid. His *Metamorphoses* depict the quiver-bearing huntress in her forest retreats, shady grottoes with flowing streams that sealed the fates of Callisto, seduced to love by Jove (*Met.* 2.409ff.) and Actaeon after he glimpsed her bathing (*Met.* 3.155ff.). These settings return in the *locus amoenus* of Boccaccio's *Hunt,* where Diana leads her nymphs to bathe in a woodland spring before deploying them as a general would. The Calydonian boar hunt (*Met.* 8.271ff.) may have contributed to the fiercely aggressive rhythm of their chase overall, as well as some detail, such as descriptions of those marshlands on the plain where waterfowl are captured. The stag-narrator's final transformation amusingly inverts Actaeon's punishment in the same way that the climactic metamorphosis of beasts en masse overturns that Ovidian archetype.

Although important features of this Italian fiction depend directly on Ovid, nowhere in the *Metamorphoses* is there a hunt that can account for the general pattern of Boccaccio's. Precedent for the structure in his strategy, previously unnoted, appears in the late-classical author Claudian, who in the Trecento ranked as a Florentine of fame. His panegyric *On Stilicho's Consulship* culminates with a global chase orchestrated by Diana to provide caged animals from every corner of the empire for spectacles in the Roman arena. Claudian's Diana, from dizzying Alpine heights, summons her companions seriatim by name, and those initially convened are then joined by a second band. On instructions from the goddess, they divide and hunt in every direction. Diana will go down to the Lybian desert; others, followed by dogs of various breeds, lead their parties east to Dalmatia and Mount Pindus; north to the lowlands of Gaul and Germany; they scour the Alps and Apennines at Europe's center, head west to the banks of the Iberian Tagus; and south to the islands of Corsica and Sicily. Claudian sums up the reach of their operation:

> Whatsoever inspires fear with its teeth, wonder with its mane, awe with its horns and bristling coat—all the beauty, all the terror of the forest is taken. Guile protects them not; neither strength nor weight avails them; their speed saves not the fleet of foot.[18]

Both borrowings and calculated departures from the Latin source are evident. In each case Diana musters a hunt; she and her captains spread out in the cardinal directions to stalk quarry of every description, hunting with hounds high and low, from mountain peak to marshy bottom. Claudian's goddess makes her appearance at the top of Italy, in the Alps; Boccaccio's comes to the bay of Naples, in the boot's foot. Claudian counts his ladies out loud: Diana plus seven chieftans in the first wave, three parties of one hundred in the second. Boccaccio, too, arranges roll calls, but instead of recording how many were present in all, he leaves it for us to count and interpret the numbers at play in his lists.

Beyond any doubt, the authority most influential in Boccaccio's poetic debut was Dante, his "first guiding light."[19] Many verses of the *Hunt* echo passages in the *Divine Comedy*. Particularly striking are parallels with the last cantos of *Purgatory,* where Dante enters Eden. Notable among them is the stag's description of his secret mistress as "that lady whose face seems always to burn with love" (4.11–12), an epithet that repeats almost verbatim Dante's allusion to Venus, "who seems always burning with the fire of love" in the third of his predawn dreams on the purgatorial mount (*Purg.* 27.96). The connection is appropriate, since it is that unnamed lady who at the end of the *Hunt* will be the one to summon Venus.

Precedent for the catalog of ladies that structures Diana's *Hunt* can also be found in Dante's *Commedia,* if one recalls his many lists of personae, such as those populating Limbo. Boccaccio's decision to compile a census of highborn Neapolitan women was prompted specifically, however, by Dante's "*sirventese* in the form of an epistle." If he did not have direct knowledge of it, his tribute to the women of Parthenope indicates the extensive borrowings he made from the *Vita nuova* itself. That small book contributed significantly to the *Hunt*'s last cantos, in which Venus quite literally brings new life both to the burning beasts captured by Diana's companions and to the poem's unhappy cervine narrator. The marvelous effects of love, described there in the manner of the *dolce stil nuovo,* are revealed to the stag by his Mystery Lady, a figure with angelic attributes inspired by Beatrice. Her newly appointed servant praises her at the end of the *Hunt* in words that recall the *Vita nuova*'s concluding promise, his final hopeful word, "salvation," being none other than Dante's focal signifier, "*salute.*"[20]

By metrical format, Boccaccio's *sirventese* is a *ternario,* that is, a composition in hendecasyllables of terza rima. Dante had invented this rhyme scheme (ABA, BCB, CDC) for his *Comedìa,* setting it into a sequence of one hundred cantos, 115 to 160 verses long, for a total of 14,233 lines. Boccaccio's small-scale poem contains eighteen cantos, all but one with fifty-eight verses (Canto 3 has sixty-one), the sum being 1,047 lines. The younger poet's appropriation of Dante's new terza rima is an important clue to the kind of poem he was writing. The *Hunt,* too, is an allegorical drama of conflicts between evil and virtue in man's soul.

## Animals in the Bestiaries and Biblical Exegesis

Antagonists to the huntresses are a forestful of beasts.[21] Over one hundred strong—the narrator tells us that they are actually too numerous for exact reckoning (Canto 8.56–57)—they number close to thirty distinct types: roebucks, hares, boars, stags, wolves, a leopard, foxes, bears, a lion cub, hedgehogs, tigers, rabbits, a unicorn, a crane, mallards, a cormorant, a *paolin* (8.55), a beaver, an elephant, seven serpents, a fallow deer, a panther, a bull, a porcupine, a hydra, two swans, and an ostrich. From the character of this list, it is clear that Boccaccio's acquaintance with most of these animals came neither from nature walks nor from outings with court hunting parties. On the contrary, he probably encountered almost all of them in the library through bestiaries and sundry florilegia of the church fathers.

Boccaccio at Naples had access to bestiaries from several of the many branches into which that popular genre had, from antiquity, been multiplied and cloned. Classical texts, such as Aristotle's *Historia Animalium* and Pliny's *Natural History,* had provided material for the ancestor of the European moralized bestiary, a curious Greek archetype dating from about A.D. 200.[22] To the Middle Ages it was known as the work of "Physiologus," or alternatively, that name was considered its title, *Physiologus*. From that source there evolved the *Physiologus* family of texts, whose voices became a sort of "standard reference," although in a richly varied, complex tradition of versions, Latin and vernacular. Through the centuries *Physiologus* was transmitted by encyclopediasts who added to and adapted it as their contexts warranted: authorities such as Isidore of Seville, Rabanus Maurus, Peter of Beauvais, Thomas of Cantimpré, and

Brunetto Latini were joined by the anonymous popular compilers of the Italian *Bestiario moralizzato*, *Il bestiario toscano*, and the *Tusco-Venetian Bestiary*.[23] Never intended as works of natural history (the unaltered text of Pliny and later, Saint Albertus Magnus's *De animalibus* filled that need), the curious and fanciful "books of beasts" were rather a source of exempla and ethical teaching and a rich font of poetic imagery throughout the Middle Ages, one from which the youthful Boccaccio eagerly drew for many of the adventures in the *Hunt*.

In Southern Italy, from the first half of the thirteenth century, when the Swabian house of Palermo began patronizing Greek and Arabic scholarship, the natural sciences had been subjects of special cultivation. Emperor Frederick II had personally encouraged a zoological tradition not only by establishing a private zoo but also by writing *De arte venandi cum avibus* (*The Art of Falconry*).[24] His treatise, which became and remains a standard even for modern hawking enthusiasts, contains scrupulously detailed information about the life cycles, habits, training, and use of many birds of prey.

With the transition from Swabian to Angevin rule, bestiaries proper began to appear, bearing testimony to ties between the French court at Naples and culture in the mother country. At least two such works are known to survive from the second half of the thirteenth century, ascribed to the Neapolitan area.[25] Exactly which texts Boccaccio may have consulted has not been established. But in spite of individual variations and occasional eccentricities, the bestiaries generally retain certain unchanging features, and these are reflected in *Diana's Hunt*, very much a product of the most traditional, enduring lore.

Typically, as *Physiologus* attests, the bestiary includes an admirable variety of animals, starting with the lion, King of Beasts. In his train come a parade of quadrupeds, bipeds, insects, various categories of birds and fish, and even fantastic composite species such as the giant hydra, the sirens, the griffin, the basilisk, the "lanzanus," and the man-eating manticore. As impressive as this range of types are the amazing habits (*naturae*) peculiar to each animal: the ferocious unicorn can only be subdued by a virgin; the elephant, with unjointed legs, topples helplessly when he leans to nap against a tree partly sawn through by the patient hunter; the beaver (*castor*), when pursued, obligingly castrates himself to give the hunters the medicinal prize they seek; the swan sings along in rhythm and harmony with the harpist; the "mild" panther attracts other animals by his sweet breath.

But wondrous species and behavior traits are only half of the Christian bestiary. To complete each entry in his zoological dictionary, or confront them in a Bible passage, an author had to moralize his animals. Sometimes the meaning was positive (*in bono* or *in bonam partem*), such as when the beast could be likened to Christ. This was true, for example, of the regal lion, who delighted in mountain heights, carefully brushed aways its tracks with its tail, and gave birth to dead cubs animated by the breath of life from their sire on the third day. In allegory this signified the Lord Christ, who sought high places for proximity with God the Father; in the lion's deception of the hunters the moralizers glimpsed the theological "pious fraud" by which Christ's divinity was concealed from the Devil to enable mankind's salvation; in the quickening of the lion cubs they saw the resurrection of Christ on the Third Day after the Crucifixion. Far more often, the beast stood for diabolical powers (symbolism *in malo* or *in malam partem*): the lion could be Satan on watch to catch the unwary sinner; the wolf signified pride and the Devil; the leopard symbolized fraud; the fox, whose name (*vulpis*) was said to derive from "twisted foot" (*volupes*), was an emblem of heresy whose trickery made him kin to the Temptor.

On these symbolisms, both *in malo* and *in bono,* turned small but critical moral dramas. Christ, Man, and the Devil performed as their three main characters. What conflict they enacted came down quite simply to the eternal struggle involving the choice between God and Satan, between good and evil. Thus, when a lion challenged the hunter he was Christ, whom all good men should diligently pursue. The leopard, decorated with spots that implied treachery, should remind any devout Christian to shun deceptions practiced by the Devil.

We can see how elaborate these morality lessons could be by examining three cases from the *Hunt*: Covella d'Anna's maniacal pursuit and strangulation of an ostrich (Canto 15); the capture and killing of rabbits and hares (Cantos 3 and 6); and Berarda's gathering up of the hedgehogs in the lap of her dress (Canto 5).

In the first case—involving, actually, the last animal to be slaughtered in the poem—Covella's ferocity seems unmotivated and incomprehensible. The fleeing ostrich, oddly out of place in the environs of Naples, seems the barest threat to her, for its only belligerence is its occasional turn to flail its wings. She is, however, aflame to destroy it, lacerating her body and clothes in her obsessive chase. Clearly, on the literal level, we are to remark the inconsistency between the provocation and reaction; clearly, too, the author means that we note it as a jarring rupture.

A full explanation comes from the conventional reputation of the ostrich among the fathers of the church. The generally favorable moral view of the bird given in the bestiaries from the *Physiologus* tradition—it ignores its eggs after laying them as a good Christian should scorn the goods of this world—was given an opposite, negative interpretation in biblical exegesis following the wide wake cut by Saint Gregory the Great. Commenting on the bird's neglect of its eggs in Job 39:13–14, Gregory saw the ostrich as the type of the fraudulent dissembler or hypocrite neglecting all for its own pride, gain, and ambition. "It raises its wings as if to fly, but yet never raises itself from the earth by flight. Thus doubtless are all dissemblers, who, while they simulate the conduct of the good, possess a resemblance of holy appearance, but have no reality of holy conduct."[26]

The widespread patristic "wings of fraud" topos springs from this passage in Gregory: compare the pseudo-Rabanus Maurus's *Allegoriae in Sacram Scripturam*: "By wings . . . is meant the purposes of the dissembler"; or Richard of St. Victor's *De eruditione* 3.12: "Do you still want to know more fully what sort of wings fraudulence has? . . . Let one be said of simulation, the second of dissimulation, the third of ostentation, the fourth of excuse."[27] Thus, the one detail that Boccaccio gives us concerning the bird, its habit of beating its wings as if to fly, is the very behavior that church doctors saw as an analogy to fraud. Fraud is the worst of sins, since it involves the misuse of man's divine mind; the huntress rips off the bird's head because the head is the seat of the intellect. Covella's fear of the flapping wings and the energy with which she decapitates this bird can be understood best in terms of the struggle between virtue and vice at the allegorical level. As the worst of sins and as the sin "peculiar to man" (as Dante had said in *Inferno* 11.25, "de l'uom proprio male"), the ostrich is fittingly last to be routed.

Similar moral situations can be seen in the capture and slaughter of the rabbits and hares. At first (Canto 3.26–27), they seem to appear simply as a realistic detail in a passing observation of the stag: "hares, headed toward the mountain." Not so, as we learn when we check the literary tradition. In Saint Albertus Magnus's *De animalibus,* and in amalgamated bestiary texts, such as that of Thomas of Cantimpré, we find the widespread item of lore that hares run uphill more easily than down: "Its back legs, by which it goes along, are longer, and therefore, it is easier for it to ascend a mountain than descend it."[28] The hare, thus, was the conventional figure, *in malam partem,* of the learned philosopher, who would mount upward in pride, yet could not descend to humility. The writer of the *Allegoria in Sacram Scripturam,* believed in Boccaccio's time to be Rabanus Maurus and widely followed, informs us with his typical logic, "The hare [rabbit] is any wicked person, yet one who is learned in the law. 'The hare, for that too cheweth the cud' [Lev. 11:6]. Because, although they are wicked, they are nonetheless learned."[29] *In bonam partem,* the creature could signify those who turned to the good in the "hind part" of their days and easily ascend to heaven!

Less arcane, perhaps, is leporine symbolism in the secular literary tradition. A mythological attribute of Venus, the prolific rabbit signified *lussuria,* or carnality.[30] Thus, to show the Virgin Mary's victory over lust, medieval and Renaissance painters would depict a white hare at her feet.[31] In *Diana's Hunt,* hares and rabbits are little creatures large with allusive possibilities: they point to Venus, to the sins of pride and lechery, and, more generally, to human sexuality, which chastity and reason must raise from sinful lapses to civilized levels of expression.

The case of the humble hedgehog (*ericius*) is again most telling. In Canto 5.55–58, Berarda makes a "novel" capture with her hounds: "She had caught six hedgehogs [*ricci*], no less, and fearful of being pricked, she was carrying them wrapped up in her lap." This episode, briefly mentioned at the close of a canto whose dominant event is the capture of two tough-hided bears, at first seems trivial, merely an addendum recounted from observation of the hedgehog's protective habit of rolling itself into a spiky ball when threatened. Religious tradition and the bestiaries, however, can again demonstrate satisfactorily how Boccaccio's *riccio* might be bound to a spiritual sense.

The spiny hedgehog habitually steals grapes by pilfering in vineyards, snapping off clusters, and then rolling on the ground to impale the pieces of fruit on his spikes. These very spines—the prickles that threaten the huntress on the literal level of the poem and that are enclosed suggestively in her lap—are the devil's traps: they can make man as sterile and empty as the vineyard thus despoiled.

The Bible and its commentators reveal even more concerning the hedgehog. The creature appears in a wrathful prophecy in Isaiah 32:2–15:

> The indignation of the Lord is upon all nations, and his fury upon their armies: he hath killed them and delivered them to slaughter. . . . And the unicorns shall go down with them, and the bulls with the mighty; their land shall be soaked with blood. . . . it is the day of vengeance of the Lord, the year of recompense of the judgment of Sion. . . . The bittern and the ericius [the hedgehog] shall possess [the land]. . . . there hath the ericius had its hole and brought up its young ones, and hath dug about and cherished them in the shadow thereof.   (Douay)

Contrary to what we would expect to be the meaning of this hedgehog at its family burrow—perhaps some model for the parent who protects threatened offspring—Saint Gregory equates the animal's behavior upon being captured with the exacerbating sin of self-exculpation, "the defense of wicked minds." The fervor and choplogic, so typical of his analogical reasoning, make that Father's arguments from the *Moralia in Job* worth citing at length:

> Under the name of "hedgehog" is designated the defense of wicked minds; because, namely, when a hedgehog is being seized, his head is seen, and his feet appear, and all his body is beheld; but presently, as soon as he has been seized, he gathers himself up into a ball, draws his feet inward, hides his head; and the whole which was before seen at once, is lost at once in the hands of him that holds it. Thus, doubtless, are wicked minds, when they are caught in their own excesses. For the head of the hedgehog is seen, because it is seen with what beginnings the sinner made his approach to sin. The feet of the hedgehog are seen, because it is seen with what footsteps his wickedness has been perpetrated; and yet the wicked mind, by suddenly adducing its excuses, draws its feet inward, because it conceals all the footsteps of its iniquity. It withdraws its head, because, by its extraordinary defenses, it gives the impression that it has never even begun anything wicked; and it remains as a ball in the hand of him that holds it, because he who reproves a sinner involved within his conscience, and he who had before seen the whole, by detecting it being deceived by the evasion of the wicked defense, is equally ignorant of the whole. The hedgehog therefore has a "hole" in the reprobate, because the wicked mind, gathering itself within itself, hides in the darkness of its defense. But the Divine discourse shews us also how the sinner—in thus excusing himself, and in thus clouding over, by his defenses which serve to obscure, the eye of the reprover which is fastened upon him—is supported by those who are like him.[32]

Other church authorities condemned hedgehogs as "duplices et dolosi" (duplicitous and crafty),[33] figures of fraud, like the ostrich. These details of animal lore, so markedly specific, suggest that Boccaccio was well acquainted with Gregory's "arsenal" of figurative language. If he did not know the *Morals on the Book of Job* in their entirety by the time he wrote the *Hunt*, he had at least acquired good portions of them as a student of canon law through excerpts, epitomes, or through uncredited patristic citations. Gregory's voluminous corpus was, along with the works of Saint Augustine, the richest source of ecclesiastical imagery in the later Middle Ages.[34] His *Morals,* not merely the standard authority on Job, but a towering column of biblical commentary that gave theologians a common discourse, was still basic for Boccaccio when he wrote the *Trattatello in laude di Dante* (*Short Treatise in Praise of Dante*) (begun ca. 1350); there he was to adapt the fundamental Gregorian definition of allegory in Scripture to his own cornerstone discussion of allegory in poetry.³⁵ Gregory's *Moralia in Job,* and the exegetical tradition that had grown around them for eight centuries, may help explain how these episodes in the *Hunt* form an integral part of the psychomachic allegoresis in which the youthful Boccaccio was working.

What most strikes us is how greatly the weighty patristic interpretations, particularly of the hedgehog and hare, contrast with the lighthearted innocence of the literal level in the poem. Yet, in the light of Boccaccio's aesthetics, as we shall presently see, such daring tension between letter and spirit was a poetic ideal.

## Antecedents and Analogs in Hunt Literature

Medieval hunt literature, a broad category of writings to which the *Hunt* belongs, has come down to us in many branches. The oldest, offshoots of prototypes composed in antiquity by Xenophon and Oppian, are cynegetic manuals. Treatises on coursing the stag, such as the Middle Eastern *Moamin et Ghatrif,* were transmitted to the Latin West around midthirteenth century through the Sicilian court of Emperor Frederick II, who was a published expert on hawking. Bookish advice, if not the sport itself, was evidently familiar to Boccaccio, since his huntswomen owe moments of success to techniques advocated by the manuals. They know, for instance, how to gauge a bird to down a chosen quarry and how to reward it, how to snare prey by spreading nets or baiting a pitfall, and how to flush fowl with beaters.³⁶

During the fourteenth century, practical and scientific texts of this sort were to evolve into a popular genre with an aesthetic and ethical intent. Most famous was Henri de Ferrières's lavishly illustrated *Livres du roy Modus et de la royne Ratio,* or *Book of King Modus and Queen Ratio* (ca. 1354–1376), a French etiquette of temperance whose embellishments include allegories of the stag and boar. A prologue tells how "Measure," or "Method," the symbolic ruler of its title, "organized all the sports of hunting to save us from laziness."³⁷ That idea, as old as Ovid's *Remedies of Love* (*Remedia amoris,* 199–210), had become a commonplace among notions associated with the hunt. Thus the *Livre de chasse* (*Book of the Hunt*) written in 1387 by Gaston Phébus, count of Foix, could stress the salubrious effects of hunting on the soul because it forestalled the sin of sloth: we should hunt eagerly "to remove cause for idleness, which is at the root of all evils."³⁸ Although these texts postdate Boccaccio's, they reflect the courtly and aristocratic climate, hospitable to "spiritualized" hunting, in which his poem was conceived. The art of venery was an easy rhetorical vehicle for allegory; hunting had parallel physical and moral benefits.

Yet not quite everyone agreed on its salubrious qualities. Danger could lie in its potential for arousing the passions, a problem attested by the sad case of Dido: the thunderstorm that disrupted her day in the forest with Aeneas (*Aeneid* 4.117ff.) drove the couple to a cave for shelter, and the queen's honor was lost. Mindful of this sensual pitfall, John of Salisbury attacked the sport as immoral, and he supposed that the ancients appointed a goddess rather than a god to preside over it because they would not have wanted to debase one of their more important immortals by assigning him a province ridden with self-indulgence and vice.[39]

Although hunting was a universal human activity, and many medieval heroes such as Saint Eustace, Siegfried, and Sir Gawain reflected its acceptance in circles both pious and courtly, John of Salisbury speaks from a long history of poetic fictions that associated the "venery" of the hunt with the "venery" of love. Ovid, who counted the chase an antidote to love in *Remedies of Love,* had by contrast in the *Art of Love* played upon the metaphor of the hunt as amatory pursuit. Similar vocabulary, casting the lover as hunter, returns in the preface to *The Art of Courtly Love* by Ovid's late twelfth-century admirer, Andreas Capellanus. The popularity of coupling the two sorts of pursuit, widely exploited in the language of lyric and narrative poetry, was reinforced by possibilities for punning in both Latin and the Romance languages alike on words such as *"venerie," "venatio," "venison," "Venus,"* and *"venereal."* In this tradition, since both Cupid and the hunter are bowmen, it is the lover who is stalker and his lady the quarry. That relationship structures the earliest French allegory of the love chase, *Li dis dou cerf amoreus (The Tale of the Amorous Stag),* composed in 326 verses around mid-thirteenth century.[40] There the hart represents the woman, forced to her knees and acceptance of love by Amours, the hunter. The image may ultimately descend from a Virgilian locus classicus, verses in which Dido, love-stricken for Aeneas, is likened to a helpless, wounded hind:

> Unhappy Dido burns, and through the city wanders in frenzy—even as a hind, smitten by an arrow, which, all unwary, amid the Cretan woods, a shepherd hunting with darts has pierced from afar, leaving in her the winged steel, unknowing: she in flight ranges Dictaean woods and glades, but fast to her side clings the deadly shaft.[41]

Medieval allegories of the "sanguinary stag," as Marcelle Thiébaux labels this bloodied, love-struck figure,[42] sometimes reverse the roles of lover and beloved. Love's victim, then, is the male stag-lover. *La prise amoureuse (Love's Capture),* dated April 1332, by the French court poet Jean

Acart (or Acars) de Hesdin, presents just such a fiction.[43] Could Acart's piece, written one year before the biennium to which *Diana's Hunt* is assigned (1333–1334), have traveled from the court of France to the French Angevin court of Naples and reached Boccaccio? Whatever the answer, Acart speaks "par mistère"—"mysteriously," that is, allegorically—to bring his readers more pleasure. His protagonist and narrator is a stag who wanders in springtime through "a forest of youth." Four routes traverse it where Love often hunts with his hounds. Most of the hounds are allegories of the lady's qualities (Beauty, Courtesy, Sweetness, and so on), the attractions that will wound and ambush the stag-narrator. His death signifies his complete surrender to her; the portions of the eviscerated quarry (in Old French, *curée*) she receives are his heart and will. The lover ends his poem with a plea for the lady to have pity and care for him.[44]

Whether Boccaccio knew Acart or not, the stag-narrators they each created are literary cousins. In *Diana's Hunt,* however, the love-wounded stag does not suffer capture and evisceration. He is rescued from love's blows and raised to a better state, changed, as if by magic, from beast into man. That moment is both a reversal and a renewal. As reversal, it may parry Acart's picture of a passion destructive unto death. It certainly counters, by the technique of narrative antithesis, Ovid's Actaeon, the man degraded to a brute hounded and doomed. As we are about to see, the stag is a symbol also of renewal, and the transformation of Boccaccio's stag alludes to that animal's legendary capacity for rejuvenation. His attainment of a "new life," based on lore in the bestiaries, reenacts allegorically the sacrament of Christian baptism.

# §§ 2 §§
# POETIC STRUCTURE

### The Reception of *Diana's Hunt* and Its Textual Integrity

Within a decade after his death in 1375, Boccaccio's life was dissolving from history into legend. According to a fictional image of the poet, already present in Filippo Villani's *Life* of Boccaccio (ca. 1390) and persisting down to our day, the author, as a young man, was an amorous fellow who made his loves the subject of his art. Popular in the two centuries after his death, those early romances and other fictions eventually were eclipsed by the *Decameron*—the "major work." Nineteenth-century philology would christen the rest "minor works," literary efforts of little sophistication. Most neglected was *Diana's Hunt,* the earliest and the shortest. So ignored was it that, although in 1521 Girolamo Claricio, a Milanese admirer, promised forthcoming publication, the first edition did not appear until Ignazio Moutier printed it among the complete works in Florence in 1832. Even so, the little-known *Hunt* had not yet entered Boccaccio's canon permanently. His chief biographers of the later nineteenth century and early decades of the twentieth continued to deny, or at least to doubt, that their master could have authored such a small, odd piece. The matter of attribution was only finally settled when Vittore Branca put the question to rest in 1938.[1]

To Romantic and early twentieth-century literary historians, nurtured on notions that Boccaccio's "minor" fiction was more confession than art, the power struggle between Diana and Venus in *Diana's Hunt* conveyed an obvious message: "Young ladies, you should prefer love to chastity," or, put in language less archaic, "Sex is much better than abstinence." From such an interpretation, it has followed that the vehicle bearing the message shows a clumsy, questionable design. Why, if Boccaccio wanted to encode love's conquest of chastity, does Diana dominate almost all of the action (nine-tenths by narrative length)? Why must we be patient through more than nine hundred verses of formulaically repetitive hunting events before at last being rewarded by the entrance of Venus? What, anyway, could lead us to expect that this grand chase would end in a debacle for Diana? Should it not rightly be called "The Triumph of Venus"? As an allegory of chastity lost, *Diana's Hunt* is hardly an achievement in subtlety or artistic economy. The poem's presumed lack of balance, unity, and logical conclusion led one of Boccaccio's most able readers to aver even quite recently that its text, as we have it today, must be lacunous.[2]

Let us assume, however, that we have *Diana's Hunt* complete, and let us see how—by crediting Boccaccio with ingenuity and artistic control as a creative writer, his calling from the cradle, as he himself claimed when complaining of the years he was forced to waste studying canon law—everything flows with its own logic.[3]

The text comes down to us in six manuscripts, and, in spite of minor gaps and variants all resolvable by comparison of the copies, none of the codices gives the slightest suspicion that the *Hunt* is incomplete.[4] The codicological group transmits the poem with two other works by Boccaccio in terza rima. Weightiest of the three is the *Amorosa visione,* an allegory fifty cantos long amusingly conceived as "half of a *Divine Comedy*"[5] and constructed in a gigantic acrostic on the letters of the words that form three prefatory *sonetti caudati* (that is, "tailed" or extended sonnets). The shortest work is a *ternario* with seventy verses, which begins "Contento quasi ne' pensier d'amore" (Content—almost—in thoughts of love) and has appended a ballad of forty-five verses, "Amor, dolce signore" (Love, O sweet Lord). Since the *Visione* and *ternario-ballata* both also catalog ladies to praise them, all three compositions conform as types to the *sirventese* as Dante shaped it. Branca has suggested that the manuscript tradition probably preserves an editorial decision made by Boccaccio himself, who wished to anthologize three related pieces in terza rima.[6] This conjecture is consistent with what we otherwise know about the author's fondness for numerological games. Numerology is more prevalent in the poetics of his Italian fiction than in his Latin works, and generally speaking, the earlier the writing, the more conspicuous the number play.[7]

## Numerology

A head and verse count in the *Hunt* marks arithmetic coordinates confirming that the text is a numerical composition and that it has come down to us intact. Those ladies whom Diana's messenger thrice summons in Canto 1 are exactly thirty-three. Since the Mystery Lady is last on the list, she is, *mirabile dictu,* the thirty-third—a position, of course, calqued directly on the numerology of the "sweet new style." In the sixth chapter of the *Vita nuova,* telling of his epistolary *sirventese* for sixty Florentine women, Dante says he mentions that poem only because the name Beatrice, marvelously, would not suffer any other place there but the ninth. The same *sirventese* must also be intended in Dante's sonnet "Guido, i' vorrei" (Guido, I would wish), where he fantasizes an enchanted sea voyage with his friends Guido and Lapo in the company of their respective ladies, "Lady Vanna and Lady Lagia along with her who stands on number thirty."[8] Who his "Thirty" was, Dante did not say. Boccaccio's anonymous "Thirty-three," quantitatively close to that secret lady, has even further and stronger numeric ties to chapter twenty-nine of the *Vita nuova,* since there Dante explains that the square root of the number persistently accompanying his most blessed lady is a Trinitarian miracle. Like the miraculous woman on whom she was modeled, the Mystery Lady of *Diana's Hunt* amounts symbolically to a 9 (33 $\Rightarrow$ 3 × 3 = 9). She is, in her maker's youthful version of an allegory for "new life," the new Beatrice.

Including their leader Diana, thirty-four women initiate the *Hunt,* distributed into four groups (9 + 9 + 8 + 8 = 34) that fan out toward the four cardinal points. In Canto 9 another wave of women joins them, this time twenty-five hunters, who again divide into four small parties (7 + 6 + 6 + 6 = 25). The two bands combined fall just one short of Dante's sixty (34 + 25 = 59), but only temporarily, for in Canto 16.26, a solitary straggler materializes. She is Zizzola d'Anna, "who unbidden, had gone hunting by herself." Zizzola brings Boccaccio's Neapolitan *sirventese* into perfectly numbered alignment with its Florentine antecedent.

Still another numerical coincidence occurs, provided the head count be limited to ladies named and mortal. They total fifty-eight, the same as the sum of the verses in each canto of the poem—or, rather, the sum of the verses in every canto but one. The single exception is Canto 3, which holds 61 verses. Its supernumerary *terzina* is accounted for by Carlo Muscetta as "a whim typical of Boccaccio, who was always violating the rules of symmetry."[9] Exceptions, though, do confirm the norm, and this one may have been strategically planned. Insofar as Cantos 1 and 2 recount preliminaries, not until the long third canto does the hunt proper begin. It closes with Canto 16, third from the end, after Zizzola d'Anna trails into view, a coda to the chase. One extra *terzina* and one extra huntress mark boundaries of a fourteen-canto sequence that is Diana's territory in the poem.

Why did Boccaccio compose just eighteen cantos, making fifty-eight the significant sum of canto lines and ladies cataloged? These combinations, not casual, attach to the other poems in his three-part anthology of triple-rhyming *sirventesi.* Three sonnets form a preface and acrostic base for the *Amorosa visione.* All longer than the standard fourteen-verse sonnet, they are *caudati,* or "tailed," consisting respectively of seventeen, sixteen, and twenty-five verses. This triad of exceptional sonnets, the alphabetic building blocks for the whole *Visione,* totals fifty-eight verses, just the same as the boundary number for canto length and named ladies in the *Hunt.*

Key numbers in Dante's reckoning were clearly a point of departure as Boccaccio laid plans for his literary debut. Like Dante, he reached back to a rich body of lore with origins in Pythagorean thought, Neoplatonism, Latin mythography, and patristic exegesis. Before we enter the matter of meanings, it will be helpful to present schematically the numbers at play in the chase.

1. Three is the root number of *Diana's Hunt.*
    Boccaccio published it as one component of a trilogy.
    It is cast in terza rima, rhyming triads that have as a base metrical unit the *terzina* ⇒ three hendecasyllables = thirty-three syllables.
    Its third canto has one extra *terzina.*
    It has three "heavenly" ladies: Diana, Venus, and the narrator's mistress.
    Diana's messenger calls thirty-three women.
    The Mystery Lady is the thirty-third.

2. Nine, as the square of three, also figures recurrently.
    The *Hunt* has eighteen cantos, which, by summing the digits, make nine: $18 \Rightarrow 1 + 8 = 9$.
    The second wave of huntresses arrives in Canto 9.
    Their arrival establishes the poem's structure as a diptych: eighteen cantos = 9 + 9.
    Inspired by Beatrice, the Anonymous Lady is also, in a sense, a Nine: $33 \Rightarrow 3 \times 3 = 9$.
    In this context, the number 58 can be understood to allude to both three and nine:

    Fifty-eight verses contain nineteen *terzine.* In the mathematics of numerology, multiplying by ten(s) does not alter basic meaning, since ten is the perfecting number, or "the number of perfection," as both the summit of the Pythagorean decad and the all-inclusive Christian Decalogue. By this "rule of ten," nineteen and nine are parallel sums.

    Fifty-eight, summing the digits, becomes a Trinitarian emblem, mystically a one and a three: $58 \Rightarrow 5 + 8 = 13; 13 \Rightarrow 1 + 3$.

3. A subdominant seven is present in the poem, associated particularly with the hunt.
    Counting Diana, in the first half of the diptych, thirty-four women hunt: $34 \Rightarrow 3 + 4 = 7$.

In the second half of the diptych, twenty-five women hunt: 25 ⇒ 2 + 5 = 7.

Canto 3, where the hunt begins, has sixty-one verses: 61 ⇒ 6 + 1 = 7.

The hunt ends in Canto 16: 16 ⇒ 1 + 6 = 7.

Diana's territory in the poem extends through fourteen, or twice seven, cantos.

If these arithmetic conundrums seem a trifle ridiculous today, they were not so by fourteenth-century standards of taste. On the contrary, numerical harmonies inhered in the powerful aesthetic analogy between God's creative activity as Author of the universe—which He had ordered "in measure, and number, and weight" (Wisdom 11:21)—and the poet's task as a "maker" of well-formed literary microcosms.[10] An intellectual of Boccaccio's age derived enhanced pleasure in reading precisely from seeking and finding those numbers artfully concealed by the author in his work, whose structural armature and contents they measure. Coupled with the delight in discovery of these numbers was the challenge that lay in deciding how to decode them. Easy one-to-one correspondences are not the rule in medieval compositions, where possibilities of meaning vary in direct proportion with the writer's talent and originality. We would shortchange Boccaccio, even at his least experienced, if we did not suspect more than a passive indebtedness to such symbolism, vigorous in the western Latin mainstream from Saint Augustine and Boethius, and channeled into Italian vernacular literature by Dante. The numbers in *Diana's Hunt* acknowledge, on one hand, values admired in Dante; on the other hand, they are figures that function integrally in the allegorical fabric of Boccaccio's personal invention, a novel fusion of received ideas.

As Boccaccio uses the three numbers three, seven, and nine, they correlate, in their most elementary meaning, with the three "heavenly" ladies. Nine as the product of three signifies the mysterious woman loved by the narrator who is unworthy, he confesses, of speaking her name. Three alludes to Venus, who, as a planet in the Aristotelian-Ptolemaic cosmos, orbits earth in the third heaven. Seven, in ancient Pythagorean acceptance the number of chastity, was associated by mythographers with the Moon, the seventh planet counting downward from Saturn. Venerable tradition sanctions the joining of the number seven with Diana, the goddess of the Moon.[11]

Considering the numbers in their secular content, we can equate three with Venus and love; seven with Diana and chastity. The nine that "names" Boccaccio's anonymous heroine, however, has, from its source in chapter twenty-nine of the *Vita nuova,* a meaning not profane but sacred:

This number was [Beatrice] herself, by analogy, I say, and here is how I understand that. The number three is the root of nine, such that, without any other number it alone makes nine, since we manifestly see that three times three make nine. Therefore, if three is of itself a factor of nine, and the factor of miracles is of itself three, that is, Father and Son and Holy Ghost, who are three and one, this woman was accompanied by this number of nine to make people understand that she was a nine, that is a miracle, whose root, namely that of the miracle, is none other than the miraculous Trinity.[12]

Thirty-third in the hunt, Boccaccio's Mystery Lady signals both her fidelity to Venus, goddess of love from the third heaven, and her likeness to Beatrice, Dante's amazing enneadic sign of the Christian Trinity. Threefold Christian Love, the serious symbolic dimension in her identity, seems then to be implied by the controlling boundary number linking verses (with but one significant exception, fifty-eight per canto) and named ladies in the *Hunt* (58 ⇒ 5 + 8 = 13 ⇒ 1 + 3).

The number seven also conveys a double sense. Subject to pluralities of meaning, seven in Christian terms is most often associated with the virtues and vices. Dante's wayfarer enters Purgatory with seven *P*'s on his forehead, each marking a capital sin (Italian *peccato*, Latin *peccatum*); all are successively erased as he climbs the mountain's seven ledges, each reserved for purging a vice. More specifically suggestive for Boccaccio would have been Dante's equation between seven and "nymphs" when, at the top of Mount Purgatory, the church comes in procession. The seven self-announced nymphs who dance about the wheels of Beatrice's chariot, four on one side and three on the other, symbolize the seven Christian virtues, cardinal and theological.[13] The Neapolitan ladies in Boccaccio's *Hunt*, covering the cardinal directions in groups (of thirty-four and twenty-five) whose digital sum is seven, figure in one sense for him the chastity of Diana's followers; less narrowly, and at the level of moral allegory, they are Virtues operant.

## The Poetic Dispute

Branca classifies *Diana's Hunt* as a "dispute" or "quarrel" (cf. Latin *altercatio, disputatio, conflictus*; Italian *contrasto*). From antiquity the formula had featured antagonisms like those between Vulcan and Mars in the *Odyssey* (8.265ff.) or Diana and Venus in Ovid's *Metamorphoses* (1.483ff.).[14] In a pastoral context, as in Virgil's *Eclogues,* it could transmit the rustic entertainment of shepherds in musical rivalry, and Boccaccio so used the form in his *Ameto* as well as in his *Bucolicum carmen*.[15] During the Middle Ages, fictional arguments gave rise to new logomachic genres. Alongside the Provençal *tenso* and *partimen*, there appeared the Old French *jeu parti* (two-sided question). Scholastic or goliardic debate-poems, in both Latin and vernacular, also continued the tradition, pitting Christ and Satan, the body and soul, the knight and cleric, the dead and living, the rose and violet, Carnival and Lent, winter and spring, water and wine.[16]

Turning on two significant oppositions, the *Hunt* is really a double *contrasto*. One axis carries the Ovidian competition between Diana and Venus, which, translated from mythic to mortal language, refers to tensions between sexual segregation—that is, not marrying—and a socialized life of procreational love. It only materializes clearly, fulfilled by a Venus ex machina, at the poem's denouement. The other conflict, on which the plot depends, is the chase itself, a sustained, fierce struggle between gentlewomen and beasts. Like its heroines, this chase should be seen with bifocal vision, profane through one lens, sacred through another. Going by the letter of the text, Boccaccio has contrived a love hunt with roles reversed, one that gives the ladies the initiative of the chase. But at the level of allegory, the huntresses are doing manly battle in the soul. They enact a psychomachia that pits virtue against vice, reason against bestial appetites.

## The Women and the Serpent

Of all the animals Diana's huntresses haul down from the hills to their bonfire, the one creature that causes these otherwise intrepid ladies to falter is a snake. They spot it, cornered in its hole by barking dogs, at the end of Canto 11: "Just then there came forth the tail of a serpent, and back inside it went at their uproar" (11.57–58). The women on the scene nearly die of fright, but reinforcements come rushing up, and they all "safely" (*salvamente*) dispatch the reptile. They set a fire in its pit to smoke out the "fierce plague" (*fiera peste*), whose snakelings soon come slithering after: "Truly six other little ones, its offspring, came out in a troublesome storm" (12.44–45).

In normal practice, hunters—or mighty huntresses—would neither be bagging snakes nor be frightened out of their wits by them. The adventure at this ophidian lair has, instead, a logic that is purely symbolic. The episode's length, lexicon, and placement make it prominent in the poem's narrative economy. Introduced just at the end of Canto 11 to create a moment of suspense when the snake's tail whips into view, it is spun to resolution through most of the canto that follows. This beast, both snake and not—both "serpent" and "fierce plague"—ambiguously threatens the women's welfare, which they guard *salvamente,* that is, both with a corporally "safe" and spiritually "saving" strategy.

But choking and clubbing to death just one serpent was not enough. There turn out to be seven. Even if snakes sometimes do slink and sleep by sevens in the wild, sevenfold families are more likely to turn up in the world of Christian signs. Seven, the sum of the virtues, is also the number of the capital vices. As agent of the Fall, the snake is the emblem par excellence of sin. More dangerous than the other animals, it embodies a satanic force to be purged. "*Serpent,*" one allegorist of the Scriptures put it, recalling Genesis 3:14, "means the Devil, as in Isaiah [65:25], 'dust shall be the serpent's food,' because those who love earthly things rather than the Lord feed the devil; by *serpents* are meant sins, as in the book of Numbers [21:6], 'Wherefore the Lord sent among the people fiery serpents' because the Lord sent sins to dominate the proud and murmuring."[17] When Boccaccio marshaled his huntresses to put "kindled fire" in the snake's hole, he must have remembered the same biblical passage, which in Saint Jerome's Vulgate refers to "kindled" or "ignited serpents" ("serpentes ignitos").

Why Boccaccio's serpent, in an Edenically "pleasant forest," should be designated as mother of six is explained by another idea. According to a theological concept advanced by Gregory the Great (d. 604), Hugh of Saint Victor (d. 1141), Peter Lombard (d. 1164), Thomas Aquinas (d. 1274), and many others, the vices form a family: Pride (or Vainglory) and her daughters, who are Envy, Anger, Sloth, Avarice, Gluttony, and Lust.[18] In other words, through filiation from Pride all evil descends.

Not inappropriately does the serpent make her appearance at the close of Canto 11. Ever since Augustine defined the connection, eleven had been the number of sin. He counts the generations from Adam to Lamech and his children as eleven, a total figuratively fit for the line descended through the felon Cain:

> Since the law is symbolised by the number ten (and hence the designation of the famous decalogue), surely then the number eleven, passing ten as it does, stands for trespassing against the law and consequently for sin.[19]

Augustine's equation of eleven with evil was accepted unanimously by the fathers and philosophers, authorities like Isidore, Bede, and Hugh of Saint Victor, who refer to the number in widely differing contexts. By introducing "sin" at *Hunt* 11, then, Boccaccio reaffirms a thousand-year-old norm. At the same time, he follows in the footsteps of his revered compatriot, dead but a dozen years, the Tuscan Dante Alighieri, who had reserved Canto 11 of *Inferno* for Virgil's exposition on the categories of sin.[20]

Were this *Hunt* scene simply an amusing case of squeamish noblewomen stumbling on something slimy, the ladies would probably have reacted to it by shrieking and running away. But Boccaccio's aristocrats overcome the "Eve" whose ancestral impulses flow in the blood of all the world's women (Genesis 3:15). Determined to confront the evil that "plagues" them, they stamp it out. Each detail in the encounter contributes to second-level meaning: the persistent huntresses "save themselves" by overcoming the "serpent," hidden with its "children" at a place in the text pointing to sin, Canto 11. The events starting in Canto 11 of the *Hunt*, then, hint at the symbolic identity of the other beasts in the forest depths, less terrifying, but evil nonetheless, whose threat Diana's chaste bands must conquer.

## The *Hunt* and the *Ameto*

The number seven *in malo* suits the *Hunt*'s snakes because of its equivalence with the sins in the family of vices. But, we have seen, as the number *in bono* of chastity and of the virtues, seven also has an affinity in the poem for Diana and her nymphs.[21] These virtue-nymphs anticipate the seven Florentine women who double as huntress-nymphs to effect the protagonist's conversion from brute to man in Boccaccio's *Comedìa delle ninfe fiorentine*, or *Ameto*.

Boccaccio wrote his pastoral "comedy of the Florentine nymphs" just after returning from Naples to live in Florence (1341–1342). Following *Diana's Hunt* by seven to eight years, this Menippean allegory is a far more sophisticated production in both style and form. Nevertheless, stripped of high rhetoric and eccentric tales, it rests on a simple plot, contoured in parallel with the *Hunt*. *Ameto*'s heroines, like their Parthenopean predecessors, begin as subjects of Diana, but end by rejecting her strictures and falling under the influence of Venus. Since the later text spells out spiritual meaning for this changeover, it can offer retrospective commentary.

The coarse shepherd Ameto, who dwells alone among the beasts of the woods and fields, chances upon seven nymphs, all with similar life stories: "Virginity, guarded by Diana, befitted me as a growing girl; then came the age for marriage, a romantically unsuitable arrangement, so that, sparked by Venus, I took myself a lover and found true happiness." After their confessions to most shameless adultery, a skirmish erupts in the sky between seven "whitest" swans and as many storks. The swans win. In answer to the portent, Venus descends, announcing herself as "gracious," Trinitarian light:

> "Io son luce del cielo unica e trina,
> principio e fine di ciascuna cosa:
> deh, qual men fu, né fia nulla, vicina?
>     E sì son vera luce e graziosa,
> che chi mi segue non andrà giammai
> errando in parte trista o tenebrosa,
>     ma con letizia agli angelici rai
> mi seguirà nelle divizie etterne"   (41.1–8)

[I am the light of heaven, one and triune, the beginning and ending of all things; pray, what was ever equal to me or ever will be? And so true and gracious a light am I, that he who follows me will never go erring in a sad or shadowy place, but in happiness he will follow me to the angelic rays in eternal riches].

Having witnessed the combat between seven against seven birds, Ameto beholds Venus on earth and recognizes in her "not that Venus whom fools call a goddess for their disordered lust, but she from whom true, just, and holy love descends among mortals" (42.1). Then Lia, the nymph whom Ameto loves, pulls off his clothes, plunges him in a "clear font," and the other nymphs reclothe him splendidly. Ameto recalls with chagrin his former, primitive life among the animals and his "concupiscent thoughts" about the women, for he has come to understand that they burn not with the fire of lust, but with the flame of Christian charity. Now purified, he can "see"; joy suffuses him, "and in short, it seems to him that he has been made from a brute animal into a man" ("e brievemente, d'animale bruto, uomo divenuto essere li pare," 46.5).

Ameto's physical transformation represents, allegorically, a shift to right order within his soul. His sensual appetites have accepted the rule of reason. In this state of rectitude, attended by God's grace and love (disguised as Venus), he enters the Faith by receiving from Lia the waters of Christian baptism. She and her sister nymphs, who tell of their own conversions from Diana to Venus, are the Seven Virtues. Each has an appropriate name—Agapes is Charity, Lia is the active life of Faith, Acrimonia is Fortitude, and so on—and the lover each takes is the contrary vice she conquers: Acrimonia takes Apaten, "the Apathetic"; Adiona, as Temperance, takes Dioneo, "the Dissolute." The combat in heaven that heralds Venus expresses the same idea visually. It is a psychomachian clash between virtues, the "whitest" swans, and their opponent vices, clacking storks. Venus herself descends as the light of saving grace, precipitating Ameto's immersion in a font, that is, his baptism. His change of clothing follows the actual ritual of baptism, during which the catechumen was stripped and reclothed in outward manifestation of Saint Paul's instructions:

> Put off your old nature which belongs to your former manner of life and is corrupt through deceitful lusts, and be renewed in the spirit of your minds, and put on the new nature, created after the likeness of God in true righteousness and holiness.   (Eph. 4:22–24)

Coming forth from the font a new man, Ameto is, in a Christian sense, reborn.

The stag who narrates *Diana's Hunt* is an early incarnation of Ameto. A solitary figure errant alone among the animals, he too comes upon nymphs in a wood and is witness to an amazing battle, women at arms killing dangerous beasts. They finally reject Diana and invoke Venus, who glides down promising "grace." Exactly thirty lines after the disappearance of Diana, Venus appears midway through Canto 17:

> . . . ignuda giovinetta
> apparve lor dicendo: "Io son colei
> da cui, pregando voi, ciascuno aspetta
>     grazia. . . ."   (17.31–34)

[There appeared a naked young woman saying to them: "I am she from whom each one of you through her prayers awaits grace"].

Through her incantatory power, the animals become men, jump into a river, and acquire fine vermilion cloaks. The same miraculous metamorphosis touches the stag:

> quasi ripien di nuova ammirazione
> mi ritrovai di quel mantel coperto
> che gli altri usciti dello ardente agone;
>     e vidimi alla bella donna offerto,
> e di cervio mutato in creatura
> umana e razionale esser per certo.   (18.7–12)

[near filled with strange awe, I found myself clothed with the same mantle as the others who had come forth from the fiery combat; and I saw myself offered to the Fair Lady, changed beyond doubt from a stag into a human being and a rational creature].

## Bestiality in the Platonic-Boethian Tradition

Like the more elegant *Ameto,* Boccaccio's lively little first work is an allegory of virtue triumphant. Once the soul has rejected vice and become rightly disposed, Grace can assure its salvation, which the sacrament of baptism will seal. Although the nymphs of Naples are fifty-nine instead of seven, and all (but one) have names real rather than symbolic, other semiotic markers point to their secret operation. We have seen how the hunt could be either an amorous or a virtuous activity. Boccaccio merges the options, creating huntresses both chaste and wise, yet led by a lady "whose face seems always to burn with love" (4.12). Since this verse echoes Dante's epithet for Venus, the dawn star that heralds his entry into Eden (*Purg.* 27.96), the lady's visage must radiate a love salvific, that same passion aflame in the seven nymphs of Florence. Whether the mystery woman of Naples might personify Charity specifically, or perhaps the virtue of wisdom, is a point open to speculation. In any event, she certainly "extinguishes" vice, as her erstwhile stag confirms: "Pride, sloth, greed, and wrath, when I see her, flee from my mind, which draws into itself their opposites" (18.34–36).

Since Pride, mother of all these vices, has already been revealed in the *Hunt,* in the guise of a maternal serpent, and since the serpent is so obviously a symbol of temptation and evil, we could assume that her fellow creatures are likewise not simply denizens of Parthenope's forest, but fauna native to a moral landscape. Thus, we should not be surprised at the presence of a unicorn, docile only to maidens and captured by chastity, in the numerically apt seventh canto. Considered tremendously strong and often as a Christ figure, the unicorn could evoke fierce, cruel Saul prior to his conversion and then Saint Paul in his new life.[22] Other antagonists in the hunt seem, at first reading, far more verisimilar and familiar as quarry than the unicorn, yet they, in turn, yield up a moral significance far stronger: one case in point is the Dantesque leopardess whose presence creates instant allegory. The beast is, notably, the target of the Mystery Lady:

> She withdrew with her women to a safe place and loosed her eagle, whose strong wings bore it almost to the sphere of fire; then, turning back down, it came circling and descending little by little. Like lightning amidst the trees and fronds, it struck so ferociously with cutting claw that it lacerated that beast's skin from head to tail. . . . The spotted

leopardess [*la variata lonza*], who felt the fierce blows, stretched out on the ground, and there in its writhing died. (4.17–30)

While the eagle's flight repeats the dreamer's rapture in *Purgatorio* 9, its victim is the poetic progeny of the "spotted leopardess" from the dark wood of *Inferno* 1. Not coincidentally, that feline's hellish companions are also close at hand in the *Hunt*: just before the spotted leopardess dies, a she-wolf has been dispatched; and shortly thereafter, the women cunningly trap a lion cub, a trophy then awarded to the anonymous heroine of the chase.

It can hardly be a coincidence that we find a wolf and a lion in close poetic proximity with Boccaccio's "Thirty-three," who is herself responsible for the demise of a she-leopard. Since Dante meant those three animals to symbolize temptations to sin, we ought to suspect that they return for the hunt endowed with a comparable capacity for evil. When seen from this literary perspective, a "raging bull" in the woods of Parthenope (Cantos 13 and 14) becomes appropriate, for in the *Divine Comedy* its counterpart, the Minotaur, and the hideous circumstances leading to his birth are twice adduced as examples of moral bestiality.[23]

Dante's reasons for coupling the evil acts of men with the natural behavior of animals derive from a tradition with deep Western roots in Plato's *Timaeus*. That creation myth envisions life perennially recycled between earth and stars, each reincarnation conditioned by previous existence:

> He who lived well during his appointed time was to return and dwell in his native star, and there he would have a blessed and congenial existence. But if he failed in attaining this, at the second birth he would pass into a woman, and if, when in that state of being, he did not desist from evil, he would continually be changed into some brute who resembled him in the evil nature which he had acquired, and would not cease from his toils and transformations until he helped the revolution of the same and the like within him to draw in its train the turbulent mob of later accretions made up of fire and air and water and earth, and by this victory of reason over the irrational returned to the form of his first and better state. (42b–c)

Thanks to the fourth-century translation and commentary by Chalcidius, a good portion of this dialogue survived for the Middle Ages. Always at the nucleus of library collections, including Boccaccio's, the *Timaeus* was a precious text because it was the only work of Plato generally available in Latin until the fourteenth century. As Chalcidius explains, at this passage Plato was not speaking literally. What he really meant was that "by indulging your passions, you will, in this present life, become more and more like an animal."[24]

Late in the fourth century, Macrobius, who flourished as an author in the medieval curriculum, recalls his Plato in the *Commentary on the Dream of Scipio*:

> When a soul allows the habits of its body to enslave it and to change man somehow to a beast, it dreads leaving the body . . . it either hovers about its corpse or it goes to seek lodging in a new body, in beast as well as man, and chooses the beast best suited to the sort of conduct it willfully adopted in the man.   (1.9.4–5)[25]

The wayfarer, beset by three beasts in Dante's prologue drama of *Inferno* 1, is hindered and driven back by his own submission to moral error. Later, on the purgatorial road to recovery, he hears Guido del Duca, a soul from Romagna temporarily blinded in his purgation from envy, describe inhabitants of the Valdarno in feral symbolism. They are "sows," "curs," "wolves," and "foxes," as if "Circe had them at pasture" (*Purg.* 14.40–54). How men can degenerate into beasts would have been evident to Dante both from the *Timaeus* and the *Commentary on the Dream of Scipio*. The animal-men in Guido's tirade, though, come to him most directly from the Christian Neoplatonist Boethius, whose *Consolation of Philosophy* Boccaccio must also have known by the mid-1330s. Men without virtue, Boethius warns, lose all semblance of humanity and can be likened to beasts:

> So it follows that you cannot adjudge him a man whom you see transformed by vices. The violent plunderer of others' wealth burns with avarice: you would say he was like a wolf. The wild and restless man exercises his tongue in disputes: you will compare him to a dog. The secret trickster rejoices that he succeeds in his frauds: let him be on a level with the little foxes. He that cannot govern his anger roars: let him be thought to have the spirit of a lion. The timorous and fugitive is afraid of things not fearful: let him be reckoned like a deer. The stupid sluggard is numb: he lives an ass's life. The fickle and inconstant changes his pursuits: he is no different from the birds. A man is drowned in foul and unclean lusts: he is gripped by the pleasure of a filthy sow. So he who having left goodness aside has ceased to be a man, since he cannot pass over into the divine state, turns into a beast.[26]

Taking his first steps as an allegorist, Boccaccio reveals himself a Platonist. With whispers of Ovid from the wings, he finds a fictional lie— lady hunters and goddesses who metamorphose animals into lovers—to veil the truth of a Platonic concept. In that idea the Renaissance would continue to recognize a commonplace. Leonardo da Vinci could record as an epigram in his *Notebooks*, "Whosoever curbs not lustful desire puts himself on a level with the animals." Still later, when in the mid-sixteenth century Giorgio Vasari compiled his *Lives of the Artists*, he would take it for granted why Giottino, back in the Florence of 1343, had put fierce animals into the city's "defaming" picture of Walter of Brienne, the duke of Athens. To humiliate publicly that vanquished tyrant, Giottino placed an image on the Bargello tower that showed him surrounded by symbols of his cruelty and inhumanity. As Vasari recorded, around the head of the duke were painted allegorical creatures, "rapacious animals . . . signifying the nature and quality of the man."[27]

The topos of human-appetites-as-animals, on which his *Hunt* allegory in good part hinges, returns in Boccaccio's later writings. There, speaking out as a humanist, he can comment openly on the iconographic rationale for that Timaean equation. Concerning the myth of Circe he supposes in his *Genealogies of the Gentile Gods* that she whorishly seduced many mortals, "and thus they assumed forms consonant with the favors they paid her, which Ulysses, that is, the prudent man, did not assume" (4.14). His earlier life of Circe in the collection of biographies *Concerning Famous Women* moralizes the seductress more openly:

> Those who through this wicked woman's deeds appeared to have lost human reason seemed to have been deservedly changed into beasts through their own crimes. . . . If we consider human behavior, we can well understand from this example that there are many Circes everywhere, and many other men are changed into beasts by their lustfulness and their vices.[28]

With Boethian philosophy to back him up, Boccaccio uncovers in his *Expositions on the Comedy* why Dante's dark forest was fraught with dangerous beasts. The wood is actually "the devil's prison," where we land for sinning. In it there is no humanity, only bestiality:

> When a man has committed sin, he becomes the beast whose habits are similar to that sin; to wit, since lust in its brutishness is likened to the pig, he who lets himself fall into the vice of lust becomes a pig, even though he retains human features; and the rapacious man becomes a wolf, because the wolf is a most rapacious animal, and hence that place is savage, being deprived of every human occupancy.[29]

A subsequent gloss on the arrival of Virgil (*Inferno* 1.63, of the *Comedy*), for Boccaccio a symbol of reason and agent of cooperant grace, could just as well apply to the final events of *Diana's Hunt*.

And of this there is no doubt at all: as many times as we become aware of our dishonest actions, so many times through divine grace do we begin again to be men, which we are not as long as we dwell in the ignorance of sins. On the contrary, having lost our reason, we have become those brute animals to which, as was said before, our defects conform. Even if there were no teaching to show us this, often poetic fictions show it to us when they speak of a certain man having been transformed into a wolf, another into a lion, another into an ass, or into some other bestial form.[30]

Since the beasts in the *Hunt* include creatures that even in the fourteenth century had no ecological business in the Neapolitan groves, their true habitat must be a "dark wood" of sin, to which they are allegorically indigenous, because like Dante's infernal beasts and many of his dehumanized malefactors, they reveal our baser instincts and, therefore, by extension, represent man himself in an irrational, degraded state of being.

Boccaccio filled his forest with animals that are actually men, but who by the stern optics of Boethian ethics no longer wear a human semblance. They have "become beasts." The *Hunt*'s stag-narrator both shares their experience and stands apart. In his distinctive aspect, he harks back to yet another Neoplatonic work of antiquity, the *Metamorphoses*, or *The Golden Ass*, by the second-century North African Lucius Apuleius. One of Boccaccio's lifelong favorite authors, Apuleius created a protagonist called Lucius who was trapped for a time in the body of an ass, the very ass that is among the fictional mutants Boccaccio remembers when he explicates how Reason rescued Dante from a forest of irrational appetites. Although this fictional Lucius relates his recovery at more length than does Boccaccio's stag, the courses of their restoration bear a close resemblance. Toward the end of Lucius's libidinous and harrowing adventures, he narrowly escapes being eaten by a wild beast in the circuses, and runs off at top speed to bathe in the sea, where he dips his head seven times beneath the waves "according to the divine Philosopher Pythagoras." Then, pouring out his heart, he makes an eloquent prayer to "the Blessed Queen of Heaven," Ceres-Proserpine-Venus-Artemis. Isis, "Nature, Universal mother," an amalgam goddess who is also Aphrodite, appears and tells the ass to eat a garland of roses. Lucius obeys and is at once transformed:

> My deformed and assy face abated, and first the rugged hair of my body fell off, my thick skin waxed soft and tender, my fat paunch became thin, my hind hoofs changed into feet and toes, my hands were no more feet but returned again to the use of a man that walks upright, my neck shrank, my head and mouth became round, my long ears shortened,

my great and stony teeth waxed less, like the teeth of men, and my tail, which before tortured me most, appeared nowhere.

A priest assisting this recuperation blames Lucius for becoming asinine because he yielded to the undisciplined desires of youth:

> Neither did thy noble lineage, thy dignity, neither thy excellent education anything avail thee from falling a slave to pleasure [*voluptates*]; thy youthful follies ran away with thee. Thou hast had a sinister reward of thy unprosperous curiosity.[31]

As metamorphosis into a lower form of life betrays the tyrannical effects of sinful, animalistic appetites upon a man's soul, "de-beastification" announces the reverse. The animal in him "dies" because his lower faculties have been brought back under the control of reason, the divine capacity that defines our humanity. Like Lucius, who let wrongly directed desires get the better of him, Boccaccio's stag also had fallen under a spell of sensuality. At the outset, he complains of Amore's painful blows, the wounds of concupiscent passion inflicted by Cupid's arrows, but after the advent of Venus at the close, his suffering and confusion vanish with the joyful discovery of a love divine. Since the stag's transformation marks moral ascent, it is appropriate that he conclude his testimony in a mood of contemplative adoration, meditating on the beauty and virtue of a woman through whom he hopes to win "salvation."

## § 3 §
# THE ALLEGORICAL STAG

### The Stag of Sensual Love

Considered from the narrator's point of view, *Diana's Hunt* is the autobiography of a lover. He often sounds like the voice speaking through memory in Dante's *Vita nuova,* praising his "most gentle lady," for her gift of "salvation." At first Boccaccio's speaker-witness is a stag, alone in dark groves, helpless before the heart-piercing blows of Amore. By the end, changed "from a stag into a human being and a rational creature," he stands in a sunny meadow, among many other new-made men and the women who have wisely "caught" them. His "éducation sentimentale," overseen by a guiding mistress, the goddess of chastity, and the celestial Venus, has brought him "out of the woods" into the world of men. What was wild in him is now tamed, ready to participate in the civilized human community. Unlike Petrarch's amorous persona, who spent the better part of a lifetime wandering "from forest to forest"—reduced to "a solitary wandering stag"[1]—Boccaccio's narrator benefits from the lesson of his Apuleian predecessor. He puts behind him the passions of youth and, a man among men, enters a life of mature rationality.

Boccaccio places his cervine storyteller squarely in the tradition of secular love and the Amorous Chase, which descends, at least in part, from Virgil's famous simile for Dido, wounded to desperation by Cupid, as if she were a hind cruelly hunted. We have seen how the motif flourished in Old French fiction, as in *The Tale of the Amorous Stag* and *Love's Capture,* poems that could have circulated at the Angevin court in Naples. For the masters of Italian lyric as well, the stag of profane love remained a powerful emblem. Late in the Quattrocento, the huntsman Iulio of Angelo Poliziano's *Stanze* is drawn to a wood, where, in "the lovely time of his green age," he will be led to Simonetta by a mysteriously compelling animal whom Amore conjures from thin air, "the image of a haughty and beautiful doe: lofty forehead, branching horns, completely white, light and slender." This elusive, untouchable apparition has a pallor and magnetism inherited from Laura, of whom Petrarch had created seductive spring epiphanies: "A white doe on the green grass appeared to me, with two golden horns, between two rivers, in the shade of a laurel, when the sun was rising in the unripe season. Her look was so sweet and proud that to follow her I left every task."[2]

In the visual arts as well the image of the stag often attends amorous moments, a symbol of lovers and sensual love itself. Take, for example, the sounding bowl of a mid-Trecento Tuscan gittern upon which are found two lovers beneath a tree, and below them, couchant at the stringed instrument's base, a stag, metaphor for the submissive lover. A coffer made in Siena in 1421, now at the Louvre, depicts Venus as queen on a cloud above three worshipful ladies; around the sides of the box, hounds pursue stags—familiar symbols of love-stricken men. Around 1420, Mariotto di Nardo would decorate a birth salver with a key scene from Boccaccio's *Teseida,* the enamorment of Arcita and Palemone: Emilia sits in a garden between a rabbit and stag. Perhaps on the coffer, as on the gittern, the stag implies sensuality. On the other hand, the pairing of the rabbit, an unmistakably erotic attribute of Venus,[3] with the stag, by rights Diana's creature, may suggest a heroine chaste until her marriage.

## The Stag as Christian Man

If a seed from Virgil's *Aeneid* ramified through medieval courtly poetry into fictions of amorous harts, another tradition from antiquity portrayed the stag as the animal that could defy death by perpetually renewing itself. This pagan lore found place in patristic wisdom as an underpinning for commentary on the Forty-second Psalm (Vulg. 41:1), "As the hart panteth after the fountains of water; so my soul panteth after thee, O God." When Augustine likened the sinner who seeks Living Waters to the thirsting hart from the Bible, the analogy became a controlling image for the liturgy of baptism. Both celebrants and catechumens chanted the psalm, which gave rise to a widespread motif in medieval religious art: stags depicted at streams of water.

Boccaccio would have learned the sacred significance of the creature from several areas of his experience. By age twenty, he had already begun studying the Fathers and Doctors, whose writings formed the core of ecclesiastical law. His knowledge of deer, however, would have derived not solely from his early reading—fiction, natural science, canons, patristics—but also from his role as a churchgoing member of the Angevin community, which frequented the baptistry of San Giovanni in Fonte, famous for its paleo-Christian mosaics. All these strands, and more, find their way into *Diana's Hunt* and surface, bound up at the finale, when a stag suddenly flashes before us, our narrator's confessed former identity.

The surprising disclosure presents us with a familiar Christian icon

*Figure 1.* Stags consuming snakes. Pseudo-Oppian, *Cynegetica,* Greek, ca. A.D. 200. Venice, Biblioteca Nazionale Marciana, MS. Gr. Z. 479, fol. 27 v. Courtesy of Biblioteca Nazionale Marciana, Venice.

whose origins go back to Greek and Roman times, when authorities on zoology agreed that the "nature" of an aging stag was to consume serpents, its enemies, by inhaling them (Figure 1). Then, to overcome the poison in this food, the stag would seek a river from which to drink. Purified by the waters, the beast shed its old horns and grew new ones, regaining vigor and youth.[4] This pseudoscientific tradition, which ex-

*Figure 2.* Stag nosing serpent from a crack in the earth. Latin *Physiologus,* Rheims, ninth century. Bern, Burgerbibliothek, MS. 318, fol. 17 r. Courtesy of Burgerbibliothek, Bern.

plains why stags pull the Chariot of Time in illustrations of Petrarch's *Triumphs,* plays a tiny but witty role in Boccaccio's own *Ameto.* One of the virtue-nymphs, Agapes/Charity, forced by her family to marry a man far her senior, caricatures him as drooling and doddering, a bed partner all shriveled up by his litigious career in the law courts, and incredibly decrepit: "having maybe seen more centuries than the renewing stag, he had been reduced by the years to practically nothing."[5]

Given its enviable ability to recover its youth, the stag was a natural exemplar in medieval bestiaries (Figure 2). About the turn of the twelfth century, Theobaldus gave a typical moralization. His metrical adaptation of "Physiologus," or *Physiologus,* the second-century ancestor of nearly all medieval bestiaries, circulated widely on the European continent:

> In his teaching on the stag, Physiologus says that he has two natural characteristics and allegorical interpretations. For with his nostrils he

pulls out snakes, no matter what their size, from their holes in the earth or their hiding-places in the rock; these he devours and, soon with the foul poison seething up, he burns to run to the limpid waters of a spring. When it happens that he has drunk them, full of them, he overcomes the poisons, and rejuvenates himself as he casts off his horns.

When, overcome by the fraud of the old serpent, we too draw up his venom and are burned with torches (that is, with lust which, like anger, begets hatred, or else with excessive greed for money), we too ought to run to Christ the living fountain who, by giving us water, rids us of the poisons we have consumed.

And we are made young by the removal of these poisons and of our deeds of pride, which are like horns when they strike the wretched.[6]

The stag, then, could stand for Christian man, vulnerable to the poison of sin, signified by the serpent. Man cleanses himself of this defilement by seeking the Living Waters of Christ, just as the stag ran to the water brook.

How had the self-renewing creature of pagan antiquity grown into a medieval emblem of the sinner purged and redeemed? Crucial to the Christianization of the symbol was Augustine's exegesis of the Forty-second Psalm (Vulg. 41:1), "As the hart panteth after the fountains of water; so my soul panteth after thee, O God." For Augustine, cognizant of the stag's dramatic eating and drinking habits, this verse applies morally to human life.

> The serpents are your vices; destroy the serpents of iniquity; then you will long yet more for the Fountain of Truth. . . . when will you desire the fountain of wisdom, as long as you labor in the poison of malice? Kill in yourself whatever is contrary to the truth; and when you see yourself dwelling in perverse cupidities, wish not to persist, as if it were what you desire. . . . Desire what will delight you; desire the river-brooks.

Equating the snakes with our iniquities, Augustine sees in the deer that devours them a twofold emblem of conversion. The stag drinking at the riverside can, in one sense, signal the turning point of baptism. But the hart's cyclical senescence and rejuvenation also repeat an ever-recurrent human experience: that is, conversion literally understood as a *turning toward* God, the source of wisdom and virtue, a process that occurs whenever in the daily course of events penitent man turns away from vice.[7]

Augustine's seminal *Expositions on the Psalms* was influential in shaping the visual tradition of stags at the river brooks.[8] As old as the earliest surviving Christian baptistries, the image spans more than a millenium and the whole of Christendom, from Eastern Europe to Britain, from Scandinavia to North Africa.[9] Striking as a high medieval synthesis of the theme is a detail in the magnificent twelfth-century apse mosaic at the Church of San Clemente in Rome (Figures 3 and 4). Its cross rises triumphant with the crucified Lord and twelve doves, signs of the Apostles, from the lush fan of an acanthus. At the base of the plant, in a direct line below the body of Christ, stands in profile a small stag nosing an enormous serpent from the ground. The snake's mid-part forms a distinct, spotted semicircle that arches over the diminutive quadruped and then curves tapering down on the right with a horseshoe-shaped tail. The scene duplicates in miniature a message of the Crucifixion: as Christ conquered sin on earth, so the stag is man who confronts the poison of vice within himself. This snake's tail is a pointer to the scene below, where two much larger stags, of natural proportions, bend toward each other to drink at a hillock from which flow four streams, symbols of the rivers of Paradise.

Jacopo Torriti's monumental thirteenth-century apse mosaic at the church of the Lateran depicts two confronted stags, similar to those at San Clemente (Figure 5). His composition links, vertically, Christ Pantocrator in heaven through a descending dove below him to a tall, jewelled cross planted windmill-like on a mount divided by four streams, full and rippling. They flow down into a horizontal river that rings the bottom of the composition as an aquatic frieze in which water fowl float and swim with genii. On either side of the mount, hollowed to contain the heavenly Holy City over which rises a Phoenix, stags and lambs line up symmetrically to lap the waters. The meek and humble lambs figure both Christ and his flock. Above them on Eden's flowering green where grows the "tree" of the Cross, the stags that graze, clearly profiled against the gold background, are mankind that purges itself of sin when it seeks the Living Waters, regenerative with virtue and the Word.[10]

Perhaps most important for understanding the nature of the narrator in *Diana's Hunt* are the scenes decorating San Giovanni in Fonte, Naples. Built around the year 400 and restored by the Angevins toward 1300, San Giovanni is the baptistry attached to the cathedral complex of Santa Restituta and San Gennaro. During Boccaccio's southern years, it was the font that served the royal court, and we can be sure that he often admired its beautiful old decorations. Between the cupola and walls, above tetramorphs symbolizing the Evangelists, are four pastoral scenes, each with a shepherd at the center. Leaning on their crooks, they preside over a pair of lambs in two facing lunettes and over a pair of stags in the alternate lunettes (Figure 6). The mosaicist Torriti chose the same combination of

*Figure 3.* Triumph of the Cross. San Clemente, Rome. Apse mosaic, twelfth century. Courtesy of Istituto Centrale per il Catalogo e la Documentazione, Rome.

*Figure 4.* Triumph of the Cross. San Clemente, Rome. Apse mosaic, detail: stag drawing forth serpent beneath an acanthus; stags drinking from the four rivers of Paradise. Courtesy of Istituto Centrale per il Catalogo e la Documentazione, Rome.

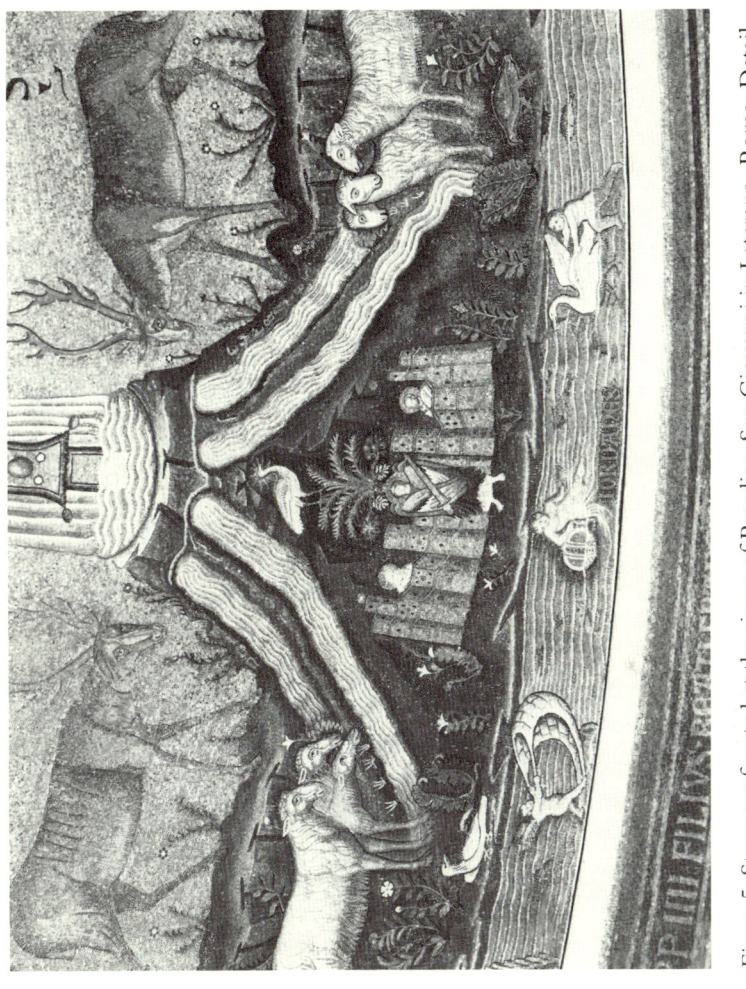

*Figure 5.* Stags confronted at the rivers of Paradise. San Giovanni in Laterano, Rome. Detail from apse mosaic, thirteenth century. Courtesy of Istituto Centrale per il Catalogo e la Documentazione, Rome.

*Figure 6.* Stags drinking from the rivers of Paradise. Baptistry of San Giovanni in Fonte, Naples, lunette mosaic, ca. 400. Courtesy of Istituto Centrale per il Catalogo e la Documentazione, Rome.

sacred animals for the Lateran basilica. While the Neapolitan stags drink amid a rocky landscape, alluding to the immersion of baptisands, their Christological guardian points to the wellsprings, where they quench their thirst for pardon and salvation in this abbreviated terrestrial paradise.[11]

The purpose of such pictures, of course, was to illustrate symbolically the liturgy of Christian rebirth. As San Giovanni's stags at the river brook attest, even before receiving sanction from Augustine's exegesis, the psalm of the thirsting hart had become a presiding scriptural presence in the rites of baptism most often administered on Easter. From early times at the Lateran, mother church of the faithful in the West, the midnight vigil of Easter would close with a reading of the Forty-second Psalm (Vulg. 41) and a prayer: "Almighty and everlasting God, look mercifully on the devotion of thy people who are born anew, who pant, as the hart, after the fountain of thy waters: and mercifully grant, that the thirst of their faith may, by the mystery of baptism, sanctify their souls and bodies. Through our Lord Amen." Then the pontiff himself would lead a procession to the baptistry, all chanting the "Sicut cervus" (As the hart).

The ceremony itself began with a blessing of the font ("Benedictio fontis"). It addresses a prayer to the Lord asking that the Holy Spirit render fruitful for regeneration the waters, which wash away the stains of all sins. Let whosoever enter them, petitions the priest, "be cleansed from the filth of the old man" and "born again new children." He prays that here, at this font of life, "all, however distinguished by age in time, or by sex in body, may be brought forth to the same infancy by grace, their mother." Following the blessing came immersion. The neophytes would be stripped naked and thrice dipped in the name of the Holy Trinity. On emerging from the waters, they were reclothed in white to display their purity and faith as new members of the church. Finally, the bishop or priest administered chrism and the baptized made their first communion.

The "Benedictio fontis," a portion of the old Gelasian sacramentary still in use in the Roman missal, seems to have been written by Leo the Great, who probably also composed an inscription of eight distichs carved on the tabernacle of the Lateran baptistry about 400, when Sixtus III rebuilt it over an older basin reputed to have been the site of the baptism of Constantine. Visible yet today, the distichs characterize baptism as the sacrament that generates the community of the faithful, born as children from waters made fertile by the Holy Ghost. Their immersion washes away sin in a renewal necessary for eternal life: "Wouldst thou be pure," the verses invite, "cleanse thyself in this bath, whether thou art oppressed by original sin or by thine own guilt. This is the fountain of life, which purges the whole world. . . . Hope for the Kingdom of Heaven, ye who are reborn in this font."[12]

Such patristic language, which set the pattern for liturgical practice, rests on two New Testament foundations. One, from Christ's words as reported by John the Evangelist, stresses the idea of birth in baptism. "Jesus answered: Amen, amen, I say to thee, unless a man be born again of water and the Holy Ghost, he cannot enter into the kingdom of heaven" (John 3:5 Douay). The other, Saint Paul's view, emphasizes rather an essential "death" in the experience: before a new man can be born, the old, corrupt one must die.

> Know you not that all we that are baptized in Christ Jesus are baptized in his death? For we are buried together with him by baptism into death: that, as Christ is risen from the dead by the glory of the Father, so we also may walk in newness of life. For if we have been planted together in the likeness of his death, we shall be also in the likeness of his resurrection. Knowing this, that our old man is crucified with him, that the body of sin may be destroyed, to the end that we may serve sin no longer.   (Romans 6:3–6 Douay)

When Boccaccio's narrator, then, leaves behind or "dies" to an old identity—as the other animals in *Diana's Hunt* do, quite literally—and then finds new life in human form, he follows an ancient tradition. That stag-turned-man, we now understand, was, in its sacred heritage, the sinner redeemed. Enemy of the serpent, the stag was ever reborn through his victories over its venom. The thirsting hart of Psalm 42:1, as Augustine taught in his *Expositions on the Book of Psalms,* was remembered at moments of conversion. At home in the art of church and baptistry, he haunted by preference rivers, meadows, and groves of the earthly paradise, in company with other creatures, among them aquatic birds. He signified man who rejects sin and turns to virtue, whether at the reception of the sacrament of baptism through which all who would be saved must be reborn, or thereafter, over and over again, in moods of repentance from repeated backsliding.

On all registers the stag spokesman is central to the *Hunt*'s meanings. By choosing a stag as protagonist—rather than, say, the amusing hybrid that Lucius became in Apuleius's *Golden Ass*—Boccaccio exploits a wonderfully rich convergence of science and fiction, pagan and Christian imagery. The stag is, in reality, a forest dweller, most noble of all hunted animals. In mythology he is an attribute of Diana,[13] hence quite correctly on hand for a tale about one of her hunts. Through a favorite Ovidian link with the goddess, this particular stag is further designated as "Not-Actaeon": instead of perishing as a beast, he survives, like Lucius, restored to wiser manhood. We see him transformed from the wounded lover of the poem's opening lines, sensuality incarnate, to a rational man in the end, one who has recovered himself through Grace, while standing near a rivulet in which the animals that share his sylvan groves find a font of new life.

## The Semantics of Baptism in *Diana's Hunt*

The semantics of baptism, which give a cervine identity to the poem's narrator, govern the whole allegorical apparatus of the *Hunt*. If the stag must survive throughout, not so the rest of the animals, who enact to the letter baptismal death and rebirth. Many "old men" die to be reborn out of fire and water.

The miracle of group resurrection occurs when, at the ladies' petition, a small white cloud poises above, platform to a diminutive Venus. Her special words murmured over Diana's holocaust elude the narrator. But no matter, what counts is what happens:

> ciascuna fiera che v'era infiammata
>   mutata in forma d'uom, di quelli ardori
> usciva giovinetto gaio e bello,
> tutti correndo sopra 'l verde e' fiori.
>   E tutti entravan dentro al fiumicello,
> e, quindi uscendo ciascun, d'un vermiglio
> e nobil drappo si facean mantello.
>   Ciascuno era fresco come un giglio.   (17.39–46)

[every beast that had been set afire came forth from that blaze, changed into the form of a man, youthful, glad, and fair, all running over the greensward and flowers. And all of them entered into the brook; and as he came forth, each one was cloaked in a cloth of noble vermilion. Each was as fresh as a lily.]

Couched in a deceptively simple style, more in the manner of a minstrel than a serious student of Dante,[14] Boccaccio's message bespeaks Christian renewal. We can pierce his false primitive veil by recalling patristic imagery, preserved in verses at the Lateran basin and in the liturgy for blessing the font: impregnated by the Holy Spirit, the virgin womb of the church generates the community of the faithful, born when life is renewed in the waters. On its mythical register, the *Hunt* permits Venus to enter chaste Diana's territory and "give birth" to youthful men. Reclothed after passing through water, they congregate on the meadow, now a community of lovers in bright red robes.

Venus descends as grace personified, a role that she makes clear, "I bring grace. . . ." In this guise, by a clever synechdoche, she herself substitutes for her attribute, the dove.[15] It is the bird of the Holy Ghost that always hovers over baptisms in Christian art to reenact the sacramental descent of the dove at the baptism of Christ (Matt. 3:16; Mark 1:10; Luke 3:22; John 1:32). Church law, codified as a body by Gratian around 1150 in Bologna, insists on the effect of the presence of the Holy Spirit. From the time of Ambrose, an author much cited on the sacraments, it was clear that water vivified by the descent of the Holy Spirit—by *epiclesis*—conveyed what plain, ordinary water could not:[16]

> Whoever passes through this water will not die, but he will resurrect. . . . Not all water heals, but only that which has the grace of Christ. The element is one thing; the consecration is another. Water does not heal unless the Holy Spirit descends and consecrates that water.[17]

But the ancient goddess's descent in the *Hunt* is, at the same time, a theophany of Venus Genetrix, and in that figuration she recalls the mother-figure to which the blessing of the waters alludes. It promises that all who enter the font, the womb of the church, no matter what their previous nature, will alike be "brought forth to the same infancy by grace, their mother." Thus Boccaccio's young men are born, very figuratively speaking, of a virgin womb in Diana's "Parthenope" through the agency of one who, amazingly, as a pre-Christian goddess of procreation can bear grace from heaven, addressing her faithful like God the Father from a cloud at the Transfiguration (Greek *metamorphosis*) of Christ.[18]

Not even the sacramental purification of a baptism by fire is absent in Boccaccio's fiery metamorphosis of beasts to men. An ancient tradition, found in the *Gospel of the Nazarenes* and in the *Diatessaron* of Tatian, reported that as Jesus went down into the waters of the river Jordan, a fire was kindled over it by the Holy Ghost. For this reason, patristic exegesis insisted that Christ's baptism fulfilled in New Testament terms the sacrifice of Elijah when God's fire descended and consumed the holocaust before the priests of Baal.[19] Thus, in the words of Gregory of Nyssa, the "vivifying, burning, inflaming" action of the Holy Spirit "consumed the impious and illuminated the faithful."[20]

And out of the flames of a holocaust leap the men of the *Hunt*, made new. Their immolation as animals intertwines several symbolic strands. Flames of desire, a concupiscence with hints of the Fall, are the metaphorical element that consumes carnal lovers. By a logic of moral and liturgical homeopathy, what characterizes the sin contributes to the cure. Fire is precisely the medium in which lust finds its medicine, as Dante's Wayfarer had discovered to his dismay on the seventh ledge of Purgatory.

Further, the holocaust in the *Hunt* crackles with "ardors" that were said to engulf snake-eating stags. Elaborating Augustine's comment on Psalm 42:1, Peter Lombard, a magisterial twelfth-century Parisian professor of theology, could rhetorically play with fire:

> Having pulled in the serpent with his nostrils, [the stag] *burns* with poison, and so *most ardently* desires a font for drinking. . . . as the hart who has attracted the serpent, *burning,* seeks a font that he might *extinguish the fire,* so the catechumen, recognizing that he *burns with the poison* of vices contracted from the world, seeks and desires a font of baptism, where he can shed his hide of vice and horns of pride, and thus rejuvenescent, be made a new man.[21]

Although, ironically, a Boccaccian reversal makes the stag the only animal in *Diana's Hunt* who is *not* true to the part that tradition had assigned him, most of the others do, in fact, take on the sacred hart's persona and burn. Only the seven snakes must be reduced to ashes at their den. The rest of the beasts, dragged down from the mountains in an allegory of humility, can successfully make the transition into better flames, where they burn partly with the "poison of vices," partly to purge their sins, partly to serve a ritual of baptism by fire and water and, pertinently upon their resurrection, to fulfill the Pauline injunction that it is "better to marry than to be burnt" (1 Cor. 7:9).

To new Christian men sprung from a burning pile of beasts, the minstrel epithets, "youthful, glad, and fair" fittingly apply. Through baptism the catechumen puts off the old man and puts on the new; he recovers an innocence that makes him an "infant," or, more simply, he becomes "young" again. Since Boccaccio's men have been stripped of the former, sinful moral ugliness that had turned them into physical brutes, they have every reason to be "glad": their outer appearance now reflects the beauty of the moral order of their souls. Following the injunctions in sermons delivered on the Paschal Vigil, they hasten toward the purifying waters, eager and impatient for salvation.

In actual practice, neophytes were stripped before immersion and then afterward reclothed with white. They ritually obeyed Saint Paul's spiritual injunction to put off the old man, and put on the new (Eph. 4:24;

Col. 3:9–10). Canon law, again excerpted from Ambrose, spells out the procedure:

> After baptism the Christian is dressed in white clothing, which signifies Christian innocence and purity; after washing away the old stains, he must preserve this garment immaculate along with his desire for sacred converse when he appears before the tribunal of Christ.

Rejection of wrongdoing is a concomitant part of the ritual, as the next canon specifies: "May you receive after baptism white vestments, that it be a sign that you will have departed from the voluptuousness of sins and put on the chaste veils of innocence." Following Tertulian in his treatise *On Baptism,* we can say that what the neophyte puts on is "the garment of faith."[22]

Boccaccio, however, clothes his new men in red, a hue wider in its allusive range than white. Red relates to baptism as the Fathers had seen it in Isaiah's Old Testament vision (63:1–3) of the Transfigured Christ: a man with glorious, crimson garments who would tread the winepress of Crucifixion, death, and Resurrection alone. Red is also the color of love; it cloaks Boccaccio's saved in outward manifestation of the charity that all who are reborn of God must hold in their hearts. But purity and faith, which white robes symbolized, have not really disappeared from Boccaccio's poem. His neophytes, who walk away from the river in their robes of vermilion, gather on the meadow, cleansed in body and soul to a pristine bloom "fresh as the lily."[23]

Exempted from the bonfire and the river brook, the stag nonetheless undergoes a renewal to earn his crimson cape.

> Near filled with strange awe, I found myself clothed with the same mantle as the others who had come forth from the fiery combat; and I saw myself offered to the Fair Lady, changed beyond doubt from a stag into a human being and a rational creature.

The verb *ritrovarsi, mi ritrovai* (I found myself) carries the same connotations here that Boccaccio thought he saw in Dante's use of that verb at the beginning of the *Divine Comedy*: a recovery of conscious awareness signaling spiritual reawakening. Thus the narrator in the *Hunt* would not be simply a catechumen now rejecting past error for the first time, but rather a baptized Christian who has lost himself because he has suffered a moral relapse and strayed from "the straight way." The implication becomes explicit when he attributes his transformation to the Mystery Lady, who, he says, brought such delight to his eyes that he was *"turned back,"* or *"turned once again,"* into a man:

> . . . agli occhi mie' diè tal diletto,
> che, donandomi a lei, uom ritornai
> di brutta belva

[She gave such delight to my eyes that I, in giving myself to her, turned back into a man from a brute beast].

What he reports then is a double recovery: literally, the restoration of his humanity, and figuratively, the recuperation from the injurious consequences of his sins.[24]

This may explain why in the *Hunt*, the Mystery Lady whose virtue helps restore the narrator to his rightful body is both "kindled" with love and "*ispegnitrice* di ogni noia" (*extinguisher* of all pain). Just as she is the one who can "put out" the illicit fire in her lover's heart, so too she can quench his thirst for salvation. Deep is the serenity she imbues in her lover, whose words of praise yield at last to adoring, reverential silence.

## From Baptism to Epithalamium

At the end of the poem, Boccaccio's stag "finds himself" with other animals in a stylized *locus amoenus*, a woodland with a hillock, a stream, and a meadow strewn with flowers. His story, from existence in pain and errancy to a life of transfiguring joy, veils a theological allegory. All the beasts share this experience, sharply divided between a "before" and an "after," which the author of the *Hunt* articulates with two distinct narrative structures. First and longest is a motif adapted from Prudentius (ca. A.D. 500), the psychomachia. Women who collectively personify virtue seek and destroy sinful appetites that skulk as animals in an umbrous forest. After their battle in the soul, when evil, or animalistic temptations to do evil, have vigorously been overcome and put to death, there occurs the passage into new life. This second event, which provides a grand finale for the nymphs' sylvan adventures, takes place as a poetic mime of baptism.

How are psychomachia and baptism, the two veiled events of the poem, compatible partners in allegory? Viewed retrospectively from the *Ameto*, where a battle of vices and virtues (the swans and storks in the sky) preceded the baptism, the conjunction in the *Hunt* seems perfectly normal, but what was there *before* that "first fiction" to serve the poet as a model? Why does he climax the struggle in a dark forest with a collective rite of baptism? Why does he not present merely a battle of virtues against vices, as Prudentius had established in the scenario of his *Psychomachia*?

One critic has called the last cantos of the *Hunt* "a gratuitous final installment, a pure expedient for resolution,"[25] and well we might wonder why Venus had to intercede at all, except that this is "a Boccaccio," albeit early. Do the women really have to betray Diana and call on her arch rival, Venus? What if they had simply conducted a successful hunt? Virtue would have defeated vice, and then the huntresses could have happily laid down their quivers and trooped home to the court for a good night's sleep.

We can once again take our guidance from liturgy and canon law. If the portion of the poem ruled over by Venus recapitulates a baptism, Diana's cantos allegorize the catechumen's preparation for that perfecting laver. The night before the sacrament was administered, those who wished to receive the waters would watch and wait in prayerful anticipation. During the long hours of this Paschal Vigil, the most solemn vigil of the year, the catechumen battled the Devil who came to make a last stand in the shadows of his soul; he struggled to expel dark forces and come forth from the fight triumphant into the light of Easter morning.

This wrestling with sin included a ritual exorcism. Like the stag, who destroys serpents with his breath by drawing them in through his nostrils, the priest used his *breath* to call forth the Evil Spirit from the sinner and from the waters of the font in the ritual "benedictio aquae," or "blessing of the water."[26] In the first instance, after the catechumen felt the air breathed on his face (*exsufflatio*), he would spit (*sputatio*) in the direction of Satan. Exorcism of the Enemy from the font, in the second instance, was absolutely necessary to proper baptism. As the Triune God hovered over the waters of primal chaos and the Holy Spirit had descended upon the Jordan in Christ's baptism, so the priest upon two occasions breathed three times over the font: "ter halat in aquam," "sufflans in aquam."[27] Canon law decreed that "without exorcisms and exsufflation no one is baptized": "Whether children or young people come to the sacrament of regeneration, let them not go to the font before the unclean Spirit has been drawn out of them by the exorcisms and exsufflation of the priests."[28] Throughout the Easter vigil, the catechumen renounced the Devil, who nonetheless stubbornly refused to give up; the struggle was thus repeated, over and again, all through the night.

During these difficult hours, the priest would encourage the neophyte. One of Augustine's *Sermons on the Easter Vigil* gives us an idea of how that moral support sounded:

> Although this night's solemn service of itself urges you to watch and pray, my dearly beloved, you are also entitled to a sermon from me so that the voice of the shepherd may rouse the flock of the Lord against envious hostile powers and rulers of darkness, as *against beasts of the night.*

For, as the Apostle says: "Our wrestling is not against flesh and blood," that is against men who are weak in mortal frame, "but against the Principalities and the Powers, against the world-rulers of this darkness, against the spiritual forces of wickedness on high" [Eph. 6:12]. . . . Therefore, since you have been separated from that darkness by the light of the Gospel and redeemed from those powers by the precious blood, "watch and pray that you may not enter into temptation" [Matt. 26:41]. For, if you have "faith which works through charity" [Gal. 5:6], the prince of the world has been cast out of your hearts, but outside, "*as a roaring lion,* [he] goes about seeking someone to devour" [1 Peter 5:8]. Do not, then, give place to the Devil, no matter where he tries to penetrate; rather, let the Lord dwell within you to oppose him whom He cast out by His sufferings. (italics added)[29]

A battle, then, always preceded baptism. Keeping vigil, the catechumen fought whatever powers of darkness hid within him like wild "beasts in the night"; he struggled with the devil, on the prowl like a ravenous, "roaring lion." The battle won, the baptisand could joyfully rush to the font.

With this field of combat as a background, Boccaccio's *contrasto* between Diana and Venus comes into clearer focus. The forest is dark, a *selva oscura* teeming with hostile powers. The huntresses, tireless, ever renew their combat. They are, so to speak, on the watch, as they keep setting new traps with their eyes ("con gli occhi ognor faccendo nuovo agguato"). In zealous pursuit, theirs is the energy of Christian vigor that Augustine demands from his flock of neophytes in his *Sermons on the Easter Vigil*.[30] At last, when they have killed a mountain of wild animals, they can emerge from the shadows and assemble under the bright noonday sun.

## Diana's Hunt and the *Filocolo*

Baptism and its doctrines return as a central part of Boccaccio's second Italian fiction, the *Filocolo* (ca. 1334–1336). Love, marriage, and conversion to Christianity are themes of that long romance, in which Diana and Venus also return, this time among a panoply of gods, again to superintend a cast of mortal characters. Not only does conversion control a plot line looped through various digressions;[31] it moves to didactic prominence as the priest Ilario catechizes the pagan hero, Florio, in the Lateran.

Florio, incognito as Filocolo, meets with many adventures before he arrives at that haven. Boccaccio previews them for us in the form of a dream imparted to Florio's father, the king of Spain (2.3). Felice dreams that he has nurtured a white doe and a lion cub; when a fierce wolf tries to kill the doe, the little lion saves her; helped by other animals, the cub later rescues her from a huge hound; they enjoy amorous union, then, finally, they jump into a fountain: "When the lion came out of it he seemed to be changed into the form of a noble and handsome young man, and the deer similarly into a lovely young woman."[32]

This vision, which the king cannot fathom, foreshadows the following story: the lion cub is his son, Prince Florio, who loves the orphan Biancifiore, the doe. Wrongly believing her a slave, the king plots with his wicked seneschal, the wolf, to have the girl murdered, but her knight, at the last minute, rides to the rescue on a charger. The hound is the Admiral, lord of Alexandria, who acquires and then releases Biancifiore. The lovers marry and afterward journey to Rome, home of Biancifiore's noble, Christian family. Florio embraces the faith, whose history and beliefs he learns from Ilario, and both husband and wife receive baptism from the pope at the Lateran font.

The several lessons in Ilario's catechism, signs of Boccaccio's own bent for scholarly lecturing,[33] together with King Felice's dream, help decode the *Hunt*. Father Ilario sums up his teachings in a *Credo* glossed with rhetorical embellishment. This sequence honors the order of the Gelasian sacramentary, which placed a homily on the *Credo* among the scrutinies for catechumens just before baptism.[34] Ilario rises to his peroration, urging Florio and his pagan companions to "run" to the font:

> Run to the holy fountain of true cleansing, which will wash the dark filth from your minds and let you know God, who grants the prayers of sinners when the time is opportune. Among wretches he is most wretched who can leave his anguish and enter into joy, and nevertheless continues in wretchedness. Come then, and wash yourselves in the holy font, and dress yourselves in those three most noble virtues, Faith, Hope, and Charity, without which no one can please God and from whomever puts these on it is impossible for the eternal realms to be barred.[35]

Although no such command is issued in the *Hunt,* the animals, as if in obedience to an order unspoken, leap from the fire and "run" to the water. Wretchedness is shed when they burst from their animal confinement and enter into joy, the reward Venus has promised. After washing in the river, they do indeed dress themselves in virtue, particularly Charity, whose symbolic color is red.

What King Felice dreamed, the *Filocolo* in a nutshell, repeats material Boccaccio had first used for *Diana's Hunt*. In the monarch's dream, the animals' identities as humans are revealed after they pass through waters that prefigure their baptism. Beasts in Parthenope also double as men, but they do not actually so emerge until grace descends and they hurry to the river brook. In each work, the vocabulary at the turning point is the same. Compare the stag's account, "vidimi . . . di cervio *mutato* in creatura / umana" (I saw myself . . . changed . . . from a stag into a human being), with the dream-prophecy of Florio's conversion at the font, "il leoncello uscendone, pareva *mutato* in figura di nobilissimo e bel giovane" (when the lion came out of it, he seemed to be changed into the form of a noble and handsome young man). Mutation from beast to man signifies a turning toward Christ. *Metamorphosis* in its literal sense means "transfiguration," and "conversion" in its spiritual sense.[36]

All of these events unfold under the influence, both angry and benign, of the "gentile" gods, whose action is tracked to serve the Christian providential design. The *Filocolo* initially pits Diana and Venus as rivals working at cross-purposes. Then, about midway through the story, Diana decides that she can stop interfering and makes a pact with Venus to protect the heroine, Biancifiore. From then on, they work together, steering events toward a happy resolution that will unite her in matrimony with Florio. Assisted by these powers of Olympus, the young pagan lovers grow into Christian man and wife, who will start a family and lead a life of model piety.

Such paradoxical elements—Diana and Venus as antagonists united in a language of myth to convey Christian meaning—inform Boccaccio's later *Ameto*. Dynamics not so different also underlie his *Teseida delle nozze d'Emilia* (*Theseiad of Emilia's Nuptials*), where the same goddesses cooperate behind the scenes to assure the proper conclusion: the wedding of an Amazon maid faithful to Diana but watched over by Venus, concluding an epic that resonates allegorically as reason's triumph over sensual appetites.[37] Boccaccio, in a sense, continued to rewrite the same tale. For *Diana's Hunt* the writer had already gathered the original, unlikely set of components: goddesses, who, although they are inimical on the surface, cooperate in allegory—pagan myth as a vehicle for a Christian moral.

The coupling of Diana and Venus as allies rather than antagonists was apparently quite accepted by Boccaccio's early Renaissance public. The two deities appear together on several fifteenth-century Tuscan nuptial chests. Such *cassoni*, which formed a customary part of a bride's dowry, were often painted with narrative scenes whose subjects could be reminders to a wife of her responsibilities of chastity and fidelity. Three such *cassoni* at the Stibbert Museum in Florence, closely related by theme, may have a Boccaccian source. One of the panels by Francesco di Giorgio Martini (Figure 7) depicts "nymphs" hunting stags in a hilly landscape.

Figure 7. Francesco di Giorgio Martini (attributed): Diana, Venus, and huntress-nymphs. Sienese *cassone*, fifteenth century. Courtesy of Opera Museo Stibbert, Florence.

Behind them throng many other elegantly dressed young ladies who gravitate around the composition's two dominant figures confronted at each side on triumphal floats. At left is Diana, her cart drawn by griffins; at right sits Venus on a vehicle pulled by swans. This *cassone* and its companions could, in fact, depict *Diana's Hunt*. If so, the transference from one medium to another is on a plane more conceptual than literal. In any event, the artists and their patrons certainly understood the Diana-Venus dualism that dominates Boccaccio's early Italian works as a mythical partnership protecting Christian virtue and marriage.[38]

## The Woods of Parthenope

*Diana's Hunt* is a polysemous invention. Most resonant is its narrating stag: in him converge Ovid's Actaeon; Apuleius's ass, Lucius; the bestiaries' renewing *elaphos,* or deer, that destroys serpents; and the thirsting hart of Psalm 42:1. A symbol of love, both sensual and sacred, he walks Boccaccio's woods as much an emblem of Diana as of Christian baptism. Diana, entitled by myth to lead the hunt, shifts from patron of chastity to the power of virtue, with hints of immaculate Marian purity. As the men at the end of the story are cloaked in vermilion, so she and her nymphs at the outset dress themselves in royal purple, another shade of red, to indicate that they are the virtues infused by Charity. Venus, who displaces chastity's guardian, descends in allegory as an agent of Grace and the Holy Ghost; she brings the fertilizing power that generates the church through the sacrament of baptism.

The forest, too, is a place of many meanings; its nature changes with the moral progress of the symbolic plot. At first its terrain is often dark and dangerous, like Dante's *selva oscura* in *Inferno* 1; yet it is at once a plaisance soothed with bird song, like Dante's *selva antica* at the top of Purgatory. Crisscrossed by steep, dusty, thorny paths, but irrigated by a beautiful fountain in its midst, this secluded landscape in Parthenope moves from labyrinth to meadow, from Hell to Paradise.

As a labyrinth, it resembles the no-man's land where the unnamed narrator of Boccaccio's *Corbaccio* loses his way in a dream-vision. That scholar, smarting from the humiliating rejection of a lustful widow, falls asleep and imagines himself strolling on a delightful path that degenerates into a valley inhabited only by savage animals. Just in time, the much-jaded but well-experienced shade of the widow's husband, stubbornly determined to cure the wounded lover of his irrational passion, arrives to demonstrate how the scholar's behavior has debased him to "a beast without intellect" ("una bestia senza intelletto"):

> I know quite well that, as yet, the ray of true light has not reached your intellect; and just as many fools do, you consider that which is sordid misery to be supreme happiness, believing that there can be some good in your concupiscent and carnal love. Therefore, pay close attention to what I will now tell you.
>
> This wretched valley is what you call "the Court of Love"; and these beasts, which you say you heard and hear growling, are the wretches—of whom you are one—who have been caught in the net of false love; while they speak of such love, their voices have no other sound in the ears of well-disposed men of discretion than that which apparently comes to yours; and because of this, I called it a "labyrinth" before, because men become trapped in it as they did in that of old, without ever knowing the way out.[39]

The Circean spell, the fate of men trapped by animal passion, downplayed to symbolic status in the scholar's nightmare, provides stuff more solid for the *Hunt*.[40] But in each tale, the first and last of his vernacular fiction, Boccaccio will break the wicked enchantment of sensuality, permitting his male protagonists the opportunity for moral recovery.[41]

The chase in the forest, exorcistic venery that destroys the serpent and its family and vanquishes the beasts in the wilderness, precedes a reenactment of redemption. Boccaccio's "virginal" Parthenope is nostalgic of Eden, and the *Hunt* closes with a poetic return to that primal garden, as couples stroll carefree on a flowering green. In retrospect we can understand that the sheer plenitude of the wood, where so many creatures coexist, had been another major clue to its polysemous, sacral nature: "Roebuck, wolves, and every other animal—bears, lions—are found in that place, and all kinds of others, the strong as well as the weak" (2.19–21). Below, a lush valley surrounded by four low-lying mountains has at its center a remarkable fountain. Those four mountains and the water orient the hunt, both geographically and morally. Just as Diana's ladies chase to the cardinal points, hinting at their operation as cardinal virtues, the hills frame a grid for the flow of the fountain, "fair, large, and with abundant water . . . that bathes all the grasses" (2.5–8). It runs on a pattern with the "fons" of Genesis 2, which "went out of the place of pleasure to water paradise, which from thence [was] divided into four heads." Boccaccio's *locus amoenus*, with the ground plan of the Garden of Creation, has, furthermore, a narrator who relates what happens there in language that depends on, more than any other single source, Dante's description of his passage through Eden, in the final cantos of *Purgatorio*.

Boccaccio's written picture of the Parthenopean fountain and forest, assimilated to the terrestrial paradise, relates to widespread iconographic conventions in the visual arts. One we have already seen in the paleo-christian baptistry mosaics of San Giovanni in Fonte in Naples, a motif later expressed splendidly in the apse decorations at San Clemente and the Lateran, where little communities of animals center on Edenic landscapes. In the peaceable kingdom of sheltering Eden, stags number among the beasts that most often betoken primal harmony. Thus, for example, illustrated Gospel Books from the Carolingian era could show, around the Fountain of Life, animals emblematic of the concord that that wellspring symbolized—among others, an antlered hart with his doe, peacocks, and a swan (Figure 8). Such imagery enjoyed long popularity, evident, for example, in the fifteenth-century French illumination depicting *The Marriage of Adam and Eve* in the encyclopedia *On the Nature of Things* (*Des Proprietez des choses*) by Bartholomaeus Anglicus (Figure 9). The first father and mother stand within a round wattled enclosure amid animals wild and tame—including the stag, unicorn, and dog—while a swan paddles in a well-stocked stream that curls away from the fountain at their feet.

As Eden, the *locus amoenus* at the end of *Diana's Hunt* is, in the mind of the twenty-one-year-old Boccaccio, a redeemed realm of a Christianized Venus, tutelary of chaste, matrimonial love. On a more worldly note, Venus may owe her triumph in the poem not merely to the young Boccaccio's love of myth, but to his blithe observation of contemporary customs as well. The court of Naples frequently enjoyed outings to Baia, a coastal watering place and country retreat near Naples, where ruins still remain of the ancient Roman Terme di Venere, or Baths of Venus. "Baia-Parthenope" was the playground where the upper classes met, parried, and wooed for matrimony. In the simplest terms, the poem's literal level also reflects the historical truth of days spent hawking, hunting, bathing, and flirting—summer pastimes that the aristocracy enjoyed around the bays of Naples, and precisely those that Boccaccio's Madonna Fiammetta would enjoy there and relate in her own mature "elegy" of amorous passion.[42]

## Poetic Tactics

Since it conceals truth beneath an imaginative fiction, Boccaccio's first work illustrates "poetry"—what we might call "creative" writing—as he defined that art three decades later in his *Genealogies*:

> This poetry, which ignorant triflers cast aside, is a sort of fervid and exquisite invention, with fervid expression, in speech or writing, of that which the mind has invented. . . . This fervor of poesy is sublime in its effects: it impels the soul to a longing for utterance; it brings forth

*Figure 8.* Stag and doe among animals and birds at the Fountain of Life. Gospels of Saint-Médard de Soissons. Carolingian, ninth century. Paris, Bibliothèque Nationale, MS. lat. 8850, fol. 6 v. Courtesy of Bibliothèque Nationale, Paris.

*Figure 9.* The Marriage of Adam and Eve. Bartholomaeus Anglicus, *De proprietatibus rerum,* trans. Jean Corbechon, *Des Proprietez des choses.* Fitzwilliam Museum, MS. 251, fol. 16. Courtesy of Fitzwilliam Museum, Cambridge.

strange and unheard-of creations of the mind; it arranges these meditations in a fixed order, adorns the whole composition with unusual interweaving of words and thought; and thus it veils truth in a fair and fitting garment of fiction.[43]

The poet-allegorist is a person who occults or secretes the truth, rather as if it were buried treasure. What sort of verity does he put undercover? It is doctrine concerning the Catholic church, Boccaccio affirms, when he enters into matter that Dante had hidden under the "rough bark of the words" in *Inferno* 1:

> Let no one regret that truth is hidden by the poets beneath fables. . . . hence our poet, like other poets, was a man who was a hider, as we can see, of a valuable jewel, none less than the Catholic truth, beneath the cortex of his poem.[44]

Poets must camouflage their communications because just as people take the greatest pleasure in things hardest won, so it is with reading: the more challenging the text, the more satisfying our discoveries.

> Customarily, whatever we acquire with difficulty is more pleasing and more carefully preserved than whatever we find without any or with little effort. . . . There being no doubt then at all that pulling forth the truth hidden under parlance in fables is most toilsome, incomparable delight must follow for whoever, through his study, sees that he has been able to find it; wherefore not only does he forget all his labors, but a sweetness remains in his mind, which, with an almost indissoluble bond, locks into the memory of him who found it, the truth that he has found.[45]

Since difficulty enhances the pleasure of reading, the deeper a poet caches his gemstone, the better. This means that the connection between literal meaning and allegorical meaning must be unexpected, even implausible. Although from our perspective today such a discrepancy between letter and spirit would violate artistic decorum, for Boccaccio it was highly desirable—in fact, essential. The wider the gap between text and intention, the more admirable a writer's originality: "Poetic fiction differs from a lie in that in most instances it bears not only no close resemblance to the truth, but no resemblance at all; on the contrary, it is quite out of harmony and agreement with the truth."[46]

To make it rewardingly arduous for his readers, Boccaccio plotted *Diana's Hunt* as a poetic fiction that actually reverses the literal truth. Huntresses oust Diana to idolize Venus, whose abracadabra gives them each a lover. Has Eros then won out over Chastity? No. The ladies are the Virtues who triumph over sensuality; Venus is Christian Grace, who baptizes their conquests into the church. Within Boccaccio's story, in other words, as he himself might have liked to think about it, the jewel lies deeply encrusted; a veil thickly envelops the fiction.

What the neophyte writer has chosen for his first fiction, no doubt with self-conscious purpose, is a tale with themes of "beginnings." In spring, nature's season of renewal, virgin girls defeat beasts that are allegorically "old men" saved with Christian "new life." The narrator of the tale is a stag, symbol of rejuvenation in the bestiaries and the Bible, whose opening words echo the first verse of Petrarch's "metamorphosis" *canzone* (no. 23), "In the sweet time of the first age." The stag is "reborn" thanks to his Mystery Lady: she who steps forward to guide the huntresses as the first among them; she who embodies the same virtues as the heavenly heroine of Dante's first work, the *Vita nuova*.[47]

For *Diana's Hunt,* a poem about beginnings by a beginning poet, Boccaccio relies on tactics of reversal and polyvalence. In a forest, both labyrinth and mythical garden, dwell animals at once diabolical and Edenic. Part of a tradition as popular as Aesop's *Fables* and as sophisticated as the pastoral, they turn into men, switching the thrust of Ovid and Boethius.[48] Women pursue them, not for lustful dalliance, but in a chaste hunt to rescue souls and find marriage partners. They are real, historical women whom the author raises to abstract virtues, but their "killing" effects come straight from the courtly lyric. Most daring are the ambiguities that play off secular and sacred semantics: spring, the season for love and literary beginnings, is also the major liturgical time for the sacrament of baptism;[49] an Ovidian stag is the psalmist's thirsting hart and an emblem of the Christian neophyte; Diana's hunt is a catechumenal psychomachia; Venus Genetrix is Grace who descends for the Holy Ghost. Opposites converge;[50] "pagan integument" conceals a "Christian design."[51]

*Diana's Hunt* is not a masterpiece, but its author is not a bad allegorist if we are good allegorical readers. To borrow D. W. Robertson's felicitous formula for the practice of medieval hermeneutics, we can say that it is "a problem to be solved."[52] Diana, with fifty-nine huntresses in Parthenope; a menagerie from the bestiaries; Venus, who gives life to young men; a narrating stag transfigured into human form—ridiculous in the realm of reality—all gather with perfect logic for the poem's moral level. Boccaccio canonist, Boccaccio courtier, and Boccaccio poet all collaborate in this precocious creation, aimed to please a pious king, flatter the ladies of society, delight scholarly peers, and honor Dante, the master, dead barely twelve years. While we smile at the surprises, humorous and serious, that he has tucked into the letter of this text, we must lift his veil of fiction with minds open to more serious meanings as they multiply in vistas of symbol and allegory.[53]

## Notes to the Introduction

### Chapter 1: The Background

1. We accept Vittore Branca's dating of *Diana's Hunt* at 1333–1334. Branca's philological studies, the first ever to treat the poem seriously, remain fundamental: "Per l'attribuzione della *Caccia di Diana* a Giovanni Boccaccio" (1938) and "Nuove note sulla *Caccia di Diana*," both in *Tradizione delle opere di Giovanni Boccaccio* (Rome: Edizioni di Storia e Letteratura, 1956; rprt. 1958), pp. 121–143; 145–198. See also V. Branca's *Profilo biografico*, published as an introductory monograph to Boccaccio's complete works (*Tutte le opere*, vol. 1 [Milan: Mondadori, 1967]), then reprinted separately (Florence: Le Monnier, 1977), and *Giovanni Boccaccio: The Man and His Works*, trans. R. Monges and Dennis J. McAuliffe (New York: New York University Press, 1976).

2. The character of Angevin culture and Boccaccio's court contacts are reconstructed by Francesco Sabatini, *Napoli angioina: cultura e società* (Naples: Edizioni Scientifiche Italiane, 1975), esp. ch. 3, "La penetrazione culturale dei Fiorentini e la presenza del Boccaccio," pp. 93–115. Useful background information on the same subject appears in Giovanni Boccaccio, *Eclogues*, trans. Janet Levarie Smarr (New York: Garland Publishing, 1987), Introduction, pp. vii–xi. See also Emile G. Léonard, *Un poète à la recherche d'une place et d'un ami: Boccace à Naples* (Paris: Droz, 1944).

3. The most famous of the French poets and musicians who lived and worked in Angevin Naples was Adam de la Halle (flourished during the second half of the twelfth century), a native of Arras. He composed in both lyric and dramatic genres and was also a professional singer. Among his best remembered works most probably composed and presented in Naples is the pastoral comedy *Le Jeu de Robin et Marion*. One measure of the popularity of such northern literature, as well as French language penetration into local culture, was the adoption of "Peronella," from a character in the *Jeu* called "Peronelle," as a fashionable Italian female surname. (See F. Sabatini, *Napoli angioina* [1975], pp. 37, 111.) There is a Peronella in the *Hunt* (consult Glossary of the Huntresses, below). The name soon filtered down to other social classes, as Boccaccio's Neapolitan "Peronella and the Tub" story (*Decameron* 7.2) bears witness.

For Villani's praise of King Robert, see *Cronaca* 12.9: "il più savio tra' cristiani già sono cinquecent'anni, sì di senno naturale, sì di scienza, come grandissimo maestro in teologia e sommo filosofo." Boccaccio calls Robert a "second Solomon" in his *Genealogie deorum gentilium* 14:9. Referring to the dynastic struggle that followed Robert's death, Boccaccio's third and fourth *Eclogues* ("Faunus" and "Dorus") had likewise praised Robert, both as a wise ruler and a talented writer. Petrarch, who chose to be examined by Robert to certify his fitness for laureation in Rome, lavishly praised this "king of kings" (*Familiares* 4.2; 12.2). These references appear in the discussion of King Robert by F. Sabatini, *Napoli angioina* (1975), pp. 67–85. Robert also wrote laws, of which 107 are known. See David Anderson on this point and for other notes concerning the Neapolitan cultural milieu of Boccaccio's early years, *Before the Knight's Tale: Imitation of Classical Epic in Boccaccio's Teseida* (Philadelphia: University of Pennsylvania Press, 1988), pp. 26–27, 58. Still useful as general background are the books by E. G. Léonard, *Un poète à la recherche d'une place et d'un ami: Boccace à Naples* (1944), and *Les*

*Angevins de Naples* (Paris: Presses Universitaires de la France, 1954), trans. R. Liguori, *Gli Angioini di Napoli* (Varese: dall'Oglio, 1967).

Dante refers to Robert of Anjou disparagingly in *Paradiso* 8:147: "e fate re tal ch'è da sermone" (and you make a king of one that is fit for sermons).

4. F. Sabatini, *Napoli angioina* (1975), pp. 58–59.

5. *Genealogie deorum gentilium* 15:6 (pp. 761–762): "Qui et etate provectus, et multarum rerum notitia doctus, fuit diu magister et custos bibliothece Roberti, Jerusalem et Sycilie regis incliti. Et, si usquam curiosissimus fuit homo in perquirendis, iussu etiam sui principis, peregrinis undecunque libris, hystoriis et poeticis operibus, iste fuit"; "Hic ingentem scripsit librum, quem Collectionum titulaverat, in quo inter cetera, que multa erant et ad varia spectantia, quicquid de diis gentilium non solum apud Latinos, sed etiam apud Grecos inveniri potest . . . quem librum maximo huius operis incomodo, Bielle, umpudice [sic] coniugis, crimine, eo defuncto, cum pluribus aliis ex libris eiusdem deperditum comperi. Puto igitur eo tempore, quo michi primo cognitus est, neminem illi in talibus equiperandum fuisse."

6. For the list and description of the earliest extant Dante manuscripts, see Mario Rotili, *I codici danteschi miniati a Napoli* (Naples: Libreria Scientifica, 1972), esp. pp. 73–93. See also F. Sabatini, *Napoli angioina* (1975), pp. 73–75.

7. Parthenope was a siren about whom ancient sources give varying accounts. According to one version of her myth, after she and her companions failed to seduce Ulysses with the magic power of their song, they threw themselves into the ocean and drowned. Her body was washed ashore and given burial at the place that was to become Naples. For Boccaccio's knowledge of Parthenope, see Commentary, 1.12, below.

Medieval legends of Virgil, who was buried in Naples, connect his sorcery with the Neapolitan "Monte Vergine" (*Mons Virginis* or *Mons Virginum*), also known as *Mons Virgilianus*. On that virginal local landmark the poet was said to have cultivated a garden with magic herbs and set up a statue trumpeting in the direction of Vesuvius to blow noxious ashes away from the city. See Domenico Comparetti, *Virgilio nel medioevo* (1872; rprt. Florence: La Nuova Italia, 1981), vol. 2, pp. 28–29.

8. *Vita nuova* 6: "sì mi venne una volontade di volere ricordare lo nome di quella gentilissima ed accompagnarlo di molti nomi di donne. . . . E presi li nomi di sessanta le più belle donne de la cittade ove la mia donna fue posta da l'altissimo sire, e compuosi una pistola sotto forma di serventese, la quale io non scriverò: e non n'avrei fatto menzione, se non per dire quello che, componendola, maravigliosamente addivenne, cioè che in alcuno altro numero non sofferse lo nome de la mia donna stare se non in su lo nove, tra li nomi di queste donne." Dante's spelling of *serventese* is atypical; *sirventese* is the usual Italian form of the word.

9. Several early Italian examples of the *sirventese,* including one possibly by Sordello da Goito, appear in Gianfranco Contini, ed., *Poeti del Duecento* (Milan: Ricciardi, 1960), vol. 1, pp. 503, 843, 877.

10. Samples of the poet's conventional appeal to women as experts on love are assembled by Victoria Kirkham, "Boccaccio's Dedication to Women in Love," in *Renaissance Studies in Honor of Craig Hugh Smyth,* ed. Andrew Morrogh et al. (Florence: Giunti Barbèra, 1985b), vol. 1, pp. 333–343.

11. Dante's final prose paragraph in the *Vita nuova* had alleged the poet's

unworthiness to continue speaking of his "most gentle one." See Commentary, 1.53–55, below.

12. The canzone "Donne ch'avete intelletto d'amore" (Ladies who have intelligence of love) in the *Vita nuova,* chapter 19, both in its specific phrasing and the broader stilnovistic concept, underlies Boccaccio's presentation of the Mystery Lady and her followers in the hunt: "Quando [Beatrice] va per via, / gitta nei cor villani Amore un gelo, / per che onne lor pensero agghiaccia e pere; / e qual soffrisse di starla a vedere / diverria nobil cosa, o si morria. / E quando trova alcun che degno sia / di veder lei, quei prova sua vertute, / ché li avvien, ciò che li dona, in salute, / e sì l'umilia, ch'ogni offesa oblia. / . . . / De li occhi suoi, come ch'ella li mova, / escono spirti d'amore inflammati, / che feron li occhi a qual che allor la guati, / e passan sì che 'l cor ciascun retrova" (When she walks along / Love drives a killing frost into vile hearts / that freezes and destroys all their thoughts; / should such a one insist on looking at her, / he becomes ennobled or he dies. / And when she finds one worthy to behold her, / that man will feel her power for salvation / when she accords to him her salvation, / which humbles him till he forgets all wrongs. . . . / Her eyes, wherever she may choose to look, / send forth their spirits radiant with love / to strike the eyes of anyone they meet, / and penetrate until they find the heart).

The imagery of love darting from the lady's eyes to penetrate the lover's heart is traced from antiquity to the Renaissance by Lance Donaldson-Evans in *Love's Fatal Glance: A Study of Eye Imagery in the Poets of the Ecole Lyonnaise* (University, Miss.: Romance Monographs, 1980).

13. Millicent Marcus argues that Boccaccio simultaneously exploits and undercuts the stilnovistic theme of love's uplifting power in her article, "The Sweet New Style Reconsidered. A Gloss on the Tale of Cimone (*Decameron,* V,1)," *Italian Quarterly* 81 (1980), pp. 5–16.

14. *De mulieribus claris,* Dedication 5: "adverterem videremque quod sexui [in]firmiori natura detraxerit, id tuo pectori Deus sua liberalitate miris virtutibus superinfuserit atque suppleverit, et eo, quo insignita es nomine, designari volueris—cum *andres* Greci quod latine dicimus *homines* nuncupent" (I realized and saw that what nature had taken away from the weaker sex, God in his generosity had compensated for by raining down on your breast amazing virile strength, and he wished that you be designated by that name which makes you outstanding, since the Greeks call *andres* what we in Latin say as *homines*).

Boccaccio's literary attitude toward women, long confused with his supposed real-life experiences, remains a subject of lively debate. Contrast, for example, Victoria Kirkham, "Boccaccio's Dedication to Women in Love" (1985), pp. 333–343, and Joy Hambuechen Potter, "Women in the *Decameron*," the latter in *Studies in the Italian Renaissance: Essays in Honor of Arnolfo B. Ferruolo* (Naples: Società Editrice Napoletana, 1985), pp. 87–103, with Millicent Marcus, "Misogyny as Misreading: A Gloss on *Decameron* VIII, 7," *Stanford Italian Review* 4, no. 1 (1984), pp. 23–40.

15. On Boccaccio's disappointing relationship with Niccolò Acciaiuoli, see V. Branca, *Profilo biografico,* pp. 100ff., esp. pp. 129–133; and *Boccaccio: The Man and His Works,* trans. R. Monges and D. J. McAuliffe, pp. 103–110, 134–139. In his fourth eclogue, Boccaccio took a fierce vengeance on Niccolò, depicting him as the greedy villain Midas. An excellent English discussion of that bitter attack

appears in Janet Levarie Smarr's translation of Boccaccio's *Eclogues* (New York: Garland Publishing, 1987), esp. pp. 224–228.

16. The fortunes of the text indicate that at least some of its latter-day readers saw in the *Hunt* an epithalamium or "marriage piece." In fact, the second edition of the poem (*La Caccia di Diana,* ed. S. Morpurgo and A. and O. Zenatti, Nozze Casini-Polsinelli [Florence: Carnesecchi, 1884]), as the bibliographical data indicates, was printed to celebrate a wedding.

17. Branca's assessment of Boccaccio's aim, first published half a century ago ("Per l'attribuzione della *Caccia di Diana,*" p. 141), still holds good: "Vagheggiava il complimento grazioso, il madrigale carezzevole alla vanità cortigiana . . . nella raffigurazione galante delle donne, nel tentativo di esaltarle facendole compagne di dee, nel tono seriamente gaudente dell'allegoria finale" (He desired a graceful compliment, a madrigal to caress courtly vanity . . . in the gallant figuration of the women, in the attempt to exalt them making them companions of goddesses, in the seriously joyful tone of the final allegory). Francesco Torraca, *Giovanni Boccaccio a Napoli* (Rome: Società Tipografica Arpinate, 1916), who remarks the repetitions of the ladies names (p. 130), also suggests that Zizzola Barrile is first on the list because of Boccaccio's friendship with Giovanni Barrile, whose role at court and in Boccaccio's writings he documents (pp. 42–48). On Zizzola, consult Glossary of the Huntresses, below.

18. *De consulatu Stilichonis* 3.317–21: "Quodcumque tremendum / dentibus aut insigne iubis aut nobile cornu / aut rigidum saetis, capitur decus omne timorque / silvarum. non cauta latent, non mole resistunt / fortia, non volucri fugiunt pernicia cursu." Claudian was a medieval curriculum author (see E. R. Curtius, *European Literature and the Latin Middle Ages,* trans. Willard Trask [Princeton, N.J.: Princeton University Press, 1973], pp. 50, 51, 56). Believed to be a Florentine, he was one of the late antique poets most widely read in the first half of the fourteenth century. Petrarch's list of famous authors and their cities of birth in *De remediis utriusque Fortunae* 2.125 identifies Claudian as a Florentine; so too Boccaccio, *Trattatello in laude di Dante* 1.99. A manuscript of "Claudianus in metris" appears in the inventory of the "parva libreria" of Santo Spirito, the nucleus of which had been Boccaccio's library. See Antonia Mazza, "L'inventario della 'parva libreria' di Santo Spirito e la biblioteca del Boccaccio," *Italia medioevale e umanistica* 9 (1966), pp. 1–71, esp. p. 48. Boccaccio quotes Claudian's description of Diana's hunt through the four corners of the world from *De consulatu Stilichonis* in his own discussion of the goddess and her attributes at *Genealogie deorum gentilium* 5.2.

19. We know from a letter written by Petrarch to Boccaccio (*Familiarum rerum libri* 21.15) that the latter considered their compatriot Dante his "primus studiorum dux et prima fax."

20. The Mystery Lady leads the huntresses on a course that will culminate in a resurrection of men new born, like catechumens in baptism, the first sacrament and a "portal," as it were, into the church and salvation (cf. Hugh of Saint Victor [*PL* 177.388–389]: "Est enim quasi janua omnibus atria Ecclesiae introentibus" [It is like a door to all entering the atria of the Church]).

21. While the hunter (*venator*), *in bono,* could signify the Apostles, religious preachers, and even Christ himself catching men's souls (see the gathering of interpretations of *venatores* by Peter Cantor, Peter Capuanus, and others in the "De

bestiis" of the *Clavis Melitonis*, ed. Jean-Baptiste Pitra, vol. 3 [Paris: Firmin Didot Frères, 1855], pp. 77–78), on the other hand, any *bestia* (beast) could figure the Devil (*diabolus*) (*Clavis*, pp. 48–49).

22. Friedrich Lauchert believed that the first versions of the work were in circulation ca. A.D. 140 (*Geschichte des Physiologus* [Strasbourg: Verlag Karl J. Trübner, 1889]); others believe that it dates from the fourth century after Christ; Francesco Sbordone concluded that it was composed around the year A.D. 200 (*Physiologi graeci singulas variarum aetatum recensiones . . . in lucem protulit F. Sbordone* [Milan: In Aedibus Societatis "Dante Alighieri"; Albrighi, Segati & C., 1936b], p. lxxviii). See also Sbordone's *Ricerche sulle fonti e sulla composizione del Physiologus greco* (Naples: Arti Grafiche G. Torella, 1936a) and "La tradizione manoscritta del *Physiologus latino*," *Athenaeum* n.s. 27 (1949), pp. 246–280. See Michael Curley's Introduction to his edition of the *Physiologus* (Austin, Tex., and London: University of Texas Press, 1979), pp. ix–xliii.

23. Florence McCulloch, *Medieval Latin and French Bestiaries*, University of North Carolina Studies in Romance Languages and Literatures 33 (Chapel Hill: The University of North Carolina Press, 1960), examines the oldest Latin versions of the *Physiologus*, the pseudo-Hugh of Saint Victor, *De Bestiis*, the metrical *Physiologus of Theobaldus*, the pseudo-John Chrysostom *Dicta Chrysostomi*, and the French bestiaries of Philippe de Thaon, Gervaise, Guillaume le Clerc, and Pierre de Beauvais. Italian examples include *Il Bestiario moralizzato*, in *Testi e Interpretazioni*, ed. Maria Romano, Studi del Seminario di Filologia Romanza dell'Università di Firenze (Milan-Naples: Ricciardi, 1978), pp. 721–888; *Il Bestiario toscano secondo la lezione dei codici di Parigi e di Roma*, ed. M[ilton] S. Garver and K[enneth] McKenzie (Rome: Società Filologica Romana, 1912; extract from *Studi romanzi* 8 [1912]); and *Il Bestiario tosco-veneziano, Ein Tosco-Venezianischer Bestiarius*, ed. Max[imilian] Goldstaub and Richard Wendriner (Halle a. S.: Max Niemeyer, 1892). For other studies and versions, see "Physiologus" in the Bibliography of Works Consulted at the end of this volume.

24. *De arte venandi cum avibus*, ed. Karl Arnold Willemsen (Leipzig: Insula, 1942); *The Art of Falconry Being the De Arte Venandi cum Avibus of Frederick II of Hohenstaufen*, trans. and ed. Casey A. Wood and Marjory Fyfe (Stanford, Cal.: Stanford University Press, 1943).

25. Florence, Biblioteca Medicea Laurenziana, MS. Laur. Plut. 73.16; Vienna, Nationalbibliothek, MS. 93.y. See Ferdinando Bologna, *I pittori alla corte angioina di Napoli (1266–1414) e un riesame dell'arte nell'età fridericiana* (Rome: Ugo Bozzi Editore, 1969).

26. Saint Gregory insists that the ostrich's wings are the wings of dissembling and fraud; the whole paragraph reads as follows: "Struthio vero pennae eorum similitudinem habet, sed volatus eorum celeritatem non habet. A terra quippe elevari non valet, et alas quasi ad volatum specie tenus erigit, sed tamen nunquam se a terra volando suspendit. Ita sunt nimirum omnes hypocritae, qui dum bonorum vitam simulant, imitationem sanctae visionis habent, sed veritatem sanctae actionis non habent. Habent quippe volandi pennas per speciem, sed in terra repunt per actionem, quia alas per figuram sanctitatis extendunt, sed curarum saecularium pondere praegravati, nullatenus a terra sublevantur" (Truly an ostrich has the likeness of the wing[s] [of other birds], but not the swiftness of their flight. For it cannot really rise from the ground, and it raises its wings, in

appearance as if to fly, but yet never raises itself from the earth in flight. Thus, of course, are all dissemblers, who, while they simulate a life of doing good, have a semblance of saintliness, but have no reality of holy conduct. Indeed, they have wings as if for flight in appearance, but in their actions, they creep along the ground—because they spread their wings in a semblance of sanctity—yet overwhelmed by the weight of earthly cares, they are never raised from the earth).

For Saint Gregory, more humane in his doctrine than the bestiaries, the abandonment of eggs and offspring is typical of the hypocrite, who, while furnishing no example to the children of a heavenly life, abandons his family, hardheartedly, for his quest for earthly gain and vain ambition (*Morals* 3.433, 435; *Moralia* 31.11, 14–17, esp. 14, *PL* 76.578, 579–580).

27. "Per alas cogitationes hypocritae" (*Allegoriae in Sacram Scripturam, PL* 112.865). Richard's Latin reads: "Vultis adhuc plenius nosse quales alas soleat fraudulentia habere? Ut igitur breviter exprimam quid sentiam: Una dicatur simulationis, alia dissimulationis, tertia ostentationis, quarta excusationis" (*PL* 196.1359). For Dante's use of the "wings of fraud" topos in the Ulysses episode *Inf.* 26, see A. K. Cassell, *Dante's Fearful Art of Justice* (Toronto: University of Toronto Press, 1984), pp. 92–95.

28. "Crura habet longiora, unde accidit, ut levius ei sit montem ascendere quam descendere" (Albertus Magnus's *De animalibus* 22.60 [110]; trans. Scanlan, pp. 153–154). Thomas of Cantimpré, "De lepore," in *LNR* 4.66.27–28; cf. Aelian 13.14. The hare does not usually figure in unaccreted *Physiologus* compilations.

29. "*Lepus* est quilibet iniquus, et tamen doctus in lege. 'Lepus, nam et ille ruminat' [Lev. 11:6], quod nonnulli iniqui et tamen docti sunt" (*Allegoriae in Sacram Scripturam* [*PL* 112.984]; cited also in the *Clavis Melitonis,* ed. Pitra, pp. 74–75). Dante uses the same odd, but conventional, image of rumination (stemming from the Christian interpretation of Levitical law [Lev. 11:3; Deut. 14:6]) while writing of canon law and spiritual rule in *Purg.* 16.99.

30. The fruitfulness of rabbits and hares is noted by Aristotle *HA* 6.33 and by Aelian 13.14—rabbits were a classical symbol of fecundity. On rabbits and hares, see also the Commentary, notes to 3.26–27 and 6.38, below. Only the European vernaculars distinguish between them; both are *lepus* in Latin.

31. Claude K. Abraham, "Myth and Symbol: The Rabbit in Medieval France," *Studies in Philology* 60, no. 4 (October 1963), pp. 589–597, and D. W. Robertson, *A Preface to Chaucer: Studies in Medieval Perspectives* (Princeton, N.J.: Princeton University Press, 1962), p. 113 et passim.

When Jean de Meung, in the *Roman de la Rose* (vv. 15135–15555), tells us of a forest full of dangers, its bushes, hounds, hares, and skirmishes leave little doubt about their secondary, sexual, earthly meaning; the battle there between "Franchise" and "Danger" may have been a further major inspiration for the *Hunt* and its psychomachic allegory.

32. "Hericii autem nomine malitiosarum mentium defensio designatur, quia videlicet hericius cum apprehenditur ejus et caput cernitur, et pedes videntur, et corpus omne conspicitur; sed mox ut apprehensus fuerit, semitipsum in sphaerum colligit pedes introrsus subtrahit, caput abscondit; et intra tenentis manum totum simul amittitur, quod totum simul ante videbatur. Sic nimirum sic malitiosae mentes sunt, cum in suis excessibus comprehenduntur. Caput enim hericii cernitur, quia quo initio peccator ad culpam accesserit videtur. Pedes hericii conspic-

iuntur, quia quibus vestigiis nequitia sit perpetrata cognoscitur; et tamen, adductis repente excusationibus, malitiosa mens introrsus pedes colligit, quia cuncta iniquitatis suae vestigia abscondit. Caput subtrahit, quia miris defensionibus nec inchoasse se pravum aliquid ostendit; et quasi sphaera in manu tenentis remanet, quia is qui corripit, cuncta quae jam cognoverat subito amittens, involutum intra conscientiam peccatorem tenet, et qui totum jam deprehendendo viderat, tergiversatione pravae defensionis illusus, totum pariter ignorat. Foveam ergo hericius in reprobis habet, quia malitiosa mens sese intra se colligens in tenebris defensionis abscondit. Sed in hoc quod se peccator excusat, in hoc quod caliginosis defensionibus fixum in se oculum corripientis obnubilat, divinus nobis sermo etiam quomodo a similibus fulciatur ostendit" (*Moralia* XXXIII, 54 [*PL* 76.707–708]; *Morals,* vol. 3, p. 606; on Job 41:7). Gregory's interpretation is dutifully reported in the *De bestiis* of the *Clavis Melitonis,* ed. Pitra, pp. 73–74, and by Vincent of Beauvais in the *Spec. nat.* 20.59: the hedgehog is the *peccator* (the sinner).

33. "Duplices et dolosi." See "Herinaceus, peccator" in the *De bestiis* of the *Clavis Melitonis,* ed. Pitra, pp. 73–74.

34. "Les compilations furent le grand arsenal patristique des auteurs médiévaux," as René Wasselynck writes in "Les compilations des *Moralia in Job* du VII$^e$ au XII$^e$ siècle," *Recherches de théologie ancienne et médiévale* 29 (1962), pp. 5–32, esp. 31; see also his "Les *Moralia in Job* dans les ouvrages de morale du haut moyen âge latin," *Recherches de théologie ancienne et médiévale* 31 (1964), pp. 5–31 (for a list of epitomes); and "L'influence de l'exégèse de S. Grégoire le Grand sur les commentaires bibliques médiévaux (VII$^e$–XII$^e$ s.)," *Recherches de théologie ancienne et médiévale* 32 (1965), pp. 157–204. See also the excellent bibliography by Robert E. Kaske, in collaboration with Arthur Groos and Michael W. Twomey, *Medieval Christian Literary Imagery: A Guide to Interpretation,* Toronto Medieval Bibliographies, vol. 11 (Toronto and London: University of Toronto Press, 1989), p. 27.

35. *Trattatello* 1.140: "[Gregorio] della sacra Scrittura dice ciò che ancora della poetica dir si puote, cioè che essa in uno medesimo sermone, narrando, apre il testo e il misterio a quel sottoposto; e così ad un'ora con l'uno gli savi esercita e con l'altro gli semplici riconforta, e ha in publico donde li pargoletti nutrichi, e in occulto serva quello onde essa le menti de' sublimi intenditori con ammirazione tenga sospese. Perciò che pare essere un fiume, acciò che io così dica, piano e profondo, nel quale il piccioletto agnello con gli piè vada, e il grande elefante ampissimamente nuoti" (What [Gregory] says of sacred scripture can also be said of the poetic, namely that as it narrates, in the selfsame speech it opens the text and the mystery underlying it; and thus it at once challenges the wise with the one and with the other it comforts the simple, and it publicly has matter to nourish babes, and privately it reserves that which holds suspended with admiration the minds of sublime connoisseurs. So that it seems to be a river, as I might say, shallow and deep, in which the tiny lamb goes wading, and the large elephant comfortably swims). The simile of the elephant and lamb stands at the start of Gregory's *Moralia in Job,* an accommodating image to convey the allegorical nature of Holy Writ.

36. A still useful history of the hunt from antiquity appears in *Encyclopedia Britannica,* 11th ed., (1910–1911), *s.v.* "hunting." The best recent source on the medieval hunt, both in practice and in poetry, is Marcelle Thiébaux, *The Stag of Love* (Ithaca, N.Y.: Cornell University Press, 1974), to which the following

discussion is heavily indebted. Useful for measuring the *Hunt's* distance in fiction from fact is Thiébaux's "The Medieval Chase," *Speculum* 42 (1967), pp. 260–274.

37. See the rhymed prologue to *Livres du roy Modus*: "Il ordena tous les deduis, / Affin que ne fussons oysis," vv. 109–110 (vol. 1, p. 6, ed. G. Tilander); cited also by M. Thiébaux, *Stag* (1974), p. 77, whose detailed study we follow closely in this section.

38. *Livre de chasse:* "pour oster cause d'ocieuseté qui est fondement de tous maulx," cit. M. Thiébaux, *Stag* (1974), pp. 27 and 78.

39. John of Salisbury is cited in Marcelle Thiébaux's edition, "An Unpublished Allegory of the Hunt of Love: *Lis dis dou cerf amoreus,*" *Studies in Philology* 62 (1965), pp. 531–545. John exaggerated a long tradition: according to Fulgentius's commentary on *Aeneid* 4, the spirit of adolescence promotes hunting, and it is inflamed by passion. See *Fulgentius the Mythographer,* trans. L. G. Whitbread (Columbus, Ohio: Ohio State University Press, 1971), p. 127.

40. M. Thiébaux, "The Medieval Chase" (1967), p. 264.

41. *Aeneid* 4.68–73: "uritur infelix Dido totaque vagatur / urbe furens, qualis coniecta cerva sagitta, / quam procul incautam nemora inter Cresia fixit / pastor agens telis liquitque volatile ferrum / nescius; illa fuga silvas saltusque peragrat / Dictaeos; haeret lateri letalis harundo."

42. M. Thiébaux, "Medieval Allegories of the Love Chase," in *Stag* (1974), ch. 4, pp. 144–153. See also Thiébaux's "An Unpublished . . . Hunt" (1965), pp. 531–545.

43. See *La prise amoureuse von Jehan Acart de Hesdin,* ed. Ernst Hoepffner (Dresden: Gedruckt für die Gesellschaft für romanische Literatur, 1910); M. Thiébaux, *Stag* (1974), pp. 153–161.

44. *La prise amoureuse* is in a tradition inspired by the *Romance of the Rose* (see above, n. 31). For a description of the poem's contents, see M. Thiébaux, *Stag* (1974), pp. 153–161. Contrary to her assumption, Acart's poem could hardly have been influenced by Froissart, who was only about six years old at the time it was written.

*Chapter 2: Poetic Structure*

1. *Diana's Hunt* is mentioned among Boccaccio's other works in a brief biography dating from the first half of the fifteenth century (Milan, Biblioteca Ambrosiana, MS. S, 72 Sup.): "Bocacius, qui dictus est Johannes de Certaldo, poeta florentinus, scripsit librum de genlogia [sic] deorum . . . item librum de visione amoris, item de venatione dyane metricos" (Boccaccio, who is called John of Certaldo, a Florentine poet, wrote the book of the genealogy of the gods . . . also the book of the vision of love, also the verses of the hunt of Diana). The reference to this biography appears in V. Branca, "Nuove note sulla *Caccia di Diana,*" in *Tradizione delle opere* (1958), p. 167. The first printed mention of the *Caccia di Diana* is in Girolamo Claricio's *Apologia contro i detrattori della poesia di messer Gio. Boccaccio,* an appendix to his edition of the *Amorosa visione* (Milan: 1521). Claricio there announced his intention of publishing "la leggiadretta et sollazzevole *Caccia di Diana,* che d'interzate Rime contiene Cant. xviii" (the little delightful and entertaining *Diana's Hunt,* which contains eighteen cantos of rhyming triplets). The *Hunt's* first editor, Ignazio Moutier (*La caccia di Diana* [Florence: Magheri, 1832]), was convinced that it was Boccaccio's work, basing his opinion

on catalogs of Florentine writers that attribute it to him, as well as internal stylistic evidence and the fact that the *Caccia* appeared together with the *Amorosa visione* in the manuscript tradition. Subsequent editions are listed in our bibliography. For Branca's contributions, see above, chapter 1, n. 1. Surveys of the literature rejecting Boccaccio's paternity appear in Giovanni Boccaccio, *Caccia di Diana,* ed. Aldo Francesco Massèra (Turin: Unione Tipografico-Editrice Torinese, 1919), p. ix; and Giovanni Boccaccio, *Caccia di Diana,* ed. Vittore Branca (Milan: Mondadori, 1967), p. 680.

2. Pier Giorgio Ricci ("Una lacuna nella *Caccia di Diana?*" in *Studi sulla vita e le opere del Boccaccio* [Milan: Ricciardi, 1985], pp. 308–310) suspected "a vast lacuna" between Cantos 15 and 16. But, he allowed, the apparent inconsistencies in the poem could also be due to the young author's inexperience rather than a defective text. The relatively little scholarly attention given the *Hunt* in overviews of Boccaccio's work has tended to be negative in slant, or at best, ambivalent. For example, Baldo Curato (*Introduzione al Boccaccio* [Cremona: Editrice "Padus," 1961], p. 50) could dismiss it in a parenthesis: "Sulla *Caccia di Diana* non occorre fermarsi; si tratta di un poemetto di 18 canti in terza rima, dove un esile invenzione mitologica serve di pretesto all'elogio di cinquantotto gentildonne napoletane" (There is no need to tarry over *Diana's Hunt*; it is a short poem in 18 cantos of terza rima, where a slim mythological invention serves as a pretext for praising fifty-eight Neapolitan gentlewomen). Carlo Grabher (*Boccaccio* [Turin: Unione Tipografico-Editrice Torinese, 1945], esp. pp. 37–39) stated flatly that the *Hunt* had no fundamental importance, either in itself or with respect to the formation of Boccaccio's major writing ("Boccaccio maggiore"), and was overall "solo un incerto tentativo" (only a hesitant effort) marred by slippage between the pagan myth and realism, which he judged a "goffo preludio" (an awkward prelude) to the *Nymphs of Fiesole* (p. 35). Giuseppe Giacalone (*Boccaccio minore e maggiore* [Rome: Avio, 1959]) found the *Hunt* defective for the contrast between its literary pretensions and popular, narrative tendency (pp. 67–68). Guido di Pino, *La polemica del Boccaccio* (Florence: Vallecchi, 1953), disapproved of the "structural deformity" that came from combining the "realistic" *sirventese* with a symbolic intention (pp. 59–60).

Generally speaking, critics have assumed that since Venus displaces Diana in the poem, Boccaccio must have had in mind a message that asserts the power of love over chastity. According to Carlo Muscetta ("Giovanni Boccaccio e i novellieri," in *Il Trecento,* ed. Emilio Cecchi and Natalino Sapegno, Storia della Letteratura Italiana, vol. 2 [Milan: Garzanti, 1965]), the poem concludes with a motif that will return repeatedly in Boccaccio's works: "The redeeming power of love is in fact exalted in this little erotic 'comedy' [*questa piccola 'commedìa' erotica*] which seems an upturning of the Circe myth" (p. 324). Similarly, Salvatore Galletti (*Patologia al Decameron* [Palermo: S. F. Flaccovio, 1969]), perceives the *Hunt* as Boccaccio's vivid depiction of his youthful hopes "in un suggestivo trionfo d'amore" (in a provocative triumph of love); the poem expresses his discovery of "gioia, sorriso, carezza, amore" (joy, laughter, caressing, love) (p. 158); it was written "senza scrupoli della seduzione de quel che è umano e piace" (without scruples for the seduction of whatever is human and pleasurable) (p. 70). V. Branca ("Per l'attribuzione della *Caccia di Diana,*" written originally in 1938, now in *Tradizione delle opere* [1958], p. 130) places the emphasis correctly when he takes a further step and argues that the triumph of love comports a triumph of virtue: "La ribellione a Diana, la invocazione a Venere, e i prodigi che ne derivano, non sono che la tradizione mitizzata di un'affermazione ripetuta in tutti i toni nelle sue prime opere: 'i giovani devono attendere ad amare, e amore li educherà alla gentilezza e alla virtù'" (The rebellion against Diana, the invocation of Venus, the amazing events that derive therefrom, are none other than the mythicized tradition of an affirmation repeated in all tones in his early works: "the young must attend to love, and love will educate them to courtesy and virtue").

One of the critics who has recently spoken out in defense of the young Boccaccio is Robert Hollander, in *Boccaccio's Two Venuses* (New York: Columbia University Press, 1977). See his reading of the *Hunt,* pp. 12–21, and his judgment, p. 12: "Its technical insufficiencies seem shameful only to those who expect Shakespeare to have composed *King Lear* in his apprenticeship rather than *Venus and Adonis* or *The Rape of Lucrece* and help explain why those who denied authenticity felt moved to do so."

3. *Genealogie* 15.10: "Verum ad quoscunque actus natura produxerit alios, me quidem experientia teste ad poeticas meditationes dispositum ex utero matris eduxit et meo iudicio in hoc natus sum. Satis enim memini apposuisse patrem meum a pueritia mea conatus omnes, ut negociator efficerer, meque, adolescentiam non dum intrantem, arismetrica instructum maximo mercatori dedit discipulum, quem penes sex annis nil aliud egi, quam non recuperabile tempus in vacuum terere. Hinc quoniam visum est, aliquibus ostendentibus indiciis, me aptiorem fore licterarum studiis, iussit genitor idem, ut pontificum sanctiones, dives exinde futurus, auditurus intrarem, et sub preceptore clarissimo fere tantundem temporis in cassum etiam laboravi. Fastidiebat hec animus adeo, ut in neutrum horum officiorum, aut preceptoris doctrina, aut genitoris autoritate, qua novis mandatis angebar continue, aut amicorum precibus seu obiurgationibus inclinari posset, in tantum illum ad poeticam singularis traebat affectio!" (Whatever the vocation of others, mine, as experience from my mother's womb has shown, is clearly the study of poetry. For this, I believe, I was born. I well remember how my father even in my boyhood directed all my endeavors towards business. As a mere child, he put me under the charge of a great business man for instruction in arithmetic. For six years I did nothing in his office but waste irrevocable time. Then, as there seemed to be some indication that I was more disposed to literary pursuits, this same father decided that I should study for holy orders, as a good way to get rich. My teacher was famous, but I wasted under him almost as much time as before. In both cases I so tired of the work that neither my teacher's admonition, nor my father's authority, who kept torturing me with ever renewed orders, nor the pleas and importunities of my friends, could make me yield, so great was my one passion for poetry) (p. 776).

Giuseppe Billanovich (*Petrarca letterato. I. Lo scrittoio del Petrarca* [Rome: Edizioni di "Storia e Letteratura," 1947], p. 73, n. 1) gives the years of Boccaccio's apprenticeship in merchandising as 1329–1335; and puts his university years between 1335–1341. Branca's chronology, which we follow, prefers to see Boccaccio already sitting in on university classes as early as 1330–1331, when Cino da Pistoia was a visiting professor in the Neapolitan *studium* (*Profilo biografico,* pp. 30–31).

4. The manuscripts are described briefly by V. Branca in *Tradizione delle*

*opere di Giovanni Boccaccio* (1958), p. 18, and are listed in the Note on the Text, *Caccia di Diana* (1967), pp. 679–680.

5. The term is Robert Hollander's, *Boccaccio's Two Venuses* (1977), p. 205, n. 67; see Hollander's useful discussions of the *Amorosa visione,* esp. pp. 77–91, 202–219, et passim. See also *Amorosa visione,* trans. Robert Hollander, Timothy Hampton, Margherita Frankel (Hanover, N.H., and London: University Press of New England, 1986).

6. *Tradizione delle opere* (1958), pp. 124–127; 148–155; *Caccia di Diana,* Introduction, in *Tutte le opere,* vol. 1, p. 11. Besides *Rime* LXIX, "Contento quasi . . . ," with its accompanying *ballata,* Boccaccio did write his "Ave Maria" as an imperfectly rhymed *ternario* (*Rime* XLI); perhaps because of its slight irregularity of rhyme and because its devotional religiosity seemed antithetical to his celebratory lists of ladies in the *sirventese* form, it did not find a place in his "this-worldly" terza rima anthology.

7. See Victoria Kirkham, "Numerology and Allegory in Boccaccio's *Caccia di Diana,*" *Traditio* 34 (1978), pp. 303–329; "Reckoning With Boccaccio's *Questioni d'amore,*" *MLN* 89, no. 1 (Jan. 1974), pp. 47–59; "'Chiuso parlare' in Boccaccio's *Teseida,*" in *Dante, Petrarch, Boccaccio. Studies in the Italian Trecento in Honor of Charles S. Singleton,* ed. Aldo S. Bernardo and Anthony L. Pellegrini (Binghamton, N.Y.: Medieval and Renaissance Texts Series, 1983), pp. 305–351; "An Allegorically Tempered *Decameron,*" *Italica* 62.1 (1985a), pp. 1–23.

8. The sonnet reads as follows: "Guido, i' vorrei che tu e Lapo ed io / fossimo presi per incantamento, / e messi in un vasel ch'ad ogni vento / per mare andasse al voler vostro e mio, / sì che fortuna od altro tempo rio / non ci potesse dare impedimento, / anzi, vivendo sempre in un talento, / di stare insieme crescesse 'l disio. / E monna Vanna e monna Lagia poi / con quella ch'è sul numer de le trenta / con noi ponesse il buono incantatore: / e quivi ragionar sempre d'amore, / e ciascuna di lor fosse contenta, / sì come i' credo che saremmo noi" (Guido, I wish that you and Lapo and I could be taken by magic and placed in a boat that, whatever the wind, would course over the sea wherever you and I chose to go, unhindered by fortune or any foul weather—our desire to be together in fact always increasing, living as we would in unceasing harmony. And then, that the good enchanter should give us for company Lady Vanna and Lady Lagia along with her who stands on number thirty, there to talk always of love; and that each of them should be happy, as I believe we would be).

9. Carlo Muscetta, *Giovanni Boccaccio* (Bari: Laterza, 1972), p. 18.

10. The analogy between God as Creator and the poet as creator was a commonplace: see, for example, Robert M. Durling, *The Figure of the Poet in Renaissance Epic* (Cambridge, Mass.: Harvard University Press, 1965), pp. 123–126; Charles S. Singleton, "The Poet's Number at the Center," *MLN* 80 (1965), pp. 1–10; Thomas P. Roche, "The Calendrical Structure of Petrarch's *Canzoniere,*" *Studies in Philology* 71 (1974), pp. 152–172.

11. On the associations between Venus and three, and Diana and seven in Boccaccio's writings as well as in the late antique tradition he had inherited (e.g., Macrobius, Martianus Cappella), see Kirkham, "Numerology and Allegory in Boccaccio's *Caccia di Diana*" (1978), and "'Chiuso parlare' in Boccaccio's *Teseida*" (1983).

12. *Vita nuova* 29: "Questo numero fue ella medesima; per similitudine

dico . . . se lo tre è fattore per sé medesimo del nove, e lo fattore per sé medesimo de li miracoli è tre, cioè Padre e Figlio e Spirito Santo, li quali sono tre e uno, questa donna fue accompagnata da questo numero del nove a dare ad intendere ch'ella era uno nove, cioè uno miracolo, la cui radice, cioè del miracolo, è solamente la mirabile Trinitade."

Boccaccio was later to spoof this threadbare, Trinitarian-miraculous connection of the number three with the beloved by having the foolish protagonist of the *Corbaccio* catch the first glance of his future harridan-wife as she is seated "third" on a bench vulgarly gossiping with other crones (*Corbaccio*, ed. T. Nurmela, p. 62; *The Corbaccio*, trans. and ed. Anthony K. Cassell [Urbana and London: University of Illinois Press, 1975], p. 17).

13. *Purgatorio* 31.106: "Noi siam qui ninfe e nel ciel siamo stelle" (Here we are nymphs and in the heavens we are stars). See Charles S. Singleton, "Rivers, Nymphs, and Stars," in *Journey to Beatrice. Dante Studies 2* (Cambridge, Mass.: Harvard University Press, 1967), pp. 159–183.

See also Anna Catharina Esmeijer, *Divina quaternitas: een onderzoek naar methode en toepassing der visuele exegese (A Study of Methods and Applications of Visual Exegesis [with a Summary in English]),* Published Dissertation, Rijksuniversiteit te Utrecht (Amsterdam, 1973).

14. See V. Branca's discussion of sources in the Introduction to *Caccia di Diana,* pp. 5–9. In addition to those we mention, he notes possible Hellenistic antecedents, and suggests a likeness with the lyrical form of the *cacce.* Muscetta believes that the *cacce* were inspired by Boccaccio's hunt poem (*Giovanni Boccaccio,* p. 21). Other critics, however, see no historical connection between *Diana's Hunt* and the "cacce in rima," which were madrigals of a sort, all dating from a later period. See Francesco Torraca, *Per la biografia di Giovanni Boccaccio* (Rome: Dante Alighieri, 1912), and his "Giovanni Boccaccio a Napoli," *Rassegna Critica della Letteratura Italiana* 20 (1915), pp. 145–245, 21 (1916a), pp. 1–80.

Boccaccio will later capitalize on the possibilities of Olympian rivalries between Diana and Venus in his romance *Filocolo,* in the epic *Teseida delle nozze d'Emilia,* and in the pastoral *Ninfale fiesolano.* In the last of these, as in the *Hunt,* the enmity remains at surface implacable; but in *Filocolo* and the *Teseida,* Diana and Venus will eventually make peace and ally forces, bringing about a happy resolution to the story.

15. Two shepherds, Alcesto and Acaten, debate the life of virtue against the life of vice, for the benefit of Ameto in *Comedìa delle ninfe fiorentine* 14. Boccaccio's thirteenth eclogue, "The Laurel Wreath," presents a similar contest between Stilbon, who pursues wealth in the busy commercial world, and Daphnis, who prefers the solitude and simplicity of a life dedicated to poetry. See J. Smarr's notes, *Eclogues,* pp. 248–251.

16. Topics of these Latin debate poems and forms of the Italian *contrasto* are reviewed by Antonio Pace in the introduction to his edition of Antonio Pucci, *Il contrasto delle donne,* ed. Antonio Pace (Menasha, Wis.: George Banta Publishing Company, 1944), pp. 4–6.

17. Pseudo-Rabanus Maurus (attributed—tenuously—to Garnier de Rochefort by Glorieux), *Allegoriae in sacram scripturam, PL* 112:1051: "*serpens,* diabolus, ut in Isaia: 'Serpenti panis pulvis est,' quod qui terrena contra Dominum diligunt, ipsi diabolum pascunt. . . . Per *serpentes* peccata, ut in libro Numeri: 'Immisit

dominus in eos *ignitos serpentes,*' quod superbis et murmurantibus peccata Dominus dominari permittit." Cf. Isaiah 65:25, "and dust shall be the serpent's food"; Numbers 21:6, "Wherefore the Lord sent among the people *fiery* [literally, 'ignited'] serpents, which bit them and killed many of them" (Douay).

18. On the "daughters of pride" see Saint Gregory, *Moralia* XXXI, 88–89; *Morals,* vol. III, pt. 2, pp. 490–491; and Saint Thomas Aquinas, *ST* II–II, qu. 118, art. 8. For a discussion of the idea of the filiation of sin, see A. K. Cassell, "The Interrelation of Sins," in *Lectura Dantis Americana: Inferno I* (Philadelphia: University of Pennsylvania Press, 1989), pp. 52–55, and *Dante's Fearful Art of Justice* (1984), pp. 48, 86, 136, 162. See also Edward Moore, *Studies in Dante,* 2nd series (Oxford: Clarendon Press, 1899), Table 1, facing p. 208.

19. Augustine, *City of God* 15.20: "Quoniam ergo lex denario numero praedicatur, unde est memorabilis ille decalogus, profecto numerus undenarius, quoniam transgreditur denarium, transgressionem legis ac per hoc peccatum significat."

20. On Dante's use of the number eleven, which Boccaccio certainly appreciated, see V. Kirkham, "Eleven is for Evil. Measured Trespass in Dante's *Commedia,*" *Allegorica* 10 (1989), pp. 27–50.

21. Boccaccio may have in mind another connotation of the number seven as it shapes the women's hunt. Seven is an established sign of wisdom, since Proverbs 9:1 tells us, "Sapientia aedificavit sibi domum, / excidit columnas septem" (Wisdom hath built herself a house; she hath hewn her out seven pillars [Douay]). Of his serpent-slayers' wisdom Boccaccio repeatedly reminds us with phrases centered on the word *senno,* (good sense, intelligence): "con senno cacciando" 2.58 (they hunted wisely); "col senno suo" 5.38 (for all her wits); "sì con senno sepper fare" 5.58 (they knew how to do it so wisely).

Boccaccio understood seven as a symbol of wisdom in other works. The seven Liberal Arts appear in his *Amorosa visione,* and seven also seems to be associated with the wisdom of Theseus in the epic *Teseida.* See V. Kirkham, "'Chiuso parlare'" (1983).

22. See Commentary, Canto 7, below.

23. *Inferno* 12.12–27; *Purgatorio* 26.41–42.

24. C. S. Lewis (*The Discarded Image: An Introduction to Medieval and Renaissance Literature* [Cambridge: Cambridge University Press, 1964; rprt. 1967], pp. 52–53) discusses Chalcidius and his commentary in the Middle Ages. The possibility of reincarnation in bestial form is also discussed in Plato's *Phaedo,* 80c–80d, of which about a dozen copies are known to have existed in medieval Europe; Francesco Petrarca's copy of Henricus Aristippus's translation is now in the Bibliothèque Nationale, Paris, B.N. lat. 6567A. The *Timaeus* was by far the more influential text; about 150 exemplars have so far been reported (to which must now be added another fifteen recently identified by James Hankins, whom we thank for this information). The *Timaeus* in Boccaccio's library is cataloged by A. Mazza in her article "L'inventario della 'parva libreria' di Santo Spirito e la biblioteca del Boccaccio," *Italia medioevale e umanistica* 9 (1966), pp. 1–71. The Circean topos appears throughout Boccaccio's literary production. His *Eclogues* mask men as beasts (see J. L. Smarr's commentary, for example, on "Faunus," where "Allobrogian wolves" signify agents of Avignon; "Molossian hounds" stand for soldiers). Striking, with similarities to both the *Hunt* and *Corbaccio,* is the

eclogue entitled "The Dark Valley"—the valley of Hell whose wretched beasts are allegorical sinners (cf. 10.101–104: "but you'd hear / quite differently our valley loud resounding / with mighty bellows, foul boars; gnashing teeth / and savage lions' roaring rage"; and vv. 156ff., where there appear in sequence "bristling hogs," "hounds," "mighty bears," "sluggish asses," and "linxes"). We may recall also Boccaccio's bucolic *Ninfale fiesolano,* in which Africo tells his father of hunting a white doe ("una cerbietta . . . bianca tutta come pura neve"), but the experienced Girafone understands that the boy refers to nymphs (stanzas 76–81). Compare also *Filocolo* 4.13, where the hero has a prophetic dream in which all the characters are various species of birds.

25. "Hinc anima, quam in se pronam corporis usus effecit atque in pecudem quodam modo reformavit ex homine, et absolutionem corporis perhorrescit . . . sed aut suum oberrat cadaver aut novi corporis ambit habitaculum, non humani tantum modo, sed ferini quoque electo genere moribus congruo quos in homine libenter exercuit." *Macrobio: Commento al Somnium Scipionis,* ed. Mario Regali (Pisa: Giardini Editori, 1983), pp. 104–105 (Lat. text and Ital. trans.); *Commentary on the Dream of Scipio,* trans. William Harris Stahl (New York: Columbia University Press, 1952), p. 125.

26. *De consolatione Philosophiae,* 4.3 Pr.: "Euenit igitur ut quem transformatum uitiis uideas hominem aestimare non possis. Auaritia feruet alienarum opum uiolentus ereptor? Lupi similem dixeris. Ferox atque inquies linguam litigiis exercet? Cani comparabis. Insidiator occultus subripuisse fraudibus gaudet? Vulpeculis exaequetur. Irae intemperans fremit? Leonis animum gestare credatur. Pauidus ac fugax non metuenda formidat? Ceruis similis habeatur. Segnis ac stupidus torpit? Asinum uiuit. Leuis atque inconstans studia permutat? Nihil auibus differt. Foedis immundisque libidinibus immergitur? Sordidae suis uoluptate detinetur. Ita fit ut qui probitate deserta homo esse desierit, cum in diuinam condicionem transire non possit, uertatur in beluam."

27. Samuel J. Edgerton, Jr., *Pictures and Punishment* (Ithaca, N.Y.: Cornell University Press, 1985), pp. 82, 84.

28. *De mulieribus claris* 38.5: "Et sic hi, quibus infauste mulieris opera humana subtracta videbatur ratio, eos ab eadem in sui facinoris feras merito crederetur fuisse conversos. Ex quibus satis comprehendere possumus, hominum mulierumque conspectis moribus, multas ubique Cyrces esse et longe plures homines lascivia et crimine suo versos in belvas" (ed. V. Zaccharia, p. 156).

29. *Esposizioni sopra la Comedìa di Dante, Inferno* 1.ii.73: "come l'uomo ha commesso il peccato, egli diventa quella bestia, li cui costumi son simili a quel peccato; verbigrazia: colui che nel vizio della lussuria si lascia cadere, per ciò che la lussuria per la sua bruttezza è simigliata al porco, esso diventa porco, quantunque effige umana gli rimanga, e il rapace diventa lupo, perché il lupo è rapacissimo animale: e così quello luogo è salvatico, sì come privato d'ogni umana stanza."

30. *Esposizioni* 2.ii.38: "E di questo non è alcun dubbio che noi, quante volte ci raveggiamo delle nostre disoneste operazioni, tante per divina grazia ricominciamo ad essere uomini, li quali non siamo quanto nella ignoranza dei peccati dimoriamo: anzi, avendo la ragione perduta, siamo divenuti quegli animali bruti, a' quali, come altra volta è detto, sono i nostri difetti conformi. Il che se altra dottrina non ci mostrasse, spesse volte ne 'l mostrano le poetiche fizioni, quando

ne dicono alcuno uomo essersi transformato in lupo, alcuno in leone, alcuno in asino o in alcun'altra forma bestiale."

31. "Protinus mihi delabitur deformis et ferina facies. Ac primo quidem squalens pilus defluit, ac dehinc cutis crassa tenuatur, venter obesus residet, pedeum plantae per ungulas in digitos exeunt, manus non iam pedes sunt sed in erecta porriguntur officia, cervix procera cohibetur, os et caput rotundatur, aures enormes repetunt pristinam parvitatem, dentes saxei redeunt ad humanam minutiem, et, quae me potissimum cruciabat ante, cauda nusquam" (Latin text from Apuleius's *Metamorphoses,* or *"The Golden Ass,"* ed., trans., W. Adlington [1566], rev. S. Gaselee, [London: William Heinemann; New York: The Macmillan Co., 1915; rprt. Cambridge, Mass.: Harvard University Press; London: William Heinemann, 1947], p. 560). "Nec tibi natales ac ne dignitas quidem, vel ipsa qua flores usquam doctrina profuit, sed lubrico virentis aetatulae ad serviles delapsus voluptates, curiositatis improsperae sinistrum praemium reportasti" (p. 562). The detailed and oblique parallels to Boccaccio's plot, beyond the metamorphosis, are evident.

*Chapter 3: The Allegorical Stag*

1. In the *Rime sparse* 23, "Nel dolce tempo de la prima etade" (In the sweet time of my first age), in a last metamorphosis, Petrarch has his lover-poet turn into a stag after he sees Laura naked at a fountain, a fate that repeats that of Actaeon, Ovid's hunter, who had espied Diana bathing: "Ch' i' senti' trarmi de la propria imago / et in un cervo solitario et vago / di selva in selva ratto mi trasformo / et ancor de' miei can' fuggo lo stormo" (For I felt myself drawn from my own image and into a solitary wandering stag from wood to wood quickly I am transformed and still I flee the belling of my hounds).

Alternatively, Petrarch's poet-persona can also be the new Dido, as in the sonnet "I dolci colli ov'io lasciai me stesso" (The sweet hills where I left myself), *Rime sparse* 209: "Et qual cervo ferito di saetta / col ferro avelenato dentr'al fianco, / fugge et più duolsi quanto più s'affretta, / tal io, con quello stral dal lato manco, / che mi consuma et parte mi diletta, / di duol mi struggo et di fuggir mi stanco" (As a hart struck by an arrow, with the poisoned steel within its side, flees and feels more pain the faster it runs, so I, with that arrow in my left side which destroys me and at the same time delights me, am tormented by sorrow and weary myself with fleeing).

See *Petrarch's Lyric Poems. The Rime Sparse and Other Lyrics,* trans. and ed. Robert M. Durling (Cambridge, Mass.: Harvard University Press, 1976).

2. *Stanze* 34: "l'imagin d'una cervia altera e bella: / con alta fronte, con corna ramose, / candida tutta, leggiadretta e snella."

See *The Stanze of Angelo Poliziano,* trans. David Quint (Amherst, Mass.: University of Massachusetts Press, 1979). Cf. *Rime sparse* 190: "Una candida cerva sopra l'erba / verde m'apparve con duo corna d'oro, / fra due riviere all'ombra d'un alloro, / levando 'l sole a la stagione acerba. / Era sua vista sì dolce superba / ch'i' lasciai per seguirla ogni lavoro."

For Branca, the doe that seduces Iulio seems to symbolize "the life of the senses, the transitory and illusory well being that we vainly follow in our earthly existence," whereas Simonetta, by a degree of Neoplatonic ascent, is "the rational soul, active life, love of earthly virtue." Although Poliziano's immediate source for the doe is Petrarch, Branca believes he might also have known the *Caccia di Diana,* taking suggestions from it for the language and rapid movement of his hunting scenes (Vittore Branca, *Poliziano e l'umanesimo della parola* [Turin: Einaudi, 1983], pp. 45, 51).

3. The examples of the iconography are from Paul F. Watson, *The Garden of Love in Tuscan Art of the Early Renaissance* (Philadelphia: The Art Alliance Press, 1979), p. 74, pl. 60, who sees Mariotto's stag as Venerean and "a traditional symbol of smitten lovers." The salver is now at the Staatsgallerie, Stuttgart. For the North Italian gittern, in the Metropolitan Museum, New York, see pp. 38–39 and pl. 18; for the Sienese *Paradise of Venus,* p. 85 and pl. 68. Cf. pp. 92–93 and pl. 76 for a Tuscan *cassone* panel of the 1430s with pairs of addorsed deer forming part of a love-hunt motif. Watson also notes the deer's association with sexual attraction in the sonnet by Lapo Gianni, "Gentil donna cortese e dibonare" (Gentle lady courteous and friendly): "Quando vostr'alto intelletto l'udìo, / sì come il cervio inver' lo cacciatore, / così a voi servidore tornò, che li degnaste perdonare" (When your noble spirit heard it, as the stag comes to the hunter, my heart returned a servant to you, because you deigned to forgive it). The text is in Gianfranco Contini, *Poeti del Duecento* (Milan: Ricciardi, 1960), vol. 2, p. 575.

For the sexual symbolism of the rabbit, see C. K. Abraham, "Myth and Symbol: The Rabbit in Medieval France" (1963), pp. 589–597; and D. W. Robertson, *A Preface to Chaucer* (1962), pp. 113, 255 (for the wordplay on *con* and *conin* in French, and the rabbit's relation to Venus); see also Commentary, 3.26–27; 6.38, below.

4. Plutarch's folk etymology for "stag" is revealing: the Greek word *elaphos* (stag) is said to derive from *helein tous opheis,* "those breathing in serpents," *De solert. anim.* 24D; see Plutarch's *Moralia,* trans. Harold Cherness and William C. Helmbold et al., vol. 12, Loeb Classical Library (London: William Heinemann; Cambridge, Mass.: Harvard University Press, 1957), pp. 420–421.

Henri-Charles Puech, in "Le Cerf et le serpent: Note sur le symbolisme de la mosaïque découverte au baptistère de l'henchir Messaouda," in *Cahiers Archéologiques* 4 (1949), pp. 17–60, esp. pp. 29–30, cites many authorities in the Greco-Roman world who had knowledge of the stag's habits involving serpents (Xenophon, *Geoponica* 19.5.3; Oppian, *Cynegetica* 2.233–252; Pliny the Elder, *Natural History* 8.32 [50], 28.9 [42]; Lucretius, *De rerum natura* 6.765–766; Martial, *Epigrams* 12.29.5; and Solinus, *Collectanea rerum mirabilium* 19.13).

5. For a particularly fine illustration of the theme, see British Library Harley MS. 3567, made at Mantua 1463–1483, in Thomas Kren, ed., *Renaissance Painting in Manuscripts. Treasures from the British Library* (New York: Hudson Hills Press, 1983), p. 97. Boccaccio, *Ameto* 32.9: "avente forse veduti più secoli che il rinnovante cervio, dagli anni in poca forma era tirato."

6. We have freely adapted the English translation from Theobaldus, *Physiologus,* ed. P. T. Eden (Leiden and Cologne: E. J. Brill, 1972), pp. 48–51, no. 6, "De cervo" (The Stag): "Cervus habere duas naturas atque figuras / Dicitur a Physio, cum docet inde, -logo. / Nam quamvis grandes cum naribus extrahit angues / De caveis terre, de latebrisve petre; / Quos vorat et tetro mox fervescente veneno / Estuat ad liquidas pergere fontis aquas. / Quas cum forte bibit, his plenus toxica vincit, / Se juvenemque facit, cornua quando jacit. / Nos quoque cum prisci serpentis fraude revicti / Virus contrahimus, urimur et facibus / (Hoc

est luxuria, que fert odium velut ira, / Aut etiam nimia eris avaritia), / Ad fontem vivum debemus currere Christum, / Qui cum nos udat, sumpta venena fugat. / Et sumus his demptis juvenes factisque superbis / Que quasi cornua sunt, cum miseros feriunt."

The text goes on to say that the second admirable characteristic (*natura*) of the stag is his compassion (*pietas*), for when the animals walk or swim in herds, they take turns letting those behind rest their heavily antlered heads on each other's haunches. In this way the stag exemplifies Paul's exhortation in Galatians 6:3, "Bear ye one another's burdens: and so you shall fulfil the law of Christ."

7. Augustine, *Enarratio in Psalmum 41.3*: "Serpentes vitia tua sunt; consume serpentes iniquitatis, tunc amplius desiderabis fontem veritatis. . . . quando concupiscis fontem sapientiae, cum adhuc labores in veneno malitiae? Interfice in te quidquid contrarium est veritati; et cum te videris tamquam vacare a cupiditatibus perversis, noli remanere quasi non sit quod desideres. . . . Desidera unde delecteris. Desidera *ad fontes aquarum*" (*PL* 36.465–466). See also "Psalm XLII [XLI]" in Saint Augustine, *Expositions on the Book of Psalms*, ed. and trans. A. Cleveland Coke, in *A Select Library of the Nicene and Post-Nicene Fathers of the Christian Church*, vol. 8 (Grand Rapids, Mich.: W. B. Eerdmans, 1974), pp. 132–133ff.

Augustine's familiarity with the stag's compulsion to eat serpents appears in his exposition of Psalm 28 (AV/RSV 29), which for him refers to "the completion of the Church in this world, where she wages war daily against the devil." Here is the text as Augustine edited it from Greek texts and glossed it: "'*Vox Domini perficientis cervos*': vox enim Domini primo perficit superatores et repulsores venenosarum linguarum. *Et revalabit silvas*: et tunc eis revalabit opacitates divinorum librorum et umbracula mysteriorum, ubi cum libertate pascantur" ("The voice of the Lord perfecting the stags." [In the Septuagint version, and in the Gallican Psalter through the Douay translation, the verse reads, "The voice of the Lord prepareth the stags." In Saint Jerome's "Hebrew" Psalter text of Psalm 28:9, there is a quite different reading.—Eds.] For the Voice of the Lord has above all led to perfection those who know how to control and discountenance venomous tongues. "And He will reveal the woods." He will then lay bare to them the obscurities of the divine books, and the mysteries hidden in the shadow, so that they may browse at large in their pastures; *PL* 36.214; *St. Augustine on the Psalms*, trans. Dame Scholastica Hebgin and Dame Felicitas Corrigan, Ancient Christian Writers, vol. 29 [Westminster, Md.: Newman Press; London: Longmans Green, 1960], p. 288).

Significantly, this passage situates the stag in darkened woods, as Boccaccio situates his narrator, who wanders the forest suffering before he is "perfected." Overcoming "venomous tongues," we now know, is a metaphorical correlative of conquering sin and the Devil. For Augustine, the forest's shadowy trees are texts with meaning to be revealed when their cortex ("bark") is removed, that is, when the veil of allegory is lifted. So, too, we as readers must "decorticate" Boccaccio's dark wood, a scene whose mysteriousness invites the light of allegorical reading.

8. The Psalms with Augustine's commentary was one of the most widely read and cited texts in the Middle Ages. Boccaccio's respect and love for it is evident from the gift he made to Petrarch of the second half of that book, when he learned that it was not part of his friend's library. Petrarch wrote in it "hoc

immensum opus donavit michi vir egregius dominus Johannes Boccaccii de Certaldo poeta nostri temporis, quod de Florentia Mediolanum ad me pervenit 1355 aprilis 10" (this immense work was given to me by the distinguished man lord John Boccaccio, poet of our time; it reached me from Florence April 10, 1355). See G. Billanovich, "Nella biblioteca del Petrarca, I: Il Petrarca, il Boccaccio e le 'Enarrationes in Psalmos' di s. Agostino," *Italia medioevale e umanistica* 3 (1960), pp. 18–21, 24, 26, and pl. 3 and 4. The manuscript is now in the Bibliothèque Nationale in Paris, B.N., MSS. Latin 1989; it bears Petrarch's abundant marginal annotations (Florence Callu and François Avril, *Boccace en France: De l'humanisme à l'érotisme* [Paris: Bibliothèque Nationale, 1975], pp. 12–13). See also Branca, *Profilo biografico,* p. 98.

9. Most magnificent and from the first period were "seven silver water-spouting stags," together with a golden lamb in a figural group, commissioned by Constantine as a gift to encircle the Lateran font constructed during Sylvester's pontificate (314–335). A fifth-century baptistry pavement from Tunisia preserves mosaic fragments with two harts confronted at a stylized date palm, each one wrestling with a snake. The Romanesque baptismal font at Freudenstad, Württemberg, shows how a stag, having devoured a serpent and purged himself by eating leaves from the Tree of Life, regurgitates the poison. A title spells out its message: "EVOMIT INFUSUM HOMO CERVUS AB ANGUE VENENUM" (MAN THE STAG VOMITS POISON POURED IN BY THE SNAKE).

The sacred stag also appears in catacombs, on sarcophagi from Gaul, carved precious stones, ceramic panels and church lamps, a lead seal, a silver coffer, a eucharistic wafer mold. For the spouting stags, see the excellent discussion by Paul A. Underwood, "The Fountain of Life in Manuscripts of the Gospels," *Dunbarton Oaks Papers* 5 (1950), pp. 41–138, esp. pp. 50–51. The Tunisian finding was published by G. L. Feuille, "Une mosaïque chrétienne de l'Henchir Messaouda (Tunisie, région d'Agareb)," *Cahiers Archéologiques* 4 (1949), pp. 9–15. For other examples of stag symbolism with rich literary documentation, see also Henri-Charles Puech, "Le Cerf et le serpent," *Cahiers archéologiques fin de l'antiquité et Moyen Age* 4 (1949), pp. 17–60. Hjörvardur Harvard Arnason, "Early Christian Silver of North Italy and Gaul," *Art Bulletin* 20, no. 1 (March 1938), pp. 193–226, reproduces a silver capsella ca. 425–450 (Museo del Vaticano) that shows a stag and roe drinking from the four rivers of Paradise below a monogrammatic cross; a Gallic sarcophagus cover (Marseilles, Musée d'Archéologie) on which two deer drink at the rivers that flow from a mount on which stands the lamb; and a sarcophagus (Marseilles, St. Victor) with stags at the rivers on its lower band and, above, lambs flanking a monogrammatic cross.

10. Similarly, at Santa Maria Maggiore, below a monumental *Coronation of the Virgin,* a stag and doe drink from the four rivers of Paradise that descend into a horizontal channel whose waters buoy genii and aquatic birds, forming a frieze across the bottom of the scene.

Primary as symbolic meanings of the number four were the cardinal points of the earth and the cardinal virtues. These pre-Christian connections were the basis for patristic expansion, which brought into alignment with the four-cornered world its four garden rivers and the four evangelists, whose message the four Gospels spread universally. See, for example, Rabanus Maurus, "De numero," in *De universo* (*PL* 111.490): the "quaternary number" pertains to the four evangelists, four cardinal virtues, four parts of the world, and the four elements of the world, of which the human body is compounded; Isidore of Seville (*Liber numerorum* [*PL* 83.179f.]) lists under "four" the evangelists, parts of the world, rivers of Paradise, and the elements. Concerning stags, the four rivers of Paradise, the four evangelists, and baptism, see also P. Underwood, "The Fountain of Life" (1950), pp. 71–73. Traditional as well were the four senses of Scriptures in the Fathers. On the cosmological, geographical ramifications of such symbolism, see also Anna C. Esmeijer, *"Divina quaternitas"* (1973).

In many artistic depictions harts appear in pairs, as they do in the mosaics of San Clemente and San Giovanni in Laterano. In the apse mosaic of the ancient Vatican church, whose design is preserved in a sixteenth-century copy, below Christ enthroned between Peter and Paul there flowed the four rivers of Paradise with stags approaching on either side. At Santa Prasseda in Rome, a lunette in the ninth-century mosaic of the Cappella della Colonna has at its center a hillock on which stands the Lamb of God; a stag and doe bend to drink at streams issuing from the mount on either side. Sometimes rather than drinking from rivers, the renewing animals flank a sacramental substitute, the chalice. The cupola mosaic of the baptistry at Florence, above the angelic order of Principalities, presents two facing stags rampant with their forelegs stretched over the edge of a water-filled basin from which grows a stylized date palm. Stags similarly stand on either side of the chalice at Salona, where the text of the psalm from which the scene derives is set on the pavement at the entrance to the baptistry and serves as its caption: SICUT CERVVS DESIDERAT AD FONTES AQVARUM ITA DESIDERAT ANIMA MEA AD TE DEVS. Among the finest and most ancient paired stags are those posed amidst thick, swirling vine tendrils from the fifth-century mausoleum of Galla Placidia in Ravenna. Photographs of the sixteenth-century copy of the apse mosaic from the old Vatican, of mosaics in Santa Prasseda, and of the Florentine baptistry are in the Fototeca Berenson, Villa I Tatti (Byzantine Mosaics, Italy and Europe). Underwood reproduces the Salona mosaic, p. 52 and pl. 28.

The various plants and trees for which stags have an affinity in art (e.g., acanthus, date palm, vine tendril) are flora of Paradise. Certain tree-seeking stags, such as those on the Romanesque baptismal fonts at Düppel (Schlesvig), Lund (Sweden), and Dalby, seem to act out a "religious hunt." Similar meaning could underlie the famous Norman mosaic frieze with hunt scenes that decorate Roger II's room in the Royal Palace at Palermo. In these contexts the stag would then allude to the human soul that pursues salvation by approaching the Tree of Life. Such visual motifs, which fuse the ideas of questing and conversion, forest and font, parallel themes of the spiritual chase in literature as Boccaccio recombined them for *Diana's Hunt*. On the "religious hunt," see Romuald Bauerreiss, "*Arbor vitae. Der 'Lebensbaum' und seine Verwendung in Liturgie, Kunst und Brauchtum des Abendlandes,*" *Abhandlungen der Bayerischen Benediktiner-Akademie* 3 (Munich: 1938), p. 37, a reference cited by Puech in "Le Cerf et le serpent" (1949), pp. 21–22.

11. Jean-Louis Maier, *Le Baptistère de Naples et ses mosaïques. Etude historique et iconographique* (Fribourg, Switzerland: Editions Universitaires, 1964). The best color reproductions of San Giovanni in Fonte, as for San Clemente, are found in Josef Wilpert, *Die römischen Mosaiken und Malereien der kirchlichen Bauten vom IV. bis XIII. Jahrhundert* (Freiburg im Breisgau: Herder, 1924). As argued by Puech, the

stags at San Giovanni in Fonte must signify the neophytes, whom their guardian, Christ, guides to the refreshing waters of baptism. On a secondary level of meaning, those waters and the fruit in the trees announce the sacramental unction and first communion that immediately follow baptism, bringing the neophyte into Christ's community of the saved.

The baptism of Christ was always depicted amid jagged rocks in the thirteenth and fourteenth centuries, reflecting the temptation in the wilderness that followed in the Gospel accounts: compare the mosaics of the event in Saint Mark's in Venice and in Saint John's Baptistry in Florence.

12. This is the baptism that Boccaccio, in his commentary on Dante's Limbo, calls: "il battesimo del fiume, cioè quello il quale attualmente ne' suoi catacumini usa la Chiesa di Dio" (baptism of the river, that is, that which in the present time the Church of God applies to its catechumens; *Esposizioni* 4.2.6); in this "river baptism," he continues, "son battezati quegli li quali noi chiamiamo rinati, de' quali dice l'*Evangelio*: 'Qui crediderit et baptizatus fuerit, salvus erit' " (are baptized those whom we call reborn, of whom the Gospel says, "He who has believed and has been baptized will be saved"; *Esposizioni* 4.2.9).

P. Underwood, "The Fountain of Life," provides an excellent discussion of the baptismal ceremony in early times. He cites the distichs (p. 55), attributing them to Leo, whose authorial hand, he argues, was probably also in the Gelasian sacramentary, source of the blessing of the font. The verses carved on the Lateran tabernacle are: "a) Gens sacranda polis hic semine nascitur almo, / quam fecundatis spiritus edit aquis. / b) Mergere, peccator sacro purgande fluento: / quem veterem accipiet, proferet unda novum. / c) Nulla renascentum est distantia, quos facit unum / unus fons, unus spiritus, una fides. / d) Virgineo faetu genitrix ecclesia natos, / quos spirante deo concipit, amne parit. / e) Insons esse volens isto mundare lavacro, / seu patrio premeris crimine seu proprio. / f) Fons hic est vitae, qui totum diluit orbem / sumens de Christi vulnere principium. / g) Caelorum regnum sperate, hoc fonte renati; / non recipit felix vita semel genitos. / h) Nec numerus quemquam scelerum nec forma suorum / terreat: hoc natus flumine sanctus erit" (a) The city, a people to be consecrated, here springs into being from fruitful seed: / which the Spirit brings forth from impregnated waters. / b) Be dipped in the sacred stream, O sinner called to purity: / whom the water will receive old, but bring forth new. / c) There is no distinction among those born again, / whom one font, one Spirit, one faith make one. / d) From her virginal womb Mother Church gives birth in the stream to her children, / whom she conceives through the breath of God. / e) Wouldst thou be pure, cleanse thyself in this bath, / whether thou are oppressed by original sin or by thine own guilt. / f) This is the fountain of life, which purges the whole world, / taking its course from the wound of Christ. / g) Hope for the Kingdom of Heaven, ye who are reborn in this font; / the blessed life does not accept those who are born only once. / h) Let not the number or the kind of his sins frighten anyone; / born of this stream he will be holy).

13. The most noble form of hunting is coursing the stag (M. Thiébaux, "The Medieval Chase" [1967]). As Diana's attribute, stags draw her chariot in Claudian's panegyric on Stillicho (3.286–287), quoted by Boccaccio for his portrait of Diana in *Genealogie* 5.2. Stags pull the chariot, he explains, because forest animals "draw" our desire to hunt. (For other examples in the poetry of antiquity and later

art, see Guy de Terverant, *Attributs et symboles dans l'art profane. 1450–1600: Dictionnaire d'un langage perdu,* Travaux d'Humanisme et Renaissance 29 [Geneva: Droz, 1958; also Supplément, 1964], vol. 1, cols. 65–66.) Diana travels through the skies in a stag-drawn chariot in painted narratives, too. See, for example, *The Realms of Love,* a *cassone* panel of ca. 1440 by Paolo Schiavo (P. Watson, *The Garden* [1979], pp. 25ff., and pls. 1 and 4).

14. In his commentary, Branca notes language typical of the *cantari,* romances in ottava rima (eight-line stanzas) recited by minstrels for folk in the piazzas.

15. Boccaccio counts the dove an attribute of Venus in *Genealogie* 3.22 (p. 142): "Addunt preterea in tutelam eius esse columbas" (They add further that doves are in her tutelage). Doves are Venus's common attribute in artistic representations throughout the Middle Ages. Cf. Venus as Luxuria in *Ymagines secundum diversos doctores,* Vat. Lat. MS. 1726, fol. 43r; *Ovide moralisé,* Copenhagen, Royal Library, MS. Thott 3399, fol. 9; *Ovide moralisé,* Paris, Bibliothèque Nationale MS. Fr. 373, fol. 207. The major *locus classicus* is *Aeneid* VI, 190–194, where Aeneas recognizes the twin doves of his goddess-mother.

16. On the doctrine of *epiclesis,* the descent of the Holy Ghost at the sacrament of baptism, see J. Daniélou, *The Bible and the Liturgy* (1956), pp. 13, 73–74, 107, et passim.

17. Gratian, *Decretum,* Part 3, "De consecratione," Dist. 4, c. 9: "Qui per hanc aquam transit, non moritur, sed resurgit. Non omnis aqua sanat, sed illa, quae habet gratiam Christi. Aliud est elementum, aliud est consecratio. . . . Non sanat aqua, nisi Spiritus sanctus descendat, et consecret aquam illam."

18. The transfiguration of Christ in the Gospel comes at the moment when the Messiah reveals to his disciples how he will fulfill the work of man's redemption through suffering, death, and resurrection (Matt. 17:1–8; Mark 17:1–13; Luke 9:28–36; 2 Peter 1:16–18). At baptism which seals conversion, Christians share in his transfiguration (2 Cor. 3:18; Phil. 3:21). In the baptismal and transfigurational events of the *Hunt,* Boccaccio closely follows the theological matrix.

19. 3 Kings 18:38, Vulgate-Douay; 1 Kings 18:38 AV. See Justin, *Dialogus cum Tryphone Judaeo,* 88 (*PG* 6.686). Carl-Martin Edsman, *Le Baptême de feu,* Acta Seminarii Neotestamentici Upsaliensis 9 (Leipzig: Alfred Lorenz; Uppsala: Lundquist, Almquist, and Wiksell, 1940), 182–186. J. Daniélou, *The Bible and the Liturgy* (1956), p. 107.

In the apocrypha, Saint Michael purifies the soul by baptism in a river of fire to make it fit for the presence of God; sacramental baptism is a prefiguration of eschatological baptism. Cf. J. Daniélou, *The Bible and the Liturgy* (1956), p. 212; see also C.-M. Edsman, pp. 65–67, and Per Lundberg, *La typologie baptismale dans l'ancienne église,* Acta Seminarii Neotestamentici Upsaliensis 10 (Leipzig: Alfred Lorenz; Uppsala: Lundquist, Almquist and Wiksell, 1942), pp. 44–45.

For the miracle of Elijah (Elias) and other typologies of baptism, see P. Lundberg, *La typologie baptismale* (1942); J. Daniélou, *The Bible and the Liturgy* (1956), esp. pp. 106–107.

20. Gregory of Nyssa, *In baptismum Christi* (*PG* 46.592).

21. Peter Lombard, *Commentarium in Psalmos* (*PL* 191.415–416): "Quo tracto naribus veneno aestuat, unde fontem ad bibendum ardentissime desiderat. . . . sicut cervus tracto serpente aestuans fontem quaerit, ut aestum extinguat, ita

catechumenus veneno vitiorum a terra contractorum, se aestuare agnoscens, fontem baptismi quaerit et desiderat, ubi vitiorum pilos atque superbiae cornua deponit, et sic rejuvenescit factus novus homo."

22. Gratian, *Decretum,* Part 3, "De consecratione," Dist. 4, c. 91: "Post baptismum traditur Christiano uestis candida, quae significat innocentiam et puritatem Christianam, quam post ablutas ueteres maculas studio sanctae conuersationis inmaculatam seruare debet ad repraesentandum ante tribunal Christi;" ibid., c. 92: "Accepisti post baptismum uestimenta candida, ut esset indicium, quod exueris uoluptatem peccatorum, et indueris innocentiae casta uelamina." Tertullian, *On Baptism,* refers to baptism as "the clothing, in some sense, of the faith which before was bare, and which cannot exist now without its proper law" (in *The Ante-Nicene Fathers,* ed. Alexander Roberts and James Donaldson, vol. 3 [Grand Rapids, Mich.: William Eerdmans, 1957], p. 676).

23. Red was indelibly associated with Baptism through Saint Paul's teaching in I Corinthians 10:1–5. Baptism's major Old Testament prefiguration was the Crossing of the Red Sea (Exodus 17): as the sinful Egyptian Pharoah and his cohorts had drowned there, as figures of Satan and his minions, so the Old Man in sin died in the waters of the font; the Hebrews, figures of the New Man in Christ, were delivered. See Isidore, *Quaestiones in Vetus Testamentum: in Exodum 19*: "Quid mare Rubrum, nisi baptismus est Christi sangue consecratus?" (What is the Red Sea but baptism consecrated by the blood of Christ?; *PL* 83.296), and Hugh of Saint Victor, *De sacramentis* II, vi, 15 (*PL* 176.460). For a discussion see J. Daniélou, *The Bible and the Liturgy* (1956), pp. 13, 107, et passim. Red is, of course, also the color of love, both sacred and profane. See Commentary, 17.44, below.

The lily was a stock symbol of purity. During the Trecento it often flowered beside the Virgin in Annunciation scenes, as, for example, in altarpieces by Simone Martini (Uffizi) and Lorenzo Monaco (Florence, Church of Santa Trinità). Often a lily is borne by the announcing angel, Gabriel, or it is found in a vase between the virgin and the angel.

In the hand of a male saint—Saint Dominic, Saint Francis, Saint Anthony of Padua, or Saint Joseph, for example—a lily also indicates virginity and chastity.

24. The concept of backsliding or recidivism and restoration in Dante's *Comedy* is discussed by A. K. Cassell, *Lectura Dantis Americana: Inferno I* (1989), pp. 8–14, 120–125, et passim.

25. Antonio Enzo Quaglio, ed. *Comedìa delle ninfe fiorentine,* in Giovanni Boccaccio, *Tutte le opere,* vol. 2 (Milan: Mondadori, 1964), p. 671: "una gratuita puntata finale, un puro espediente risolutivo."

26. L. Duchesne, *Origines du culte chrétien,* 2nd ed. (Paris: A. Fontemoing, 1898), pp. 284–285. See also J. P. Christopher's notes to his edition and translation of Saint Augustine's *The First Catechetical Instruction* [*De catechizandis rudibus*], Ancient Christian Writers (Westminster, Md.: The Newman Bookshop, 1946), pp. 108, 146.

27. Thus reads the Benediction of the Waters on Holy Saturday in the *Missale Romanum* (Ratisbon: Pustet [1963], pp. 238–248)—clearly a combination of at least two original liturgies at this point. Compare the *Missal* of Isidore of Seville in the *Liturgia mozarabica* (*PL* 85.105): "insufflet tribus vicibus" (he breathes thrice; see also *PL* 85.465).

See also P. de Puniet, "La Bénédiction de l'eau," in *Dictionnaire d'archéologie et de liturgie,* ed. Fernand Cabrol, vol. 2, pt. 1 (Paris: Létouzey et Ané, 1910), cols. 685–713.

28. Gratian, *Decretum,* Part 3, "De consecratione," dist. 4, c. 53: "Sine exorcismis et exsufflationibus nullus baptizetur": "Siue paruuli, siue iuuenes ad regenerationis ueniunt sacramentum, non prius fontem uitae adeant, quam exorcismis et exsufflationibus clericorum Spiritus inmundus ab eis abigatur."

The initiatory ceremonies of the catechumen consisted of exsufflation with a formulary of exorcism, the signing with the cross upon the forehead, the imposition of hands, and the administration of exorcized salt, symbolic of cleansing and preserving. See L. Duchesne, *Origines du culte chrétien* (1898), pp. 284–285; J. P. Christopher's notes in his translation of Saint Augustine's *The First Catechetical Instruction* (1946), pp. 108, 146; and Henry Ansgar Kelly, *The Devil, Demonology, and Witchcraft: Christian Beliefs in Evil Spirits* (Garden City, N.Y.: Doubleday, 1968; rev. 1974), pp. 39–43.

29. Augustine, *Sermo 222 de tempore,* "In Vigiliis Paschae" (*PL* 38.1091): "Ad vigilandum et orandum ipsa solemnitas sanctae hujus noctis hortetur; etiam nostrum vobis tamen solemniter debetur alloquium, ut adversus contrarias et invidas potestates rectoresque tenebrarum, velut contra nocturnas bestias, dominicum gregem etiam vox pastoralis exsuscitet. *Non est enim nobis conluctatio adversus carnem et sanguinem,* sicut Apostolus dicit; id est, adversus homines mortali corpore infirmos: *sed adversus principes et potestates, et rectores mundi tenebrarum harum, contra spiritualia nequitiae in coelestibus* [Eph. 6:12]. . . . Ab illis ergo tenebris evangelica luce distincti, et ab illis potestatibus sanguine pretioso redempti, vigilate et orate, ne intretis in tentationem [Matt. 26:41]. Nam quicumque habetis fidem quae per dilectionem operatur [Gal. 5:6], missus est princeps hujus mundi foras a cordibus vestris [Johan. 12:51]: sed forinsecus tanquam leo rugiens circuit quaerens quem devoret [1 Pet. 5:8]. Non ergo detis locum diabolo, quacumque ex parte penetrare volenti: sed qui cum foras misit patiendo pro vobis, adversus eum habitet intus in vobis." "For the Vigil of Easter," translation cited from Saint Augustine, *Sermons on the Liturgical Seasons,* trans. Sister Mary Sarah Muldowney, R.S.M. Fathers of the Church 38 (Washington, D.C.: The Catholic University of America Press, 1959), pp. 179–181.

30. "In Vigiliis Paschae," *Sermones* 19, 20, 21, and esp. 22 (*PL* 38.1087–1091).

31. Victoria Kirkham relates conversion as a theme to the structure of the romance and its principal digressional episodes in "Reckoning with Boccaccio's 'Questioni d'amore'," *MLN* 89, no. 1 (1974), pp. 47–59.

32. *Filoc.* 2.3.11: "della quale il leoncello uscendone, pareva mutato in figura di nobilissimo e bel giovane, e la cerbia simigliantemente d'una bella giovine."

33. The didactic urge in Boccaccio that is basic to his Latin encyclopedias also finds expression in his fiction. The *Filocolo* opens with a Christian history of the world, compacted into Scholastic manual form. A similar lesson informs the eleventh eclogue, "Pantheon," a brief universal history cast in the language of myth and pastoral.

34. P. Underwood, "The Fountain of Life," p. 61.

35. *Filoc.* 5.57.3: "Correte al santo fonte del vero lavacro, il quale, lavando l'oscura caligine delle vostre menti, vi lascerà conoscere Iddio, il quale l'orazioni de' peccatori essaudisce nel tempo opportuno. Assai è tra' miseri miserabile colui che può uscire d'angoscia e entrare in festa, se in quella pur miseramente dimora.

Venite adunque e lavatevi nel santo fonte, e di quelle tre virtù nobilissime, Fede, Speranza e Carità vi rivestite, sanza le quali niuno può piacere a Dio."

36. On the Transfiguration as metamorphosis, see p. 52 and this chapter, n. 18, above.

37. Boccaccio's *Teseida delle nozze d'Emilia* is read as an allegory of Reason's triumph over concupiscent and irascible appetites by Janet Levarie Smarr in "The *Teseida*, Boccaccio's Allegorical Epic," *NEMLA Italian Studies* 1 (1977), pp. 29–35; and, in a more extensive study, by V. Kirkham, "'Chiuso parlare' in Boccaccio's *Teseida*" (1983), pp. 305–351.

38. The best recent discussion of *cassoni*, their use, and meaning, especially those with subjects that depict Diana and Venus, is P. Watson's *The Garden of Love* (1979). There is no certain illustration of *Diana's Hunt*. None of the six manuscripts that preserve the text has accompanying miniatures. Ellen Callmann has suggested that a Florentine *cassone* front of ca. 1420 with scenes that may depict a *Myth of Diana* (Florence, Museo Stibbert, cat. no. 165 of vol. 2, pt. 1 with pl. 12 of vol. 2, pt. 2) represents Boccaccio's *Caccia di Diana*. Connections between the two works, however, are hard to discern. See her essay "The Growing Threat to Matrimonial Bliss as Seen in Fifteenth-Century Florentine Poets," *Studies in Iconography* 5 (1979), pp. 73–92. There are other *cassoni* panels at the Museo Stibbert, including the one we reproduce (Figure 7), that would better qualify as Boccaccian. If these paintings illustrate *Diana's Hunt*, they must reflect some iconographic influence from the *Amorosa visione* and Petrarch's *Triumphs*, because each goddess appears in a triumphal chariot: Diana's drawn by griffins, Venus's pulled by swans. See Giuseppe Cantarelli, ed., *Il Museo Stibbert a Firenze*, 4 vols. (Florence: Cassa di Risparmio, 1974), cat. no. 9 and no. 162 of vol. 2, pt. 1 with pls. 21 and 22 of vol. 2, pt. 2; cat. no. 12 of vol. 4, pt. 1 with pls. 21 and 22 of vol. 4, pt. 2; especially the discussion and bibliography in 4.1, pp. 29–31. The possibility of a connection between the Stibbert Museum panels and Boccaccio's hunt poem is accepted by Paul F. Watson in his "A Preliminary List of Subjects from Boccaccio in Italian Painting, 1400–1550," in Vittore Branca, Paul F. Watson, Victoria Kirkham, "Boccaccio visualizzato," *Studi sul Boccaccio* 15 (1985–1986), pp. 153, 161.

39. *Corbaccio*, ed. Tauno Nurmela, *Annales Academiae Scientiarum Fennicae*, Ser. B 146 (Helsinki, 1968), pp. 57–58: "'Assai bene conosco che ancora il raggio della vera luce non è pervenuto al tuo intelletto, e che tu quella cosa la quale è infima miseria, come molti stolti fanno, estimi somma felicità, credendo che nel vostro concupiscibile e carnale amore sia alcuna parte di bene; e per ciò apri gli orecchi a quello che io ora ti dirò.

"'Questa misera valle è quella corte che tu chiami "d'amore" e quelle bestie, che tu di' che udite hai e odi mugghiare sono i miseri, de' quali tu se' uno, dal fallace amore inretiti; le boci de' quali, in quanto di così fatto amore favellino, niuno altro suono hanno negli orecchi de' discreti e ben disposti uomini che quello che mostra che pervenga alle tue; e però dianzi la chiamai laberinto, perchè così in essa gli uomini, come in quello già faceano, senza saperne mai riuscire, s'avviluppano.'"

40. The nightmarish landscape in the *Corbaccio* clearly means "Carnal love is hell." On this point we concur with Robert Hollander, who analyzes Boccaccio's first and last Italian fictions as a pair in *Boccaccio's Two Venuses* (New York: Columbia University Press, 1977), ch. 1, see esp. p. 26. See also Hollander's

*Boccaccio's Last Fiction: "Il Corbaccio"* (Philadelphia: University of Pennsylvania Press, 1988), esp. pp. 2–3.

41. Unlike the renewed stag of the *Hunt,* the foolish aging lover of the *Corbaccio* will ironically fail in his conversion: the ending of that work, with the protagonist still enmeshed in love-hatred and revenge, provides, perhaps, a negative exemplum, yet one which erudite, rollicking satire and bawdy laughter ultimately overwhelm. See A. K. Cassell, Introduction, *The Corbaccio* (1974), pp. xxv–xxvi.

42. For the Terme di Venere at Baia, the history of the archeology and information on the extant remains, see *The Princeton Encyclopedia of Classical Sites,* ed. Richard Sitwell et al. (Princeton, N.J.: Princeton University Press, 1976), pp. 137–138, and the entry "Baia" in the *Enciclopedia Italiana,* complete with photographs of the Terme.

Boccaccio's reminiscences of his youthful days at that seaside resort find their way into his *Rime* (XXXVI, XLVIII, LX, LXII, LXV) and into the fiction of his *Elegia di madonna Fiammetta* (in Giovanni Boccaccio, *Decameron, Filocolo, Ameto, Fiammetta,* ed. Enrico Bianchi, Carlo Salinari, Natalino Sapegno [Milan: Ricciardi, 1952], p. 1131): "Donna, come tu sai, poco di là dal piacevole monte Falerno in mezzo dell'antiche Cume e di Pozzuolo sono le dilettevoli Baie sopra li marini liti, del sito delle quali più bello né più piacevole ne cuopre alcuno il cielo. Egli di monti bellissimi tutti d'alberi varii e di viti coperti è circundato, fra le valli de' quali niuna bestia è a cacciare abile, che in quelle non sia; né a quelli lontana la grandissima pianura dimora, utile alle varie caccie de' predanti uccelli e sollazzevole" (Lady, as you know, slightly beyond pleasurable Mount Falerno, between ancient Cumae and Pozzuoli, there are the delightful Bays on marine shores, nor does heaven cover any site more beautiful or more pleasurable. It is surrounded with most beautiful mountains all covered with various trees and vines; their valleys lack not a single beast fit for hunting, and not far from them lies the vast plain, useful and fun for various hunts with birds of prey).

However, as we can see from the outcome of events in the *Elegia,* at some time Boccaccio began to view the enchanting watering place, which he once thought so virginal, as a den of libidinous corruption; was it a reading of Cicero's *Pro Caelio* (15.35), where the orator makes the retreat synonymous with "libidines, amores, adulteria" (debauchery, amours and adultery) that made the betrayed lover of Boccaccio's early Sonnet LXXII spit his hellish curse? "Perir possa il tuo nome, Baia, e il loco, / boschi selvaggi le tua piagge sieno, / e le tua fonti diventin veneno, / né vi si bagni alcun . . . / in pianto si converta ogni tuo gioco, / . . . / . . . e'l sereno / in te riversin fumo, solfo e fuoco; / ché hai corrotto la più casta mente / che fosse'n donna, con la tua licenza" (May your name perish, Baia, and your site; may your beaches be wild woods, and your fountains turn to poison; nor let anyone bathe there . . . may all your frolic turn to woe, . . . and your clear skies turn to smoke, sulphur and fire: for with your licence you have corrupted the chastest mind there ever was in woman; *Opere minori in volgare,* ed. Mario Marti, pp. 100–101).

43. *Genealogie* 14.7 (p. 699): "Poesis enim, quam negligentes abiciunt et ignari, est fervor quidam exquisite inveniendi atque dicendi, seu scribendi, quod inveneris. . . . Huius enim fervoris sunt sublimes effectus, ut puta mentem in desiderium dicendi compellere, peregrinas et inauditas inventiones excogitare,

meditatas ordine certo componere, ornare compositum inusitato quodam verborum atque sententiarum contextu, velamento fabuloso atque decenti veritatem contegere."

44. *Esposizioni* 1.2.17–18: "non si ramarichi alcuno, se da' poeti è sotto favole nascosa la verità. . . . Fu adunque il nostro poeta, sì come gli altri poeti sono, nasconditore, come si vede, di così cara gioia, come è la cattolica verità, sotto la volgare corteccia del suo poema."

45. *Esposizioni* 1.2.10–11: "Suole quello, che con difficultà s'acquista, piacer più e guardarsi meglio che quello che senza alcuna fatica o poca si truova. . . . Non essendo adunque senza alcun dubbio esser molta malagevoleza il trarre la nascosa verità di sotto al fabuloso parlare, dee seguire essere incomparabile diletto a colui che, per suo studio, vede averla saputa trovare; laonde non solamente ogni affanno avutone se ne dimentica, ma ne rimane una dolcezza nell'animo, la quale quasi con legame indissolubile ferma, nella memoria di colui che ritrovata l'ha, la verità ritrovata."

46. *Genealogie* 14.13 (p. 718): "uti mendacium est, fictiones poetice, ut plurimum, non sunt nedum simillime, sed nec similes veritati, imo valde dissone et adverse." Cf. *Trattatello* II.102–105: "confesso le fizioni poetiche nella prima faccia avere niuna consonanza col vero. Ma, se per questo elle sono da dannare, che diranno costoro delle visioni di Daniello, che di quelle di Ezechiel, che dell'altre del vecchio Testamento scritte con divina penna, che di quelle di Giovanni evangelista? Diremo, però che simiglianza di vero in assai cose nella corteccia non hanno, sieno, come stoltamente dette, da rifiutare? Nol consentirà mai chi ficcherà gli occhi dello 'ntelletto nella midolla" (I confess that poetic fictions, at first sight, have no consonance with the truth. But if for that people should condemn them, what will they say about Daniel's vision, what about Ezechiel's, what about the others written with divine pen in the Old Testament, what about those of John the Evangelist? Are we to say, because they have no resemblance to truth in many things in their bark, that we should, as some foolishly say, reject them? No one will ever agree to that who with the eyes of his intellect pierces to the pulp).

47. Our reading is diametrically opposite to that of Gordon Poole, "Boccaccio's *Caccia di Diana*," *Canadian Journal of Italian Studies* 5, no. 3 (Spring 1982), pp. 149–156: "The 'salute' his beloved gives him has nothing to do with Christian salvation."

48. Franco Fido, arguing against an ironic reading of the *Hunt,* sees irony instead in Boccaccio's treatment of his sources, the "myths that he overturns"—Diana and Actaeon, Circe, Lucius—"not to mention the exquisite Ovidian 'remake' of Petrarch in 'Nel dolce tempo de la prima etade.'" He makes these points in his review of Robert Hollander's *Boccaccio's Two Venuses,* reprinted in *Il regime delle simmetrie imperfette. Studi sul Decameron* (Milan: Franco Angeli, 1988), pp. 141–147.

49. As autumn is the season of the Last Judgment, so spring renews the spirit of man. See Rabanus Maurus, *De universo*, 10.11 in *PL* 111; cited by Emile Mâle, *The Gothic Image,* p. 31. Canon law reserves for general baptism Easter Saturday and Pentecost. See *Decretum,* part 3, dist. 4, canon 11: "Generale baptisma non nisis sabbato sancto Pascae et Pentecostes celebretur"; ibid., canon 15: "In solempnitate pascali et Pentecostes catecumini baptizentur."

50. Janet Levarie Smarr rightly terms the work "a conjunction of opposites,"

in *Boccaccio and Fiammetta. The Narrator as Lover* (Urbana, Ill.: University of Illinois Press, 1986), p. 14.

51. See R. Hollander's chapter "Pagan Integument and Christian Design" on the *Comedia delle ninfe fiorentine* and the *Amorosa visione,* in *Boccaccio's Two Venuses* (1977), pp. 66–91.

52. D. W. Robertson, *A Preface to Chaucer* (Princeton, N.J.: Princeton University Press, 1962), p. 5.

53. As medievalists now are teaching us, the Middle Ages had a remarkable "tolerance for inconsistency." For one example of a reading that polemically opposes radical reduction of the text's complexity, see Don A. Monson, "Andreas Capellanus and the Problem of Irony," *Speculum* 63, no. 3 (1988), pp. 539–572.

*Caccia di Diana*
*Diana's Hunt*

## CANTO 1

    Nel tempo adorno che l'erbette nove
rivestono ogni prato e l'aere chiaro
ride per la dolcezza che 'l ciel move,
    sol pensando mi stava che riparo
5 potessi fare ai colpi che forando
mi gian d'amor il cuor con duolo amaro;
    quando mi parve udir venir chiamando
un spirito gentil volando forte:
"Donne leggiadre," in voce alta gridando,
10     "venite omai, venite alla gran corte
dell'alta iddea Diana, che elette
v'ha in Partenopè per sue consorte."
    E poi ch'egli ebbe tre fiate dette
queste parole, sanza più voltare,
15 ad una ad una chiamandole ristette.
    E, se non m'ingannò 'l vero ascoltare
che far mi parve, Zizzola Barrile
la prima fu ch'io gli senti' chiamare;
    poi Ciancia l'altra, nobile e gentile,
20 Cecca Bozzuta e poi Principessella
Caracciola e Letizia Moromile,
    de' Gattoli Berarda con Linella,
Beritola Carafa, e 'n compagnia
degli Scrignar Mignana ed Isabella,
25     e Isolda di Giaquinto e Lucia
Porria e Berita e Caterina
de' Brancazzi e de' Melii Maria.
    E seguitò Caterina Pipina
e Sobilia Capece; e chiamò Fiore
30 Curial bella, di colei vicina,
    Verdella di Berardo e Biancifiore
de' Caffettini e Ceccola Mazzone
ed Alessandra d'Anna con valore.
    Caterina di Iacopo Roncione
35 chiamò, e Caterina Caradente;
poi la Crespana seguì nel sermone
    e di Bolin Caterina piacente
e Caterina di Serpando, e poi
Caterina Fellapan similmente.

## CANTO 1

In that fair season when the new grasses reclothe each meadow, and the bright air smiles for the sweetness that moves the heavens, I stood alone giving thought to what shelter I might take against the blows of Love that were piercing my heart with bitter pangs, when I seemed to hear a gentle spirit come flying fast, calling, "Lovely ladies!" and crying aloud, "Now come, come to the great court of the high goddess Diana, who has chosen you as her companions in Parthenope!"

And when he had thrice said these words, he paused, hovering on the wing, to call them one by one. And unless my ears deceived me—and I think they did not—Zizzola Barrile was the first I heard him call, then Ciancia second, noble and gentle; then Cecca Bozzuta and Principessella Caracciola and Letizia Moromile, Berarda de' Gattoli with Linella, Beritola Carafa, and in her company, Mignana degli Scrignar and Isabella, and Isolda di Giaquinto and Lucia Porria, both Berita and Caterina de' Brancazzi, and Maria de' Melii. And he went on to Caterina Pipina and Sobilia Capece; and boldly he called the fair Fiore Curiale, her neighbor Verdella di Berardo, and Biancifiore de' Caffettini and Ceccola Mazzone and Alessandra d'Anna. He called Caterina di Iacopo Roncione and Caterina Caradente; next in his recital came La Crespana and the charming Caterina di Bolino and Caterina di Serpando, so too Caterina Fellapane. Then he summoned Giovannola de' Coppoli and after her, La Lucciola, and with his next words he called Fiore Canovara, and further, Vannella de' Gambatelli found a place beside them, as I heard from the sounds to which he gave voice.

But last to be called was that Lady whom Love honors more than any other for her lofty virtue, which to every other virtue gives strength and increase; and for the other women's welfare, she went much like a guardian to the head of the group to guide them safely; and in the company of Diana's messenger

40      Giovannola de' Coppoli ampoi
        si chiamò e la Lucciola dop'essa,
        e Fiore Canovara ne' dir suoi
            chiamò appresso, e oltre con lor messa
        de' Gambatelli Vannella fu ancora,
45      come intesi nella voce espressa.
            Ma quella donna cui Amore onora
        più ch'altra per la sua somma virtute,
        che tutte l'altre accresce e rinvigora,
            fu l'ultima chiamata, e per salute
50      dell'altre, quasi com'una guardiana,
        avanti gio per guidarle tute:
            e 'n compagnia del messo di Diana,
        che più non ne chiamò (né nomo lei,
        perché a suo nome laude più sovrana
55      si converria, che qui dir non potrei),
        sen gì in parte ov'io le seguitai
        con l'altre insieme, infin ch'io discernei
            ciò ch'elle fer, come appresso udirai.

## CANTO 2

        In una valle non molto spaziosa,
        di quattro montagnette circuita,
        di verdi erbette e di fiori copiosa,
            nel mezzo della qual così fiorita,
5       una fontana chiara, bella e grande,
        abbondevole d'acqua, v'era sita,
            e l'acqua che superflua si spande
        un rivo fa che tutte l'erbe bagna,
        poi n'esce fuor da una delle bande:
10          d'alberi è piena ciascuna montagna,
        di frondi folti sì ch'a pena il sole
        tra essi può passar nella campagna:
            diversi uccelli cantan lor carole
        sopr'essi, e quivi un'aura sottile
15      move le frondi, come mover sole
            nel tempo estivo zefiro gentile,
        quando il calor diurno più non sale,
        ma quando fa, calato, l'aere umile:
            caprii, lupi ed ogni altro animale,

(who called no more of them—nor do I name her, since praise more sovereign would suit her name than I could here set forth), she went off to a place together with the others, and I followed them until I could make out what they did, as you will presently hear.

## CANTO 2

There was a valley, not very broad, encircled by four low-lying mountains, bountiful with green grasses and flowers, and in its flowering midst there stood a clear fountain, fair, large, and with abundant water; and the water that overflows spreads out and makes a stream that bathes all the grasses; then it runs off to one side. Each mountain is covered with trees with fronds so thick that the sun can scarcely pass through them to the fields; upon them various birds perch to pipe their carols, and a slight breeze stirs the boughs there, just as in summertime a gentle zephyr is wont to stir when the heat of the day no longer rises, but when it has declined and humbles the air. Roebuck, wolves, and every other animal—bears, lions—are found in that place, and all kinds of others, the strong as well as the weak.

Here Diana, who keeps the tepid fire in chaste breasts, assembled those who were invited to her sport. Then she commanded them to enter those lim-

20   orsi e leoni si trovano in quel loco,
     e qualunque altro che più o men vale:
        quivi Diana, che 'l tiepido foco
     ne' casti petti tien, ricolse quelle
     che invitate furono al suo gioco.
25      Poi comandò che esse entrasser nelle
     chiarissime onde e de' freschi liquori
     lavando sé si rifacesser belle.
        E poi, come a lei piacque, uscite fori
     si rivestir di purpurea veste,
30   inghirlandate d'uliv'e di fiori.
        Diana quattro parti fé di queste,
     ed alla bella donna disse: "Andrai
     sopra 'l monte a meriggio con coteste,
        e tu, Isabella, al ponente sarai,
35   e Fiore a tramontana; ed alla caccia
     ciascuna pensi di valere assai."
        E, dati i cani e forti reti d'accia,
     girfalchi, astori ed archi con saette
     e spiedi aguti che' cinghiari impaccia,
40      quelle che ella avea per sé elette
     (cioè Cecca Bozzuta e Caterina
     Fellapane, con le qua' poi seguette
        insieme Biancifiore Caffettina,
     la Crespana e Catrina Caradente
45   e quella di Serpando e la Pipina,
        e Marella Melia similmente)
     sopra 'l più picciol monte se n'andaro,
     ch'era disteso verso l'oriente.
        Quivi la caccia prime incominciaro
50   le quattro sopra 'l monte, e l'altre al basso
     avevan fatto con reti riparo
        acciò che nulla fiera ad alcun passo
     lor potesse fuggir sanza esser presa
     o ferita da' ferri del turcasso.
55      Poi passar dentro, e ciascheduna intesa
     andava per la selva riguardando
     per l'altrui danno e per la lor difesa,
        sì, come segue, con senno cacciando.

pid waters so they could refresh their beauty, washing in the cool liquid. And then, as was her pleasure, they came forth to dress again in gowns of royal purple, garlanded with olive leaves and flowers. Diana divided them into four parties and to the Fair Lady said, "You shall go with these women up the southward mountain; and you, Isabella, shall be on the west; and Fiore to the north; and let each one strive to hunt very bravely."

And when Diana had given them dogs and strong flaxen nets, gyrfalcons, goshawks, bows and arrows, and sharp spears to stay wild boars, those huntresses whom she had chosen for herself (that is, Cecca Bozzuta and Caterina Fellapane, together with whom there followed Biancifiore Caffettina, La Crespana; and Caterina Caradente and her namesake di Serpando; and La Pipina and Marella Melia as well) went off up to the lowest mountain, which stretched toward the east. There the four ladies high on the mountain were first to begin the hunt, and the others, at its base, formed a screen with nets, so that no wild beast could escape at any turn without being caught or wounded by darts from their quivers. Then they passed within, and each one went on the watch through the forest, intent on the destruction of other things and defending themselves. So they hunted wisely, as shall follow.

## CANTO 3

Aveva Diana nella man sinestra
un arco forte, noderoso e grosso,
tal che daria fatica ad ogni destra,
  e nel cacume del monte rimosso
5 gia con Cecca Bozzuta, che portava
la sua faretra piena dietro al dosso.
  E dietro ad un macchion s'ascose, e stava,
fin ch'ella vide un capriol venire,
che un can, che lasciò Cecca, cacciava.
10  L'aprir l'aspro arco e 'l cavriuol ferire
in un momento fu, ond'e' si fisse,
e quivi cadde e non poté fuggire.
  Diana volta a Cecca allora disse:
"Quando discenderemo il prenderai,
15 e siesi tuo." E Cecca nol disdisse.
  Ma alla Pipina, disiosa assai
con la Crespana: "A prender delle fiere,"
disse, "da questa parte te n'andrai,"
  (e a sinistra le mostrò un sentiere)
20 "ed io terrò di qua, e, quando senti
fremir le frasche, lascia il tuo levriere."
  Così divise andavan pedetenti,
ogni cespuglio con l'occhio cercando,
co' cani appresso, al loro officio attenti.
25  Ma guar non erano ancor ite, quando
due lepri si levar correndo forte
non di lunge da loro, al monte andando.
  Di queste fur le giovinette accorte,
e l'una all'altra gridò: "Lascia i tuoi!
30 non possono scampar che non sien morte."
  "Ciuffa!" gridando, ciascheduna i suoi
lasciò, correndo dietro a' passi loro,
fin che presa la preda stetter poi.
  A picciol passo poi dopo costoro
35 veniva Caterina Caradente,
guardando un porco, che' can di coloro
  avean levato, e sé tacitamente
dietro ad un alber pose, e ver di lui
uno spiedo drizzò lungo e tagliente.

## CANTO 3

In her left hand Diana held a powerful bow, so knotty and thick that it would weary any right hand, and on the summit of the far-off mountain, she strode with Cecca Bozzuta, who carried a full quiver upon her back. And she hid behind some dense scrub and stayed until she saw a roebuck coming, chased by a dog that Cecca unleashed. The bending of her rugged bow and the wounding of the buck occurred in an instant; whereupon he was transfixed, and there fell down, and could not escape.

Then, turning to Cecca, Diana said, "When we descend, you are to take it, and yours it shall be!" And Cecca did not decline. But to Pipina, all eagerness beside La Crespana, she said, "You shall go off to catch wild beasts in this direction" (and she showed her a path to the left), "and I shall stay back here, and when you hear the branches shake, let loose your greyhound!"

Thus divided up, step by step they went peering into every thicket, with their dogs following intent on their task. But they had scarcely set out, when not far from them there rose up two swiftly running hares, headed toward the mountain. The young girls caught sight of them and one cried to the other, "Let your dogs loose! They cannot escape except by death!" "Sic!" each cried, as she loosed her dogs, then she ran after in their tracks, until they stopped with their captured prey.

Then to their rear came creeping Caterina Caradente, watching a boar that their dogs had flushed, and she silently slipped behind a tree and leveled a long, sharpened spear at him. Bristle-covered, he came raging, bitten all over by the dogs and hotly bent on doing injury. And he so angrily struck the spear brandished before him that he ran himself through on it, shafted from end to end.

Biancifiore Caffettina, who had spread nets with Catella at the foot of the mountain, fiercely attacked three horned stags whom the dogs had driven straight

40  Di squama pien, furioso costui
 venia, da' can d'ogni parte addentato
 ed infiammato di nuocere altrui;
  e nello spiedo a lui innanzi parato
 ferì con rabbia sì che vi rimase
45 da una parte in altra trapassato.
  Biancifior Caffettina, che ispase
 avea le reti insieme con Catella
 a piè del monte, fieramente invase
  tre gran cerbi cornuti, che in ella
50 incappati eran dalli can cacciati,
 e con loro a pigliarli fu Marella
  de' Melii; e poi che fur pigliati,
 voltate a di Serpando Caterina,
 che 'ntorno al monte co' cani affannati
55 era gita di 'nfin dalla mattina
 sanza aver presa fiera e nella valle
 che tra l'un monte e l'altro si declina,
  seguiro un lupo, e nelle dure spalle
 Caterina gli gittò col suo forte arco
60 una saetta che impedì il suo calle;
  e questo preso ritornaro al varco.

## CANTO 4

  La bella donna, il cui nome si tace,
 con un'aquila in man prese la via
 su per lo monte ch'al mezzodì giace.
  Zizzola e Ciancia menò in compagnia,
5 e dopo queste la Principessella;
 Beritola Carafa le seguia
  e Berita Brancazzi gia con ella,
 e Sobilia Capece con Berarda
 e Caterina a Berita sorella.
10  Ciascuna presta, gioconda e gagliarda,
 cantando andavan di dietro a colei
 che nel viso d'amor sempre par ch'arda.
  Non fu salita molto alto costei,
 ch'a sé lontano vide uno animale
15 fiero ed ardito e presto sopra i piei.
  Acciò che nuocer potesse nè far male,

into her path, and with them for the catch was Marella de' Melii. And when those were caught, the huntresses went back to Caterina di Serpando, who since morning had been circling the mountain with her panting dogs, and had not yet taken any beasts. And in the valley that sloped between one mountain and the next, they followed a wolf, and with her strong bow Caterina shot into its tough shoulders an arrow that stopped him in his tracks; and when he was taken, they returned to the mountain pass.

## CANTO 4

The Fair Lady, whose name is not spoken, with an eagle in hand made her way up the mountain that lies to the south. Zizzola and Ciancia were the companions she led, and after them Principessella. Beritola Carafa followed them, and with her went Berita Brancazzi and Sobilia Capece with Berarda and Caterina, sister to Berita. Fleet, gay, and lively all, they went singing behind that Lady whose face seems always to burn with love.

She had not climbed very high, when she saw at a distance a beast fierce, bold, and fleet of foot. So that it could neither harm nor hurt, she withdrew with her women to a safe place and loosed her eagle, whose strong wings bore it almost to the sphere of fire; then, turning back down, it came circling and descending little by little. Like lightning amidst the trees and

sé e le sue ritrasse in salvo loco
e l'aquila lasciò, le cui fort'ale
   la trasportaron quasi infino al foco,
20 e poi rivolta in giù venia rotando
e discendendo sé a poco a poco.
   Fra gli albori e le frondi folgorando
percosse quella sì ferocemente,
che dal capo alla coda laniando
25    l'andò la pelle con l'unghion tagliente,
e risalita ancor la riferio
un'altra volta vie più fieramente.
   La variata lonza, che sentio
i fieri colpi, in terra si distese
30 e quivi dibattendosi morio.
   La bella donna il forte uccel riprese
ed alla lonza trasse il caldo cuore
e l'aquila pascé; e poi discese
   del monticel, faccendo un gran romore
35 Zizzola e Ciancia, e dicean: "Piglia, piglia!"
dietro ad un bianco cervio, che di fore
   d'un cespuglio fuggiva a maraviglia
per molti can che dietro si sentia,
de' qua' ciascuno a prenderlo si spiglia.
40 Ma Ciancia, che conobbe la sua via,
traversò il monte e riuscigli appresso
sopra uno balzo ove 'l monte finia;
   e poi ch'ell'ebbe all'arco lo stral messo
ch'ella portava in mano, apersel forte
45 e lui ferì in quello punto stesso.
   Quivi, vermiglio ritornato, a morte
ferito si sentì, né più potero
portarlo avanti le sue gambe accorte.
   Zizzola si tornò per lo sentiero
50 e richiamando i can sonava un corno,
fin che di loro il numero ebbe intero.
   Così andando e mirandosi intorno,
due volpi vide, e ciascuna fuggendo
andava a fare a sua cava ritorno.
55    Tanto le gio Zizzola seguendo,
che prese quelle e ver la donna onesta

fronds, it struck so ferociously with cutting claw that it lacerated that beast's skin from head to tail; and after soaring again, again it struck, far more fiercely the second time. The spotted leopardess, who felt the fierce blows, stretched out on the ground, and there in its writhing died. The Fair Lady caught up the strong bird again and pulled out the leopardess's hot heart and fed the eagle.

And then she came down from the low-lying mountain, as Zizzola and Ciancia, making a great uproar, were calling "Get him! Get him!" after a white stag that fled from a thicket in wonder at the many dogs he heard behind, each one rushing to catch him. But Ciancia, who knew her way, crossed the mountain and soon came out again upon a promontory where the mountain ended; and when she had set an arrow to her bow, which she bore in hand, she drew it back powerfully and struck the stag at that very instant. There, turning vermilion, he felt the mortal wound, nor could his nimble legs bear him onward any longer.

Zizzola came back down the path and recalled the dogs, sounding a horn until she could count them all. Thus walking along and gazing about, she saw two foxes, and each one fled, running to regain its lair. Zizzola kept following them until she caught them, and laughing about this to herself, she returned to the Honorable Lady, and it made the latter merry too.

se ne tornò, di questo in sé ridendo;
e quella ancor di ciò si fece festa.

## CANTO 5

Beritola Carafa infra la folta
e dilettevol selva con un arco
s'andava pian, dicendo: "Ascolta, ascolta!"
    a Sobilia Capece, "ché al varco
5   mi par le frasche dimenar sentire
e a' cani far grandissimo rammarco.
    Voltianci là; ché, se nel mio udire
non prendo inganno, alcuna bestia fia,
che di leggiere la potrem ferire."
10  Non disser più; ma, subito la via
presa, pervenner là dove 'l rumore
avean sentito ciascheduna pria.
    Quivi trovaron pieni di furore
due orsi grandi e negli occhi focosi,
15  tal che ciascuna n'ebbe allor tremore.
    Ma Beritola pria rassicurossi,
e, amettendo i can, della faretra
trasse saette e alquanto allungossi
    e l'un ferì; ma quanto in una petra
20  v'entrò il ferro, ed ella l'altra trasse,
ma quella come l'altra ancor s'arretra.
    Parve ch'allor Beritola sdegnasse
insieme con Sobilia, e adirorsi
non potendoli avere, ed eran lasse.
25  Le cocche de' loro archi in man voltorsi
e d'ira accese più s'assicuraro
e più si fer vicine all'un degli orsi,
    e 'n sulla testa sì forte i donaro,
che cadde semivivo; e l'altro poi
30  con più vigore i lor cani addentaro.
    Ciascuna con romore atava i suoi,
fin che 'l secondo, da' cani abbattuto,
presero, e se n'andar con ambeduoi.
    Principessella, quantunque era suto
35  del giorno, tanto con reti e con arte
aveva un leoncel prender voluto;

## CANTO 5

Beritola Carafa, deep in the thick and delightful wood, was walking along slowly with a bow, saying to Sobilia Capece, "Listen, listen! For at the pass I think I hear the branches shaking and greatly provoking the dogs. Let us head back there, for unless my hearing deceives me, it must be some beast we can easily shoot." They said no more, but took the path forthwith, reaching the place where each had heard the noise before. There they found two huge bears, so full of fury and fiery eyed that the ladies were seized with trembling. Beritola, first to regain confidence, brought on the dogs, drew arrows from her quiver, and stood back at a distance to shoot one of them. But the arrow entered no further than into a stone, and she shot again, but again that one recoiled like the first. This then seemed to exasperate Beritola as well as Sobilia, for they were weary, and it angered them not being able to catch the beasts. They grasped their bows by the notched ends, and as they burned with wrath their confidence grew; they moved closer to one of the bears and gave him such a blow on the head that he fell down half dead; and then, with more vigor, the dogs sank their teeth into the other. Each lady loudly urged hers on, until they captured the second bear, brought low by the dogs, and they went off with both of them. Principessella had spent the whole day up to then trying to catch a lion cub, using nets and skill alike; but for all her wits, she had not yet been able to corner one so that it would fall straight into the outspread nets. Suddenly, a cunning turn of thought stirred her, and she took a roebuck caught by the others and threw its carcass in the net-lined pit. The lion cub saw the roebuck lying dead in the pit, then ran to it, suffering perhaps from hunger, and began to eat the buck, but the lady so nimbly pulled the nets that he was caught there and had to stay.

ma non l'avea potuto ancora in parte
col senno suo recar, sì che si fosse
punto incappato nelle reti sparte.

40  Sottile avviso subito la mosse
e prese un cavriol dall'altre preso:
morto 'l gittò nelle 'nretite fosse.

Vide quel cavriol morto disteso
il leoncello nella fossa stare;
45  corsevi allor, da fame forse offeso,

e cominciò del caprio a mangiare;
ma quella accorta tirò sì le reti,
che quivi preso li convenne stare.

Non li giovò perché in que' pareti
50  mugghiasse forte; ché 'ngegnosamente
ella il legò con sembianti lieti.

Alla donna gentil ne fé presente,
dicendo: "Te', più ch'altra valorosa!"
E quella il prese graziosamente.

55  Ma Berarda avea fatta nuova cosa,
che con suoi bracchi ben sei spinosi
aveva presi, e 'n grembo, paurosa
   non la pungesser, li portava chiusi.


### CANTO 6

Caterina Brancazza e la sorella,
quasi nel luogo del monte più alto
giva ciascuna baldanzosa e snella

e due tigre leggere, che di salto
5  forte fuggivan, salendo trovaro,
alle quali esse e i can dieron l'assalto.

Per lungo spazio queste seguitaro
ma alla fin le presero i can loro,
perché in tese reti elle incapparo.

10  Gioconde si tornaron poi costoro,
liete di preda tanto nominata
qual quella fu che fu presa da loro.

Isabella Scrignara e sua brigata
(con la qual giva Ceccola Mazzone
15  con la Mignana insieme accompagnata,
   Isolda ancor di Giaquinto vi fune,

Roaring as loudly as he might inside those walls availed him not, for she tied him up cleverly, beaming with delight.

To the Gentle Lady she made a present of him, saying, "Take it, you who are more worthy than any other!" and the latter took it graciously.

But Berarda had done something novel, for with her hunting dogs she had caught six hedgehogs, no less, and fearful of being pricked, she was carrying them wrapped up in her lap.

CANTO 6

Caterina Brancazza and her sister, bold and quick, were coming close to the highest part of the mountain, and, as they climbed, they found two swift tigers that fled leaping fast, on which they and their dogs pressed the attack. They followed the beasts for a long way, but finally their dogs caught them, for they fell into the taut nets. Gaily the two returned, delighted by prey as illustrious as was that which they had caught.

Isabella Scrignara and her group (with her went Ceccola Mazzone, together in the company of La Mignana; and there also were Isolda di Giaquinto, Vannella Gambatella, and Caterina, daughter of the notary Iacopo Roncione: and with them, Alessandra) approached the mountain—and Linella did likewise—whose valleys incline westward.

  Vannella Gambatella e Caterina
figlia di notar Iacopo Roncione,
 e con loro Alessandra) s'avvicina,
20 e simil fa Linella, verso il monte
ch'all'occidente i suoi vallon declina.
  Ceccola prima con ardita fronte
prese il cammin, né ristette giammai
fin che su la portar le gambe pronte.
25  Ed eravi già istata suso assai,
chiamando le compagne e rimirando
s'alcuna fiera fosse fra que' mai,
 e un fiero cinghiar, che riposando
si stava, in una macchia vide fitto,
30 forse cacciato, inverso lei guardando.
  Andonne questa a lui tutto dritto,
e 'n sulla testa il ferì d'una scure
sì forte che morì sanza respitto.
  Mignana ed Isabella nelle dure
35 piagge avean tese reti e gian dintorno
frugando con bastoni le grotte oscure.
  Con esse era Vannella; ed in quel giorno
preser conigli assai e lepri grosse,
e 'ndietro si tornar sonando un corno.
40  Ma Isolda di Giaquinto percosse
sì forte un lupo da due can tenuto
con un bastone, che mai più non si mosse.
  Ma dopo, sé rivolta, ebbe veduto
un altro con due figli; onde a gridare
45 incominciò: "Compagne, aiuto, aiuto!"
  Linella corse là, sanza più stare,
con due gran cani e con un arco in mano,
e Alessandra ancor vi volle andare.
  Aperse l'arco quella e non invano:
50 ché l'un de' tre ferì sì che rimase,
e' can assalir l'altro a mano a mano.
  Fuggissi il terzo, e Alessandra invase
con uno spiedo in man quel che tenieno
i can feroci per l'orecchie rase,
55 e quasi morto già fra lor l'avieno;
questa il condusse a fine, e, preso lui,

First, bold-browed Ceccola struck out walking; never did she pause until carried to the top by her ready legs. And she had already been up there some time, calling her companions and gazing around to see whether any wild creature might possibly be down in the valleys, when she saw, resting stock-still in a thicket, where perhaps he had been chased, a fierce wild boar looking toward her. She went straight to him and struck him so hard on the head with her axe that he died then and there.

Mignana and Isabella had stretched nets over the flinty slopes and were going about, poking with their clubs through the dark caves. With them was Vannella; and on that day they caught lots of rabbits and large hares, and they headed back sounding a horn.

Isolda di Giaquinto, though, struck a wolf, held by two dogs, so hard with a club that it never stirred again. But afterward, turning around, she saw another with two cubs; whereupon she began to shout, "Comrades, help! Help!" Linella came running as fast as she could with two large dogs and bow in hand, and Alessandra, too, insisted on coming. Linella drew her bow, and not in vain, for she so wounded one of the three that it stopped, and at the same time, the dogs assailed the second. The third fled, and, spear in hand, Alessandra attacked the one whom the dogs held fast by his shorn ears and whom, between them, they had nearly killed already. This huntress made an end of him; and when she had picked him up, the companions went off together to take a rest from their toils.

con le compagne insieme sen venieno
per pigliar posa degli affanni sui.

## CANTO 7

Fior Curial guidava altra compagna,
delle qua' parte il monticel saliro
e parte ne rimase alla campagna.
   Quelle che lei, sagliendo, seguiro
5 fur queste: pria Letizia Moromile
e Lucia Porria fu, e con disiro
   Fior Canovara di dietro seguile;
ed il primo animal ch'elle scontraro
un leocorno fu, non miga vile.
10   I cani arditamente il seguitaro
guardando sé dal suo aguto corno,
al cui ferir non aveva riparo.
   Più volte s'aggirò il monte intorno:
né saetta né correr ci valea
15 che prender si potesse l'unicorno.
   Fior Curiale, che d'ira dentro ardea,
l'altra Fior prese e vestilla di bianco,
e disse: "Fa che tu in sul monte stea
   sanza paura, e con aspetto franco
20 con questa fune lega l'animale,
che verrà a te quando sarà istanco.
   Né dubitar di lui, ché non fa male
per tempo alcuno ad alcuna pulcella,
ma stassi con lei, tanto gli ne cale."
25   Salivvi Fior, sì come disse quella,
e, per ispazio lungo lui cacciato,
quivi aspettò tanto che venne ad ella.
   Temette quella prima, fin ch'allato
colcar sel vide, e poi rassicurossi
30 e tosto con la fune ebbel legato.
   Fior Curiale allora rallegrossi
veggendol preso, e l'altre insiememente;
e' passi loro in altra parte mossi,
   cominciaro a seguir velocemente
35 due cerbi grandi, i quali, avviluppati
le corna a' rami, preser tostamente.

## CANTO 7

Fiore Curiale led another company, some of whom climbed the low-lying mountain, while some of them remained in the plain. Those who followed her in the climb were these: first was Letizia Moromile with Lucia Porria, and Fiore Canovara eagerly followed on behind. And the first animal that they encountered was a unicorn, far from cowardly. The dogs daringly pursued it, wary of its pointed horn, from whose wound there was no protection. Several times the unicorn circled round the mountain, yet neither arrow nor chase availed: they could not catch the unicorn.

Fiore Curiale, who was burning inside with wrath, took the other Fiore and dressed her in white, and she said, "See that you stay, unafraid, atop the mountain, and with a trusting look and this rope tie up the animal, who will come to you when he tires. Do not fear him, for he never does harm to any maid; rather he keeps to her side, such is his fondness for her."

Up climbed Fiore, as she had been told, and after chasing him for quite a while, she waited there until he came to her. She was at first afraid, until she saw him lie down beside her; and then, reassured, she soon had him tied up with the rope.

Fiore Curiale was gladdened then at seeing him captured, and the others together with her. And turning their steps in another direction, they began rapidly pursuing two large stags, who were quickly taken when their horns got tangled in the branches.

Scarcely had the dogs left the deer, when a tumult of wild pigs on the run was heard through the forest. Branches and fronds they broke as they passed, snarling loudly, proud and bristly, panting so much that each seemed weary. At that uproar, Letizia turned with a spear in hand and let most of the furious herd

Né gli avean quasi i cani ancor lasciati
che per la selva si sentì un fracasso
di fieri porci da altrui cacciati.

40  Rami e frondi rompeano nel trapasso,
forte rugghiando, superbi e squamosi,
ansando sì che ciascun parea lasso.

A quel romore Letizia voltossi
con uno spiedo in mano e lasciò gire
45  la maggior parte d'essi furiosi;

ma l'ultimo di questi, che venire
vide, aspettò ad un alber fermata,
in parte che 'n lo spiedo il fé ferire.

Di dietro a questo forse una tirata
50  d'arco venivan cani, ond'e' fu preso;
e tosto all'altre con el fu tornata.

Verdella di Berardo, che asceso
non avea 'l monte, ma rimasa s'era
con sue compagne al pian d'acqua difeso,
55  con un falcone in mano alla riviera
si stava, e Caterina di Bolino
con un girfalco; e con esso loro era
la Lucciola, seguendo il lor cammino.

CANTO 8

Andando queste intorno al fiumicello,
e Giovannola Coppola con loro,
per far levar malardo o altro uccello,
del lito si levò sanza dimoro
5  una gran gru e volando salio
tanto ch'a pena la vedean costoro.

Ma il girfalco tosto la seguio,
e più presto di lei salito ad alto,
in giù volando, forte la ferio.

10  Né cadde però quella al verde smalto,
ma, ripigliato vol, più prestamente
si dipartia per cessar l'altro assalto.

Ma il fuggir non le giovò niente,
chè la seconda volta fu ferita
15  ben ch'ella sostenesse fortemente.

E, pur ripreso il volo, fu salita

go by, but she stood waiting still by a tree for the last one of them she saw coming, so placed that she made him strike her boar-spear. Behind him, perhaps as far as an arrow flies, the dogs were coming, and so he was taken; and soon Fiore had returned with him to the other huntresses.

Verdella di Berardo, who had not gone up the mountain, but had remained with her companions in the moated plain, stood on the bank with a falcon in hand, and so, too, Caterina di Bolino with a gyrfalcon; and together with them was La Lucciola, following in their footsteps.

## CANTO 8

These ladies, and Giovannola Coppola with them, were going about by the brook to flush mallard or other fowl, when suddenly, a huge crane flew up from the bank, soaring so high they could hardly see it. But the gyrfalcon was quick to follow, and climbing aloft faster than she, downward it flew to wound her gravely. In spite of this the crane still did not fall to the enameled green, but she again took flight, making off the faster to avoid the next attack. But she fled to no avail, and for the second time she was wounded, although she bravely withstood. And yet again she took flight, climbing far higher than before, so high that the ladies lost sight of her. The gyrfalcon was far above her in regions sublime, and striking her again, drove her to regions ever so further downward. Then returning above her once more, he sank his strong

più alta che non era assai in prima,
tanto ch'agli occhi di quelle fu smarrita.
    Era 'l girfalco in parte più sublima
20  di quella assai, e, riferita lei,
la pinse in parte vie troppo più ima;
    poi ritornato ancor sopra costei,
in sul groppone i forti artigli fisse
e giù discese in piè con esso lei.
25      Presa la preda, Caterina sfisse
i sanguinosi unghioni, lui pascendo,
allegra in sé delle passate risse.
    In questo mezzo Verdella, vedendo
levati più malardi, lasciò gire
30  il suo falcon, con l'occhio lui seguendo.
    E' cominciò quanto poté a fuggire,
poi rivoltato in giù veloce venne
e un per forza ne corse a ferire.
    Non gli rimase in sulla schiena penne
35  né pelle che non fosse laniata;
e con gli unghion fortemente il ritenne.
    Tirollo giù sanza far ritornata
in su per più ferir, perché già morto
l'aveva pur nella prima calata.
40      Verdella corse là con atto accorto,
riprese quello e recollosi in mano;
e a cintola il malardo s'ha attorto.
    La Lucciola e Giovannola nel piano,
sopr'un braccio del chiaro ruscelletto,
45  tese avean reti, e non miga in pantano.
    E ciascheduna in mano un bastonetto
portava, l'acque dintorno frugando,
talor toccando di quel fiume il letto,
    e con voci alte talora gridando,
50  con diversi atti, acciò ch'uscisser fuori
gli uccei ch'ascosi gian per l'acqua andando.
    Un marangon, che prima a' lor romori
uscì dell'acqua, nelle reti preso
fu, ch'elle tese avean tra l'acque e' fiori.
55      Un paolino ancora vi fu offeso;
malardi ed altri uccelli, i qua' contare

talons into her back, descended, and alighted with her. Taking the prey, Caterina unfastened the falcon's bloody claws and fed it, feeling inward joy at the clashes that had taken place.

In the meantime, Verdella, who had seen several mallards flushed, let go her falcon, following him with her eye. He took wing as fast as he could; then, turning back downward, came rushing swift and strong to wound one of them. Neither plume nor hide was left untorn on its back, and the falcon held it hard with his talons. He brought it down without making the return aloft to strike again because he already had killed it with the very first swoop. Verdella, quick to act, rushed to the spot, caught the falcon, and gathered him to hand, tying the mallard to her waist.

On the plain, La Lucciola and Giovannola had spread nets, not in the marsh at all, but across a branch of the clear little brook. And each bore a beater in hand, stirring the waters round about, now touching the bed of that river, now shouting in a loud voice and making various motions, so that the fowl going hidden through the waters would come forth. A cormorant, first to leave the water at their uproar, was caught in their nets stretched over the waters and flowers. Again, a *paolin* was injured there; mallards and other fowl—too many for proper reckoning right now—they captured there, since they knew how to do it so wisely.

lungo sarebbe in ordine testeso,
vi preser, sì con senno sepper fare.

## CANTO 9

Mentre con gli occhi fra le verdi fronde
mirando giva la caccia, che 'n esse
talor si mostra e talor si nasconde,
    convenne che altrove mi volgesse
5 per nuovo suon ch'agli orecchi mi venne,
che lo 'ntelletto a sé tutto riflesse;
    né 'l mio veloce sguardo si ritenne
fin ch'a quel loco, dond'erano entrate
le prime donne, subito pervenne.
10    E quivi vidi con difficultate,
per lo spazio lontan, gran gente entrare
dentro dal pian dell'erbette bagnate.
    E 'l suon de' corni e de' can l'abbaiare
e 'l romor loro facean quella valle
15 tutta mirabilmente risonare.
    Io mi ristrinsi tutto nelle spalle,
credendo nel pensier ched altra gente,
forse malvagia, fosse per quel calle.
    Ma poi che l'occhio più agutamente
20 ficcai fra loro, conobbi che era
di donne compagnia bella e piacente.
    E come a me quell'amorosa schiera
si fisse appresso, ch'io potea vedere
apertamente ciascuna chi era,
25 tututte le conobbi al mio parere,
e 'mmaginai che poi chiamate foro
che l'altre, che cacciavano a potere.
    Venute allato alla fonte, costoro
stavan sospese al cacciare, ascoltando;
30 ma così cominciò una di loro:
    "Chi va per questi monti ora cacciando?"
La Lucciola rispuose, ch'era presso,
sopra la chiara riva, al suo dimando.
    Come ella questo udio, disse: "Adesso
35 dubitavam noi forte che nel loco
altri non fosse, come suole spesso

## CANTO 9

While I went gazing through the fronds with my eyes on the hunt that now appeared then disappeared amidst the greenery, I was forced to look elsewhere by a strange sound that came to my ears, one that claimed for itself my whole intellect. Not until my swift glance had quickly reached that spot where the first ladies had entered did it rest. And there, far in the distance, I was just able to catch sight of a great throng entering the wet, grassy plain. And the sound of the horns and baying of the dogs and their commotion made that whole valley resound wondrously.

My shoulders stiffened, for it crossed my mind that another group of people, perhaps evil-minded, was on that path. But when I fixed my gaze more keenly upon them, I knew it for a company of fair and charming ladies. And that amorous troop drew to a stop close by me, so I could plainly see who each lady was; I recognized, I think, every single one; and I imagined that they had been called after the others, who were hunting with all their might.

Once alongside the fountain, they gave pause to their hunt and listened. And one of them began thus, "Who goes now hunting through these mountains?" From nearby, La Lucciola, on the sunny bank, answered her question. When the lady heard this, she said, "Just now we were all quite worried that someone else might be in this spot—as often happens." And she withdrew aside a little to call Cecca and Zizzola Fagiana, faces fair with amorous fire, and Vannella Bolcana, Lariella Caracciola, and Serella Brancazza, of countenance humble and gentle. And she who called was Marella Caracciola, and with them, I believe, there was also Peronella d'Arco. Then Marella said, "My wish is to hunt within these narrows!" to which everyone said, "So is mine!" And eastward through the fair meadow they made their

addivenire." E sé ritrasse un poco
da parte; Cecca e Zizzola Fagiana,
belle nel viso d'amoroso foco,
40    chiamò, ancora Vannella Bolcana,
Lariella Caracciola e Serella
Brancazza nello aspetto umile e piana.
   E questa che chiamava fu Marella
Caracciola, e con loro al parer mio
45 vi fu ancora d'Arco Peronella.
   Disse Marella allora: "Il mio disio
è di cacciar fra questi luoghi stretti!"
a cui ciascuna disse: "Sì voglio io!"
   E 'nver levante per le belle erbette
50 preser la via, guernite a quella guisa
che fa mestieri a sì fatti diletti.
   Fatta dall'altre dovuta divisa,
gì, ed io torsi l'occhio e lascial'ire
a veder che dall'altre si divisa.
55    E vidi là cominciare a salire
al mezzodì Iacopa Aldimaresca,
e a cinque altre la vidi seguire,
   ciascuna inghirlandata d'erba fresca.

## CANTO 10

   Quella ch'avante all'altre la seguiva
mi par ch'era Marella Passerella,
a cui Gostanza Galeota giva
   di dietro e Mariella Piscicella;
5 Dalfina di Barasso ancora v'era,
e dopo lei de' Brancazzi Vannella,
   salendo per la nuova primavera.
Ma a quel monte ch'è inver ponente
si dirizzava più piacente schiera;
10    ch'io vidi all'altre andar principalmente
Zizzola Faccipecora, la quale
vidi seguir, se ben mi torna a mente,
   ardita assai Tuccella Serisale,
e Biancola Carafa dopo lei
15 con Caterina, nello andare eguale.
   Veniva appresso di dietro a costei

way, equipped with whatever is needed for pleasures such as these. Making due departure from the others, Marella went off; and I turned my eye and let her go, so as to see what the others were devising. And there to the south I saw Iacopa Aldimaresca begin climbing; and five others I saw follow her, each garlanded with fresh greenery.

CANTO 10

She who followed her ahead of the rest was, I believe, Marella Passerella, behind whom went Gostanza Galeota and Marella Piscicella; Dalfina di Barasso was there besides, and after her Vannella de' Brancazzi, climbing through the new spring growth. But toward that mountain that lay to the west, a troop more charming was setting out, for heading the others I saw Zizzola Faccipecora, following whom, if memory serves me well, I saw the dauntless Tuccella Serisale, and after her Biancola Carafa with Caterina walking apace. Next behind her came Giacopella Embriaca, and I recognized gracious Tanzella dell'Acerra.

But, if my memory errs not, Caterina Sighinolfi stayed by choice in the lowlands and took to the plain. Covella d'Anna accompanied her, and so did Mitola Caracciola, Berita Galeota, and Zizzola d'Alagna;

Giacopella Embriaca, e dell'Acerra
Tanzella graziosa conoscei.
　　Ma, se la mia memoria non erra,
20　Catrina Sighinolfi alla campagna
si volse rimaner, pigliando terra;
　　a cui Covella d'Anna s'accompagna
e Mitola Caracciola e Berita
Galeota e Zizzola d'Alagna:
25　　Covella d'Arco ancor v'era, fornita
di buono uccel ciascuna, e se n'andaro
all'altre che nel luogo avean partita.
　　Marella e l'altre ardite incominciaro
la caccia forte dietro ad un castoro,
30　che nel vallon, dove giron, trovaro.
　　Ma Vannella Bolcana fra costoro
più presta fu con buon can seguitando,
per ch'ella 'l prese prima di coloro.
　　E mentre che l'andavan sì cercando,
35　Mariella si fisse ed ascoltava
che fosse ciò ch'ell'udiva mugghiando.
　　E quanto più nella foresta entrava
più il mugghiar vicin li si faceva,
di ch'ella forte si maravigliava.
40　　Né conoscer di lor nulla poteva
ciò che là fosse; ma Serella disse
ch'uno olifante udir le pareva
　　giacere in terra: onde ciascuna fisse
il passo dubitando, e dilivrarsi
45　per gire ad esso, che che n'avvenisse.
　　E come alquanto ver quello appressarsi,
giacendo in terra lo videro stare,
né si poteva in modo alcun levarsi.
　　Cessossi allor da loro il dubitare,
50　e correndoli sopra con la scure
lance e saette 'ncominciargli a dare.
　　Ucciso quello, ritornaron sicure,
ed a Marella presentar la testa,
che lor guida era nelle vie oscure.
55　　Quella ne fece mirabile festa,
dicendo: "I cacciator, ch'ebbero affanno

there, too, was Covella d'Arco, each one furnished with a fine falcon; and they went off to the others whose party was in that place.

Marella and the other brave ladies began chasing hard after a beaver that they found in the wide valley where beavers roam. But Vannella Bolcana, following with a fine dog, was quickest among them, so that she caught it before they did. And while they were off in search of it, Marella stopped still and listened to whatever it was that she heard bellowing. And the farther into the forest she went, the closer to her the bellows came, and that greatly amazed her. None of the ladies could tell what was there, but Serella said she thought she heard an elephant lying on the ground. At that each lady stopped fearful in her tracks, and they made up their minds to go after it, come what might. And as they drew quite near, they saw it lying on the ground, nor was there any way for it to stand up. Then the fear among them ceased, and they charged, besetting it with axes, lances, and arrows. After the kill, they safely returned and presented its head to Marella, guide to them on the dark paths. She rejoiced over it in wonderment, saying, "The huntsmen who had toiled cleverly perhaps to catch this beast will be sorry to find it has been caught."

con loro ingegni forse a prender questa,
trovandola esser presa si dorranno."

## CANTO 11

　　Di frondi coronata, in mezzo cinta,
col corno al collo e col turcasso allato,
di bellezza piacevole dipinta,
　　e con un arco insieme accompagnato
5　con due saette, sen giva Marella,
con gli occhi ognor faccendo nuovo agguato;
　　e 'n simil forma seguiva Serella,
quando trovar le reti, onde già tratti
li cerbi avien Biancifiore e Catella:
10　le qua' prestar si fenno, e ne' burratti
di que' luoghi più folti le spiegaro,
in guisa ch'assa' tosto vi fur catti
　　ben quattro cervi, i qua' poi saettaro,
perché non ne potean nessun pigliare;
15　e di quel luogo seco glien portaro.
　　Ma Peronella faceva un gridare
dietro a due can ch'un capriol seguieno,
che tutto il bosco facean risonare;
　　e questo appena quelli giunto avieno,
20　che ella sopraggiunse e lui ferio,
da lui cacciando li can che 'l tenieno.
　　E Zizzola Fagiana, con disio,
con Cecca insieme due n'avevan presi
e 'n collo li recavano, quand'io
25　forte gridare: "Piglia, piglia!" intesi
di dietro a me: per ch'io mi rivoltai
subito al pian, dov'io vidi discesi
　　tre gran cinghiar, de' quali io dubitai,
fiata fu, ma più di venti cani
30　dietro lor vidi, ond'io m'assicurai.
　　E dietro a questi, con piene le mani
di archi e di saette, correr vidi
tre donne preste con tre grandi alani,
　　lasciando que' con altissimi gridi,
35　com'io già dissi, e sopra que' giro
feroci assai; né in prima m'avvidi,

CANTO 11

 Crowned with fronds, belted at the waist, a horn at her neck and quiver at her side, and with two arrows to accompany her bow, off there went Marella, a picture of charming beauty, her steady eyes setting new ambushes. And in like fashion Serella was following, when they found the nets with which Biancifiore and Catella already had hauled in their stags. These they asked to borrow, and in the densest ravines of those parts they spread them so that, quite soon there were fully four stags captive, which then they shot with arrows, because they could not lay hold of a single one, and they carried them off from that place.
 But Peronella was raising a cry behind two dogs that were following a roebuck and making the whole wood resound. And no sooner had they brought it to bay than she overtook them and wounded it, driving off the dogs that were holding it. And Zizzola Fagiana had, together with Cecca, eagerly taken two others, and they were carrying them on their shoulders, when behind me in loud cries I heard, "Get them! Get them!" So I straightaway turned to the plain, where I saw three great boars bearing down, who frightened me for a moment, but I saw more than twenty dogs behind them, and so felt reassured. And behind the dogs, I saw three swift ladies, their hands full of bows and arrows, running with three Great Danes; and releasing them with shrill cries, as I said before, they fell upon the boars most fiercely. No sooner had I noticed that than I saw Vannella Brancazza eagerly descend upon one, who was overcome by the dogs and wearying torment. And she dragged it away, most of its body all darkened with blood. But then I saw Dalfina kill the second one; and to the third, overwhelmed by the dogs, Gostanza struck a savage blow with a lance so fierce that she made it feel the

          che Vannella Brancazza con disiro
      vidi discender sopra l'un, che vinto
      era da' cani e dal greve martiro.
40        E quel, di sangue quasi tutto tinto,
      se ne tirò; ma poi vidi Dalfina
      uccidere 'l secondo; e 'l terzo, avvinto
          da' can, Gostanza con fiera rapina
      ferì con uno spiedo sì feroce
45    che di morte li fé sentir ruina.
          Poi, richiamando i cani ad una voce,
      tutti raccolsero, addietro tornando
      con loro insieme, con romore atroce.
          Iacopa Aldimaresca, che cercando
50    con Mariella Passerella andava
      per la piacevol selva riguardando,
          com'ella ad una ripa trapassava,
      a costa i can si fermar di presente
      ad una buca, e ciascuno abbaiava.
55        Quella guardava e non vedea niente;
      li can volea cacciar, ma ecco fore
      di quella uscia la coda d'un serpente,
          e dentro ritornossi al lor romore.

### CANTO 12

          Marella Piscicella, che vicina
      a costoro era, udì il lor romore,
      e con le sue compagne ancor Dalfina.
          Corsero adunque tutte con furore
5     in quella parte, e trovaron coloro
      quasi smarrite tutte del tremore.
          Allora s'accostò Dalfina a loro,
      dicendo: "Che vedeste, che non pare
      che 'n questa vita facciate dimoro?"
10        Iacopa allora cominciò a parlare:
      "Omè, che 'n questa buca è un serpente,
      terribil cosa pure a riguardare."
          Disse Dalfina: "Non dubbiar niente:
      noi siam qui con buon cani e ben armate:
15    ben lo potremo uccider salvamente."
          Iacopa, le compagne assicurate,

ruin of death. Then, in chorus, calling the dogs, they collected them all, going back together with them amidst an atrocious uproar.

Iacopa Aldimaresca was going along with Marella Passerella, watchfully searching the pleasant forest, when, as she crossed a hillside, the dogs stopped suddenly at a hole on its slope, and every one was barking. She looked and saw nothing; she wanted to chase off the dogs, but just then there came forth the tail of a serpent, and back inside it went at their uproar.

## CANTO 12

Marella Piscicella, who was near them, heard their uproar, and Dalfina with her companions did, too. So all ran to the spot in a furor, and they found the others fairly trembling with dismay. Then Dalfina approached them, saying, "What have you seen to make you look more dead than alive?" Iacopa then began to speak, "Alas! for there is a serpent in this hole, a thing terrible even to look at!" Dalfina said, "Have no fear in the least! We are here with good dogs and well-armed; we can certainly kill it safely."

Iacopa, her companions reassured, then replied, "If it be your pleasure, follow some of my advice." Said Dalfina, "Tell us what you think." Then Iacopa stood and thought a little, and then replied, "This is my wish. Let us put fiery coals in this hole; the flame and the smoke will kill the snake or chase it out into

        allor rispuose: "Sed e' v'è in piacere,
        alquanto el mio consiglio seguitate."
           Disse Dalfina: "Dì il tuo parere."
20      Iacopa stette allora e pensò un poco,
        e poi rispose: "Questo è 'l mio volere:
           mettiamo in questa buca acceso foco;
        la fiamma e 'l fumo lui uccideranno
        o 'l cacceranno fuor di questo loco.
25         Se forse fuor di qua uscir lo fanno,
        le vostre lance e le saette preste
           con voi aggiate, se non vogliam danno."
           A tal consiglio s'accordaron queste,
        e ritirar li cani e fiamme accese
30      misser nel luogo della fiera peste.
           Sostenne quella alquanto queste offese;
        poi, non potendo avanti sofferire,
           fuori furioso si gittò palese.
           Ciascuna allora il cominciò a ferire,
35      e' cani l'addentar, de' quali assai
           dintorno a sé co' denti fé morire.
           Ma non gli valse; ché gli ultimi guai
        gli apparecchiava quella che seguita
           era dall'altre, com'io avvisai.
40         Con greve colpo gli levò la vita
        con una lancia Iacopa, e la testa
           gli tagliò poi vigorosa e ardita.
           E mentre che di ciò facevan festa,
        ben sei altri n'usciron piccioletti,
45      figliuoi di quel, con noiosa tempesta.
           Con lieve affanno a morte fur costretti,
        perché gia' el fumo gli avea consumati
           mentre da quel nel buco eran distretti.
           Così da queste tututti pigliati
50      li vidi e morti; ond'io ad altra cosa
           rivoltai gli occhi già di quel saziati;
           e, al ponente, vidi valorosa
        Zizzola Faccipecora andar suso,
           leggiadra, bella, gaia e poderosa.
55         Ma nel bel monte delle frondi chiuso
        non andò guar con li suo' can guardando,

the open. If by chance the fire does force it out of here, be quick with your lances and arrows, unless we want to be hurt."

To this advice the ladies agreed, and they called off the dogs and put burning flames into the fierce plague's hole. For some time it withstood these assaults, then, unable to suffer them any longer, it furiously threw itself into full view. Every lady then began to strike it, and the dogs bit into it—many of those around it met death at its fangs. But nothing availed it, for the lady whom the others followed was, as I gathered, preparing its final woes. With a heavy blow of her lance, Iacopa took its life, and, vigorous and bold, she then cut off its head. And while they were celebrating this, truly six other little ones, its offspring, came out in a troublesome storm. With little effort they were put to death, for the smoke had already enfeebled them while it pinned them in the hole.

So I saw every one of them caught and killed by these ladies, whereupon I turned my eyes, now sated with that, to other things. And to the west I saw worthy Zizzola Faccipecora wending upward, graceful, fair, gay, and vigorous. But she, watching with her dogs, had scarcely gone far on the fair, bough-enclosed mountain, when in front of her, there appeared a leopard, far fleeter than we are used to, coming in her direction.

ch'un leopardo, lieve oltre a nostro uso,
l'apparve avanti, ver di lei andando.

## CANTO 13

Ella non dubitò, ma l'arco aperse
e quel ne' fianchi ferì sì profondo
che le sue forze tutte gli disperse,
    ed allo primo stral giunto il secondo,
5   che dandoli nel petto toccò il core,
onde morì: e li can, cerchio tondo
    fatto gli avean, faccendo romore
li s'appressaro e preser, con costei
oltre correndo, mostrando valore.
10      Ma Biancola Carafa innanzi a lei,
coronata di fior (tanto piacente
quanto alcun'altra che fosse con lei),
    giva correndo sì velocemente
dietro ad un daino ch'avanti li giva,
15  che parea che volasse veramente;
    e con lei insieme alcun can lo seguiva,
ma non perciò che giunger si potesse,
tanto era presto que' che si fuggiva.
    O che lui ramo o altro ritenesse,
20  non so; ma ella il giunse e lui ferio
d'un dardo nella gola, donde spesse
    guizzate diede e poi pur si morio
davanti a lei, che altro non parea
ch'ella attendesse con tutto 'l disio.
25      Alto nel bosco al mio parer vedea
due leggiadre e belle giovinette,
le qua' ciascuna assai ben conoscea,
    inghirlandate di due ghirlandette
di rose rosse, tanto relucenti
30  che a veder parean due fiammette,
    vestite strette, sì belle e piacenti
che facean rider tututto quel loco,
dond'elle andavan con li passi lenti.
    Le quali, andandosi a poco a poco,
35  d'archi e di saette bene armate,
fra sé cantando e faccendosi gioco,

CANTO 13

    She did not hesitate but drew her bow and struck him so deep in the flanks that she drained all his strength; and as the second arrow joined the first, hitting him in the breast, it touched his heart and killed him. And the dogs had made a circle around him; raising a hue and cry, they closed in and seized him, rushing forward with her, showing their courage.

    But, ahead of her, Biancola Carafa crowned with flowers (as pleasing as any who were with her!) went coursing so fast after a fallow deer on the run before her that she fairly seemed to fly. And along with her a dog or two pursued him but not quickly enough to catch up with him, so swift was he that fled. Whether a branch or something else impeded him, I know not, but she caught up with him and struck him in the throat with an arrow; whereupon he quivered in rapid spasms, then just died in front of her—she who looked to be hoping for nothing else with all her heart.

    High up in the woods, as it seemed to me, I saw two comely and fair young girls, each of whom I knew very well, engarlanded with little garlands of red roses so bright that to behold them they seemed two little flames; with gowns girded, they were so lovely and charming that they gladdened the whole of that place where they trod with slow steps.

    As these ladies went off slowly, well-armed with bows and arrows, singing together and frolicking about, they saw a panther descend from the highest reaches of the mountain; at this Covella Embriaca sounded her horn several times; and Tanzella did the same, calling the dogs who had no sooner arrived than they charged the agile beast.

    Covella ran forward and with three sharp arrows struck him on the brow, and her arrows went in so far

vider discender della stremitate
del monte una pantera; onde Cobella
Embriaca sonò molte fiate
40  il corno, e 'l somigliante fè Tanzella,
chiamando i cani, li qua', po' venuti
fur, si drizzaro ver la fiera snella.
   Covella corse avanti e con tre aguti
istrali ferì quella nella fronte,
45  e sì v'entrar, ch'a pena eran veduti
   fuor che le penne; laonde le pronte
gambe della pantera non potero
portarne lei, ma cadde a piè del monte.
   Diece can, credo, o più ve l'assagliero,
50  ed a Covella, che già là giunta era,
in terra morta e vinta la rendero.
   Ma a Tanzella più usata fiera
apparve avante, andando per atare
Iacopella nel loco dov'ell'era:
55  ch'un piccol fosso volendo passare
si attraversò un furioso toro,
rompendole la via nel suo andare;
   ond'ella fé per quel quivi dimoro.

## CANTO 14

   Salvossi questa alquanto in alto loco,
sonando un corno, raccogliendo i cani,
ch'erano avanti, qual molto e qual poco,
   impingendoli al toro con le mani:
5  "Ciuffa!" gridava, "piglial, buon Pezzuolo,
piglial, Dragone, e piglial, Graffiacani!"
   E poi ch'adosso l'abbaiante stuolo
gli ebbe drizzato, quale per la coscia,
chi per l'orecchie li porgeva duolo;
10  e da tutti la mortale angoscia
cacciava a suo potere, or coll'un corno
ferendo l'uno ed or coll'altro poscia;
   e simile co' calci a sé dintorno
non ne lasciava nullo appressimare;
15  sì passò prima gran parte del giorno.
   Tanzella non facea se non gridare

that hardly more than the feathers showed. Whereupon the panther's ready legs could not carry him off, and he fell at the foot of the mountain. Ten dogs or more, I believe, attacked him there; and to Covella, who had already reached the spot, they delivered him, dead and defeated on the ground. But a more common beast appeared before Tanzella as she was heading to the spot where Giacopella needed help, for just as Tanzella wanted to pass over a little ditch, a raging bull came across, blocking her way, so that she came to a halt there because of him.

## CANTO 14

She took refuge for a while on high ground, sounded her horn and assembled the dogs that were on ahead, some far, some near, urging and waving them on to the bull; "Sic!" she cried, "Get him, Pezzuolo, good dog! Get him, Dragone! Get him, Graffiacani!"

And then, when she had set the baying pack upon him, some of them inflicted him with pain at his haunches and others at his ears: and he fended off mortal anguish from them all as best he could, now striking one with one horn and then with the other, and so, too, by kicking about him, in the same way, he let none of them come too close.

Thus, at first, passed a good part of the day. Tanzella did nothing but shout and often shot her arrows amiss, never able to land him a blow. Tuccella

e spesso in fallo saette gittava,
non potendoli mai colpo donare.
   Tuccella Serisal, che quindi andava,
20 un dardo le prestò, e quella allora
con tutta la sua forza li gittava.
   Nel mezzo de' duo corni, un poco fora,
li colse con tal forza che si fisse
e quivi si morì sanza dimora.
25    Trasseli quella il core, e poscia disse:
"Tuccella, andiamo ove ti piace omai,
ch'io me n'andrei contenta s'i' morisse."
   Disse Tuccella: "Certo ragion hai,
sì fatta pugna hai vinta." E preser via
30 al traverso del monte, e giro assai
   pria che trovasser bestia, tuttavia
mirando ogni cespuglio; e, sì andando,
Caterina Carafa in compagnia
   preser con loro; e givan ragionando
35 del lor cacciare e de' loro accidenti,
una parola poi l'altra tirando.
   Ma con le punte agute in sé battenti
videro a loro un istrice vicino,
che ruppe loro i lor ragionamenti;
40    e, fermatasi quivi nel cammino,
Tuccella aperse l'arco e lui ferio,
e di quel colpo si morì il tapino.
   Caterina Carafa allor seguio
con li suo' cani un caprio, che fuggiva
45 quanto potea al monte con disio;
   ma li can di Covella, che reddiva
al pian, trovaron quello, onde fu morto
da Caterina, che forte il seguiva.
   Prendeva al piano mirabil diporto
50 Catrina Sighinolfi sopra il lito
del fiumicello, il cui correre è corto.
   Ell'avea funi nel fondo pulito
del fiume poste con lacci ravvolte
per un'idra pigliar da lei sentito;
55    la quale, dando per lo fiume volte,
incappò in quella, onde costei ridendo

Serisale, who was then going by, lent her a spear, and Tanzella flung it at him with all her might. She caught him with such force between and a little beyond his two horns, that he stopped short and there died forthwith. She pulled out his heart and then said: "Tuccella, now let us go where it pleases you, for I'd be happy to go if I died!"

Tuccella said: "How right you are! You have won quite a battle!" And they took their way across the mountain and circled wide, peering all the while into every thicket before they found a beast. And as they went along like this, into their company they took Caterina Carafa, and they went along talking about their hunt and about their mishaps, one subject leading to another.

But near them, they saw a porcupine, with its sharp quills clattering together, which cut short their conversation. And stopping there on the path, Tuccella drew her bow and struck him, and the wretched thing died from that blow. Then, with her dogs, Caterina Carafa pursued a roebuck that was anxiously fleeing up the mountain as fast as he could. But, as she was returning to the plain, Covella's dogs found him; whereupon he was killed by Caterina who was in hot pursuit.

Down in the plain Caterina Sighinolfi was having marvelous sport upon the bank of the brook that runs but a short way. She had placed ropes with twisted snares in the river's smooth bed to catch a hydra she had heard. Tumbling through the river, it bumped into her trap; at this she laughed and pulled it up; and many ladies laughed along with her when they saw her ingenuity.

la tirò suso; e risersene molte
con lei insieme, lo 'ngegno vedendo.

## CANTO 15

  Covella d'Arco a piè del monte s'era
tra giunchi e canne con Berita ascosa,
Galeota, al lito di quella riviera.
  E ciascheuna con nota amorosa
5 sonava un'arpa graziosamente,
in voce che il suono è dilettosa.
  E mentre elle sonavan dolcemente,
due cigni bianchi si calar nel loco,
assai vicini a lor, tacitamente.
10 Col capo ad alto giano a poco a poco
appressandosi al suon che piacea loro,
faccendo in atti di quel suono il gioco.
  Non s'appressaro a lor quasi costoro
ch'essi incapparo ne' tesi lacciuoli,
15 e dalle donne poi sanza dimoro
  pigliati furon, rimutando in duoli
i lor diletti; e altri a quel romore
se ne fuggiron con non lenti voli.
  Ma Mitola Caracciola un astore
20 portava in mano, ardito nello aspetto,
di più vol ch'altro e di maggior valore;
  e giva andando sopra il ruscelletto,
e Zizzola d'Alagna era con lei,
un naccaro sonando con diletto.
25 E mentre che sonando gia costei,
usciron più malardi di quelle acque
forte fuggendo davanti da lei:
  per che lasciar l'astore allor le piacque,
il qual, montato, uno ne ferio,
30 sì che in sull'erba morendo si giacque;
  e senza tardar punto risalio:
mentre se ne scendeva giù calando
infino in terra con un altro gio.
  Mitola, andando dietro a quel gridando,
35 e Zizzola con lei, l'astor riprese,
co' due malardi al fiume ritornando.
  Covella d'Anna i suo' passi distese

## CANTO 15

At the foot of the mountain Covella d'Arco had hidden herself on the bank of that river among the reeds and canes with Berita Galeota. And each was gracefully playing a harp with such amorous strain that the sound was a delightful melody.

And while they played sweetly, two white swans floated silently down to a spot very near them. With their heads held high, little by little the birds neared the sound that delighted them, swaying in time to the sound of the music. No sooner had they neared the huntresses, than they fell into the outspread snares, and then the ladies captured them without pausing, turning their pleasure to grief. And at that noise others were not slow in flying away to escape.

But Mitola Caracciola was bearing on her hand a goshawk, bold of mien, stronger in flight and greater in worth than any other. And she was going along beside the brook, and Zizzola d'Alagna was with her, joyfully playing a naker.

And while she went playing along, several mallards came up from those waters, fleeing hard before her, so that it pleased her to release her goshawk; and, he, climbing high, struck one of them so that it lay dying on the grass.

And without a moment's delay he rose again; as he came swooping down, he brought another to the ground. Mitola, crying out and going after her goshawk along with Zizzola, recaptured him and returned to the river with the brace of mallards.

Covella d'Anna lengthened her stride behind an ostrich, who went fleeing along the plain in fear of injury. But she could not pursue him without his fleeing all the more, and often he would turn around, flailing with his wings.

So much running through the thick brush had torn and twisted all Covella's clothes; and thus, both out of breath and filled with rage, she burned all over

  di dietro ad uno struzzo, che fuggendo
gia per lo piano, temendo l'offese.
40  Ma nol poteva tanto andar seguendo
ched e' più non fuggisse, e spesse volte
si rivoltava con l'ali battendo.
  Il molto correre e le frasche folte
avevano a Covella tutti i panni
45  quali stracciati e quali a sè ravvolte;
  ond'ella, piena e d'ira e d'affanni,
tututta ardeva nella faccia accesa,
di quello uccel desiderando i danni.
  Con più vigor, nuova forza ripresa,
50  seguitandol, si fé prestare un arco,
fra sé dolente di cotale impresa;
  ma dopo molto andare ad un gran varco
il colse e saettollo, e quegli allora
quivi morì con dolente rammarco.
55  Covella il prese sanza più dimora,
e tirollosi dietro infino al piano,
riferendol da capo ad ora ad ora,
  istroncandoli il capo con la mano.

## CANTO 16

  Ma già il sol saliva a mezzo giorno
e l'aere calda ai corpi dilicati
noia facea: per che sanza soggiorno
  Diana disse a quelle: "A' freschi prati
5  scendiamo omai e lasciam riposare
i nostri uccegli ed i cani affannati.
  Non è ora ben tempo da cacciare;
riposiamoci omai, però che lasse
semo, e facciamo quest'altre chiamare."
10  E comandò ad una che andasse
sull'alto monte, e tutte ad una ad una
le donne e le pulcelle richiamasse.
  Quella n'andò in sull'eccelsa cruna
del monticello, ed a chiamar costoro
15  incominciò per nome ciascheduna.
  Sì come agli orecchi di coloro
da lunga venne il chiamar di colei,

with her face aflame, yearning to injure that bird. Following him with more vigor and regaining new strength, she had someone lend her a bow, feeling sorrowful for such a deed. But after going a long way, she caught him in a wide mountain pass and shot him; and there he died with sorrowful regret.

Covella caught him without further ado and dragged him behind her down to the plain, striking him again, over and over, and wringing off his head with her hands.

## CANTO 16

But the sun was already rising to midday, and the hot air troubled their delicate bodies, so that Diana promptly said to the ladies: "Let us now go down to the cool meadows and allow our falcons and panting dogs to rest. Now is not a good time to hunt; now let us rest, for we are weary; and let us have the others called back."

And she commanded one of them to go up the high mountain and call back all of the ladies and maidens one by one. The huntress went off up to the lofty gap of the low-lying mountain and began to call each one by name. As her call came from afar to their ears, each one prepared without delay to come down to her quickly; and taking their dogs, and bows, and outspread nets, and whatever each took up with her, and with the game they had caught, some carrying it on their shoulders and others dragging it, down they came to the flowering meadow.

  tutte s'apparecchiar sanza dimoro
   di scender tostamente giuso a lei,
20 e presi i cani ed archi e reti stese
  e ciò ch'ognuna vi portò con lei,
   e con le prede ch'elle avean prese:
  chi le portava in collo e chi tirando
  giuso al fiorito prato se ne scese.
25   E già eran discese tutte, quando
  Zizzola d'Anna venne, che soletta
  sanza richiesta era gita cacciando;
   molti animali avea con sua saetta
  feriti e presi, ma nessun tenere
30 n'avea potuto né seguir con fretta.
   Con l'altre questa si pose a sedere,
  che della preda avean fatto un gran monte,
  come a Diana suto era 'n piacere.
   Levossi Diana poi con lieta fronte
35 dicendo: "Donne gentili e donzelle,
  ch'ardite e vigorose, liete e pronte,
   avete prese queste bestie snelle
  sotto mia provvedenza e con mio ingegno,
  io vo' che voi sacrificio d'elle
40   facciate a Giove, re dell'alto regno,
  ed a onor di me, che esser deggio
  reverita da voi in modo degno.
   Così vi priego e così vi richieggio
  quanto più posso, onde non siate lente,
45 acciò che nel mio coro aggiate seggio."
   Udito questo, la donna piacente
  si dirizzò turbata nello aspetto,
  dicendo: "E' non sarà così niente!
   Infino a qui, sì come avete detto
50 e comandato a noi qui adunate,
  così abbiam seguito con effetto.
   Or non vogliam più vostra deitate
  seguir, però ch'accese d'altro foco
  abbiamo i petti e l'anime infiammate."
55   Come Diana questo udì, nel loco
  non stette guari più, ma sen salio,
  partendosi turbata, a poco a poco,
   fin che nel ciel tornò ond'ella uscio.

And they all had already descended when Zizzola d'Anna came, she who, unbidden, had gone hunting by herself. With her arrows she had wounded and caught many animals but none had she been able to keep hold of or pursue with any speed. She sat down to rest with the others who had made a great mound of their game as had been Diana's pleasure.

Diana then rose, saying, with a joyful expression on her face: "Noble ladies and damsels, who, under my tutelage and art, boldly, vigorously, joyfully and swiftly have captured these lithe beasts, I now want you to make a sacrifice of them to Jove, King of the Lofty Realm, and in my honor, for by you must I be revered in worthy manner. Thus I pray you and require of you as far as it is in my power; therefore, be not slow about it, that you may have a seat in my chorus."

Upon hearing this, the Charming Lady arose saying with a stormy look: "It won't be that way at all! Up until now, all of us here gathered have followed exactly everything you have said and commanded. Now we no longer wish to follow your divine power since our breasts are enkindled with another fire and our souls are aflame."

When Diana heard this, she tarried in that spot no longer, but departed stormily, ascending little by little until she returned to the heaven whence she came.

## CANTO 17

    Rimaser queste adunque quivi; e quando
più non poteron Diana vedere,
chinaron gli occhi tacite aspettando.
    Poi la donna gentile, che a sedere
5 già s'era posta, si dirizzò e loro:
"Così farete," disse, "al mio parere,
    chiamando in voce pria l'aiutoro
di Venus santa Dea, madre d'Amore;
e, coronata ciascuna d'alloro,
10     sacrificio faremo al suo onore
della presente preda lietamente,
sì che s'accresca in noi il suo valore."
    A tutte piacque; onde liberamente,
acceso il foco nella preda, a dire
15 cominciar tutte assai divotamente:
    "O santa Dea, poich'è nostro disire,
per la virtù del nostro sacrificio
non isdegnar le nostre voci udire,
    ma pietosa al tuo giocondo officio
20 per merito de' nostri preghi umili
ricevi noi e per tuo beneficio.
    Caccia de' petti nostri i pensier vili,
e per la tua virtù fa eccellenti
gli animi nostri e' cor larghi e gentili.
25     Deh, fa sentire a noi quanto piacenti
sieno gli effetti tuoi, e facci ancora,
alcuno amando, gli animi contenti."
    Così pregando, non fé gran dimora
che una chiara e bella nuvoletta
30 venendo si fermò sovr'esse allora;
    sopra la quale ignuda giovinetta
apparve lor dicendo: "Io son colei
da cui, pregando voi, ciascuno aspetta
    grazia; e prometto a voi, per gli alti dei,
35 che ciascheduna avrà la dimandata,
ch'è degna di seguire i passi miei."
    E poi, verso del foco rivoltata,
non so che disse: se non che di fori,
ciascuna fiera che v'era infiammata

## CANTO 17

Therefore, the ladies remained there; and when they could no longer see Diana, they lowered their eyes in silent expectation. Then the Noble Lady, who had already taken her seat, arose and said to them: "In my opinion, this shall you do: after calling aloud first for the help of Venus, the holy goddess, mother of Love, and then after each has put on a crown of laurel, we shall joyfully make a sacrifice of this kill in her honor so that her power may increase within us."

This pleased them all, so that when the fire was lit under the kill, they all freely began to say most devoutly: "O holy Goddess, since it is our desire, through the power of our sacrifice, disdain not to hear our voice but receive us mercifully into your joyful rite through the merit of our humble prayers and through your beneficence. Banish base thoughts from our breasts and through your power make excellent our spirits and generous and noble our hearts. Yea, let us feel how pleasing are your effects and again, make our spirits content with someone to love."

While thus they prayed, it was not long before a bright and beautiful cloud came and then settled over them; upon it there appeared a naked young woman saying to them: "I am she from whom each one of you through her prayers awaits grace; and I promise you, by the gods above, that each one who is worthy to follow in my footsteps shall have what she asks."

And then, turning back toward the fire, she said I know not what, but every beast that had been set afire came forth from that blaze, changed into the form of a man, youthful, glad, and fair, all running over the greensward and flowers. And all of them entered into the brook; and as he came forth, each one was cloaked in a cloth of noble vermilion. Each was as fresh as a lily.

To them Venus turned and said: "By my command and by useful counsel, be subject to these ladies and love them until you shall merit victory and mercy for your suffering."

40     mutata in forma d'uom, di quelli ardori
usciva giovinetto gaio e bello,
tutti correndo sopra 'l verde e' fiori.
    E tutti entravan dentro al fiumicello,
e, quindi uscendo ciascun, d'un vermiglio
45     e nobil drappo si facean mantello.
    Ciascuno era fresco come un giglio;
a cui Venus rivolta disse: "State
per mio comando e per util consiglio
    suggetti a queste donne, e loro amate
50     fin che meriterete aver vittoria
del vostro affanno insieme con pietate."
    E questo detto, al ciel della sua gloria
veloce se 'nvolò, lasciando a' petti
di tutti segno d'etterna memoria.
55     Nel verde prato diversi diletti
alcun prendeano, e sospirando alcuni
givan cogliendo diversi fioretti,
    tutti aspettando li promessi doni.

## CANTO 18

    Io, che veduto lungamente avea
le nuove cacce e 'l ritornare al piano
e 'l rimontar della turbata dea
    e lo scender dell'altra ed il sovrano
5     miracol fatto in non lunga stagione,
maraviglioso ad intelletto umano,
    quasi ripien di nuova ammirazione
mi ritrovai di quel mantel coperto
che gli altri usciti dello ardente agone;
10     e vidimi alla bella donna offerto,
e di cervio mutato in creatura
umana e razionale esser per certo:
    ma non ingiustamente, ché natura
non mise mai valor né gentilezza
15     quant'è in lei, onestissima e pura.
    Il viso suo angelica bellezza
del ciel discesa veramente pare,
venuta a dare agli occhi uman chiarezza:
    discreta e saggia nel suo ragionare

And having said this she flew swiftly off to the heaven of her glory, leaving in the breasts of all a sign of eternal remembrance. In the green meadow some took part in various delights and, sighing, others went about gathering various flowers, while all awaited the gifts she had promised.

CANTO 18

I—who had long been watching this strange hunt, the return to the plain, the ascent of the stormy goddess and the descent of the other, and the supreme miracle, wondrous to human intellect, wrought in no time at all—near filled with strange awe, I found myself clothed with the same mantle as the others who had come forth from the fiery combat; and I saw myself offered to the Fair Lady, changed beyond doubt from a stag into a human being and a rational creature; and not unjustly, for nature never bestowed more worth or nobility than upon her, so chaste and pure.

Her face seems truly angelic beauty descended from heaven, come to give clarity to human eyes; discreet and wise in speech, she is a lady of commanding mien, blithe and bold in gait; wherefore, if she gave such delight to my eyes that I, in giving myself to her, turned back into a man from a brute beast, no man of intellect will ever find it unjust or amazing, for

20  e signorevol donna nello aspetto,
    lieta e baldanzosa nello andare;
        onde, s'agli occhi mie' diè tal diletto,
    che, donandomi a lei, uom ritornai
    di brutta belva, a uomo d'intelletto
25      non pare ingiusto né mirabil mai,
    ché l'etterno Signor credo che gioia
    abbia dicendo in sé: "Io la formai!"
        Ell'è ispegnitrice d'ogni noia:
    e chi la mira ben negli occhi fiso
30  torna pietoso o convien che si moia.
        Quanta sie la virtù che il bel viso
    spande in quella parte ove si gira,
    sollo io, che per dolcezza son conquiso.
        Superbia, accidia ed avarizia ed ira,
35  quando la veggio, fuggon della mente,
    che i contrari lor dentro a sé tira.
        Ond'io priego ciascun divotamente,
    che subbietto è, com'io, a quel signore
    che ingentilisce ciascuna vil mente,
40      ched e' prieghin per me che nell'amore
    di questa donna lungamente io sia,
    e che io d'onoralla aggia valore;
        ché simile orazion sempre mai fia
    fatta per me in servigio di quelli
45  che allegro possiede o che disia;
        e per coloro ancor che son ribelli
    con le lor donne, acciò ch'egli abbian pace
    e che angoscia più non li flagelli.
        Il più parlare omai qui non mi piace,
50  però che in parte più di lode degna
    serbo di dir con laude più verace
        quella biltà che l'anima disegna
    di quella, per cui son l'altre onorate
    e cui servire il cor sempre s'ingegna.
55      E torno a contemplar quella pietate
    ne' verdi prati e l'altra gran virtute
    che questa donna fregia di biltate,
    da cui ancora spero aver salute.

the Eternal Lord, I believe, rejoices in it, saying to Himself: "I made her!"

She banishes every woe. And whoever gazes fixedly into her eyes becomes merciful or else must die. How great the virtue that her fair face pours forth wherever it turns, I know, for I am conquered by its sweetness.

Pride, sloth, greed, and wrath, when I see her, flee from my mind, which draws into itself their opposites. Therefore, I devoutly pray every man who is subject, as I am, to that Lord who ennobles every base mind, that he pray for me, that I may long abide in the love of this Lady and that I may have the worth to honor her; for the same orison henceforth will always be made by me in the service of whoever happily possesses or desires—and even of those who are rebellious to their ladies, so that they may have peace and that their anguish may scourge them no more.

It pleases me now to speak no further, because for a place more praiseworthy I reserve my words to praise more truthfully that beauty that her soul traces upon her, she through whom other women are honored and whom my heart ever contrives to serve. And I go back to contemplate in the green meadows that mercy and the other great virtue that adorns with beauty this Lady from whom I yet hope to have salvation.

# COMMENTARY TO THE POEM

## Canto 1

*Caccia di Diana (Diana's Hunt)*: The *Hunt* is preserved in six manuscripts, none with illustrations. We concur with Branca in his division of the manuscripts into "α" and "β" groupings, but we believe that the "β" group very occasionally preserves more accurate readings lost or no longer dominant in "α":

**"β" group:**

L   Florence, Biblioteca Mediceo-Laurenziana. MS. Pluteo XC sup. 93 (Gaddiano 851). Paper, fifteenth century. (Verses 6:40–44, 14:52–53 missing.)

F   Florence, Biblioteca Nazionale Centrale. MS. II,IX,125. Paper, fifteenth century. (Missing verses 12:49–51; manuscript incomplete from 14:51 to the end.)

FR  Florence, Biblioteca Riccardiana. MS. 1059 (O,III,2). Paper, fifteenth century. (The most defective manuscript. Verses missing: 2:34–36; 6:16–18; 12:45–48; 16:44–17:50.)

**"α" group:**

FR[1]  Florence, Biblioteca Riccardiana. MS. 1060. Paper, fifteenth century. (Branca lists it as MS. 1069 in the edition that appears in *Tutte le opere di Giovanni Boccaccio* vol. 1 (1967), p. 679, a misprint.)

FR[2]  Florence, Biblioteca Riccardiana. MS. 1066 (O,IV,39). Paper, fifteenth century (1433). (Missing verses 7.34–36.)

WE   Wellesley College Library, Plimpton Collection, Wellesley, Mass. MS. 854 (Fabbroni; Minutoli-Tegrini; Battaglini). Parchment, fifteenth century (1430). Acephalous; last page of *Amorosa visione*, first page of *Caccia*, that is, 1.1–18, and *Caccia* 17.17–18.7 are missing. (The most accurate manuscript.)

The Latin title *Venatio Dianae* appears in three of the six manuscripts; *Caccia di Diana* in two: L ("Incipit Venatio Diane," "Explicit Venatio Diane"); F ("Incipit primus cantus Venacio Diane"). F ends abruptly at line 51 of Canto 14. FR bears no title or incipit. FR[1] bears "Incipit Venatio Diane" and "Explicit Venatio Diane." FR[2] has a title page inscribed "*Cac-*

*cia di Diana*," and an explicit reading, half in Italian and half in Latin, "compiuto capitoli Diane." WE is acephalous; the explicit reads: "Qui finisce la caccia di Diana e sue compagne."

See also V. Branca, *Tradizione* (1958), pp. 148–157; and his graph and notes to *La Caccia di Diana* in *Tutte le opere*, vol. 1, pp. 679–680.

Most important for the history of Italian literature is the fact that *Diana's Hunt* is the first Italian work that we know of that imitates Dante's invention of terza rima. The *Hunt*'s metrical form is that of a *ternario* in eighteen cantos of hendecasyllabic *terzine*. By genre it can be considered as a variant of the *sirventese*, a lyric type of Provençal origin, which originally consisted of strophes of three hendecasyllable verses plus a *quinario*, but which varied widely in structure and content (see Introduction, pp. 12–13, 23–24); perhaps, in adopting Dante's terza rima, Boccaccio considered that metric structure a contemporary variation omitting the *quinario*. In any case, the author's understanding of the *sirventese* as a vehicle for naming and praising many ladies derives from Dante's mention of an epistle he had written "in the form of a *sirventese*" (*Vita nuova* 6).

The *ternario* and *sirventese* are both learned or "high" literary modes. In addition to them, the popular *cantare* influenced the *Hunt*, particularly on the register of poetic diction. The *cantari* were narratives of adventure and love composed in stanzaic octaves closed by a rhyming couplet (ottava rima). Recited from memory in the piazzas by minstrels (*cantastorie*), these long romances, whose octave form Boccaccio used for his *Teseida delle nozze d'Emilia* and *Ninfale fiesolano*, were ancestors of the Renaissance chivalric epic.

In composition, *Diana's Hunt* is a diptych. After the ladies summoned by Diana's messenger have hunted as four parties in the four cardinal directions, at the center of the poem a second group of women enters the forest and closely repeats that pattern of action. Within the iterated structure of the poem's two halves, a symmetry that provides a kind of frame pattern, the concatenated episodes of the chase occur. Modern readers may scan these little scenes with some impatience, where, one after another, the huntresses repeatedly capture and kill their prey. But such insistence is not a sign of immature or impoverished imagination. It presents, rather, an opportunity for Boccaccio to display his virtuosity in the technique of the "catalogue with *variatio*," much practiced and, therefore, much prized in late medieval literature. Boccaccio's admired elder friend, Petrarch, used the idea to great advantage in the "vario stile" (varied style, variations) of his *Rime sparse*, begun only a few years before the *Hunt*.

**1.1–3** *In that fair season when the new grasses reclothe each meadow, and the bright air smiles* ("*Nel tempo adorno che l'erbette nove / rivestono ogni prato e* *l'aere chiaro / ride"*): The opening lines are calqued on the first verse of Petrarch's metamorphosis canzone of 1333–1334 (*Rime sparse* 23), where the narrator, in his last transformation, becomes a stag, "Nel dolce tempo della prima etade" (In the sweet time of the first age).

Boccaccio still had the same seasonal setting in mind twenty years later when he envisioned Dante and Beatrice meeting and falling in love as children at Folco Portinari's traditional Florentine May Day party (*Trattatello* 1.30): "Nel tempo nel quale la dolcezza del cielo riveste de' suoi ornamenti la terra, e tutta per la varietà de' fiori mescolati fra le verdi frondi la fa ridente, era usanza della nostra città, e degli uomini e delle donne, nelle loro contrade ciascuno in distinte compagnie festeggiare" (In the time when the sweetness of heaven reclothes with its ornaments the earth, and makes her everywhere smile with the variety of flowers mingled among green boughs, the custom in our city was for men and women, each in his neighborhood, to gather festively in separate companies). Cf. also the setting of Africo's love for Mensola in *Ninf. fies.* 18, "Era 'n quel tempo del mese di maggio, / quando i be' prati rilucon di fiori" (it was in that time the month of May, when the fair meadows sparkle with flowers); and *Ameto* 7.10, where the return of spring inspires Ameto to sing of his love for Lia: "Ma poi che Febo, venuto nel Monton frisseo, rendé alla terra il piacevole vestimento di fiori innumerabili colorato . . . e gli alberi, di graziose fronde e di fiori ricoperti, sostennero i lieti uccelli . . . e tutta la terra, dipinta, da argentali onde rigata, si mostrò lieta, e a Zeffiro soavissimo fra le nuove foglie sanza sturbo furono rendute le fresche vie" (But when Phoebus entered into the Phrygian ram and gave the earth a lovely dress colored with innumerable flowers . . . and when the trees were covered again with graceful branches and flowers and housed the happy birds; . . . and all the earth, striped with silver waters, looked happy; and when among the new leaves the cool paths were opened to soft Zephyr without hindrance).

More generally, the powerful topos connecting spring with love and literary beginnings—a cornerstone for the *Divine Comedy*, Petrarch's *Rime sparse*, Chaucer's *Canterbury Tales*—prompts the *Hunt*'s lyric exordium. Here, as in Dante's *Comedy*, nature's season of birth marks a time of moral rebirth.

**1.5–6** *the blows of Love that were piercing my heart*: Cupid is shooting the narrator with his arrows. Influential in shaping the conventional image was Ovid's tale of Apollo and Daphne, *Met.* 1.452ff.

**1.8** *a gentle spirit come flying fast*: The verse recalls, at a distance, the courteous spirits who fly on the terrace of envy in Dante's *Purg.* 13.25–33 (Marti).

**1.9** *Lovely ladies!*: The ladies are listed and identified alphabetically, with the various forms of their names, in the Glossary of the Huntresses.

While we have preserved, as far as possible, the original form of the names in the Italian text, we have tried, for the benefit of the reader, to use the following forms consistently in the Introduction, Translation, and Commentary: Marella (rather than the variant: Mariella), Giacopella (variant: Iacopella), Covella (variant: Cobella), Caterina (variant: Catrina). Similarly, names that appear in both apocopated and non-apocopated forms have been given full spelling: for example, Fiore, Biancifiore, Bolina, Curiale, Fellapane, and Serisale, rather than Fior, Biancifior, Bolin, Curial, Fellapan, and Serisal.

None of the manuscripts, not even the accurate Wellesley codex, is consistent in the spelling or usage of the huntresses' names. To make matters more difficult for the modern English reader, the name and nickname appear indiscriminately (both Giacopella and Covella, Caterina and Catella, for example).

The many variations in the references to the Mystery Lady ("Fair Lady," "Gentle Lady," "Noble Lady," and so forth) have all been capitalized in English for better comprehension.

**1.12** *Parthenope*: Naples and its environs, a place of woodlands and of watering places; especially popular with the fourteenth-century Angevin court were the resorts, such as Baia with its famous Roman baths, where such ancient Romans as Crassus, Lucullus, Cicero, Varro, Hortensius, and the Caesars once had villas. See Introduction, p. 63. In the *Ameto* 35.2–18, Fiammetta has the honor of telling how the city was settled and named. Its Greek founders happened to unearth a marble tomb with an inscription that read, "Qui Partenopes vergine sicula morta giace" (Here lies the dead Sicilian virgin Parthenope). They were eventually able to interpret it as a favorable omen of fertility for both the land and their people, since virginity and death had been buried with the maiden. The story seems to have been suggested less by Livy (*Ab urbe condita* 8.22.5–65) than by local legend.

As Boccaccio elsewhere reveals, Parthenope had been one of the Sirens. See, for example, Boccaccio's *Rime* 36.1–8: "Scrivon alcun Partenopè, sirena / ornata di bellezze e piena d'arte, / aver sua stanza eletta in questa parte / tra il colle erboso e la marina rena; / e qui lasciat'ancor d'età non piena / le membra sua, che or son cener sparte, / e il nome suo" (Some say that Parthenope, a siren beautiful and artful, chose to dwell in these parts, between the grassy hill and the sands of the shore; and they say that here, still young, she departed her body, which now is scattered ashes, and left her name). Cf. *Rime* 48 and, for the poet's later learned explanation of the myth and her name's meaning, *Genealogie* 7.20 (p. 355): "prima [Syrena] vocatur Parthenopia a parthenos, quod est virgo" (the first Siren is called Parthenopia from *parthenos,* that is, *virgin*).

The designation "Parthenope" reflects Boccaccio's scholarly fondness for names derived from Greek. It appears in the more erudite vernacular fictions—and always to the exclusion of "Napoli"—as part of their elevated, Latinate rhetorical style. For example, the aspiring author's "coup de foudre" for Fiammetta struck in "a beautiful temple in Parthenope"; within a nearby garden that lady rules the love debate joined by Filocolo after his fortuitous shipwreck "in the port of ancient Parthenope"; woods around "ancient Parthenope" harbor Boccaccio's fictional double Idalogo, an amorous poet whom Venus turned into a pine tree (*Filoc.* 1.1.17, 4.9ff., 5.4.7ff.). Again, the *Fiammetta* sets its protagonist's sad tale against contrastingly merry "Parthenope." But in writings of popular or more realistic style, the mythological allusion disappears altogether. Naples stays simply "Napoli" in the proem of the *Filostrato,* and so too in the *Decameron*'s Neapolitan tales: Andreuccio da Perugia's adventure (2.5); a comeuppance at the baths for jealous Catella Sighinolfi (3.6—that same Caterina-Catrina who enters the *Hunt* at 10.20!); Peronella's hindside visit from her lover (7.2); King Carlo's temptation (10.6). Generally speaking, Parthenope seems to have been one of Boccaccio's youthful affectations, since the scholarly works, even those in Latin, will opt for Naples: *Trattatello* 1.105 (concerning Octavian's tomb for Virgil in Naples; P. G. Ricci ed., p. 606); *De mulieribus* 105.11; *De casibus* 9.14.7, 9.19.22, 9.24.3, 9.26.2.

**1.13** *when he had thrice said these words*: The triple summons called out by the "gentle spirit . . . flying fast," who is referred to below (1.52) as "messo di Diana" (Diana's messenger), recalls the angelic herald of *Purg.* 30.10–12: "e un di loro, quasi da ciel messo, / 'Veni, sponsa, de Libano' cantando / gridò tre volte" (and one of them, as if sent from Heaven, singing cried thrice, '*Veni, sponsa, de Libano*').

**1.15** We have restored the reading "ad una ad una" attested in five of the six major manuscripts. The Wellesley manuscript lacks its first page. Cf. 15.57, 16.11 for evidence of Boccaccio's preference for the intervocalic dental between words.

**1.16–17** *unless my ears deceived me—and I think they did not*: The claim of such scrupulously truthful accuracy is typical of the *cantari* (Branca). Cf. *Tes.* 1.51: "ma bene era risposto, se non erra / la mente mia, a lor da tutti i canti" (but on all sides, if my memory errs not, they met their match); *Filostr.* 1.16: "e spesse volte i Greci, s'el non erra / la storia, givano assai fieramente" (and, if history err not, the Greeks often went out very fiercely); *Ninf. fies.* 329:5–7 "e secondo che 'l mio avviso stima, / era la sua caverna, . . . / forse un trar d'arco sopra 'l fiumicello" (and according to my reckoning, her cave . . . was about an arrow's shot above the rivulet).

**1.46** *that Lady whom Love honors*: She is the narrator's beloved; her historical identity is unknown. See below, 4.1.

**1.53** *nor do I name her*: The Italian text is ambivalent at this point, either "né nomò lei" (nor did he [i.e., the messenger] name her), which is Branca's reading, or "né nomo lei" (nor do I name her). There are no accent marks in the manuscripts. We prefer the latter reading in the first person, parallel in meaning to the passage that was Boccaccio's source, Dante's *Vita nuova* 42. There, it is the *narrator* who confesses his unworthiness to speak of his lady.

**1.54–55** *praise more sovereign . . . than I could here set forth*: The verses echo *Vita nuova* 42: "Appresso questo sonetto apparve a me una mirabile visione, ne la quale io vidi cose, che mi fecero proporre di non dire più di questa benedetta, infino a tanto che io potessi più degnamente trattare di lei" (After I wrote this sonnet there came to me a miraculous vision in which I saw things that made me resolve to say no more about this blessed one until I would be capable of writing about her in a nobler way).

## Canto 2

**2.1–15** This idyllic place sweetened by bird song recalls "la divina foresta spessa e viva" (the divine forest green and dense) of Dante's terrestrial paradise (*Purg.* 28). Boccaccio's "reclothed" landscape (1.1–3) and spring zephyr (2.16) also point back to the season of Saint Dominic's birth (*Par.* 12.46–48). A similar secluded retreat with surrounding mountains will return in the *Decameron* (Concl., Day 6) as "la Valle delle Donne" (the Valley of the Ladies). But the *locus amoenus,* in one variation or another, plays important roles for most of Boccaccio's fictions. Indicative are the walled garden of the love debate (*Filoc.* 4.17); the castle garden of vanities (*Am. vis.* 37–39); the meadow by Venus's temple (*Ameto* 9). See P. Watson, *The Garden of Love* (1979), pp. 30ff.

**2.9** *the water that overflows . . . makes a stream*: This stream returns as the "clear little brook" (*chiaro ruscelletto*) in 8.44, "the brook [*fiumicello*] that runs but a short way" of 14.51, and the "brook" (*fiumicello*) of 17.43.

**2.17** *when the heat of the day no longer rises* ("*quando il calor diurno più non sale*"): Cf. *Purg.* 19.1: "Ne l'ora che non può 'l calor dïurno / intepidar più" (At the hour when the day's heat . . . can no more warm).

**2.22–23** *Diana, who keeps the tepid fire*: Lukewarm fires, as opposed to hotter flames fanned by Venus, are signs of the chaste life that Diana fosters. So in *Filoc.* 2.4.8, Florio and Biancifiore's tutor realizes only belatedly that Venus has made the children fall in love over the "holy book of Ovid" (i.e., *Art of Love*) from which they are learning to read in a scene amusingly reminiscent of Dante's *Inf.* 5: "E già il venereo fuoco gli avea sì accesi, che tardi la freddezza di Diana li avrebbe potuti rattiepidare" (And they already so burned with Venerean fire that Diana's coldness would have been too late to make them tepid again).

**2.24**  *to her sport* ("*al suo gioco*"): The hunt is, literally, a game, play. In this it can be compared to other entertainments described by Boccaccio, such as the love debate ruled by Fiammetta, *Filoc.* 4.27.1.: "per la potenza del nostro giuoco, vi priego che utile consiglio diate a' miei dimandi" (by the power of our game, I pray that you give useful counsel to my questions); and the "amorous battle" tournament, *Tes.* 7.13.1: "Questo sarà come un giuoco a Marte" (this will be like a game to Mars).

**2.25–27**  *she commanded them to enter those limpid waters so they could refresh their beauty* ("*comandò che esse entrasser nelle / chiarissime onde e de' freschi liquori / lavando sé si rifacesser belle*"): Cf. *Ameto* 3.13–15: "all'ombra di piacevoli albuscelli, fra' fiori e l'erba altissima, sopra la chiara riva [Ameto] vide più giovinette; delle quali alcune, mostrando nelle basse acque i bianchi piedi, per quelle con lento passo vagando s'andavano; altre, posti giuso li boscherecci archi e li strali, sopra quelle sospesi i caldi visi, sbracciate, con le candide mani *rifacean belli* con le fresche onde" ([Ameto] saw several young maidens, sitting on the bright bank in the shade of saplings among some tall grown grass and flowers. Some of these maidens bared their white feet in the low waters and were wading there with a slow step. Others, having laid down their rustic bows and arrows, with their sleeves tucked up, were bending their warm faces over the clear brook and *refreshing their beauty* with their white hands and the cool waters [italics added]). Cf. also *Ameto* 9.11: "sopra chiara fontana con sua compagnia [Lia] si pose a sedere; e sé alquanto sopra quella mirata, asciugati i caldi sudori, *si rifé bella* dove mancava" ([Lia] set herself with her company before a clear fountain. And when she had admired herself in this fountain for a while, and had dried her perspiring brow, *she refreshed her beauty where it fell short* [italics added]). Cf. also *Purg.* 2.75: "quasi oblïando d'ire a *farsi belle*" (as though forgetting to go and *make themselves fair* [italics added]).

The bosky bath is Ovidian. It recalls both Actaeon's luckless day at Diana's grotto when the hunter was silenced as a quarried stag (*Met.* 3.155ff.), and Callisto's expulsion from the chaste goddess's band at the stream where all disrobed to wade (*Met.* 2.441–464). Both myths will return repeatedly in Boccaccio's writings. See, for example, *Tes.* 5.57 gl. for the commentator's account of Actaeon, and *Tes.* 7.50 gl. for Callisto's story.

Nude bathers are a favorite Boccaccian fantasy. Prominent in the *Hunt* and its Florentine counterpart *Ameto*, they are central to the *Nymphs of Fiesole*, which culminates midway with Africo's rape of Mensola at a rustic pool (st. 234ff.), and the *Decameron*, where Boccaccio's female narrators retreat to bathe in the limpid pool at the heart of the Valley of the Ladies (Concl., Day 6). Similar scenes are glimpsed in *Fiammetta*, around the bay of Naples, ch. 5.

**2.29** *dress again in gowns of royal purple* ("*si rivestir di purpurea veste*"): The four cardinal virtues in the procession that meets Dante as he enters the earthly paradise are "in porpore vestite" (clothed in purple; *Purg.* 29.131).

The ritual bath and dressing in royal purple of the women here under the tutelage of Diana is repeated with the ritual immersion and dressing in vermilion cloaks of the men under Venus in Canto 17.

**2.30** *garlanded with olive leaves*: Cf. *Purg.* 30.31: "sovra candido vel cinta d'uliva / donna m'apparve" (olive-crowned over a white veil a lady appeared to me).

**2.33** *up the southward mountain*: South is the best direction in secular love, as we deduce from an illustrative tale in the fifth dialogue of Andreas Capellanus's *Art of Courtly Love*. The nobleman who there presses his suit describes a palace at the center of the world with four splendid facades. Love holds the eastern gate; groups of ladies the other three. On the west side are women who will indiscriminately admit any man, on the north those who coldly deny entrance to all, but the ladies at the south door exercise judicious authority, welcoming deserving lovers and driving away the unworthy (Parry, trans., p. 73). Boccaccio seems to have had Andreas in mind, when, at the symbolic fountain and garden trivium of *Am. vis.* 39, he sends his dreamer strolling in a southerly direction.

**2.40** *those huntresses whom she had chosen for herself*: The first group, who hunt to the east are:
 1. Diana
 2. Cecca Bozzuta
 3. Caterina Fellapane
 4. Biancifiore Caffettina
 5. La Crespana
 6. Caterina Caradente

7. Caterina di Serpando
8. Caterina Pipina
9. Marella Melia (or, Maria, or Mariella de' Melii)

**2.50** *the four ladies high on the mountain . . . the others, at its base*: Of Diana's nine-member party, the four who hunt high on the mountain are Diana herself, Cecca Bozzuta, La Pipina, and La Crespana; behind them, perhaps halfway up, comes Caterina Caradente. The net-spreaders below are Biancifiore Caffettina, Catella, and Marella Melia, who then team in the valley with Caterina di Serpando.

**2.51** *a screen with nets*: Typically, in medieval hunts, beaters drove the game into a corral through an ever-narrowing funnel.

**2.58** *they hunted wisely ("con senno cacciando")*: The phrase "con senno" (with wisdom), which can at first sound simply formulaic, slips into the literal text from its allegorical premise. It implies not just "sensibly" but "wisely," with reference to the highest intellectual virtue of "wisdom" possessed by the huntresses, who especially follow bestiary law in their methods of capturing animals, and who are morally prudent in subduing beastly forces.

The sagacity of the hunter was also a common motif especially in the Ovidian love tradition, where the hunt was a metaphor of amorous pursuit. The *Ars amatoria* 1.45 sets it forth thus: "The hunter knows well where to spread his nets for the stag, well knows he in what glen the boar with gnashing teeth abides; familiar are the copses to the fowlers, and he who holds the hook is aware in which waters many fish are swimming."

See also M. Thiébaux, *Stag* (1974), p. 97. For other samples of Boccaccio's programmatic use of the term *senno,* see V. Kirkham, "An Allegorically Tempered *Decameron*" (1985a).

## Canto 3

**3.1–3** *Diana held a powerful bow*: The Diana of the *Hunt* is typical of the goddess as she appears in tradition and in Boccaccio's other works, a maid always bearing weapons of the hunt. See, for example, *Genealogie* 5.2: "Hanc veteres insignem virginitate perpetua voluere, et quoniam spreto hominum consortio silvas inhabitaret, venationibusque vacaret, eam arcu pharetraque accinctam descripsere" (the ancients took her as a sign of perpetual virginity, and since she disdained the fellowship of men to live in the woods and spend her time hunting, they described her as girded with bow and quiver).

The *Hunt*'s Diana is a much more primitive goddess than the regal blond beauty who from time to time looks in on her nymphs in Fiesole: "e' cape' crespi e biondi, non com'oro, / ma d'un color che vie meglio sta loro. / E le più volte sparti li tenea / sopra 'l divelto collo, e 'l suo vestire / a guisa d'una cioppa il taglio avea; / d'un zendado era ch'a pena coprire, / sì sottil era, le carni potea. / . . . / Venticinque anni di tempo mostrava / sua giovinezza, sanz'aver niun manco; / nella sinistra man l'arco portava, / e 'l turcasso pendea dal destro fianco, / pien di saette, le qua' saettava / alle fiere selvagge, e talor anco / a qualunque uom che lei noiar volesse" (Her hair was curled and blond, yet not like gold but of a shade that suited it far better. And most of the time she wore it parted over her slender neck. And her apparel, cut in the manner of a robe, was made of sendal so fine that it scarcely concealed the flesh. . . . In years she seemed a youthful twenty-five. She carried a bow in her left hand, while from her right side hung a quiver full of arrows which she discharged at savage beasts or, at times, even at any man who might want to molest her); *Ninf. fies.* 11–13.

**3.4** *on the summit of the far-off mountain* ("*nel cacume del monte rimosso*"): Cf. *Par.* 17.113: "per lo monte del cui bel cacume" (upon the mountain from whose fair summit).

**3.8** *roebuck* ("*un capriol*," "*cavriuol*"): The roebuck is the first animal to be killed in the poem, and fittingly, it is Diana who shoots it. According to Isidore (*Etym.* 12.1.15–16), the roe's name, *caper*, is derived from the verb *capio* because it "occupies [Latin, *captet*] mountain peaks." In the Physiologus tradition as well, the roe loves, and dwells on, the tops of mountains (cf. Guillaume le Clerc, "De caprea": "amat altos montes," "*captent* aspera," ed. M. F. Mann, p. 53). The animal, whose keen-sightedness represents "the wisdom of God," combines the idea of the Logos with the verse from the Song of Songs 2:8: "He cometh leaping upon the mountains, skipping over the hills. My beloved is like a roe." Thus the roebuck becomes an emblem of Christ, for it loves mountain peaks as does Christ, metaphorically, in loving prophets, angels, and patriarchs (*Physiologus*, ch. 22, ed. and trans. M. J. Curley, pp. 33–34; J. Carlill, pp. 198–199; *Le Best. divin,* ed. C. Hippeau, pp. 137–140; 247–250 [French]; ed. M. F. Mann, p. 53 [Latin]; cf. T. H. White trans. of the pseudo-Hugh of Saint Victor, *De bestiis* in *The Bestiary*, pp. 42–43).

The roe appears also in Cantos 5, 11, and 14.

**3.11–12** *he was transfixed, and there fell down, and could not escape*: "Reversal of the sequence of events, sometimes for reasons of euphony, is traditional in the *cantari*" (Branca). Boccaccio would have known this rhetorical figure, hysteron proteron (last first), from Dante, too, who makes striking use of it in the *Commedia* in, for example, *Par.* 2.23–24: "e forse in tanto in quanto un quadrel posa / e vola e da la noce si dischiava" (and perhaps in that time that a bolt strikes, flies, and from the catch is released).

**3.20, 22, 24**  We have preferred the reading of manuscripts F, FR, and L: "*senti*," "*pedetenti*," "*attenti.*"

**3.20–21**  *when you hear the branches shake* ("*fremir le frasche*"): Cf. *Inf.* 13.112–114: "similmente a colui che venire / sente 'l porco e la caccia a la sua posta, / ch'ode le bestie, e le frasche stormir" (like one aware of the wild boar and the chase approaching his post, who hears the beasts and the branches crashing).

**3.26–27**  *hares, headed toward the mountain* ("*lepri . . . al monte andando*"): Animal lore has it that hares and rabbits run uphill more easily than down; on the rabbit as a symbol of the pride of learning, see our discussion in the Introduction, pp. 16–17. As we note concerning the other beasts, Boccaccio will always center on the one specific habit or trait of the animal that signifies some sort of sinfulness in tradition. Again in the case of the hares, we can observe the erudition of our precocious author, always dependent upon a subtext for his meaning. On hares and rabbits see also 6.38.

**3.36–40**  *a boar* ("*un porco*") *. . . bristle-covered*: Five of the manuscripts read "di squama pien" (covered with bristles); only FR reads "di schiuma pien" (foaming at the mouth). Cf. *Hunt* 7.42; *Teseida* 7.119. Although we have adopted the reading "squama," the reading "schiuma" would have overwhelming bestiary support. For almost all of his beasts, Boccaccio carefully selects one feature from bestiary lore; it is odd that the boar's bristles are never mentioned in the books of beasts. However, the pseudo-Hugh of Saint Victor, in *De bestiis* (3.17 [*PL* 177.89]; *The Bestiary,* p. 76), reports that the words "aper, id est porcus, vel sus silvester" derives "a nomine Graeco ἀφρὸς, quod est spuma, eo quod spumam ore emittat" (from the word . . . "foam" because it emits foam from its mouth). Isidore had derived the etymology of the word "boar" (*aper*) "from its savagery (*a feritate*), by omitting the letter 'f' and substituting a 'p' instead" (*Etym.* 12.1.27)—a derivation also noted by the pseudo-Hugh. See also McCulloch, pp. 97–98; and below, 6.28, the note on the wild boar.

The hunting dogs in this canto repeat the actions of Dante's black bitches as they punish the wastrels in *Inf.* 13.124–127, "Di rietro a loro era la selva piena / di nere cagne, bramose e correnti / come veltri ch'uscisser di catena. / In quel che s'appiattò miser li denti" (Behind them the wood was full of black bitches, eager and fleet, like greyhounds loosed from the leash. On him who had squatted they set their teeth). Notice also the detail of "ogni cespuglio" (every thicket) in *Hunt* 3.23 and "cespuglio" (bush) in

*Inf.* 13.123 and 131. Boccaccio returns to the language of the gruesome chase through Dante's wood of the suicides for Nastagio degli Onesti's infernal apparition in *Dec.* 5.8.15–16: "Vide venire per un boschetto assai folto d'albuscelli e di pruni, correndo verso il luogo dove egli era, una bellissima giovane ignuda, scapigliata e tutta graffiata dalle frasche e da' pruni, piagnendo e gridando forte mercé; e oltre a questo le vide a' fianchi due grandi e fieri mastini, li quali duramente appresso correndole spesse volte crudelmente dove la giungnevano la mordevano" (He saw a very fair young woman come running, naked, through a thicket all full of underwood and briars, toward the place where he was, weeping and crying loudly for mercy and all disheveled and torn by the bushes and brambles. At her heels ran two huge and fierce mastiffs, which followed hard upon her and oftentimes bit her cruelly, whenever they overtook her). Is it coincidence that the figures marking this tale's position (5.8) duplicate the *Hunt*'s recurrent verse totals, fifty-eight per canto?

**3.47**  *Catella*: That is, Caterina Fellapane.

**3.49–52**  *three horned stags*: These are the first of the ten stags captured in the *Hunt* (cf. 4.36: "a white stag"; 7.35–36: "two large stags, who were quickly taken when their horns got tangled"; 11.13: "four stags"). Isidore in the *Etym.* 12.1.18 states: "Cervi dicti ἀπὸ τῶν κεράτων, id est a cornibus; κέρατα enim Graece cornua dicuntur. Hi serpentium inimici cum se gravatos infirmitate persenserint, spiritu narium eos extrahunt de cavernis, et superata pernicie veneni eorum pabulo reparantur" (The name for stags derives from ἀπὸ τῶν κεράτων, that is to say, from "horns," since in Greek horns are called κέρατα. Being enemies of serpents, when they feel themselves heavy with old age, they draw serpents forth from caves with the breath of their nostrils, and once they have overcome the danger of the poison, they are restored by that food).

See also J. Williamson (1986), pp. 98, 108–109.

For the stag as a symbol *in bono* of baptism, see Introduction, pp. 40–57.

In patristics, the stag, *in malo*, also figures the sinner, and its horns (like the horns of other beasts) represent pride (see *Clavis Melitonis*, ed. J.-B. Pitra, pp. 69–71).

**3.58**  *a wolf, and . . . into its tough shoulders* ("*un lupo, e nelle dure spalle*"): In the bestiary tradition the rapacious and cunning wolf (cf. Vincent of Beauvais, *Spec. nat.* 20.82: "Lupus est animal rapacissimus et fraudulentus" [The wolf is a rapacious and fraudulent animal]) is allied to pride and to the Devil, who fell from pride (*Il best. tosc.*, p. 25; T. H. White, trans. *The Bestiary*, p. 59). The tough-shouldered creature here shot is specifically consistent with medieval lore, which reputes that beast to be strongest in its foreparts, but weak in the flanks. These are among the features that liken it to the Devil, who "before" was an angel in heaven, but "after," by falling, became wicked. See Pierre de Beauvais (ed. G. Bianciotto, p. 64); Thomas of Cantimpré, *LNR*, 4.60, pp. 143–145; F. McCulloch (1960), pp. 188–189. Boccaccio was later to identify Dante's "she-wolf" (*lupa*) of *Inf.* 1 with avarice (*Esposizioni* 1.2.92).

This wolf in the third canto initiates a ternary pattern: it is the first of three captured in the *Hunt;* the second comes three cantos later; and the third (6.44) is taken with two cubs, making for a further trio. This wolf is also the first of the three Dantesque animals in three successive cantos calqued on *Inf.* 1: Canto 3 has a wolf, Canto 4 a *lonza,* Canto 5 a lion.

# Canto 4

**4.1** *The Fair Lady, whose name is not spoken*: Earlier critics assumed that she was actually the poet's beloved, a passing youthful fancy before Fiammetta entered his life. Thus Massèra (1919, p. 8) suggested that she could be one of the ladies alluded to under the pseudonyms Pampinea and Abrotonia in *Ameto* 35, where Fiammetta's lover tells her his story. For more along late Romantic lines of speculation, see below, 4.12.

Readers today prefer a less precise accounting: "The conventional literary character of her attributes and all the references to her can incline one to consider her a literary figure, or rather a *silhouette,* created along the lines of the stilnovistic or generic medieval tradition that underlies the *Hunt*" (Branca). The courtly poet typically, of course, shielded his lady's true identity, through such tactics as substituting for her given name a poetic code name—the Provençal *senhal*—or deflecting attention to a screen lady. Dante, who used the latter ploy in this *Vita nuova,* had also created a hardhearted "Petra" (Stony Lady) for the *Rime petrose.* Secrecy as a necessary condition to love was listed by Andreas Capellanus in his rules in the *De amore:* "When made public love rarely endures" (trans. Parry, p. 185).

**4.2** *with an eagle in hand*: Diana's companions in Parthenope use gyrfalcons and goshawks (2.38), except for the Mystery Lady, whose fowl befits her preeminence. In the hierarchy of falconry, the eagle is the noblest of birds, the prerogative of kings (A. Illiano [1984], p. 322). Anecdote has it that when a falcon belonging to Frederick II attacked and killed an eagle, he had the falcon beheaded because "it had killed its lord" (*Novellino,* ed. C. Alvaro, p. 90). The emblem of empire in *Par.* 6, it appears in Boccaccio's subsequent fiction as the sign of imperial authority. See, for example, *Am. vis.* B, 10.25–36: "Nobile nell'aspetto si vedea /

possente oltre venir intra costoro / Cesar, che 'n vista quasi ancor ridea / d'aver a forza avuto da coloro / nome d'imperio / .... / Mirabilmente bello a campeggiare / in ampio scudo il giovial uccello / li vidi in oro" (Noble of aspect appeared, / mighty among the rest, / Caesar, whose face still smiled / because he had by force / the name of emperor / .... / On his shield, marvelously beautiful to behold, / I saw the bird of Jove in gold).

**4.3** *to the south* ("*al mezzodì*"): Recall 2.33, where Diana sends the Mystery Lady "up the southward mountain." By emphasizing her association with this cardinal point of the compass, Boccaccio adds to the psychomachean aim of the poem. On the positive value of south ("up" in the view of the cosmos presented by the *Timaeus* through Chalcidius), in Aristotle and Saint Thomas Aquinas and others, see John Freccero, "Dante's Pilgrim in a Gyre," in *Dante: The Poetics of Conversion,* ed. Rachel Jacoff (Cambridge and London: Harvard University Press, 1986), pp. 70–92, esp. p. 73.

**4.12** *that Lady whose face seems always to burn with love* ("*che nel viso d'amore sempre par ch'arda*"): Cf. *Purg.* 27.96: "che di foco d'amor par sempre ardente" (who seems always burning with the fire of love). The epithet will return to accompany other Boccaccian ladies, notably Fiammetta.

With piecemeal reconstruction of such passages, late romantic criticism produced abundant speculation, but no satisfactory conclusions, concerning the identity of the *Hunt*'s anonymous heroine. Some interpreters believed that she was the same person as the first lady noticed in the garden of love by the dreamer in the *Am. vis.* 40.64–66, one so beautiful that he initially mistakes her for Venus: "Nel viso che d'amor sempre par ch'arda / affigurai, guardando con diletto, / che costei era la bella lombarda" (Glancing delightedly into the face / which seems to burn always with love, / I saw that she was the beautiful Lombard). F. Torraca (*Per la biografia,* pp. 117–118) went so far as to argue that "the fair Lombard," whose given name, Vanna, is revealed in Boccaccio's *Ternario* "Contento quasi ne' pensier d'amore" (Content—almost—in thoughts of love [see the text and translation of the *Ternario,* esp. vv. 46–47, below, pp. 221–227]) was "la formosa ligura," the shapely Ligurian—Acrimonia/Fortitude of the *Ameto*. But even if this chain of "clues" means that her name was Vanna, we still remain in the realm of poesy, for Guido Cavalcanti's mistress was also Giovanna, a fact on which Dante capitalizes in *Vita nuova* 24. Alternatively, the recurring epithet may simply mean that Boccaccio tended to repeat himself, whenever a formula, image, myth, and so forth pleased him.

The women in the second group, who hunt to the south, are:
1. Mystery Lady
2. Zizzola Barrile
3. Ciancia
4. Principessella Caracciola
5. Beritola Carafa
6. Berita Brancazzi
7. Sobilia Capece
8. Berarda de' Gattoli
9. Caterina Brancazzi

**4.14–15** *a beast fierce, bold, and fleet of foot* ("*uno animale / fiero ed ardito e presto sopra i piei*"): This "variata lonza" (spotted leopardess) (see below, v. 28) is the literary offspring of the first beast in Dante's *Inf.* 1.32–33: "una lonza leggiera e presta molto, / che di pel macolato era coverta" (a leopardess light-footed and very fleet, covered with a spotted hide). A caged *lonza* is recorded in Florence in 1285; it was one of a number of leopards and lions kept in Florence as mascots for many years. See A. Scolari, "*Inferno* I, 49–54," *Studi Danteschi* 54 (1982), pp. 1–14, and A. K. Cassell, *Lectura Dantis Americana: Inferno I* (1989), pp. 59–65, for Florentine custom and Dante's use of medieval bestiaries.

That poetic license here overrides venatic realism finds supporting external evidence in the treatise on falconry by Frederick II. Trained birds of prey, presumably including even the rare eagle, hunt only other birds or smaller, weaker forest creatures, such as hinds, roebucks, hares, and rabbits (*De arte venandi* 1.29).

Theologically, the leopard had a terrible reputation: "pardus, Antichristus" (the pard, the Antichrist), "diabolus, vel peccator" (the Devil, the sinner), it signified a vast array of sins, among them hypocrisy, heresy, and cruelty. See the entry in pseudo-Rabanus Maurus's *Allegoriae in Sacram Scripturam PL* 112.1022, and the *Clavis Melitonis,* ed. J.-B. Pitra, pp. 38–39. It was a symbol of fraud and fraudulence in Richard of Saint Victor's influential *De eruditione hominis interioris* 3.11 (*PL* 112.1358) and in Dante's *Commedia*. Boccaccio, however (*Esposizioni* 1.2.92), interprets the leopard of *Inf.* 1 as lust. Thus, in the *Hunt,* the eagle's capture of this beast would most likely signify the overcoming of lust by temperance, justice, and just rule.

**4.19–23** *almost to the sphere of fire . . . it came circling. . . . Like lightning amidst the trees and fronds, it struck so ferociously*: The bird given to Boccaccio's leading lady learned its flight pattern from the eagle in Dante's dream of his rapture to Purgatory's gate. Cf. *Purg.* 9.28–30: "Poi mi parea che, poi rotata un poco, / terribil come folgor discendesse, / e me rapisse suso infino al foco" (then it seemed to me that, having wheeled a while, it descended terrible as a thunderbolt and snatched me upwards as far as the fire).

In the *Physiologus,* the eagle's fabled ability to fly to extraordinary heights has an allegorical meaning based on Psalm 102.5 (Douay): "Thy youth shall be renewed like the eagle's." When it grows old, the eagle restores itself by flying to the sphere of fire, or even to the heavenly circle of the sun, before bathing in a fountain to restore its youth. Its remarkable molting and rejuvenation symbolized baptism. In that capacity for renewal it is spiritually akin to the stag. See *Physiologus,* ch. 8, ed. and trans. M. J. Curley, pp. 12, 72; J. Carlill, pp. 209–210; "De cervorum natura," in the pseudo-Hugh of Saint Victor, *De bestiis* 2.14 (*PL* 177.64); *The Bestiary,* p. 105. *Le Best. divin,* ed. C. Hippeau, pp. 100, 211 (French); M. F. Mann, p. 42 (Latin): *Il best. tosc.* 35, pp. 57–58; the *Tusco-Venetian Bestiary,* pp. 62–63; *LBAR,* vv. 1058ff., p. 37; *Li Tresors,* 1.145.

**4.32** *pulled out the leopardess's hot heart and fed the eagle*: "The extraction of the heart, to feed the bird of prey, rule and custom in ancient falconry, was applied more or less analogously to game of other types." So reports A. Illiano (1984), p. 322, who cites an instance involving a crane from Frederick's falconry treatise: "et extrahatur id membrum, quod per se movetur intrinsecus, id est cor, quod etiam extractum diu movetur moto suo naturali . . . et id membrum det falconi ad comedendum super gruem" (and one extracts the member that beats by itself on the inside, that is, the heart, which even after extraction still beats with its natural movement . . . and that member should be given to the falcon to eat on the crane; *De arte venandi* 2.93).

**4.36** *white stag*: See above, "three horned stags," and Commentary, 3.49–52.

**4.46** *turning vermilion*: It had become covered with its own blood. Cf. *Inf.* 28.68–69: "innanzi a li altri aprì la canna, / ch'era di fuor d'ogne parte vermiglia" (before the others [he] opened his gullet, which was all red outside).

**4.53** *two foxes*: Isidore, *Etym.* 12.2.25, and Saint Gregory in his *Moralia* 19.2 (*PL* 76. 96; *Morals,* vol. 2, p. 395) say that the fox always runs in circles, never in a straight line. In fact, Isidore derives fox (*vulpis*) from *volupes* (twisted foot). (In his usual scientific way, Saint Albertus Magnus corrects that etymology, saying that it derives from *voli-pes* [fleet-footed], *De animalibus* 22.110; trans. J. Scanlan, p. 182.) For the fox in Latin and French bestiaries, see McCulloch, pp. 119–120. In ecclesiastical tradition "the little foxes that destroy the vines" (Song of Songs 2:15) were, as in Saint Bernard's exegesis of the verse, identified as heretics (*Sermones 63–66* in *Cantica Canticorum*). Herod is compared to a fox in Luke 13:22, a fact noted in the *Physiologus* and by the compiler of the *Clavis Melitonis* (ed. J.-B. Pitra, p. 65). In the *Physiologus* and other forms of the bestiary tradition, the fox, because of its wiles (cf. Vincent of Beauvais, *Spec. nat.* 20.121–122: "Vulpis est animal dolosum" [The fox is a crafty animal]; "Vulpis est animal ingeniosum" [The fox is a wily animal]), also signifies "lo dimonio" (the Devil; *Il best. tosc.* 40, p. 61), who tempts mankind (*Le Best. divin*, ed. C. Hippeau, pp. 122, 232 [French]; ed. M. F. Mann, pp. 48–49 [Latin]). Following the long wake of tradition, Vincent of Beauvais (*Spec. nat.* 20.122) describes how the fox feigns death when hungry. He rolls in the mud to look bloody, lies down on the ground with paws stuck in the air, holds his breath, and lets his tongue dangle from a wide-open mouth. This way he catches the birds who, thinking him dead, come to perch on his body. He is the Devil, and his victims are those who live and die by the flesh, as described by St. Paul (see also Peter of Beauvais in G. Bianciotto, ed., p. 38); the tale is found in the various *Physiologus* versions, such as in Book 2 of the pseudo-Hugh of Saint Victor, *De bestiis* (*PL* 177.59; see the loose translation in *The Bestiary*, pp. 53–54). Saint Albertus Magnus repeats it in the *De animalibus* 22. Cf. Philippe de Thaon, pp. 66–67.

See *Physiologus*, ch. 18, ed. and trans. M. J. Curley, pp. 27–28, and p. 78, for a historical list of early *Physiologus* references.

The detail of the lair of the animals in the poem alludes to the patristic interpretation of fox in Jesus' words in Matt. 8:20 ("Vulpes foveas habent" [The foxes have holes]), as "dolosi quilibet" (any sort of crafty man). (Cf. the *Allegoriae in Sacram Scripturam*, *PL* 112.1084; *Clavis Melitonis*, ed. J.-B. Pitra, p. 65.) As usual, the one feature that Boccaccio points to in the text is the key to the traditional allegoresis.

**4.56**  *the Honorable Lady*: that is, "the lady whose name is not spoken."

## Canto 5

**5.28**  *a blow on the head*: Although bears were fabled for the strength of their loins and legs, used for standing upright (compare the American bestiary legends of "sasquatch" today), in the bestiary tradition transmitted via Pliny (*NH* 8.54) they were said to have vulnerable heads. The legend is pressed into service here as the arrows glance off the bear's flanks; the huntresses are successful only when they flog the beast's head in most unladylike fashion, using their bows as clubs. Their "wisdom" here is surely of a kind learned from the "Books of Beasts." One most respected bestiarist, Thomas of Cantimpré, affirms: "Caput autem infirmum habet et debile" (He has an infirm and weak head), "De quadrupedis," *LNR* 4.105.3 (ed. Boese, p. 168); cf. also Vincent of Beauvais, who, after Thomas, cites Pliny in his influential *Spec. nat.* 20.119: "Invalidissimum est urso caput" [The head of the bear is very weak]). See also the pseudo-Hugh of Saint Victor, *De bestiis,* Book 3.6 (*PL* 177.35); and *The Bestiary,* p. 45. We must note that wild bears were common in mountainous Italy at the time Boccaccio was writing; they are found today in the Abruzzi, protected in the national park.

*In malo,* the bear signifies the Devil ("Ursus, diabolus," *Clavis Melitonis,* ed. J.-B. Pitra, p. 61). Petrus Capuanus identifies the animal with "Gehenna, heretics, the devil, or vice" (cited in the *Clavis,* p. 61). Saint Ambrose, in *Hexameron* 6.18, had seen the bear as deceit, basing his interpretation on Lamentations 3:10.

**5.34–48** *trying to catch a lion cub:* Principessella surely knows her business in bagging this lion. Cf. *De consolatu Stilichonis* 3.339–343, where Claudian lists the customary hunt methods, only to announce that Diana did not need them, since her sheer Olympian magnetism compelled the beasts to surrender: "non illos taedae ardentes, non strata superne / lapsuro virgulta solo, non vocibus haedi / pendentis stimulata fames, non fossa fefellit; / ultro se voluere capi gaudentque videri tantae praeda deae" (To catch them had been used no blazing torches, no twigs strewn over turf undermined; the voice of a tethered kid had not allured their hunger nor had a diggèd pit ensnared them: of their own free will they gave themselves up to capture and rejoiced at being seen the prey of so great a goddess). Bartholomaeus Anglicus describes the same method of the bated pitfall using a lamb (*Medieval Lore,* ed. R. Steele, p. 161).

On trapping in a pit, which was dug wider at the bottom than the top to prevent the animal's escape, cf. also Gaston Phoebus (or Phébus), *Le Livre de chasse,* "Ci devise comment on peut chassier sanglers et autres bestes as fosses" (How to hunt wild boar and other animals with pits), "Ci devise comment on puet prendre les lous as fousses au train" (How wolves can be trapped in a pit by dragging pieces of carrion), ed. Tilander, pp. 257, 266; Bibliothèque Nationale, MS. 616ff., 85, and 90.

It is appropriate that Principessella (literally, a diminutive of *principessa,* a "little princess"), catch the beast (here a diminutive *leoncello* to fit his huntress) whom Isidore calls "*princeps* omnium bestiarum" (the *prince* of all animals; *Etym.* 12.1.2; cited in the *Clavis Melitonis,* ed. J.-B. Pitra, p. 55)—the *Hunt* reflects a primacy built into the structure of most bestiaries, which nearly always begin with a chapter on the lion (but see, for example the *Tusco-Venetian Bestiary,* pp. 24–26). Principessella's wisdom and ingenuity in using a dead roebuck recall bestiary stories of the "leontophonus," whose ashes are spread upon meat set out to catch lions (Isidore, *Etym.* 12.2.34; McCulloch, p. 138). The difficulty she experiences in capturing him may also owe something to the legend that the lion, who delighted in mountain heights, carefully brushed away its tracks with its tail. The deception perpetrated on the hunters was interpreted as an allegory of the theological "pia fraus" in which the divinity of Christ was hidden from the Devil to enable the salvation of mankind (see, for example, the *Tusco-Venetian Bestiary*, pp. 24–25). The lion cub is born dead, but, guarded by its mother for three days, it is then brought to life by its sire, who breathes life into it. See also *Le Best. divin*, ed. C. Hippeau, pp. 74, 193; *Il best. tosc.* 13, pp. 33–35; *Physiologus*, ch. 1, ed. and trans. M. J. Curley, pp. 3–4; *The Bestiary*, pp. 7–11. On the lion, see also *Physiologus*, ch. 1, ed. and trans. M. J. Curley, p. 68; Thomas of Cantimpré, *LNR* 4.54 (ed. Boese, pp. 139–141); *LBAR*, "li lyoncel" vv. 1632ff., p. 55; lion and pride, v. 1773, p. 59; *Li Tresors* 1.174; George Clarence Druce, "The Lion and Cubs in the Cloisters," *Canterbury Cathedral Chronicle* 23 (April 1936), pp. 18–22.

Although the lion could symbolize Christ *in bono* (cf. Apoc. 5:5: "the lion of the tribe of Juda"), it was most fabled for its ferocity. Vincent of Beauvais devotes a whole chapter just to this aspect of the beast ("De leonis ferocitate") in his *Spec. nat.* 20.68; for the lion's savagery in tradition see J. Williamson, *The Oak King* (1968), pp. 113–114. The *in malo* aspects are most important for the *Hunt*. The lion is the second Dantean animal taken; in the *Divine Comedy*, he was the beast associated with sins of force and violence (see A. K. Cassell, *Lectura Dantis Americana: Inferno I* [1989], pp. 65–66). From Psalm 56:5 ("God . . . hath delivered me from the midst of the young lions" [Douay]), the church fathers and doctors saw in the "catulus leonis" (the lion cub), "daemones, vel mali homines" (demons or evil men) who fall into the very pit they set for others (Psalm 56:7); cf. *Clavis Melitonis*, ed. J.-B. Pitra, pp. 52–53. The lion's roar is interpreted by the pseudo-Rabanus Maurus as the Devil and the Antichrist: "Antichristus in fallacia sua. 'Leo ipse diabolus rugiens tremit, quod diabolus' semper rapere studet fideles (I Pet. 5:8)" (Antichrist in his falsity. "[Your adversary] the Devil himself trembles as a roaring lion, [goeth about seeking whom he may devour (Douay)]" because the Devil always strives to capture the faithful); *Allegoriae in Sacram Scripturam*, PL 112.983. Compare also the passages on the lion cub, including those from Saint Gregory the Great, in the *Clavis*, p. 53.

In the poem, the nature of the capture in a pit and the vain roaring of the beast are both calculated to stir in the reader's mind the traditional negative significance found in biblical exegesis.

**5.52** *the Gentle Lady*: The narrator's mistress.

**5.55–58** *six hedgehogs* ("*spinosi*"): There was some confusion in the bestiaries concerning the hedgehog (*ericius*), the porcupine (*histrix*), and the sea urchin (*echinus*). But those uncertainties do not trouble the young Boccaccio, who is writing here as much from personal experience as from bestiary lore. As nearly every European child experiences, the hedgehog (*riccio*), when frightened, rolls into a spiky ball for protection so that one cannot touch it without being pricked. Berarda's "novelty," recommended by the bestiaries, permits her to overcome this problem by wrapping them in a cloth.

The *Tusco-Venetian Bestiary* says that it represents "una maniera de zente malvasia de questo mondo" (one kind of wicked people of this world). Other texts, particularly those deriving from Saint Gregory, are more specific: see Introduction, pp. 17–18. The patristic *in malo* symbolic significance would have been open to those who could pierce the symbolism and allegory. See Pliny, *NH* 8.56; Plutarch, *De sollert. an.* 971F. Saint Ambrose, *Hexameron* 6.4.20. *Physiologus*, ch. 16, ed. and trans. M. J. Curley, pp. 24, 77; Fournival, *Le Bestiare d'amour*, pp. 34–35. See also, for example, Thomas of Cantimpré, "De erinacio," *LNR* 4.39 (ed. Boese, pp. 134–135); and Philippe de Thaon, "heriçun," pp. 64–65; McCulloch, pp. 124–125.

## Canto 6

**6.1** *her sister*: Berita Brancazzi.

**6.4–5** *two fleet tigers that fled leaping fast* ("*due tigre leggere, che di salto forte fuggivan*"): Isidore tells us in *Etym.* 12.2.7: "Tigris vocata propter volucrem fugam; ita enim nominant Persae et Medi sagittam. Est enim bestia variis distincta maculis, virtute et velocitate mirabilis; ex cuius nomine flumen Tigris appellatur, quod is rapidissimus sit omnium fluviorum" (The tiger takes its name from the swiftness of its flight; the Persians and Medes use tiger as the word for arrow. It is, in fact, a beast with various distinctive markings, amazing for strength and speed, after which the Tigris river is named, because it is the most rapid of all rivers). Cf. the pseudo-Hugh of Saint Victor, *De bestiis* 3.1 (*PL* 177.33); *The Bestiary*, p. 12; McCulloch, pp. 176–178.

**6.13** *Isabella Scrignara and her group*: They are:
1. Isabella Scrignara
2. Ceccola Mazzone
3. Mignana degli Scrignari
4. Isolda di Giaquinto

5. Vannella Gambatella
6. Caterina di Iacopo Roncione
7. Alessandra d'Anna
8. Linella Gattoli

**6.28**  *a fierce wild boar* ("*un fiero cinghiar*"): Boccaccio chooses the word "fierce" with some care. Isidore, who derives the etymology from Varro's *De lingua latina,* tells us that the boar (*aper*) "is named from its savagery [*a feritate*], by omitting the letter 'f' and substituting a 'p' instead" (*Etym.* 12.1.27; cited in the pseudo-Hugh of Saint Victor, *De bestiis* 3.17 [*PL* 177.89]; *The Bestiary,* p. 76). See also McCulloch, pp. 97–98. Boars (*cinghiali*) are also mentioned in the *Hunt* in Cantos 3 (*un porco*), 6, and 11.

The rustic protagonist of Boccaccio's Florentine hunt pastoral also chases these animals (*Ameto* 5.24). The visual narrative in a pair of early fifteenth-century salvers by Apollonio di Giovanni, now at the Metropolitan Museum of Art, includes a hunt scene with Ameto, Lia, and her nymphs pursuing the boar (P. Watson and V. Kirkham, "Amore et virtù" [1975]).

**6.38**  *large hares* ("*lepri grosse*"): They are "big," not "plump." Many classical and medieval sources state that wild hares do not fatten—a truth observable in nature. See, for example, Pliny ("nunquam pinguescit"), and others, in the texts cited by Thomas of Cantimpré, "De lepore," *LNR* 4.65 (ed. Boese, pp. 146–147). See Introduction, pp. 16–17, and Commentary to Canto 3.26–27 for the symbolic meaning of hares and rabbits.

**6.41–44**  *a wolf . . . with two cubs*: This is the third wolf in the poem (see text and Commentary to Canto 3.58). Of all the animals in the *Hunt,* only she and the serpent of Cantos 11–12 have offspring. The fact is allegorically significant, as explained in the Introduction. Again the almost gratuitous violence of the huntresses on the literal level can be explained allegorically by the *in malo* significance of the wolf as "diabolus" and "homines inhumani" (inhuman men) who seek to spill human blood: "lupus figuram gerit diaboli" (the wolf bears the figure of the Devil); he is Satan feeding on sinners (cf. the *Clavis Melitonis,* ed. J.-B. Pitra, pp. 62–64). For Peter Capuanus the animal is "cruentus, fraudulentus et violentus" (bloodthirsty, fraudulent and violent), *Clavis,* p. 63. Altogether seven wolves are killed in the hunt (in Cantos 4 and 6); the number probably is meant to reflect the seven "deadly" sins.

# Canto 7

**7.1**  *another company*: They are:
1. Fiore Curiale
2. Letizia Moromile

3. Lucia Porria
4. Fiore Canovara
5. Verdella di Berardo
6. Caterina di Bolino
7. La Lucciola
8. Giovannola Coppola

**7.9–12** *unicorn, far from cowardly. . . . no protection* ("*un leocorno fu, non miga vile. . . . non aveva riparo*"): Although the "non miga vile" sounds like a metrical filler or an afterthought, Boccaccio knew the unicorn's reputation for ferocity. In *Etym.* 12.2.13, Isidore informs us: "Tantae autem esse fortitudinis ut nulla venantium virtute capiatur" (He is of such great strength that he cannot be captured by any ingenuity of hunters). The *Tusco-Venetian Bestiary* says that it signifies "una maniera di zente fiera e crudele" (a kind of people who are fierce and cruel); p. 32. It is "one of the cruellest beasts that exists," according to *Il best. tosc.* (20, pp. 41–42) and, along with the *Tusco-Venetian Bestiary* (pp. 32–33), the Tuscan bestiarist sees in it a figure of the fierce Saul before his conversion as Saint Paul. Brunetto Latini (*Li Tresors* 1.188, p. 170) says he is "si aspres et si fiers" (so savage and fierce) that no man can bind him. Fournival tells us that "nule beste [est] si cruels a prendre" (*Il best. d'amours*, ed. C. Segre, p. 43).

The *unicornus*, conflated with and probably deriving from the rhinoceros, is mentioned in the Vulgate four times; a comparison of the Gallican (Vulgate) Psalter and Jerome's "Hebrew" Psalter shows that the former mentions the "unicorn" three times (Psalms 20:22; 28:6; 91:11), while the latter uses it only in the first instance. Boccaccio was probably most familiar with the Gallican version used in the liturgy; in any case, the unicorn was not considered a mythical beast in Boccaccio's time. See Robert Brown, Jr.'s modest study, *The Unicorn: A Mythological Investigation* (London: Longmans Green, 1881), usefully superseded by Odell Shepard, *The Lore of the Unicorn* (Boston: Houghton Mifflin; George Allen and Unwin, 1930; rprt. New York: Avenel Books for The Metropolitan Museum of Art, 1982), For the tradition of the unicorn in the visual arts, and particularly concerning the Cloister tapestries in New York, see John Williamson, *The Oak King, the Holly King, and the Unicorn* (New York: Harper and Row, 1986), esp. pp. 40–57; for the unicorn as a symbol of Christ, pp. 83–85.

Once again in the poem, the unicorn's *in malo* significance plays the initial major role, while the possible *in bono* senses remain concealed until the final conversion–metamorphosis of all the beasts. The compiler of the *Clavis Melitonis* (ed. J.-B. Pitra, p. 57) informs us: "Unicornes, superbi"

(Unicorns, the proud); he cites Saint Gregory the Great and the pseudo-Rabanus to the effect that the beast is also symbolic of the powers of the earth. From Psalm 74:4 (75:4 AV), the horn of the unicorn became the symbol of proud elation: "I said . . . to the sinners: Lift not up the horn" (Douay); cf. *Clavis,* pp. 57–58. Fiore Canovara allegorically humbles pride.

**7.17** *the other Fiore*: that is Fiore Canovara.

**7.22–23** *he never does harm to any maid*: According to one of the most popular items of bestiary lore, only a virgin can catch the unicorn, luring him with the irresistable power of her chastity. The *Bestiario toscano* (cited also by Branca), assures us, for example: "sua propria [del liocorno] natura si è che quando elli vede una pulcella virgene, sì li vene sì grande ulimento [ = vilimento] della virginitade, che se lli adormenta a piede e in questa maniera lo prende lo cacciatore e occide" (the unicorn's nature is such that when he sees a virgin maiden, he is so weakened by her virginity that he goes to sleep at her feet, and in this manner the hunter catches and kills him). See also "l'unicorno" in *Il bestiario moralizzato,* ed. M. Romano: "verginitate: / la quale tanto lo core li affina, / ke ve se adorme e la morte ne pate" (virginity, which so refines his heart that he lies down there and suffers death; pp. 745–746).

Isidore, and all the bestiaries, go on to describe as necessary the curious way in which the unicorn must be caught. See Fournival, *Le Bestiaire d'amour,* p. 23; *LBAR,* vv. 1252ff., p. 43; *Li Tresors* 1.188, p. 170. In the Physiologus tradition, the unicorn is a symbol of Christ, who descended into a virgin's womb. See *Physiologus,* ch. 36, ed. and trans. M. J. Curley, pp. 51, 86–87; ed. J. Carlill, pp. 199–200. The pseudo-Hugh of Saint Victor, *De bestiis,* "De monoceronte, sive unicorni animali," Book 2.6 (*PL* 177.59–60); *The Bestiary,* pp. 20–21. *Le Best. divin,* ed. C. Hippeau, pp. 126, 235 (French); "'monoceros' . . . vero unicornis" in the Latin version, ed. F. M. Mann, pp. 49–50. See also McCulloch, pp. 179–183.

The lore of the unicorn had widespread appeal. Massèra's commentary on *Hunt* 7 cites poetic examples from Chiaro Davanzati: "come lo lunicorno che si prende / A la donzella per verginitate" (as the unicorn who is caught by a maiden because of her virginity); and from *Il mare amoroso*: "et nolli fa male, / Sichome l'unichorno a la pulzella" (and he does not hurt her, like the unicorn with a maiden).

As with other animals, there was, however, a traditional *in malo* sense, one which led to a meaning *in bono*: conversion. The *Bestiario toscano* explains: "Questo unicornio significa una maniera di fieri homini e crudeli di questo mondo, che sono stati tanto fieri e tanto crudeli che non era homo ch'elli non conquidesseno co la loro impietudine, sì come fu sancto Paolo che perseguitava fieramente tucti li Christiani" (This unicorn signifies a kind of men who have been fierce and cruel, so that they are so fierce and cruel that there was no man they did not vanquish with their impiousness, just as was Saint Paul who persecuted all Christians fiercely; p. 41).

**7.52** *Verdella di Berardo*: The scene now shifts to the marshy area alongside the river brook, where the hunt continues with the ladies who are hawking.

## Canto 8

**8.5** *a huge crane*: The crane's ability in flight and its distant perception of its course and landing spots are mentioned in some sources: *The Bestiary*, pp. 110–112; Thomas of Cantimpré, *LNR* 5.55, "De gruibus" (ed. Boese, p. 203); *Li Tresors* I, 163, p. 148; McCulloch, pp. 105–106.

Just how cranes take flight is a question that Boccaccio turns to humorous account in quite a different context in the tale of Chichibio (*Dec.* 6.4).

**8.7** *gyrfalcon*: After dividing falcons into four groups, the Tuscan bestiarist (pp. 54–56) claims the fourth to be the noble kind, "and the first year they take ducks, and the second year they nobly strike cranes in the heart." The *Tusco-Venetian Bestiary* gives only three "schiatte," or species (pp. 56–57). Brunetto Latini says that the gyrfalcon exceeds all other falcons in size, and is "strong, vehement fierce and clever and happy in chasing and capturing" (*Li Tresors* 1.149, p. 140).

**8.10** *to the enameled green* ("*al verde smalto*"): Cf. *Inf.* 4.118; "sovra 'l verde smalto" (on the enameled green), and *Tes.* 9.1.8, "sovra il verde smalto."

**8.23–24** *he sank his strong talons into her back, descended*: The treatise by Frederick II describes in considerable detail how a falcon can capture a crane, one of its most typical targets.

**8.30** *falcon*: Thomas of Cantimpré (*LNR* 5.51, ed. Boese, pp. 201–202) has this to say: "Falco avis est nobilissima. Ad predam directa impetuosissime volat et est minus cauta in custodiam sui. Ideo cum ad predam dirigendus est falco, retardatur a domino suo nec ei avis capienda ostenditur, nisi prius aliquantulum elongetur, ut predam cum moderato impetu subsequatur. In captura vero ardee cum duo falcones relaxantur, socialiter volant. Unus summa petit, alius iuxta terram in imo volat, videlicet ut ille qui in summa contendit ardeam volantem impulsu precipitet, et ille qui in imo volat precipitatem accipiat" (The falcon is a most noble bird. It flies impetuously straight at its prey and does not take care to look after itself. Thus when the falcon is to be directed toward its prey, he must be held back by his master and the bird he is to catch should not be shown to him until it has first distanced itself a bit, so that he will pursue the prey with a moderate impetus. In the capture of a heron, when two falcons are released, they fly cooperatively. One seeks the height, the other flies low close to the ground, so that the one who is pursuing the heron on high can strike it down with a push as it flies, and the one who is flying low can catch it as it falls).

**8.45** *not in the marsh at all* ("*non miga in pantano*"): Here, in contrast to 7.9, the words *non miga* (not at all), attested in all the manuscripts, seem to be a metrical filler.

**8.55** *a paolin* ("*paolino*"): "name of a bird" (Massèra); "aquatic bird with a long beak" (Branca). Given the context, it is some form of shore or water fowl, but its precise identity is unclear. The name appears to derive from a diminutive of *pavone* (Lat. *pavo, pavonis* [peacock]), but that fact will not aid us in its identification: *pavo, pao* is a name applied in Romance languages (and cf. German *Pfau*) to other birds because of a supposed resemblance in attributes. For example, it refers to birds as different as the European crested plover or lapwing (*pavoncella* in Italian), a species of sandpiper, and later, in Spanish, to the turkey (*pavon real*). The word underwent a redevelopment through the assimilative pressure of the name "Pagolo" (Paul), becoming *pagolino*.

Cf. *Dec.* 8.7.8–9, where the widow Elena scornfully misjudges Rinieri as someone she can wrap around her finger, or "lead by the nose," as the Italian idiom has it: "se non io erro, io avrò preso un paolin per lo naso" (If I am not mistaken, I have got this bird by the beak). Branca (1976, p. 1432, n. 1) also mentions Sacchetti's use of the term, citing F. Ageno, "Nomignoli e personaggi immaginari, annedottici, proverbiali," *Lingua nostra* 19 (1958), pp. 73–77, esp. p. 73.

**8.58** *they knew how to do it so wisely*: Cf. above 2.58, "so they hunted wisely."

## Canto 9

**9.1–2** *While I went gazing through the green fronds with my eyes on the hunt* ("*Mentre con gli occhi fra le verdi fronde / mirando giva la caccia*"): The narrator in the forest, amazed as more huntresses arrive, has much in common with Dante in Eden as he witnesses the approaching procession of the church and Beatrice. Cf. *Purg.* 29.31, "Mentr' io m'andava tra tante primizie" (While I went on among so many first-fruits); 29.35, "sotto i verdi rami" (under the green boughs); 29.64–65, "Genti vid'io allor, come a lor duci, / venire appresso" (Then I saw people, following as after their leaders).

See also *Purg.* 23.1–2, "Mentre che li occhi per la fronda verde / ficcava ïo" (while I was peering thus intently through the green foliage). Compare below, *Hunt* 9.19–20, "when I fixed my gaze more keenly upon them" (poi che l'occhio più agutamente / ficcai fra loro).

**9.22** *that amorous troop* ("*quell'amorosa schiera*"): Cf. *Inf.* 5.85, "la schiera ov'è Dido" (the troop where Dido is).

**9.26–27** *called after the others*: The others are the huntresses summoned in Canto 1.

**9.33** *the sunny bank* ("*la chiara riva*"): Cf. *Tes.* 5.78, "alla chiara rivera."

**9.38ff.** These are the ladies in the first group of the second installment, whose hunt will take them toward the east:

1. Marella Caracciola
2. Cecca Fagiana
3. Zizzola Fagiana
4. Vannella Bolcana
5. Lariella Caracciola
6. Serella Brancazza
7. Peronella d'Arco

**9.39** *faces fair with amorous fire* ("*belle nel viso d'amoroso foco*"): an attribute similar to the Mystery Lady's epithet. See above, 4.12: "whose face seems always to burn with love."

**9.42** *of countenance humble and gentle* ("*nello aspetto umile e piano*"): "typical pairing of adjectives in Boccaccio" (Branca). Cf. *Inf.* 2.56, "soave e piana." The terminology is, of course, stilnovistic.

**9.44** *I believe* ("*al parer mio*"): Literally, "so it seemed to me." The formula is from the *cantari* tradition (Branca). Variants, all expressing the idea "if I am not mistaken," occur throughout the poem (cf. 1.16: "and unless my ears deceived me—and I think they did not"; 10.19: "if my memory errs not").

**9.54ff.** Here, proceeding southward, is the second group of ladies in the second phase of the hunt:

1. Iacopa Aldimaresca
2. Marella Passerella
3. Gostanza Galeota
4. Mariella Piscicella
5. Dalfina di Barasso
6. Vannella de' Brancazzi

## Canto 10

**10.9ff.** The third and westward group in the second part is listed:
1. Zizzola Faccipecora
2. Tuccella Serisale
3. Biancola Carafa
4. Caterina Carafa
5. Giacopella Embriaca
6. Tanzella dell'Acerra

**10.19** *if my memory errs not* ("*se la mia memoria non erra*"): Cf. *Inf.* 2.6, "la mente che non erra." Branca points to *Purg.* 20.147: "se la memoria mia in ciò non erra" (if my memory err not in this).

**10.20ff.** *stayed by choice in the lowlands*: Her party will hunt and fish at the stream on the plain. Fourth in the second half of the *Hunt,* and presumably the northern party, its members are:
1. Catrina Sighinolfi
2. Covella d'Anna
3. Mitola Caracciola
4. Berita Galeota
5. Zizzola d'Alagna
6. Covella d'Arco

**10.28** *Marella*: Caracciola.

**10.29** *chasing hard after a beaver*: The beaver is a valley dweller familiar in the bestiaries. It is worth noting that—but quite obvious why, given the nature of his allegory—Boccaccio omits the famous classical and medieval lore surrounding the beaver here: when pursued, the legendary *castor* castrates itself, obligingly casting its "medicinal" testicles to the hunter and dogs in order to escape (Pliny, *NH* 8.47; Isidore, *Etym.* 12.2.21). Thereafter, it turns supine to demonstrate its lack to later hunters; cf. Aelian, *On Animals* 6.34; *Physiologus,* ed. and trans. M. J. Curley, p. 52; *Le Best. divin,* ed. C. Hippeau, pp. 129–231, 238–241 (French); ed. M. F. Mann, pp. 50–51 (Latin). Philippe de Thaon, pp. 42–44. *Il best. tosc.,* pp. 52–53; the *Tusco-Venetian Bestiary,* pp. 51–52; "De castoris natura," in the pseudo-Hugh of Saint Victor *De Bestiis* II, 11 (*PL* 177.61–62); *The Bestiary,* pp. 28–29. *Li Tresors* 1.181, p. 159. McCulloch, p. 95. In Fournival's *Bestiaire d'amour,* p. 31, and in the *LBAR,* vv. 1937ff., pp. 64–65, the beaver's testicles become the lady's heart, for which the lover pursues her! Perhaps, since these beasts are men conquered by their ladyloves, Boccaccio intends his silence here to be an unspoken joke.

**10.30** *where beavers roam*: ("*giron*"). Only the Wellesley manuscript (WE) reads *giro* (I wander) at this point; the other five manuscripts read *giron* or *girō* (the tilde over the *o* indicating an abbreviated *n* [= they roam]). The verb is predicated of the beavers, which inhabit, "roam," mountain valleys where they make their lodges in the water (cf. Thomas of Cantimpré, *LNR* 4.14: "domum suam super aquas faciens," ed. Boese, p. 117). The former stag tells the events of his tale in retrospect; at the point of narration he has returned to being a man; he, therefore, is *not* still wandering in a valley of the hunt, although, within the fiction, he can make "authorial" decisions in the present tense such as that of not naming his lady ("né nomo lei" [nor do I name her], 1.53).

This interpretation also agrees with Boccaccio's strategy of choosing one traditional attribute or habit (*natura*) to characterize each of the animals in the *Hunt*.

**10.42–48** *an elephant. . . . nor was there any way for it to stand up*: The elephant's weakness is its "unjointed" legs. Theobaldus's *Physiologus*, for example, teaches: "It does not have the power to rise, because it never bends its legs: this is the mother's fear—that by some accident she may fall down. When it wishes to rest, or to refresh itself with sleep, it leans on a small trunk of a tree: this the hunter marks and cuts and hides with a covering, and he sits and watches in secret until the elephant comes again to rest. When the elephant comes to the shade of the tree, unsuspecting, as before, it leans against it and falls down as the tree falls. If no man is nearby it groans and then finally bellows" (ed. P. T. Eden, pp. 64–67; see also *Physiologus,* ed. and trans. M. J. Curley, pp. 29–32). Judging from Marella's words, the ladies must get their elephant by taking advantage of just such an arboreal trap, one that had been prepared by rival male hunters. Cf. also *Mare amoroso*: "E non mi credo mai poter levare / Più chon può lo leofante ch'è chaduto, / Che non si può levar s'altri nol leva" (And I do not believe I shall ever be able to get up any more than the elephant who has fallen, who cannot get up unless someone helps him [Italian text modified vv. 59–62]; ed. Vuolo, pp. 24–25, 120–121).

The extraordinary legend of the elephant's jointless legs obviously predates Aristotle's disagreement on the matter (*HA* 2.1 [498a]; 9.46 [630b]), and the cutting down of trees to deceive it as it rests appears in all the bestiaries. See *Physiologus,* ch. 20, ed. and trans. M. J. Curley, pp. 30–31; ed. J. Carlill, p. 202; *The Bestiary,* pp. 26–27; *Il best. tosc.,* pp. 62–63; the *Tusco-Venetian Bestiary* ("lo lionfante"), pp. 60–61. Thomas of Cantimpré, *LNR* 4.33.44–164; Philippe de Thaon, pp. 53–54. *LBAR,* vv. 1686ff., p. 57; *Li Tresors* 1.187, pp. 164–165. Saint Ambrose mentions the legend as fact in his *Hexameron* 5.32. Julius Caesar, in the *Gallic Wars* 6.27, and Pliny, *NH* 8.15, describe the same method of capture for the elk. See also Aelian, *HA* 8:17 (who mentions the elephant's extraordinary gift of temperance); Strabo 16.4.10 [772]; Diodorus Siculus 3.27; Plutarch *De sollert. an.* 977D; *Physiologus,* ch. 20, ed. and trans. M. J. Curley, p. 79; *Best. divin.,* ed. M. F. Mann (Latin), p. 67; ed. C. Hippeau, pp. 181–182, 291–295 (French). McCulloch gives a full account of entries in Latin and French bestiaries, pp. 115–119. See also George Claridge Druce, "The Elephant in Medieval Legend and Art," *Archeological Journal* 76 (1919), pp. 1–73.

The amusing variants in the spelling of "elephant" in the manuscripts are worth noting: L: *elefante*; F: *olifante*; FR: *leofante*; FR¹: *olifante*; FR²: *lionfante*; and WE: *oliofante*.

Along with its symbolic meaning of chastity, incorruptibility, and fortitude, the elephant also had its *in malo* interpretation: the *Clavis Melitonis* informs us: "elephas, immanis peccator" (the elephant, an immense sinner)! See ed. J.-B. Pitra, pp. 59–60.

**10.54** *dark paths ("le vie oscure")*: A calque on Dante, *Inf.* 1.1–3.

## Canto 11

**11.1** *Crowned with fronds ("Di frondi coronata")*: Cf. *Purg.* 29.93, "coronati ciascun di verde fronda" (each crowned with green leaves). The formula returns in *Am. vis.* 43.11, "d'erbe e di frondi tutte coronate" (all crowned with leaves and grass).

**11.3** *a picture of charming beauty ("di bellezza piacevole dipinta")*: Cf. *Par.* 29.7, "col volto di riso dipinto" (her face illumined with a smile). Marella foreshadows the Amazon princess Emilia, described as a huntress in *Tes.* 5.79: "Ell'era sopra d'un bel pallafreno / co' can dintorno, e un corno dallato / avea e dalla man contraria al freno, / dietro alle spalle, un arco avea legato / e un turcasso di saette pieno, / che era d'oro tratto lavorato; / e ghirlandetta di frondi novelle / copriva le sue treccie bionde e belle" (She was on a fine palfrey, with dogs around her, and she had a horn at her side, and over her shoulder, opposite the hand on the rein, she had tied a bow and an arrow-filled quiver worked in beaten gold, and a chaplet of new fronds covered her tresses blond and fair).

**11.5** *Marella*: Caracciolo.

**11.9–10** *with which Biancifiore and Catella already had hauled in their stags*: See 3.46–50. Catella is Caterina Fellapane.

**11.30** *felt reassured*: That the stag-narrator feels oddly reassured here, instead of threatened by the hounds—a purposeful reversal of the Actaeon myth (*Met.* 3.198ff.)—as he does also by the appearance of the new huntresses in Canto 9.21, is one of the ruptures in the literal sense that point to the allegorical meaning of the poem.

**11.57** *the tail of a serpent*: The serpent's first appearance in the eleventh canto is no accident. The number eleven, like the serpent, symbolized sin. Dante underlines that equation in *Inf.* 11, reserved for Virgil's exposition on the categories of sin in Hell. The tradition originates in Augustine, *City of God* 15.20. See Introduction, and Victoria Kirkham, "Eleven is for Evil. Measured Trespass in Dante's *Commedia*," *Allegorica* 10 (1989), pp. 27–50.

## Canto 12

**12.15** *we can certainly kill it safely* ("*ben lo potremo uccider salvamente*"): The word *salvamente* carries a double connotation. On the one hand, it implies "with safety, security," that is, with no risk of physical harm, which is its literal meaning here. On the other hand, it may be "salvation" in a Christian sense. The latter is probably implied by Boccaccio in this passage, given the serpent's powerful association with the Fall, hence damnation. Cf. Dante's bivalent use of *salute* (greeting, or salvation) in the *Vita nuova*.

**12.22** *put fiery coals in this hole* ("*mettiamo in questa buca acceso foco*"): Literally, "let us put kindled fire in this hole." For the biblical and allegorical importance of the wording, "acceso foco," see Introduction, pp. 28–30. The creature's habitat is not only zoologically but also etymologically correct: Isidore tells us (*Etym.* 12.4.3) that "the serpent takes its name from the fact that it crawls [*serpit*] through hidden places and not along open paths." In the Physiologus tradition, the serpent, in old age, uses narrow cracks in the rocks to slough its skin and renew itself after a forty-day fast (ch. 13, ed. and trans. M. J. Curley, pp. xxiii–xxiv, 16; ed. J. Carlill, pp. 233–234). *Li Tresors* 1.137, pp. 132–133; McCulloch, pp. 170–171.

**12.27** *aggiate*: We have preferred the reading of all six manuscripts, *aggiate*, rather than the *abbiate* of printed versions; cf. text of Canto 16.45.

**12.30** *the fierce plague* ("*la fiera peste*"): The term, symbolic in its semantics, as is *salvamente* (safely, with salvation), emphasizes the snake's generic association with evil and destruction. The word may have been suggested initially by Virgil's *Georgics* 3.419, where fumigation of animal stalls is advised to rid them of snakes, especially the adder, the "sore plague" (*pestis acerba*) of cattle.

**12.41–42** *she then cut off its head*: Why the serpent should have been decapitated can be accounted for by the *Physiologus* family of bestiaries, where we learn that a snake's head is its vulnerable part: "When a man approaches seeking to kill him, the serpent surrenders his entire body to the blows but protects its head" (ed. and trans. M. J. Curley, p. 19; cf. ed. J. Carlill, pp. 233–234). (Amusingly, the Tuscan bestiarist gets it wrong: "Lo serpente difende lo suo corpo col suo cozzo" [The serpent defends its body with its head], *Il best. tosc.*, p. 66.) The tradition probably arose from, or was strengthened by, the curse on the snake in Genesis 3, that woman after the Fall "shall crush [its] head."

**12.45** *offspring* ("*figliuoi*"): Allegorically, the serpent is the symbol par excellence of sin and recalls the origin of sin through the Fall in Genesis 3 (cf. *The Bestiary*, p. 167, where it is allied to pride and the Devil). Notably, only the serpent and the wolf have offspring in the poem. In theological metaphor, pride and avarice, the beginning and the root of all sin, were said to have "offspring," the "filiae superbiae" and "filiae avaritiae," the vices which spring from them. Cf. Saint Gregory, *Moralia* 31, pp. 88–89; *Morals,* vol. 3, p. 490; Saint Thomas Aquinas, *ST* II-II, qu. 118, art. 8. See Introduction p. 29 for the interrelation, or "filiation," of sins in theology.

**12.54** *graceful, fair, gay, and vigorous*: A string of adjectives in the style of the *cantari*. Cf. also above, 12.42, "vigorous and bold" (Branca).

**12.57** *leopard* ("*leopardo*"): For Pliny (*NH* 8.42), the leopard was an inferior hybrid, born of a cross between a lioness and a pard; he is cited by Isidore (*Etym.* 12.2.11); by Vincent of Beauvais (*Spec. nat.* 20.102); and by Bartholomaeus Anglicus (ed. R. Steele), pp. 162–163. See also McCulloch, pp. 150–151. In Thomas of Cantimpré (*LNR* 4.86, p. 159), the leopard signifies the heretic of spotted, stained dogma. See above for the *lonza* (leopardess, or female pard), 4.28.

## Canto 13

**13.11–12** *as pleasing as any who were with her* ("*tanto piacente quanto alcun'altra che fosse con lei*"): We have preferred the reading "tanto piacente" that is attested in all six manuscripts, not "tant'è piacente" of printed versions.

**13.14** *a fallow deer on the run before her* ("*un daino*"): "The fallow deer [damnula] is so named," says Isidore, "because it flees from your hand," "de manu effugiat" (*Etym.* 12.1.22). Since it engenders through its ears and because it can bring life to its stillborn fawns, the *Tusco-Venetian Bestiary* tells us that it represents "the good preacher" (p. 26). Even with this tiny and timid creature, however, the *in malo* interpretation seems to be uppermost. Its very fleeing tells "Rabanus," in the *Allegoriae in Sacram Scripturam* (*PL* 112.906), that the "damula" is "diabolus, ut in Isaia [13:14]:

'Quasi damula fugiens'" (the devil, as in Isaiah [13.14], "fleeing like a fallow deer"; [in the Douay version "as a doe fleeing away"]), and the "Anonymus Clarevallensis" concurs: "Damula, diabolus.—Contemtor mundi" (The Devil, contemner of the world). Both are cited by the compiler of the *Clavis Melitonis* (ed. J.-B. Pitra, p. 72). Once again, Boccaccio centers on the one "nature" of this beast that he knows is interpretated as vice in patristics.

**13.29–30** *so bright that to behold them they seemed two little flames* ("*tanto relucenti / che a veder parean due fiammette*"): This is a "characterization typical in Boccaccio's lyrics" (Branca). See Boccaccio's *Rime* 97: "Sovra li fior vermigli e' capei d'oro / veder mi parve un foco alla Fiammetta" (Upon the vermilion flowers and golden hair, I thought I saw a fire on Fiammetta); *Filoc.* 4.43.10–11; "Io son del terzo ciel cosa gentile. . . . E vo di fronda in fronda a mio diletto, / intorniando gli aurei crini, me di me accendendo: / e 'n questa mia fiammetta con effetto mostro la forza de' dardi divini" (I am a gentle creature from the third heaven. . . . And I go from branch to branch in my delight, circling her golden tresses, kindling myself with myself, and in this little flame of mine I effectively show the force of the divine darts); *Am. vis.* 15.61–63: "In fronte a cui serena e spaziosa / due begli occhi lucean, sì che fiammetta / parea ciascuno d'amor luminosa" (In her serene, wide forehead shone / two lovely eyes; each one seemed / a little flame of luminous love).

**13.34** *these ladies went off*: we read "*andandosi*" not "*andando sì.*" The "si" clitic, or so-called pleonastic *si*—a misnomer—serves to isolate and separate the subject (cf. "andarsene"). Compare Dante, *Inf.* 7.94, on Fortune's indifference to man's revilings, "ella s'è beata e ciò non ode" (she is off there blessed and hears not).

**13.38** *a panther*: Physiologus bestiaries understand the panther as Christ, for after the beast has eaten, three days later he arises from sleep with such a sweet fragrance in his mouth that he attracts all other animals, except the serpent. "Our Lord Jesus Christ who is the true panther draws to Himself all humankind . . . through His Incarnation" (*Physiologus,* ch. 30, ed. and trans. M. J. Curley, pp. 43, 82–83; *Le Best. divin,* ed. C. Hippeau, pp. 145–148, 256–260 [French]; ed. M. F. Mann, pp. 56–57 [Latin]). Cf. *Il best. tosc.*, pp. 42–43, where the panther represents the persuasive preacher who inwardly digests the mystery of Christ's divinity. The imagery is based on Hosea 5:14: "I have become a panther to Ephraim, and like a lion to the house of Judah."

That the panther of the *Hunt* is killed by three ladies garlanded with red roses seems to reflect the tradition of allegorical depictions of Christ put to death by the virtues (see Hanns Swarzenski, *Die lateinischen illuminierten Handschriften des XIII. Jahrhunderts in den Ländern an Rhein, Main und Donau* [Berlin: Deutscher Verein für Kunstwissenschaft, 1936]). Cf. Alanus de Insulis: "In passione, inquam, fuit misericordia, quae filium Dei . . . affixit patibulo" (In the Passion, I say, there was mercy, which affixed the son of God to the cross) in *Sermo II in S. Croce, PL* 210.224, cited by Adolf Katzenellenbogen, *Allegories of the Virtues and Vices in Medieval Art from Early Christian Times to the Thirteenth Century* (London: The Warburg Institute, The University of London, 1939; rprt. New York: W. W. Norton, 1964), pp. 38–39.

For the detail of the ladies' red head wreaths (they are "engarlanded with little garlands of red roses") Boccaccio seems to have conflated two scenes from the Procession of the Church in *Purg.* 29: first, the nymphs figuring the virtues, dressed in royal purple to signify that they are not merely acquired political virtues but the God-given infused virtues of Christianity (*Purg.* 29.131), and second, the seven New Testament writers with garlands of roses on their heads (*Purg.* 29.147–148).

**13.42** *the agile beast* ("*la fiera snella*"): Cf. *Inf.* 12.76, where the adjective and noun are applied to the centaurs in Hell: "Noi ci appressammo a quelle fiere isnelle" (We drew near to those fleet beasts).

**13.53–54** *Giacopella . . . help* ("*per atare / Iacopella*"): That is, Giacopella Embriaca. For variants of her name see the Glossary of the Huntresses, below.

**13.56** *raging bull* ("*un furioso toro*"): Although the bull is the familiar victim in a Spanish *corrida*, to find him as the quarry of a hunt may seem odd at first; again, however, the bestiary tradition and the mythical-allegorical senses can quicken our understanding. The bull's attributes are reported in the entry "De juvenco et tauro" in the pseudo-Hugh of Saint Victor's *De bestiis*, III (*PL* 177.89–90; *The Bestiary*, pp. 76–77): the "Indicus taurus" (Indian bull) is said to be of terrible ferocity, totally losing its mind if anyone tries to capture it. For Dante the bull was a symbol of violence and lust; in the *Commedia, Inf.* 12.12ff., it appears in its ancient hybrid mutation as the Minotaur embodying senseless rage: "Qual è quel toro che si slaccia . . . mentre ch'e' 'nfuria" (As a bull that breaks loose . . . while he is in fury). In *Purg.* 26.41–42, heterosexual penitents remind their homosexual ledgemates of that hybrid beasts' parentage, "Ne la vacca entra Pasife, / perché 'l torello a sua lussuria corra" (Pasiphaë enters the cow, that the bull may hasten to her lust). Commenting on *Inf.* 12 in the *Esposizioni* 12.2.7, Boccaccio allegorizes Pasiphaë's love for the bull as the human soul in which reason failed to control concupiscible and irascible appetites: "Ne' quali appetiti, se noi passiamo i termini della ragione, pecchiamo per incontinenzia . . . per ciò che, poi, qualunque s'è, l'uno de' due appetiti ha tratto il freno di mano alla ragione, non essendo chi ponga modo agli stimoli, si lascia l'anima transportare ne' disideri bestiali" (In these appetites, if we go beyond the boundaries of reason, we sin by incontinence . . . because then, whichever appetite it was that pulled the bridle out of reason's hand, since there is no one to impose measure on the goadings, we let our soul be carried away by bestial desires).

## Canto 14

**14.5–6** *"Get him, Pezzuolo, good dog! Get him Dragone! Get him, Graffiacani!"*: The dogs, distributed by Diana (2.37), move side by side with their mistresses throughout the hunt. They are loyal companions, essential for success, as the poet repeatedly reminds us in, for example, 3.26, "with their dogs following intent on their task"; 3.31, "'Sic!' each cried, as she loosed her dogs"; 3.54–55, "circling the mountain with her panting dogs"; 4.35–36, "'Get him! Get him!' after a white stag"; 4.49–51, "Zizzola . . . recalled the dogs, sounding a horn until she could count them all"; 5.32, "the second bear, brought low by the dogs"; 6.6, "they and their dogs pressed the attack"; 7.10, "The dogs daringly pursued it"; 9.13; "And the sound of the horns and baying of the dogs"; 12.35–36, "and the dogs bit into it—many of those around it met death at its fangs."

This is the only passage in which some are named. They are the trio Pezzuolo (a diminuitive of *pezzo*: bit), Dragone (dragon), and Graffiacani (dogscratcher). The last is the name of one of Dante's Malebranche devils, doggish predators—among them a "Cagnazzo," or "Bad Dog"—whom their chief, Malacoda (*Inf.* 21.118–123), marshals in a manner to which Boccaccio amusingly alludes when he has Tanzella sic her dogs on the bull: "'Tra'ti avante, Alichino, e Calcabrina,' / cominciò elli a dire, 'e tu, Cagnazzo; / e Barbariccia guidi la decina. / Libicocco vegn' oltre e Draghignazzo, / Cirïatto sannuto, e Graffiacane, / e Farfarello, e Rubicante pazzo'" ("Come forward, Alichino and Calcabrina," he began to say, "and you, Cagnazzo; and let Barbariccia lead the ten. Let Libicocco come too, and Draghignazzo, and tusked Ciriatto, and Graffiacane and Farfarello and crazy Rubicante"). Cf. *Inf.* 22.34.

Classical precedent for naming the hounds came to Boccaccio from Ovid's hunts. See *Met.* 3.206ff.: "But while he [Actaeon] stands perplexed he sees his hounds. And first come Melampus and keen-scented Ichnobates, baying loud on the trail—Ichnobates a Cretan dog, Melampus a Spartan; then others come rushing on swifter than the wind: Pamphagus, Dorceus, and Oribasus, Arcadians all; staunch Nebrophonus, fierce Theron and Laelaps." Boccaccio settles for a more modest pack than the thirty-three with noble Greek bloodlines that come baying after Cadmus's grandson.

The dogs in *Diana's Hunt,* such staunch helpmates, also descend from the bestiaries, where they are not only praised for their faithfulness, but, especially, for their wisdom. See J. L. Schrader, "A Medieval Bestiary," *The Metropolitan Museum of Art Bulletin* 44, no. 1 (Summer, 1986), p. 26: "No animal is more sagacious than CANIS the Dog: for he has more perception than other animals, for he alone recognizes his own name. He esteems his master highly. . . . When a dog comes across the track of a hare or a stag, and reaches the branching of the trail, or the criss-cross of the trail because it has split into more parts, then the dog puzzles silently with himself, seeking along the beginnings of each different track. He shows his sagacity in following the scent, as if enunciating a syllogism. By rejecting error, the dog finds truth. . . . Its way of life is reported to be perfectly temperate."

**14.7-8** *when she had set the baying pack upon him* ("*E poi che adosso l'abbaiante stuolo / gli ebbe drizzato*"): We have preferred the *lectio difficilior* "adosso" (upon him), although the "α" manuscripts read "adesso" (now, immediately)—the latter reading makes less logical and temporal sense after "poi che." Branca, in support of reading "adesso," points to *Filostrato* 7.51 and *Teseida* 8.83, cases where "adesso" clearly means "immediately."

**14.18** *never able to land him a blow*: Apart from the obvious echoes of Dante's Minotaur (*Inf.* 12), bullocks "can resist every weapon by the thickness of their hides" (pseudo-Hugh of Saint Victor, *De bestiis* [*PL* 177.89]; see also *The Bestiary*, p. 77). Thomas of Cantimpré cites Aristotle to the effect that the head and neck of the bull are its strongest parts (*LNR* 4.98, p. 164). Indeed, the neck is the traditional target of the picador in wearing down the bull in Spanish bullfights. The aquatic setting in which the bull in the *Hunt* makes his appearance might bear a relation to descriptions of the ferocious Indian bulls that sleep in rivers—water buffalo—such as are recorded, for example, in the pseudo-Hugh of Saint Victor's *De bestiis* ("bubali atrocissimi" [*PL* 177.90]) and in Brunetto Latini's *Tresors* (1.177, pp. 156–157); cf. Isidore, *Etym.* 12.35 and the *Clavis Melitonis,* ed. J.-B. Pitra, p. 18. See also F. McCulloch, pp. 98–99. Boccaccio's bull is a strange, mythical agglommerate.

The compiler of the *Clavis* cites many identifications of the bull with vices: for the Anonymus Dominicanus: "Tauri sunt animal luxuriosum" (Bulls are lustful animals). The bull's horns and neck, emphasized in the poem, both signify pride (ed. J.-B. Pitra, pp. 18, 22–23): it is allegorically fitting, therefore, that the bull would be slain precisely by a spear hurled into his upper neck, just behind his horns.

**14.37–38** *they saw a porcupine, with its sharp quills clattering together* ("*un istrice*"): The detail is not from direct observation, but from a reading of Isidore's *Etymologiae*, 12.2.35: "Histrix animal in Africa erinacii simile, vocatum ab stridore spinarum" (The porcupine is an African animal similar to the hedgehog, named for the rattling of its spines). When Tuccella fires an arrow to kill the porcupine, Boccaccio perhaps has in mind a reversal of the legend, transmitted by Pliny (*NH* 8.53) through Isidore and the bestiaries, that the porcupine could shoot its quills. In his entry, "De istrice, qui et porcus spinosus dicitur," Thomas of Cantimpré (*LNR* 4.52, p. 138) records that, because the porcupine is a hidden, secretive animal, it symbolizes the heretic, while its spines symbolize the heretic's barbed arguments. Medieval books on animal lore often confuse porcupines with the hedgehog and sea urchin. See Commentary to Canto 5.55–58 above.

**14.54–56** *a hydra . . . bumped into her trap* ("*idra . . . / incappò in quella*"): Although the hydra regularly appears in bestiaries, particularly in the Physiologus family, Boccaccio seems to use no element of its description, except its river habitat. Isidore defines the name: "Hydros aquatilis serpens" (The hydra is an aquatic serpent); Hercules' many-headed hydra lived in the Lernaean swamps (*Etym.* 12.4.22–23). Normally in bestiaries, the hydra is described as the enemy of the Nile crocodile, into whose mouth it leaps and whose viscera it tears as it comes forth. *Physiologus* allegorizes this as Christ harrowing the bowels of Hell. See commentary on "Niluus," *Physiologus*, ed. and trans. M. J. Curley, pp. 53–54. Cf. F. McCulloch, pp. 129–130; pseudo-Hugh of Saint Victor, *De bestiis*, Book 2.7 (*PL* 177.60); *The Bestiary*, p. 179; *Le Best. divin*, ed. C. Hippeau, pp. 134–137, 244–246 (French); ed. M. F. Mann, pp. 52–53 (Latin); Fournival, *Le Bestiaire d'amour*, p. 36.

Branca notes the similarity between this episode and other of Boccaccio's fishing scenes, for example, *Dec.* 6, Concl.; *Dec.* 10.6.

"In quella," of verse 56, must refer to *fune* or to the idea of *trappola* implicit in the text. *Quella* and *costei* are pronouns indicating two different physical locations in Tuscan usage (cf. the difference in sense of *là* and *costà*).

## Canto 15

**15.8** *two white swans*: The swan was lauded for its musical talent (cf. Aelian, *On animals* 2.32). Isidore writes: "Cygnus a 'canendo' est appellatus, eo quod carminis dulcedinem modulatis vocibus fundit. . . .

Ferunt in Yperboreis partibus precinentibus cytharoedis olores plurimos advvolare apteque admodum concinere" (It is called swan from the word "to sing" because it produces the sweetness of its song with harmonious sounds. . . . They say that in northern regions, when the lyre players have started to play, a great number of swans fly up and sing along in strict measure; *Etym.* 12.7.18–19). Thomas of Cantimpré cites the same text, *LNR* 5.26, p. 188, as does pseudo-Hugh of Saint Victor, *De bestiis* (*PL* 177.51; *The Bestiary,* p. 119). Cf. *Li Tresors* 1.161, p. 147, where instead of lute, lyre, or zither the instrument is a harp, as it also is in the French bestiaries of Pierre de Beauvais (3.233) and Richard de Fournival (*Le Bestiaire d'Amour,* p. 7, "Li cisnes"; ed. C. Segre, p. 13): "Qu il est .1. païs là où li cisne chantent si bien et si volontiers que qant on harpe devant aus il s'acordent à la harpe" (There is a country where the swans sing so well and so willingly that when the harp is played in their presence, they sing in tune to the harp). The detail suggests that Boccaccio was using some form of a French animal encyclopedia. McCulloch errs in saying that the version of Pierre de Beauvais was the only French bestiary to include the swan (p. 176). *Il best. toscano* (p. 27) also knows about the proper instrument for swan songs: "Lo cecino . . . quando homo li sona uno stormento che si chiama arpa, sì s'accorda con esso in cantare" (The swan . . . when a person plays an instrument called the harp, sings in harmony with it).

This bird was not without a negative symbolism. The pseudo-Rabanus Maurus's *Allegoriae in Sacram Scripturam* defines the swan as a symbol of pride (*PL* 112.894).

**15.15** *without pausing* ("*sanza dimoro*"): Rhyme formula frequent in the *cantari* and often repeated in the *Hunt*—for example, 14.24, 16.18 (Branca).

**15.19** *goshawk* ("*astore*"): "Low-flying bird of prey used especially for hunting partridge, quail, and pheasant" (Branca).

Isidore tells us, "the hawk [*accipiter*] is a bird more endowed with spirit than talons, bearing greater worth in a smaller body. It takes its name from *accipiendo,* that is to say, from 'capturing.' It is avid in capturing other birds, for this it is called 'capturer' [*accipiter*], that is, 'raptor' [*raptor*]" (*Etym.* 12.7.55). Brunetto Latini also describes the greater *ostour* as *hardis* (brave) and tells us that it delights mightily in taking other birds (*Li Tresors* 1.149, p. 137). See F. McCulloch, pp. 123–124.

**15.24** *a naker*: The word comes from an Arabic root that can be expanded to mean either "trumpet" or "kettledrum." Cf. Chaucer's *Knight's Tale,* 2511–2512: "Pypes, trompes, nakers, clariounes, / That in the bataille blowen bloody sounes." Although the context suggests the former meaning, standard commentary on Chaucer (ed. F. N. Robinson) opts for the latter, noting that in English, "*Naker* always seems to mean a drum." The term *naccaro* (or *nacchero*) in the *Hunt* most surely means "drum," a good noisemaker for frightening ducks from the water; indeed, Marti glosses it, "In olden times it was a sort of drum."

Classical legends blame the trumpet for disfiguring the face, causing not only the wise Minerva to spurn wind instruments, but even the vain Alcibiades as well. About two hundred years later in his advice to the lady of the court, Baldassare Castiglione puts the topos to good use in *Il Cortegiano* (*Book of the Courtier*). Would not Diana's classicizing companions here be as circumspect?

Later use of the same word by Boccaccio is suggestive of both explosive bangs and glissandos puffed by brass players. It occurs in *Dec.* 8.9.75, where the painter Bruno punningly announces Master Simone's forthcoming tryst with a countess resident in "Laterino" (translatable, perhaps, as "Latrineland"), that is, the doctor's fall into a cesspit. So Bruno praises the scatological target as "una troppo gran donna, e poche case ha per lo mondo nelle quali ella non abbia alcuna giurisdizione, e non che altri, ma i frati minori a suon di nacchere le rendon tributo" (a very great lady and there are few houses in the world wherein she has not some jurisdiction. To say nothing of others, the Minor Friars themselves render her tribute, to the sound of kettledrums). But, perhaps, rather than the bawdy suggestion of repeated sexual percussion, Boccaccio might have intended the sound of brass in his reference to the friars' noisy habits—if he had in mind Dante's musical demon, Malacoda, in *Inf.* 21.139: "ed elli avea del cul fatto trombetta" (and he had made a trumpet of his arse).

See also Sacchetti, *Rime* 159.187, for *nacchere* (Branca).

**15.38** *an ostrich*: Tradition attests that the ostrich can outpace a horse (Thomas of Cantimpré, *LNR* 5.90, pp. 226–227). For the bestiary ostrich, see also Isidore, *Etym.* 12.7.20; *Physiologus*, ch. 42, ed. and trans. M. J. Curley, pp. 54–55; *Le Best. divin*, ed. C. Hippeau, pp. 163–169, 272–274; *Il best. tosc.* 38, pp. 59–60; the *Tusco-Venetian Bestiary*, pp. 57–58; J. Carlill, pp. 220–222; *The Bestiary*, pp. 121–122; *Li Tresors*, 1.172, p. 153. For the negative allegorical-symbolic meanings of the ostrich in patristics, and the reason for Covella d'Anna's otherwise inexplicably vehement pursuit, see Introduction, pp. 15–16, above.

# Canto 16

**16.1–3** *but the sun was already rising to midday*: Cf. *Filoc.* 4.17: "Era già Appollo col carro della luce salito al meridiano cerchio e quasi con diritto occhio riguardava la rivestita terra, quando le donne e' giovani . . . diversi diletti per diverse schiere prendevano, fuggendo il caldo aere che li dilicati corpi offendeva" (Already Apollo had risen with his chariot of light to the meridian sphere, and with virtually perpendicular gaze viewed the restored earth, when the ladies and youths . . . [chose] pleasant shades and various delights in different groups, fleeing the hot air that offended their delicate bodies). Branca notes similar moments in *Ameto* 17.4–5; *Dec.* Intro. 106–110.

**16.13–14** *the lofty gap of the low-lying mountain* ("*sull'eccelsa cruna / del monticello*"): Cf. *Purg.* 10.16: "quella cruna" (that needle's eye). The youthful Boccaccio seems not to find it amiss that a *monticello* (mountainlet) could have a towering peak.

**16.26** *Zizzola d'Anna*: She is the sixtieth, and last, of the huntresses to join the company; entering at line 26, she is the twenty-sixth of the second party. For her numerical significance to the structure, see the Introduction, pp. 24–26.

**16.46** *the Charming Lady* ("*la donna piacente*"): This charming ringleader in the revolt to expel Diana is, of course, the Unnamed Beloved of the stag-narrator, she who is the guardian and guide of the others (cf. *Hunt* 1.49–51).

## Canto 17

**17.3** *they lowered their eyes in silent expectation* ("*chinaron gli occhi tacite aspettando*"): Cf. *Purg.* 31.65: "con li occhi a terra stannosi, ascoltando" (with eyes on the ground, listening; Branca).

**17.16** *O holy Goddess*: Mortals frequently call on the gods in Boccaccio's early fiction. See, for example, Filostrato's prayer to Venus (*Filostr.* 3.74–89), esp. 77: "Tu 'l fiero Marte al tuo piacer benegno / ed umil rendi, e cacci ciascuna ira; / tu discacci viltà e d'alto sdegno / riempi chi per te, dea, sospira; / tu d'alta signoria merito e degno / fai ciaschedun, secondo ch'el disira; / tu fai cortese ognuno e costumato / che del tuo foco alquanto è infiammato" (You render fierce Mars humble and benign to your pleasure, and you chase out all wrath; you banish baseness and you fill any who sigh for you, goddess, with lofty scorn. You make everyone worthy and deserving of lofty dominion according to his desire. You make each one, who is fairly inflamed with your fire, courteous and well mannered). Note also Palemone's orison to Venus (*Tes.* 7.43): "O bella dea, del buon Vulcano sposa, / per cui s'allegra il monte Citerone, / deh, i' ti priego che mi sii pietosa / . . . / e la mia voglia per te amorosa / contenta" (O fair goddess, wife of good Vulcan, through whom Mount

Citheron rejoices, O, I pray that you have mercy on me, and content my desire that you have made amorous), and Ameto's thanks to Venus (*Ameto* 47): "O diva luce che in tre persone / e una essenza il ciel governi" (O divine light, which in three persons and one essence governs the heavens).

**17.29–30** *a bright and beautiful cloud came and then settled over them; upon it there appeared a naked young woman*: Cf. *Filoc.* 4.134.2, when Venus descends to save Florio and Biancifiore from death at the Admiral's stake: "E involta in una bianchissima nuvola, coronata delle frondi di Pennea, con un ramo di quelle di Pallade in mano, lasciò i cieli e discese sopra costoro" (And wrapped in a white cloud, crowned with Peneian leaves, and with a branch of Pallas' leaves in her hand, she left the heavens and came down over them); and *Ameto* 40.7, where she comes hidden in a column of fire, herald to Ameto's purification and conversion: "subita nuova luce videro uscire del cielo . . . di quella a' suoi orecchi pervenne una voce soave" (they suddenly saw a new light emerge from the sky . . . from there a soft voice reached his ears). For the biblical and spiritual resonances of this episode, see above, Introduction, pp. 30–31, 51–52, 67, 89 n. 18.

**17.34** *I am she from whom each one of you through her prayers awaits grace* ("*grazia*"): Cf. *Ameto* 41: "Io son luce del cielo unica e trina, / principio e fine di ciascuna cosa: / deh, qual men fu, né fia nulla, vicina? / E sì son vera luce e *graziosa*, / che chi mi segue non andrà giammai / errando in parte trista o tenebrosa, / ma con letizia agli angelici rai / mi seguirà nelle divizie etterne" (I am the light of heaven, one and triune, the beginning and ending of all things; pray, what was ever equal to me or ever will be? And so true and *gracious* a light am I, that he who follows me will never go erring in a sad or shadowy place, but in happiness he will follow me to the angelic rays in eternal riches).

The Italian *grazia* (grace) here in its literal context of courtly love means "favor," but allegorically, as the scene's replay in *Ameto* makes clear, Venus is bringing Christian grace.

**17.40** *changed into the form of a man*: Cf. *Filoc.* 2.3 for King Felice's prophetic dream, in which Florio and Biancifiore are disguised as animals, but turn into human beings after baptism. By the time Boccaccio wrote *Ameto*, the transformation is a figurative one, from rustic to enlightened gentleman (see Introduction, and below, 18.12). The same motif returns in the tale of Cimone (*Dec.* 5.1), made wise by love.

**17.44–45** *cloaked in a cloth of noble vermilion* ("*vermiglio*"): The gowning of Diana and her nymphs in purple (2.29) prefigures the men's ritual immersion and manteling in red, the color of love, sacred and profane. In Filocolo's vision of the seven Virtues, it marks Charity (both her dress and complexion!) as the first of the theological Virtues (*Filoc.*

4.74.18): "delle quali tre vedea l'una tanto vermiglia e nel viso e ne' vestimenti quanto se tutta ardesse" (one of the three had so much *vermilion* in both her face and her vestments that she seemed to be all on fire). Cf. also *Ameto* 42, where Agapes is symbolically aflame.

In a detail of Sassetta's *Exaltation of Saint Francis* (Florence, Berenson Collection, Villa I Tatti), Lust reclines in a scarlet gown. A fifteenth-century manuscript of the *Filocolo* in Venice (Biblioteca Nazionale di San Marco, MS. It. X.31) shows the lovesick protagonist cloaked in solid red. For other examples of red as the color of love, see P. Watson (1979), p. 111, and P. Watson and V. Kirkham (1975), pp. 44–45.

**17.52** *the heaven of her glory*: The third heaven, the planetary sphere of Venus in the Aristotelian-Ptolomaic cosmos.

**17.55–57** *some took part in various delights . . . others went about gathering various flowers* ("*diversi diletti / alcun prendeano . . . alcuni / givan cogliendo diversi fioretti*"): Cf. *Purg.* 28.40–41: "Una donna soletta che si gia / e cantando e scegliendo fior da fiore" (A lady all alone, who went singing and culling flower from flower). The *brigata* in a bucolic setting becomes a favorite Boccaccian motif: *Filoc.* 4.17, quoted above at 16.1–3, and *Dec.* 1, Intro. 103: "li giovani insieme con le belle donne, ragionando dilettevoli cose, con lento passo si misero per un giardino, belle ghirlande di varie frondi faccendosi e amorosamente cantando" (The merry company . . . went straying with slow steps, young men and fair ladies together, about a garden, blithely conversing and diverting themselves with weaving goodly garlands of various leaves and singing amorously).

## Canto 18

**18.8** *I found myself* ("*mi ritrovai*"): Boccaccio alludes to *Inf.* 1.1–3. In Dante's *Commedia,* the verb *ritrovarsi* (*mi ritrovai* [I found myself (again)]) bears intentional theological ambiguity, as A. K. Cassell has shown (*Lectura Dantis Americana: Inferno I* [1989]), pp. 8–14). From Boccaccio's echo in the *Hunt,* however, we can infer that our poet, along with several other later Renaissance commentators, took Dante's self-finding in the second verse of the *Commedia* only in a positive sense. Boccaccio's own *Esposizioni* 1.2.51–56 confirm that for him *mi ritrovai* clearly signaled the awakening from mortal sin that comes when grace already has descended: "La quarta cosa, la qual propuosi da essere da investigare, fu quale cosa potesse esser quella che l'autore movesse a ravedersi che esso avesse la diritta via smarrita. E questa, senza alcun dubbio, si dee credere che fosse la grazia di Dio, il quale ci ama assai più che non ci amiamo noi medesimi e sempre è alla nostra salute sollicito. . . . Ma, acciò che noi cognosciamo qual fosse la grazia di Dio, dalla quale l'autore tocco si movesse a destarsi del sonno mortale, nel quale la mente sua era legata, e a ravedersi in qual periculo fosse l'anima sua, è da sapere, sì come il Maestro delle *Sentenze* afferma, essser quatro grazie quelle che la divina bontà ci presta alla nostra salute.

"Delle quali la prima è chiamata grazia 'operante.' . . . E dico che la prima grazia senza alcun merito di colui che la riceve si dona; di che dice san Paolo: '*Non secundum opera que fecimus nos, sed secundum suam misericordiam salvos nos fecit.*' La qualità delle quali grazie considerate, assai manifestamente apare la prima delle quatro essere stata quella che al nostro autore, e similemente a ciascun altro che in simile caso si truova, fu conceduta da Dio, per la quale esso il suo misero stato conobbe" (The fourth thing that I proposed for investigation was what could have moved the author to realize that he had lost the straight way. And it must be believed beyond any doubt that this was the grace of God, who loves us much more than we love ourselves and is always mindful of our salvation. . . . But in order that we may know by which grace of God the author, once touched, was moved to awaken from the mortal sleep that bound his mind and realize what danger his soul was in, it must be known, as the Master of the *Sentences* affirms, that there are four graces that divine bounty lends to our salvation.

Of these the first is called "operant" grace. . . . And I say that the first grace is given without any merit of he who receives it, about which St. Paul says, "Not according to our works, but according to his mercy he saved us." Considering the qualities of these graces, it appears most manifestly that the first of the four was the one that was granted by God to our author, and similarly to everyone else who finds himself in a similar situation; by this grace he recognized his miserable state).

**18.9** *fiery combat* ("*ardente agone*"): The two words combine the suffering of the animals both during the hunt and in the flames. The suffering is now revealed, in a sensuous sense, as the burning sufferings occasioned by love; in the poem's more social and moral sense, as the "burning" rejected in favor of a Christian celebration of marriage now about to be consecrated; in the spiritual sense we see the words signifying the struggle for purification, in the pattern of the climax of a neophyte's "combat" during the nocturnal vigil prior to baptism.

The terms' metrical placement, ninth verse of the eighteenth canto, is probably meant to allude to beatific love.

**18.11–12** *changed beyond doubt from a stag into a human being and a rational creature* ("*di cervio mutato in creatura / umana e razionale esser per certo*"): Cf. *Ameto* 46.5: "brievemente, d'animale bruto, uomo divenuto essere li pare" (in short, it seems to him that he has been made from a brute animal into a man).

**18.16** The final, full description of the Mystery Lady is a stilnovistic mosaic fashioned from the tessera of Dante's praise-language for Beatrice in the *Vita nuova*. Compare, for example, 18.16–18: "Il viso suo angelica bellezza / del ciel discesa veramente pare, / venuta a dare agli occhi uman chiarezza" (Her face seems truly angelic beauty descended from heaven, come to give clarity to human eyes) with the sonnet of *Vita nuova* 26: "par che sia una cosa venuta / da cielo in terra a miracol mostrare" (she seems to be a creature come from Heaven / to earth, to manifest a miracle).

**18.26** *the Eternal Lord . . . rejoices*: Coming from a stag-man saved by Venus in Diana's Parthenopean groves, this reference to the deity points up Boccaccio's brazen mixture of pagan and Christian elements intended to challenge the reader into discovering the allegory.

**18.29–30** *whoever gazes fixedly into her eyes becomes merciful or else must die*: Cf. *Vita nuova* 19.9: "E qual soffrisse di starla a vedere / Diverria nobil cosa, o si morria" (and whoever might suffer to look upon her long / would become a noble thing, or he would die).

**18.34–35** *pride, sloth, greed, and wrath . . . flee from my mind*: Cf. *Vita nuova* 21.2: "fugge dinanzi a lei superbia ed ira" (anger and pride flee before her); *Inf.* 6.74–75: "Superbia, invidia e avarizia sono / le tre faville c'hanno i cuori accesi" (Pride, envy, and avarice are the three sparks that have inflamed their hearts).

**18.49ff.** *It pleases me now to speak no further, because for a place more praiseworthy I reserve my words*: Cf. *Vita nuova* 42, "Vidi cose che mi fecero proporre di non dire più di questa benedetta infino a tanto che io potesse più degnamente trattare di lei" (I saw things that made me resolve to say no more about this blessèd one until I would be capable of writing about her in a nobler way).

**18.52** *beauty that her soul traces*: The notion that virtue shines from within is Aristotelian. Hence the lady's moral perfection is reflected in her physical appearance. The tradition continues through Petrarch and his followers. The body of the *Hunt*'s Mystery Lady images her mind, for allegorically she may be Wisdom, the Aristotelian virtue that "precedes" all the others. She anticipates the virtue who "comes first" in the *Ameto*, Prudence, and who similarly may lie behind Pampinea, the leader of the *Decameron brigata* (see V. Kirkham, "An Allegorically Tempered *Decameron*" [1985], pp. 1–23).

The Christian ideal of the soul externally revealed is a subject Saint Bernard discusses in *Sermones in Cantica Canticorum:* "When the brightness of beauty has replenished to overflowing the recess of the heart, it is necessary that it should emerge into the open, just like the light hidden under a bushel. . . . The body is an image of the mind, which, like an effulgent light scattering forth its rays, is diffused through its members and senses, shining through in action, discourse, appearance, movement—even in laughter" (cited by Umberto Eco, *Art and Beauty in the Middle Ages,* trans. Hugh Bredin [New Haven: Yale University Press, 1986], p. 10). As Ambrose had earlier put it, "Itaque vox quaedam est animi corporis motus" (the movement of the body is a sort of voice of the soul; *De officiis ministrorum* I, xviii, 71 [*PL* 16.44]; cited in Marilyn Migiel, "Between Art and Theology: Dante's Representation of Humility," *Stanford Italian Review* 5, no. 2 [Fall 1985], pp. 144–145).

**18.58**   *salvation ("salute")*: See above, 12.15. There *salvamente* meant both "with safety" and "with salvation." Here the sense has shifted, finally, to the latter meaning, "spiritual well being."

# GLOSSARY OF THE HUNTRESSES

Besides briefly indicating the role that each woman plays in the action of the poem, our principal aim here has been to emphasize the high social rank of the *Hunt's* participants, the power of their families, and their tight interrelation through blood and marriage. Knowledge of their rank, wealth, and kinship adds much not only to an appreciation of the aims of the poet and his poem but also to an understanding of his intended audience. Boccaccio's poetry here is not disinterested—but, we must remember, neither was the best art of the High Renaissance.

In this listing, we have noted to which of the two hunting parties (that of *Hunt* 1–8, or that of *Hunt* 9–16) each huntress belongs, along with her venatic triumphs. The huntresses are, we surmise, divided by their degree of sexual maturity: the almost total segregation of the two groups ("le donne e le pulcelle" [the ladies and maidens, *Hunt* 16]) is essential to the youthful Boccaccio's celebration of the purification of love, that is, of the marriage sacrament toward which his allegory points. The action of the *Hunt* adumbrates, in one sense, an epithalamium.

Only in the second party are any of the huntresses called by their married names (Iacopa Aldimaresca, *Hunt* 9.56, and Caterina Sighinolfi, 10.20). Except in *Hunt* 9, where La Lucciola greets Marella Caracciola and the new arrivals, and in *Hunt* 11, where Biancifiore de' Caffettini and Catella Fellapane, two of Diana's personally restricted band of the first hunt, lend hunting nets to Marella Passerella and Serella Brancazza of the second team (notably, to catch four stags, Diana's symbols), no member of the first hunting party actually joins with the second until they all are called back by Diana in *Hunt* 16—and then, only to revolt against her. The segregation probably makes it clear, for example, why the unicorn should be trapped by the virginal Fiore Canovara during the first hunt, and why in the second chase are there two huntresses with faces "fair with amorous fire" (Cecca and Zizzola Fagiana, in *Hunt* 9), or who are not "garlanded with olive leaves and flowers" (*Hunt* 2), but adorned with fiery red roses (Covella [Giacopella] Embriaca and Tanzella Acerra), the flower of Venus and the color of love. Only the first group is summoned personally by

Diana's messenger. The straggler, Zizzola d'Anna, hunts "unbidden." There is no word on how the second party is gathered.

We list the participants in the *Hunt* in alphabetical order according to their first name, nickname, or diminutive, and then their family name as it occurs in the English translation. When there is more than one woman with the same first name, they are then listed alphabetically following the patronymic or family name.

In most cases identification is difficult both because of a lack of historical evidence and because of the intense popularity of most of the given names.

We have preserved Italian convention in not changing family names when they are used in the plural: for example, "the Fellapane" rather than "the Fellapanes."

The historical information is adapted primarily from Vittore Branca's notes to his edition of the *Caccia di Diana,* with some additions and references from A. F. Massèra, Mario Marti, and from the partial edition by Pier Giorgio Ricci; we refer the reader to those editions for full references to the primary and secondary sources.

## Diana, the goddess, and the Fair Lady

In addition to the goddess Diana, there are fifty-nine mortals; of the latter, one remains anonymous—the poet's Special Lady who is first introduced as "quella donna cui Amore onora / più ch'altra" (that lady whom Love honors more than any other); she, along with Diana herself, Isabella Scrignara, and Fiore Curiale are the leaders of the four groups into which Diana divides the first gathering of huntresses. These three and the rest, in both hunting parties, bear the names of fifty-eight noble ladies attached to the Angevin court of Naples. For the role of the goddess Diana, the identification of the beloved, and the significance of the number sixty, see the Introduction, pp. 23–27.

## Alessandra d'Anna

A member of the first group, Alessandra helps Isolda di Giaquinto and Linella de' Gattoli kill the second of three wolf cubs in *Hunt* 6.

Despite the fame of her family, nothing has come down to us about Alessandra personally; this silence is itself important as a social comment upon the position of women in contemporary society. Boccaccio was one of the few who realized the need for a history of women and was later to attempt to remedy the deficiency by writing his *De mulieribus claris* (*Concerning Famous Women*).

Alessandra belonged to one of the most prominent Neapolitan families, important to the Angevin court from its earliest days because of its commercial interests. The d'Anna were related to the Pignatelli, Pignone, Ugo, Tufo, and Transo families. Among the squires of the Duchess of Calabria, we find Nicola d'Anna in 1325; in the next century, one Indico d'Anna was grand seneschal to Queen Giovanna II, who ruled from 1419 to 1495.

See also Covella d'Anna, the huntress who makes the last and allegorically important kill of the ostrich (*Hunt* 15), and Zizzola d'Anna who straggles in as the last huntress in *Hunt* 16.

## Berarda Gattoli, or de' Gattoli

Summoned to the first group of huntresses in *Hunt* 1, Berarda catches six hedgehogs at the end of *Hunt* 5.

As in so many cases with the protagonists of the poem, this lady is otherwise not known. The Gattola were a noble family of the Portanova quarter and had their private chapel in the Church of Sant' Agostino. References to the family go back to the time of Carlo I, who reigned from 1282 to 1285. They appear frequently in lawsuits with such families as the Pignatelli. Goffredo Gattola enjoyed the favor of King Robert and was royal criminal judge in the Abruzzi. A Bernardo (d. 1348) and a Giovanni (d. 1351) appear at the court of Robert's successor, Queen Giovanna I.

Linella Gattoli (q.v.) also numbers among the huntresses of the first party.

## Berita Brancazza, or de' Brancazzi

With her sister Caterina, Berita is called to hunt in the first canto; the siblings kill two tigers in *Hunt* 6.

Of the woman herself nothing is known, but the Brancaccio (variously spelled Brancazzi or Brancazza) family was extremely prominent in Naples, being one of the forty-seven noble families of the See of Capua. Many of its members held important posts under King Robert and under his heir Queen Giovanna: Alessandro; Giovanni, captain of Monopoli; Guglielmo, captain at Capua; Landolfo; Marino, Lord of Casola; and Masello.

Taking part in the second hunt are two other members of the clan, Serella (Canto 9.41–42; and see below) and Vanella Brancazzi (10.6; and see below).

## Berita Galeota

Playing her harp along with Covella d'Arco among the reeds by a river, Berita entices two swans into her snares in *Hunt* 15.

The Galeota belonged to the forty-seven noble families of the See of Capua, they were a branch of the Capece, related by marriage to the Barrisio family. Gualtiero Galeota was well known at the time and probably known to Boccaccio personally through their mutual friend, Dionigi da Borgo San Sepolcro. Various others held offices and enjoyed honors at the Angevin Court: particularly, the illustrious Arrigo Galeota, vice treasurer of the Kingdom, counsellor and ambassador of King Robert; and Francesco, member of the household and captain to Queen Giovanna I.

Gostanza Galeota is also one of the huntresses of the second party of twenty-five huntresses in the poem.

## Beritola Carafa

A member of the first party called in the first canto, Beritola clubs two bears to death with Sobilia Capece in *Hunt* 5.

"Berita," or "Beritola," was a common name at the time, as we can see from the three who take part in the poem (cf. *Hunt* 1.26, Berita de' Brancazzi, 10.23, and Berita Galeota, 15.2–3). Branca suggests that, since there was a family Carafa-Caracciolo, this lady may be the protagonist of *Dec.* 2.6. Members of the famous and noble Carafa clan held high positions at the Angevin court and great responsibilities in the Kingdom of Naples: Bartolomeo III was criminal judge in Bari in 1309 and 1324 and was governor of various cities.

Her kinswomen, Biancola and Caterina Carafa, are both members of the second party of huntresses who arrive in *Hunt* 9.

## Biancifiore de' Caffettini

Biancifiore de' Caffettini (or Caffettina), among the first group of huntresses that Diana reserves for her own personal party (*Hunt* 2), spreads her nets with Catella Fellapane and Marella Melia to capture three horned stags in *Hunt* 3.

As usual, "Biancifiore" (and its variants, such as Biancofiore) was such a common name at the time as to make identification nearly impossible. The Cafatino, or Caffettini, were a noble family of the See of Portanova, related to the Arcamone; they are mentioned at the Angevin court from the time of Carlo I (1266–1285).

## Biancola Carafa

Biancola, who appears crowned with flowers, pursues and shoots a fallow deer with her hounds during the second hunt (*Hunt* 13).

See Beritola Carafa (of the first hunt) and Caterina Carafa (of the second) for information on her family.

## Caterina Bolino

Caterina, a member of the first party called by Diana's messenger, kills a crane with her gyrfalcon in *Hunt* 8.

Nothing is known personally about this woman. Branca notes that the Bolino family was originally of Salerno and related to the Cavaselice family, descendents of the Langobard princes of Salerno. Massèra, apparently unaware of the existence of the family otherwise, cites a friar, "Andrea de Bolino," an oblate in 1346 of the Monastery of San Pietro a Castello, and in 1365, a "Martucello de Bolino."

## Caterina de' Brancazzi

This Caterina and her sister Berita, both members of the first hunt, kill two swift tigers in *Hunt* 6.

For the Brancazzi, Brancazza, or Brancaccio family, see under Caterina's sister, Berita Brancazza. Serella and Vannella Brancazza take part in the second hunt that begins in *Hunt* 9.

## Caterina Caradente

Selected from the first group as one of Diana's personal troop (*Hunt* 2), Caterina impales a boar in *Hunt* 3.

Of this Caterina we have certain record. In 1338 she married Stefano Sueth, earlier squire of Carlo I and later one of the most eminent courtiers of the household of Andrea, Duke of Calabria, first husband and consort of Queen Giovanna I. An Angevin registry records a wedding gift to her in 1338: "a girdle of silver thread given on behalf of the Duchess of Calabria . . . to the wife of the Hungarian, Stephan Sueth." Caterina is probably "la cortese donna" to whom Boccaccio refers in the *Am. vis.* 42.22ff., beside Dalfina di Barasso, another Neapolitan noblewoman appearing in *Hunt* 10 and 11.

## Caterina Carafa

Like her kinswoman Biancola, Caterina hunts with the second, twenty-five member party; she kills a roebuck in *Hunt* 14.

A tombstone in Santa Maria Maggiore in Naples attests that a Caterina Carafa died 10 June 1383; and there is record of a Caterina de Sangro Carafa, wife of Matteo, who died in 1315.

See also Beritola and Biancola Carafa.

## Caterina, or Catella, Fellapane

This Caterina, nicknamed "Catella," is among those huntresses of the first group that Diana keeps as her own special band in *Hunt* 1 and 2.

The Fellapane were a noble family of the See of Portanova. During the reign of Carlo I (1266–1285), Niccolò Fellapane had been investigator of the feudal lords; he held minor posts at the court of Robert the Wise and Queen Giovanna I.

On the nickname "Catella," see also Caterina Sighinolfi.

## Caterina Pipina

"La Pipina" is among those select few of the first hunting group chosen to hunt personally with Diana (*Hunt* 2). She catches two hares with La Crespana in *Hunt* 3.

The Pipini were of recent nobility, having established their fortune through Giovanni Pipino, a supporter of Carlo I and Carlo II who was knighted by them; Giovanni became count of Lucera, Potenza, Troia, and Vico. However, between 1338 and 1340, his *nipoti*, Giovanni, count of Altamura and Minervino, Pietro, count of Vico and lord of Troia, and Ludovico, count of Potenza, all rebelled against King Robert who in turn, after a hard struggle to subdue them, imprisoned them for life in the Castle of Capua. Clearly, as Branca indicates, the reference to Caterina Pipina here among such illustrious company must predate the ignominy of that rebellion. We find no record of a Caterina born to this family, but the maternal aunt of one of the conspirators, Giovanni of Altamura, was named Caterina; his mother was the wife of Niccolò Pipino II. Branca believes that our huntress was a sister of one of the three rebels and christened in honor of her aunt.

## Caterina di Iacopo Roncione

A member of the first party, Caterina hunts with the band hunting toward the west under the direction of Isabella Scrignara; her adventures are not otherwise described (*Hunt* 6).

In *Hunt* 6.17, Caterina is said to be specifically the *daughter* of the notary, Iacopo Roncione, but unfortunately, as Branca notes, the Naples Archives do not contain notary records for the fourteenth century. Branca discounts the possibility of her connection with the Sicilian branch of the Roncione counts.

## Caterina di Serpando

This Caterina is among the first group of huntresses whom Diana selects for her personal band (*Hunt* 2). She kills a wolf in the third canto.

As usual, we know more about the men of the family than the lady in question. The Serpando, or Seripando, were feudal lords from the time of King Manfred (crowned 1258, d. 1266). This well-known clan was among the forty-seven aristocratic families of the See of Capua, having a private chapel in the cathedral. Like so many families mentioned in the *Hunt,* the Serpando held high offices: a certain Berardo was master ostiary and member of King Robert's household in 1338; another, Riccardo, was captain of Aquila and vicar at Taranto under King Robert; a Giovanni was chancellor to both King Robert and his granddaughter, Queen Giovanna I; and a Giannotto was supporter and member of the household of Robert of Taranto.

## Caterina, or Catrina, Sighinolfi

Caterina is not called by Diana's messenger, but "merrily" takes part in the aquatic adventures of the second hunt; her expertise in fishing is stressed as she ingeniously places a rope trap in the river to catch a hydra at the end of *Hunt* 14.

Caterina-Catrina shares the name of the once-virtuous protagonist of *Decameron* 3.6, the jealous wife of Filippello Sighinolfi, nicknamed Catella, who is tricked into adultery in a seaside bagnio by Ricciardo Minutolo. Although, perhaps, a serious objection to this intriguing identification of the lady in the *Hunt* with that of the *Decameron* may arise from the fact that a real Filippo Sighinolfi, who held various offices and various benefices at the court of Queen Giovanna I, was married to Mattea d'Aprano, we cannot discount the possibility that he took another wife at another time. That Boccaccio would celebrate Caterina in the *Hunt* and tarnish her reputation in the masterpiece makes for interesting speculation on his maturer views of the "virginal" Parthenope of his youth.

Torraca makes too general a claim that "the women of the *Hunt* all bear the surnames of the families in which they were born, not into which they married" (*Giovanni Boccaccio a Napoli,* p. 154). This "rule," as Branca observes, is not without its exceptions. We might add that these exceptions occur only among the huntresses of the second party, that is, among those who are not called by the messenger of the goddess of chastity. Against the opinion of other historians, Branca rejects the identification of Catella or Covella di Loffredo as the Catella named as the second wife of Filippo Sighinolfi.

The Sighinolfi or Siginolfi family belonged to the upper Neapolitan nobility and held great power at King Robert's court, especially with Bartolomeo, count of Caserta and grand treasurer; he had been an intimate of both Carlo I and Carlo II. Boccaccio certainly knew the family personally since they were related to his friends: Perrillo Sighinolfi, son of the knight Enrico and of Egidia di Berardo, was married to Regale Barrile, daughter of Giovanni Barrile.

## Cecca Bozzuta

Cecca is part of the first group of huntresses called in *Hunt* 1 and hunts with the special group whom Diana chooses as her own (*Hunt* 2). The allegorical—or social—significance of her being awarded the first animal shot in the chase, a roebuck (*Hunt* 3), remains a mystery.

"Cecca" is a shortened form of Francesca, a common given name among the Bozzuto family. The latter were feudal lords at the time of Queen Giovanna I; they were a branch of the Capece (see Sobilia Capece) and one of the forty-seven noble families of the See of Capua, having a private chapel in the cathedral. Among the most famous of them were Giovanni, criminal judge of Capitanata (Lucania) in 1314; Andrea, governor of Amalfi in 1328; and Giacomo, archbishop of Naples.

## Cecca Fagiana

With her kinswoman, Zizzola, both are huntresses of the second party entering in *Hunt* 9; Cecca captures two roebucks in *Hunt* 11.

The Fagiano, or Fasano, originally of Amalfi, were Sicilian nobles. Several gained power at the court of King Robert: Riccardo (d. 1333), a knight and professor in the *studium,* was personal physician to the King;

Giovanni, a member of the king's household, had protected the Infante Ferdinand of Majorca in 1332 and sat among the highest dignitaries at the homage ceremony for Queen Giovanna I.

Torraca believed that the name "Fagiana," meaning pheasant, given to Alleiram in the *Filocolo,* alludes to a lady of this family; Branca disagrees, saying that in love treatises the pheasant was the conventional emblem of any beloved's noble family.

## Ceccola Mazzone

One of the first huntresses called, Ceccola hacks a wild boar to death in *Hunt* 6.

The Mazzone family were related to the Abenante family of Calabria; they are recorded as nobles in the records of the See of Porto. At the courts of Robert the Wise and his successor, Queen Giovanna I, several members, Giovanni, Sergio, and Martino, held important posts, such as bailiff and constable.

## Ciancia

Ciancia is the second huntress to be called in the first canto of the poem; with Zizzola Barrile, she slays a white stag in *Hunt* 4.

The name "Ciancia" or more commonly, "Sancia," was in vogue at the time in Naples, perhaps, Branca believes, as a homage to the wife of King Robert. Léonard cites several: Sancia de Lupiano, Sancia de Magdalono, Sancia Gantelme, Massèra and Marti identify Boccaccio's Ciancia with Sancia de' Cabanni, granddaughter of Raimondo and Filippa de' Cabanni, a family well-known to Boccaccio and mentioned prominently in the *De casibus* 9.26. Boccaccio refers to her indirectly in the *Am. vis.* 41.1ff., and at length in the *Buccolicum carmen* 3, mentioning her marriage to Carlo, count of Morcone. Torraca rejected the identification on the grounds that Sancia was too young at the time when the *Hunt* was written and that she was not noble. Branca points out that we know nothing of her date of birth—only that Boccaccio in the *De casibus* indicates that there was little difference in age between her and Queen Giovanna I, born in 1326. Since the poem does not give her last name, Torraca believed her to be a member of the Barrile family; Branca believes the omission of the family name would indicate rather the more famous Sancia de' Cabanni.

## Covella d'Anna

Covella's wild pursuit, throttling, and decapitation of an ostrich is the last kill of the poem (*Hunt* 15); for the bird's allegorical meaning as fraud and dissembling, see Introduction, pp. 15–16.

The diminutive "Covella," or "Cobella," from "Iacopella" or "Giacopella," was common usage: compare also the poet's alternation of the name and nickname in the case of her namesake, Giacopella Embriaca.

All three kinswomen of the d'Anna clan seem to receive some textual, symbolic, and numerological prominence: Alessandra d'Anna, called in the thirty-third verse of *Hunt* 1 (who kills the second, "Dantesque" wolf offspring in *Hunt* 6); and Zizzola d'Anna, the last straggler to arrive in *Hunt* 16.

For the social importance of Covella's family, see under Alessandra d'Anna.

## Covella d'Arco

With the sound of her harp, Covella, a member of the second hunt, lures and snares two swans in *Hunt* 15.

Branca suggests that since this Covella's family, or at least one branch of it, was from Sorrento, we might identify her with Covella di Sorrento, the wife of Masuccio Masso, who was a member of the household of Queen Giovanna I and nurse to the queen's firstborn son, Carlo; noblewomen were often called to such a duty. Branca insists, however, that this identification is purely hypothetical.

The d'Arco clan, a patrician family of Amalfi, were nobles of the Sees of Portanova and Montagna, related to the Caputo; they are recorded from the time of Carlo I (1266–1285). Under King Robert, Marino d'Arco held offices and honors; as, in the first years of the reign of Giovanna, did Landolfo, a soldier, together with his sons, Niccolò, Giovanni, and Giannetto.

See also Peronella d'Arco below.

## La Crespana

La Crespana is among the special few that Diana selects from the first group of huntresses as her own. With "La Pipina," Caterina Pipina (q.v.), she captures two hares in *Hunt* 3.

Boccaccio does not give "La Crespana" 's first name in the text. The

Crespano, or Crispano, family were nobles of the See of Capua, with a private chapel in the cathedral; they had been feudal lords from the time of Manfred (crowned 1258, d. 1266). At King Robert's court, Francesco held the post of lieutenant to the grand treasurer, and Pietro Crispino's doctorate was celebrated in a sermon by the king himself. Two others, Floriano and Landolfo, rose to power under Queen Giovanna I. Landolfo was an illustrious expert in jurisprudence, a knight, auditor of accounts, and, in 1348, lieutenant to the grand public treasurer, Enrico Caracciolo.

## Dalfina di Barasso

Dalfina, of the second party, kills the second of three boars in *Hunt* 11.7.

This Dalfina is probably represented also in the *Amorosa visione* by the "lady who bears the name of the helper of Arion," Arion being the mythical poet saved by dolphins (*delfino* or *dalfino* means "dolphin") that he had tamed by the power of his song (see the *Am. vis.*, ed. and trans. R. Hollander, T. Hampton, and M. Frankel, p. 242). Dalfina, the wife of Francesco Caracciolo, lord of Pisciotta, was left a widow before 1353; her second marriage was to Berardo Caracciolo. In the Duomo of Naples she is recorded on the tombstone of her son, Jacopo Caracciolo. In 1341, a Dalfina Barassio, probably her granddaughter, was promised, at the age of seven years, to Giovanello Barrili, grandson of Giovanni, the close friend of Boccaccio and Petrarch. The Barras family (the name is Italianized in many documents into "Barasso" or "Barrasio") were among those of the Provençal nobility who had immigrated to Naples, King Robert being also count of Provence. The Barras appear often in connection with the Bardi and Peruzzi banking families, and were related to the Galeota. Raimondo di Barras, Dalfina's father, was one of the first to pay homage to Queen Giovanna I when she was proclaimed heir by King Robert the Wise. Luigi Barras was seneschal in Piedmont from 1344. Barras de Barras, a courtier of Giovanna, had married Taddea di Castelpagano.

## Fiore Canovara

A member of the first huntresses assembled in *Hunt* 1, she is dressed in virginal white by Fiore Curiale to catch the unicorn in *Hunt* 7.

Identification is, as usual, difficult, because "Fiore" was a very common name in contemporary Naples (see below for Fiore Curiale; and cf. *Dec.* 2.5). The Canovara, or Cannovaro, were known in Naples from the time of the first Angevin king, Carlo I.

## Fiore Curiale

Leader of one of the four smaller bands into which Diana divides the first gathering of huntresses, this Fiore sets Fiore Canovara out as virginal bait to catch the unicorn in *Hunt 7*.

The Curiale or Correale, originally from Amalfi, were a noble family in the See of Porto, related to the Bozzuto, the Capece, the Carafa, the Moromile, the Scrignaro, and the Serisale clans, among others. They had enjoyed important posts since the reign of Carlo I (1266–1285). Several had positions under King Robert the Wise: Marino became *protontino*, the admiral in charge of the fleet at Amalfi; Guglielmo was judge of the criminal court in the Abruzzo from 1318; and Pietro was a judge and legal expert entrusted with confidential missions to Amalfi.

## Giacopella ("Iacopella," "Covella," or "Cobella") Embriaca

Like her companion of the second hunt (Canto 10), Tanzella Acerra, Giacopella-Covella appears with her head adorned with red roses (*Hunt 13*). This flaming red garland (suggesting the flame of love and charity) and the fact that neither she nor the other twenty-five ladies of the second hunting party are personally called by the messenger of the goddess of chastity may indicate that Giacopella is enamored and betrothed, or even wed. As "Covella," she shoots a panther in *Hunt 13*.

The Embriaca, Embriachi, or Imbriachi were a branch of the Brancazzi clan; they were nobles of the See of Nido and inscribed in the *Libro d'Oro*, or *Registry of the Nobility*. One Sandalo had great influence at the court of Queen Giovanna I; he was entrusted with some of the most important and delicate missions on behalf of her court.

## Giovannola de' Coppoli

Giovannola, summoned in *Hunt 1*, helps La Lucciola to spread nets and flush fowl in Canto 8. Wise in the techniques of fowling, they capture a cormorant, a *paolin*, mallards, and other water birds.

The Coppola clan, originally from Amalfi, was listed from the time of Carlo I (1266–1285) among the noble families of Portanova and Montagna; its members fulfilled financial tasks in close cooperation with the Bardi and Peruzzi banking companies on behalf of King Robert. Among its most notable scions were Cesario, who was a professor of medicine; Filippo, who, with Giovanni Barrile, was one of the eight elected *capi* of the city when Louis of Hungary arrived in 1347; Giacomo and Francesco, courtiers and counselors to Queen Giovanna I; Bartolomeo, member of the households of Louis of Taranto and Jean Estendart; and Matteo, lieutenant of the grand treasurer in 1353.

Lucciola de' Coppoli (q.v.) appears in *Hunt* 1 and 9.

## Gostanza Galeota

One of the second hunting party, Gostanza spears the last of three wild boars in *Hunt* 11.

Concerning her family, see Berita Galeota.

## Iacopa Aldimaresca

A member of the second gathering of huntresses, she leads her own small band to the south in *Hunt* 9. With Marella Passerella, Iacopa first catches sight of the serpent's tail in *Hunt* 11, advises using "fiery coals" to drive this "fierce plague" from its lair, and finally lances and decapitates the reptile in *Hunt* 12.

In the will of Queen Maria (1323), a Jacopa Aldimoresca (again, there are variant spellings of both first and last names) is listed as the recipient of a legacy of an ounce coin; and in 1330, a Jacopa di Matteo Caruba is recorded as the wife of the soldier Giovanni Aldomoresco, a member of the household of Louis of Taranto and Queen Giovanna I. We do not know if it is the same woman. Obviously, the second reference would represent an exception to Boccaccio's usual practice of giving a huntress her father's surname. Perhaps there is some significance to the fact that none of the second party of huntresses are called by Diana's messenger (this is explicit in the case of the straggler, Zizzola d'Anna, who goes hunting "unbidden"); the poem's silence on this count may mean that some are already wed or betrothed.

The Aldimaresca or Aldemaresco family, nobility of the See of Nido, flourished especially at the courts of Robert and Giovanna and, later, at the court of Ladislao (1400–1414). Through one of their members, Giovanni, a counselor and vicar of King Robert, they held great authority in the court, and even more so through Paffello, *maestro di marescialleria,* or military captain, one of the most influential courtiers before the rise of Niccolò Acciaiuoli, Boccaccio's boyhood friend and later enemy, in the court of Queen Giovanna I. Another member of the family, Matteo, was also a favorite of Queen Giovanna, especially after his marriage to Gisolda Poderica.

Iacopa's mature authority in the poem matches the authority of her family in history.

## Isabella Scrignara, or degli Scrignar

Leader of the second troop into which Diana divides the first hunting party summoned in *Hunt* 1, Isabella hunts with her kinswoman Mignana to catch rabbits and hares in *Hunt* 6.

The Scrignara family numbered among the feudal lords of Nola during the 1200s; in the mid-1300s they had seats at Portanova, Montagna, and Porto. Illustrious members were: Bartolomeo, a knight of Carlo II; Ligorio, knight of King Robert; and Ligorio's three sons, Giovanni, Niccolò, and Ciccillo; the last was one of the supporters of Queen Giovanna and Louis of Taranto. Giannello, supposedly a member of the Scrignara family, is protagonist of the *Dec.* 7.2. The Scrignara had family ties to the Curiale and Serisale clans: see *Hunt* 1.30 (Fiore Curiale); 10.13 (Tuccella Serisale).

See also Mignana Scrignara.

## Isolda di Giaquinto

As a member of the first hunt, Isolda clubs a wolf to death in *Hunt* 6.

The name "Isolda" (and its variants "Gisolda" and "Isolta") was very frequent at the Angevin court in Naples (cf. *Dec.* 10.6). The Isolda of the *Hunt* was probably one of the ladies-in-waiting and favorites of Princess Giovanna. Massèra proposed identifying her with Gisolda Poderico, nurse, companion, and great favorite of the future queen. Gisolda married Matteo Aldamaresco about 1339 (see above, and *Hunt* 9.56, for Iacopa Aldimaresca); since, as Branca indicates, this Isolda's father's name is uncertain, however, positive identification is not possible. Still, as this Isolda appears in the company of others who were favorites of the future queen, Massèra's thesis cannot be totally dismissed.

Notices of the Poderico family date back to the 1200s; their private chapel was in San Lorenzo. Many family members held important posts: Sergio Poderico was captain of Durazzo in 1348–1349; Folco was an intimate and a knight of Louis of Taranto, consort of Queen Giovanna I; Landolfo was ostiary of Giovanna and governor of Manfredonia. Under King Robert, Giovanni had been chief bailiff of Naples, and Lorenzo had been treasurer of the court and procurator in Piedmont.

Branca gives references to other members of this family, but prefers to identify Isolda as a daughter of the di Giaquinto (variously, de Jaquinto) family because Boccaccio gives her last name each time he mentions her in the poem (see *Hunt* 6.16, 6.40); obviously the poet wishes to flatter the whole clan of that name. Since Isolda is summoned with "le pulcelle" (the maids) of the first hunting party, we believe Branca to be correct. A Giaquinto family was known in Angevin Naples and held positions at court from the reign of Carlo I (1266–1285) to that of Ladislao (or Lanzilao), who was king from 1400 to 1414; they were related to the De Rossi, nobles of the See of Sommapiazza.

## Lariella Caracciola

A member of the second hunt, Lariella (named in *Hunt* 9), is one of four Caracciola women in the poem. Since, historically, she was a woman who could care for her affairs, we can identify her, Marella, and Mitola more easily than Principessella, the fourth. She was Aloara, or Alagora, Caracciola, daughter of Filippo (who died in 1334), and married to one of the Piscicelli clan. About 1334 or 1335 she had a turbulent lawsuit with the sisters of the convent of San Gregorio Maggiore. The diminutive or pet name "Lariella" was common in the Caracciolo household.

See also Marella, Mitola, and Principessella Caracciola.

## Letizia Moromile

Letizia is among the first party to be called in *Hunt* 1; she climbs the "low-lying mountain" in *Hunt* 7; there she fails in the huntresses' first attempt to capture the unicorn with Lucia Porria and Fiore Canovara, but she spears a boar in the same canto.

We have no precise information about the historical Letizia, but of her family we know much: they were among the nobility of the See of Portanova. One Tommaso Moromile was a courtier and knight at the courts of King Robert and Queen Giovanna I. In recompense for his services, another Moromile, Perrino, bodyguard and member of the royal household, was given a burial crypt in the territory of Avorio, where the *Dec.* 7.2 is set.

## Linella Gattoli, or de' Gattoli

Linella, part of the first group drafted by Diana's messenger in *Hunt* 1, comes to Isolda di Giaquinto's aid and, with Alessandra d'Anna, shoots one of three wolf cubs in *Hunt* 6.

For the family, see Berarda Gattoli, above.

## Lucciola de' Coppoli ("La Lucciola")

Lucciola is summoned in *Hunt* 1 and responds to the queries of the second assembly of huntresses who enter in *Hunt* 9.

For her family, see Giovannola de' Coppoli.

## Lucia Porria

Lucia is called in *Hunt* 1 and forms part of Fiore Curiale's troop in Canto 7 in the hunt for the unicorn.

No personal information has come down to us about Lucia, but the Porria family flourished in Naples during the reign of King Robert and had been prominent from the time of Carlo I (1266–1285).

## Marella Caracciola

Marella, a member of the second party, is the first to express a wish to hunt on the site chosen by the huntresses of the first party (*Hunt* 9); as spokeswoman, she calls out to "La Lucciola" to assure the safety of all.

Most probably, Marella was the daughter of Giovanni and niece of Ludovico Caracciola; she died on 8 July 1374 and was buried in San Lorenzo. Alternatively, she is to be identified with the sister of Lariella (*Hunt* 9.41), daughter of Filippo. Given the frequency of the name and diminutive one cannot completely exclude other possible identifications proposed by Massèra: Maria, born Capece Scondito, wife of Filippo Caracciolo, already widowed by 1339; Maria di Matteo Orimino, wife of Lodovico Caracciolo. Although the women in the *Hunt* are generally given their fathers' surnames, as we have noted, there are possible exceptions among those of the second hunting party not personally summoned by Diana's herald. Obviously, if 1328 is the correct date of the death of Maria di Berardello Caracciolo Pisquizi, she must be excluded.

Branca points, rather, to Torraca's hypothesis that Maria-Marella is present also in the *Filocolo* through a complicated biblical allusion to her name, echoing the angel's annunciation to the Blessed Virgin Mary, "Hail, full of grace" (Luke 1:28): "I, descended of noble parents, was born in this city, and was named with a name full of grace, although my surname, Cara, may identify me to the hearers" (*Filoc.* 4.27.2).

See also Lariella, Mitola, and Principessella Caracciola.

## Marella Melia (Maria, or Mariella de' Melii)

Marella, called variously "de' Melii Maria" in *Hunt* 1.27 and "Marella de' Melii" in 3.51–52, is named "Marella Melia" in Canto 2.46, where she figures among the personal band selected by Diana herself; she helps in the capture of three horned stags in Canto 3.

The Melia (or de' Melii) were a noble family of Naples related to the Toraldo. Various members were courtiers and functionaries at the court of King Robert and his successor, Queen Giovanna: Matteo was judge of the criminal court in the Otranto territory; Jacopo was lieutenant of the treasurer; Angelo Melia was among the most illustrious abbots of San Demetrio.

## Marella Passerella

Marella enters with the second group of huntresses in *Hunt* 9; after the capture of a beaver, Marella first hears the elephant bellowing in *Hunt* 10, and, with Iacopa Aldimaresca, first catches sight of the serpent's tail in *Hunt* 11. Like Serella Brancazza, Marella appears crowned with green fronds in *Hunt* 11, suggesting, perhaps, that she represents the burgeoning of springtime love and the virtue of hope.

The Passerella family were nobles of Monopoli and Catanzaro. A branch of the Sighinolfi, they were related also to the Carafa, Filomarino, and Caracciolo families. We find historical evidence of them especially from the end of 1200 to the mid-fifteenth century. They traced their ancestry to Passerello Sighinolfi; they held the baronies of Brocentoro, Motta, and Paganica; in Naples they lived in the See of Capua. Among the chamberlains of King Robert there figures a Giovanni Passerella and among the king's feudatories, one named Errico Passerella.

## Mariella Piscicella

One of the twenty-five huntresses of the second party, Mariella joins Iacopa Aldimaresca, Marella Passerella, and Dalfina di Barasso at the snake's hole in *Hunt* 12.

Mariella was probably related to Lariella Caracciolo (q.v.). The Piscicelli also belonged to the forty-seven noble families of the See of Capua and later became united with the Capece family; they had a chapel in the Duomo, and held high offices at the time: Caraccio, Filippo, and Arrigo were members of the household and barons to King Robert; Bartolomeo was ambassador; Niccolò was criminal judge of the Abruzzo under the king; Riccardo was squire of Carlo, duke of Calabria; Tommaso was knight of Queen Giovanna and captain of the Abruzzo.

## Mignana Scrignara

Mignana, a member of the first hunt, catches rabbits and hares with Vannella Gambatella and with her kinswoman Isabella (q.v.) in *Hunt* 6.

For the family, see under Isabella Scrignara.

## Mitola Caracciola

Mitola, who appears in the second hunt, flushes mallards as prey for her goshawk in *Hunt* 15.

Branca cites a historical record of a Mitola or Margherita, daughter of Filippo Caracciolo (called "Bullone"); she was still a minor at the death of her father in 1327 and probably died herself before 1334, since she does not appear in the pact dividing the estate of her great-grandmother, Teodora del Gaudio. Branca disagrees with Massèra's proposal identifying this Mitola with the Mitola who was the daughter of Giovanni Caracciolo and wife of Giacomo Acciapaccia, lord of Cerchiara. The name "Margherita" and the diminutive, Mitola, were common among the Caracciolo family.

See also Lariella, Marella, and Principessella Caracciola.

## Peronella d'Arco

Hunting as a member of the second party, Peronella and her dogs capture and wound a roebuck in *Hunt* 11.

"Peronella" was a very fashionable name at the time in Naples. A "Péronelle" had recently appeared as a character in the popular pastoral comedy *Le jeu de Robin et Marion,* by the French poet Adam de la Halle, a one-time resident at the Angevin court in Naples. Appearing first, as here, among the aristocracy, the name soon became adopted by other classes of society. Boccaccio presents us with a very different Neapolitan Peronella in *Dec.* 7.2.

For the family, see Covella d'Arco.

## Principessella Caracciola

Part of the group called in *Hunt* 1, Principessella traps a lion cub (the traditional "Prince of Beasts") in a pit and presents it to the Mystery Lady in *Hunt* 5.

"Principessella" is her given name, not her title; names such as "Imperatrice" and "Principessa" were common at the time and especially so in her family, much as "Earl," "Prince," and "Duke," as given names, or "Princess," as a pet name, are in our time. The Caracciolo were one of the outstanding noble families among the forty-seven of the See of Capua and were divided into several branches. Unfortunately, no "Principessella" appears among the genealogical tables published.

See also Lariella, Marella, and Mitola Caracciola.

## Serella Brancazza

A member of the second hunting party, Serella identifies the bellowing in *Hunt* 10 as that of an elephant.

Serella Brancaccio (or, variously, "Brancazzi") married Gualtiero Galeota; she died in November 1339, as a tombstone in San Domenico attests. In October 1339, her husband Gualtiero had donated land for the convent and church of San Giovanni to Boccaccio's great friend, Padre Dionigi da Borgo San Sepolcro. When the *Hunt* was written, Serella was unmarried, since she still has her maiden name; but, as Branca points out, there is some inconsistency in use of patronymics, family names, and married names in the poem.

See also Berita, Caterina, and Serella's sister, Vannella.

## Sobilia Capece

With Beritola Carafa, likewise a member of the first hunt summoned in the first canto, Sobilia clubs two bears to death in *Hunt* 5.

Of Sobilia, or Sibilla, Capece we have precise information: she was the daughter of Corrado Capece and married Matteo Mansella, knight and courtier of King Robert, who was present at the wedding. Her family was among the most aristocratic of Naples and had various ties with the forty-seven families of the See of Capua, where the Capece themselves had their seat in Vico dei Castaldi.

## Tanzella Acerra, or dell' Acerra

Like her companion Covella (Giacopella) Embriaca, Tanzella appears with her head adorned with red roses in *Hunt* 13; in *Hunt* 14 she borrows a spear and dispatches a fierce bull. The flaming red garland that she wears, and the fact that neither she nor the other twenty-five members of the second hunt are personally called by the messenger of the goddess of chastity, may signify that she is married or betrothed.

Tanzella is a diminutive of Costanza, "Costanzella." Her family belonged to the nobility of the Sees of Nido, Capua, and Portanova. They were related to the Carafa and had tombs in San Domenico. They held offices and enjoyed privileges at the Angevin court from the time of King Carlo I (1266–1285) until that of Ladislao (1400–1414). Branca does not believe that the name refers to a lady belonging either to the princely house of Taranto, among whose titles was the countship of Acerra, or to the d'Aquino family of Acerra; both families are cited at the beginning of the fourteenth century by the name of their feudal domain.

## Tuccella Serisale

During the second hunt (*Hunt* 14), Tuccella lends Tanzella Acerra a spear to dispatch the bull; whereupon, in the company of Tanzella and Caterina Carafa, she shoots a porcupine.

The pet name "Tuccella" was common at the time, and a precise identification of this huntress has not been made. Her family members were nobles of the See of Nido and were known in Naples from the time of Carlo I (1266–1285). Matteo Serisale was counselor and member of the households of King Robert and Queen Giovanna I; Bartolomeo was criminal judge in the Abruzzi; Nicola was a household member and counselor of Robert and Giovanna; and Antonio married Imperatrice Caracciolo near the date of the poem.

## Vannella Bolcana

One of the second group, Vannella incites her hound to catch a beaver in *Hunt* 10.

As we can see from the entries immediately below, Vannella was a common diminutive of an even more common first name, Giovanna—a phenomenon that we would expect, given that it was the baptismal name of the crown princess.

The Bolcano or Vulcano family, originally of Sorrento, was one of the forty-seven noble families of the See of Capua; one of its branches also dwelt in the See of Nido. A great many of its members held important posts at court. Tommaso was governor of Capua for King Robert. When his relative, Landolfo, the king's jurisconsult and counselor, received his doctoral insignia, he was paid honor by King Robert himself. Marino was one of the most faithful and trusted courtiers of Queen Giovanna I, who had him accompany her on her flight from Naples on 15 January 1348. The family appeared so tied to Giovanna that, during the popular revolt of February 1347, a Bolcano was put to death as a contemptuous affront to the monarch.

The Bolcana or Bolcano were related by marriage to the Caracciolo family—as the close proximity of the two women in the poem might indicate. Probably Boccaccio had some relationship with a member of this family. Branca points out that in a letter to Francesco de' Bardi, attributed to Boccaccio, a certain Martucello Borcano or Bolcano (and not "Orcano" as other editors read) is mentioned among their friends.

## Vannella Brancazzi

Like Serella Brancazzi, she is a member of the second hunt; she slays one of the three boars in *Hunt* 11.

For the derivation of the diminutive "Vannella," see the note above on Vannella Bolcana. Massèra believes this lady to be Giovanna Brancaccio Embriachi (see also *Hunt* 10.17, and Giacopella Embriaca), wife of a certain Petrillo Caracciolo who was still a minor in 1339; she died on 15 August 1358. For the Brancaccio, Brancazza, or Brancazzi family, see also Serella and the sisters, Berita and Caterina.

## Vannella Gambatelli, or de' Gambatelli

The second-from-last to be called to the first hunt in *Hunt* 1, she captures rabbits and hares with Mignana and Isabella degli Scrignar in *Hunt* 6.

For the lady's first name, see the preceding notes on her namesakes. The Gambatelli, or Gambitella, were nobles of the See of Portanova related to the Caputo family.

## Verdella di Berardo

A huntress of the first hunting party, she goes hawking with her falcon in *Hunt* 7, killing a mallard in *Hunt* 8.

"Verdella," or "Berdella," was not an unusual name at the time in Naples. There was a Berardi family mainly involved in law and jurisprudence: Guglielmo Berardi was criminal judge in charge of the confiscation of the property of rebels; Egidia Berardi was wife to Enrico Sinigolfo, lord of Felesa. The appellation "di Berardo," however, may be a genuine patronymic: men named Berardo were numerous at the Angevin court:

among them, Berardo d'Aquino, count of Loreto; Berardo Serpando; Berardo Caracciolo, palatine seneschal, or majordomo; Berardo di San Flaviano, tribunal judge; and Berardo Moromile.

## Zizzola Barrile

This Zizzola has considerable textual prominence: she is the first to be summoned by Diana's messenger in the first canto of the *Hunt*. She hunts among the first troop deployed to the south, where, led by the Mystery Lady, she helps Ciancia shoot a white stag, and personally kills two foxes in *Hunt* 4.

"Zizzola" (variously, "Zeza," "Zizza," and "Zezzerella") was a diminutive of "Lucrezia" (see the four other Zizzolas below); however, since the diminutive could be formed from any woman's name ending in "-za," or "-zia," (thus we find it used for "Costanza"), positive identification is difficult. "Lucrezia" was a name popular among the Barrile, or Barrili, family, one of the best known and powerful in Naples in the first half of the fourteenth century. The family was one of forty-seven noble clans of the See of Capua with its own chapel in the cathedral. Among the most famous of the Barrile were Nicola, ambassador to Queen Giovanna I, and Giovanni, a good friend of Boccaccio and the one chosen to be King Robert's stand-in at Petrarch's crowning on the Campidoglio in Rome in 1341—although Giovanni failed to arrive at that occasion because he was ambushed by brigands.

## Zizzola d'Alagna

Zizzola flushes mallards with her naker as she goes hawking with Mitola Caracciola (*Hunt* 15).

We have a record of a Costanza (of which "Zizzola" can be a diminutive), the daughter of Baldovino d'Alagna, called Baldetto. She married Niccolò della Marra, lord of Stigliano, who was of the noble family of Berletta (they too are named in an Angevin registry from 1327). Alternatively, the name may derive from "Lucrezia," another name common in the d'Alagna family. A later Lucrezia d'Alagno is said to have been the beloved of Alfonso d'Aragona.

The Alagna family were nobility of the See of Nido, related to the Caracciolo, Carafa, Crispano, Moromile, Piscicelli, and Bolcana (Vulcano) clans. They had considerable power at the court of King Robert and his heir, Queen Giovanna I, especially thanks to Franzone, lieutenant of the grand treasurer; Andrea, criminal judge of the Abruzzo from 1321;

and Ovillo, auditor of the Gran Corte della Vicaria (the supreme civil and criminal tribunal) under Queen Giovanna.

## Zizzola d'Anna

This Zizzola is the last straggler of the huntresses, and perhaps the youngest; at the last minute, she brings their number to a perfect Dantesque total of sixty (see Introduction, pp. 7, 24). Introduced only as late as *Hunt* 16.26, she is not called by the "gentle spirit" of Canto 1, nor does she form part of the second party of huntresses who enter in *Hunt* 9. As noted above, "Zizzola" is a typical Neapolitan diminutive of "Lucrezia" or "Costanza."

## Zizzola Faccipecora

This Zizzola, hunting with the second group, sights the male leopard in *Hunt* 12 and dispatches him with an arrow in *Hunt* 13.

Again, nothing is known specifically about this lady historically. The Faccipecora, one of the branches of the Capece family, related to the Serpando (or Seripando) and Gattini clans, belonged to the forty-seven families of the See of Capua. Giovanni Faccipecora was a right-hand man of King Robert, Queen Giovanna I, and Louis of Taranto; to him were entrusted delicate missions, among them, one to the king of England.

## Zizzola Fagiana

Both members of the second hunt, Zizzola and her kinswoman, Cecca, kill two roebucks in *Hunt* 11.

For the diminutive of her first name, see the note on Zizzola d'Anna above. For her family, see Cecca Fagiana.

*Appendix*

# TERNARIO AND BALLATA WITH ENGLISH TRANSLATION

### Ternario e Ballata

    Contento quasi ne' pensier d'amore,
soletto un giorno in essi dimorava,
immaginando il suo alto valore;
    e, mentre dolcemente più pensava,
5  Amor m'apparve con gioioso aspetto
ver me dicendo: "Qual pensier ti grava?
    Non istar qui, ch'amoroso diletto
ti mosterrò, se tu mi seguirai,
di belle donne in fresco giardinetto."
10  Allora in piedi ritto mi levai,
seguendo lui, che diritto sen gio
in un giardin dilettevole assai.
    Lasciommi quivi, e disse: "Mentre ch'io
a tornar penerò, fa che m'aspetti";
15  e volando da me si dipartio.
    Ma e' non stette guari, ch'io vedetti
lui ritornar con dodici donzelle
gaie, leggiadre e con gentili aspetti.
    Tutte eran fresche, dilicate e belle,
20  d'erbe e di frondi verdi coronate,
negli occhi lor lucenti più che stelle.
    Tutte danzando venieno ordinate
su un bello prato d'erbette e di fiori,
nel qual danzando Amor l'avea menate.
25  Fessi ver me Amor: "Tu, che di fori
della danza dimori, riguardando
ne' belli occhi a costoro i miei ardori,
    odile nominare, sì che quando
forse sarai di fuor da questo loco,
30  d'onorarle disii per mio comando.

## *Ternario* and Ballad

Content—almost—in thoughts of love, I all alone dwelt on them one day, as I pondered on Love's lofty power:

and, while I continued thinking sweetly, Love appeared to me, with joyous aspect, and said to me, "What thought grieves you?

Tarry not here, for, I shall show you, if you will follow me, the amorous delight of fair ladies in a fresh little garden."

Then I arose straight to my feet to follow him, for straightway he went off to a garden of great delight.

There he left me and said: "While my return is delayed, see that you wait for me." And he flew away from me and departed.

But he hardly tarried a moment for I saw him return with twelve damsels, joyful, graceful, and of noble mien.

All were fresh, delicate and fair, crowned with herbs and verdant fronds; their eyes shone more than stars.

They all came dancing in file onto a fair meadow of herbs and flowers to which Love, dancing, had led them.

Love approached me: "You who stay outside the dance gazing at my ardor in their eyes,

hear their names, so that, perhaps, when you are far from here you may desire to honor them at my command.

Tra l'altre, che più guarda il nostro foco
con senno e con virtù, costei è quella,
allato a cui con allegrezza gioco.
   Di Giachinotto monna Itta s'appella,
35 de' Tornaquinci, e Meliana è colei,
di Giovanni di Nello, ch'è dop'ella.
   E la Lisa e la Pecchia, che con lei
vengono appresso, amendue figliuole
di Rinier Marignan son saper dei.
40    A nostra danza quinta è il tuo sole,
cioè quella Fiammetta, che ti diede
con la saetta al cor, ch'ancor ti dole.
   Ell'è più bella ch'altra, ma nol crede
chi non riguarda lei con gli occhi tuoi,
45 però che tanto avanti alcun non vede.
   E la bella lombarda segue poi,
monna Vanna chiamata, e, se tu guardi,
nulla più bella n'è con esso noi.
   Di Filippozzo Filippa de' Bardi
50 seguita bella, e poi monna Lottiera
di Neron Nigi con soavi sguardi.
   La Vanna di Filippo, Primavera
da tal conosci tu degna chiamata,
vedila poi seguir nostra bandiera.
55    Allato allato a lei vedi onorata
Sismonda di Francesco Baroncelli,
e poi, appresso lei, accompagnata
   Niccolosa è di Tedice Manoelli
insieme appresso con Bartolomea
60 di Giovanni: Beatrice cre' s'appelli.
   E ben che 'n fine della danza stea,
non è men bella, ma vien per riscossa,
come tu vedi"; ed io ben lo vedea.
   Tacquesi allora, e la danza fu mossa
65 sopra bei fiori e sotto verde fronda,
che a' raggi solar toglieva possa.
   Onde ciascuna di quella gioconda
e bella danza, gaia e leggiadretta,
a cantar cominciò, come seconda,
70    questa leggiadra e bella canzonetta:

Among the others, she most guards our fire with judgment and with virtue, is she beside whom I most joyfully disport.

Monna Itta di Giachinotto is she called, of the Tornaquinci, and Meliana is she of Giovanni di Nello who is behind her.

And you must know that La Lisa and La Pecchia, who, with her, come after, are both daughters of Rinier Marignan.

Fifth in our dance is your sun, Fiammetta, that is, she who struck you in your heart with an arrow which afflicts you still.

She is fairer than any other, but anyone who does not look upon with your eyes, does not believe it, since no one sees so far beyond.

And the fair Lombard follows next, called Monna Vanna, and if you look, in our company none is fairer.

The fair Filippa of Filippozzo de' Bardi follows; and then Monna Lottiera of Neron Nigi with gentlest looks.

La Vanna di Filippo—'Primavera'—you know her worthily called by someone—see her, then, follow our banner!

Close beside her see the honored Sismonda of Francesco Baroncelli; and then, after her,

Niccolosa is accompanied by Tedice Manoelli, together, afterwards, with Bartolomea of Giovanni—Beatrice I believe she is called.

Although she is at the end of the dance, she is not less fair, but comes in vindication, as you see." And I did surely see her.

He then fell silent, and the dance moved off upon the fair flowers and beneath the verdant fronds that stole power from the rays of the sun.

Wherefore each one in that joyful and lovely dance, graceful and fair, began to sing

this charming and beautiful song, as follows:

[*Ballata*]

"Amor, dolce signore,
che hai il nostro core
in tua balia, per Dio, fanne contente.
    Tu se' nostro signor caro e verace,
5   e noi così volemo;
tu se' colui che ne puo' render pace
nel gran disio ch'avemo:
però quanto potemo
preghiam tua signoria
10  che 'nvèr di noi si porti umilmente.
    Noi siam qui giovinette, e tu 'l ti sai,
che poca di grevezza,
che noi sentiam, ci par sentire assai;
però la tua grandezza
15  a chiunque la sprezza,
signor, falla sentire,
ch'a noi non cal, che siam tue veramente.
    Fa sentire a coloro il tuo valore,
che si fanno chiamare
20  innamorati sanza farti onore:
ché, se tu fai provare
lor quanto tu puoi fare,
saranno innamorati,
e noi ti loderem più degnamente.
25      Noi ardiam tutte per la tua virtute
nel tuo cocente foco.
Per Dio, mercé; deh, donaci salute
anzi che mutiam loco,
    ché già a poco a poco
30  per te ci consumiamo,
se tu non ci soccorri tostamente.
    Fa, signor nostro, gli animi pietosi
degli nostri amadori;
raffrena alquanto i lor atti orgogliosi
35  con più aspri dolori,
che non hanno ne' cori,
sì che la nostra pena
e' provi come noi chi non la sente.

## [The Ballad]

"Love, O sweet Lord,
you have our hearts
in your power, through God, make us content.
You are our lord dear and true
and that is as we want it;
you are he who can grant us peace
in the great desire that we have:
therefore with all our might
we beg your Lordship
that you bear yourself toward us humbly.
We here are damsels, and you well know
that the little grief
that we do feel, we seem to feel greatly;
therefore whoever scorns
your greatness,
Lord, make him feel it,
for we do not need to, who are truly yours.
Make those feel your worth
who call themselves
enamored without honoring you,
for if you make them experience
how much you can do,
they shall be enamored
and we will praise you more worthily.
We all burn because of your power
in your scorching fire.
For the sake of God, mercy! Ah! Give us salvation
before we pass away,
for already, little by little
we are consumed for you,
unless you hasten to give us succor.
Make pitying, O Lord of ours,
the minds of our lovers;
restrain somewhat their proud acts
with harsher pains
than they have in their hearts,
so that whoever does not feel our suffering
may experience it as we do.

Entra en gli orecchi qui, ballata, avanti
40   ad Amor nostro siri,
e, come tu pietosamente canti
i nostri aspri martiri,
fa che pregando il giri
a darci tosto gioia,
45   prima ched ei n'uccida crudelmente."


The text is from Giovanni Boccaccio, *Rime e Caccia di Diana,* ed. Vittore Branca (Padova: Liviana Editrice, 1958), pp. 68–77.

Enter here into their ears, Ballad, before
Love our Sire,
and, as you piously sing
of our bitter torture,
by praying make him turn
swiftly to give us joy,
before he slays us cruelly."

# BIBLIOGRAPHY OF WORKS CONSULTED

Main-entry authors and titles are listed alphabetically. Multiple listings for modern authors (post-1850) are listed chronologically under their names, so that the contributions of scholars and critics may be consulted more conveniently.

English translations immediately follow the listing of works in the original foreign language.

Abraham, Claude K. "Myth and Symbol: The Rabbit in Medieval France." *Studies in Philology* 60, no. 4 (October 1963): 589–597.
Acars [or Acart], Jean de Hesdin. *La prise amoureuse von Jehan Acart de Hesdin*. Ed. Ernst Hoepffner. Dresden: Gedruckt für die Gesellschaft für romanische Literatur, 1910.
Aelian [Aelianus Claudius]. [*De sollertia animalium.*] *On the Characteristics of Animals*. Trans. A. F. Schofield. LCL. 3 vols. Cambridge: Harvard University Press; London: William Heinemann, 1958–1959.
Ageno, Franca. "Nomignoli e personaggi immaginari, anneddotici, proverbiali." *Lingua nostra* 19, no. 3 (September 1958): 73–77.
Albertus Magnus, Saint, Bishop of Ratisbon. *De animalibus libri XXVI: Nach der kölner Urschrift*. Ed. Hermann Stadler. In *Beiträge zur Geschichte der Philosophie des Mittelalters* (series), vols. 15–16. Münster: Aschendorffschen Verlagsbuchhandlung, 1916–1920.
———. *Opera omnia*. Ed. Bernhard Geyer. Monasterii Westfalorum [Münster]: Aschendorff, 1951; rprt. 1972. (Many reprintings.)
———. *Man and the Beasts: De animalibus (Books 22–26)*. Trans. James J. Scanlan. Binghamton, N.Y.: MRTS, 1986.
[Albertus Magnus, Saint, Bishop of Ratisbon, attributed.] *The Book of Secrets*. Ed. Michael R. Best and Frank H. Brightman. Oxford: Clarendon Press, 1973.
Ambrose, Saint. *Hexameron, Paradise, and Cain and Abel*. Trans. John J. Savage. Fathers of the Church, 42. New York: Fathers of the Church, Inc., 1961.
Anderson, David. *Before the Knight's Tale: Imitation of Classical Epic in Boccaccio's Teseida*. Philadelphia: University of Pennsylvania Press, 1988.
Andreas Capellanus. *The Art of Courtly Love by Andreas Capellanus*. Intro. and trans. John Jay Parry. Records of Civilisation. Ed. Austin P. Evans. New York: Columbia University Press, 1941; rprt. New York: Frederick Ungar, 1959, 1970.
Apuleius. *The Golden Ass*. Trans. W. Adlington, rev. S. Gaselee. LCL. London: William Heinemann; New York: The Macmillan Co., 1915; rprt. Cambridge, Mass.: Harvard University Press; London: William Heinemann, 1947.

Aristotle. *Historia animalium*. Trans. A. L. Peck. LCL. Cambridge, Mass.: Harvard University Press; London: William Heinemann. Vol. 1, 1965; vol. 2, 1970.

Arnason, Hjörvardur Harvard. "Early Christian Silver of North Italy and Gaul." *Art Bulletin* 20 (March 1938): 193–226.

Augustine, Saint. *S. Aureli Augustini Hipponensis episcopi De catechizandis rudibus liber unus*. Trans. with intro. J. P. Christopher. Catholic University of America Patristic Series 8. Washington, D.C.: Catholic University of America Press, 1926. *The First Catechetical Instruction [De catechizandis rudibus]*. Trans. J. P. Christopher. Ancient Christian Writers 2. Westminster, Md.: The Newman Bookshop, 1946.

———. *City of God Against the Pagans: In Seven Volumes*. Trans. George E. McCracken, David S. Wiesen, William Chase Green, William M. Green et al. LCL. Cambridge, Mass.: Harvard University Press; London: William Heinemann, 1957–1972.

———. *Enarrationes in Psalmos*. PL 36–37. *Saint Augustin: Expositions on the Book of Psalms*. Ed. A. Cleveland Coxe. A Select Library of the Nicene and Post-Nicene Fathers of the Christian Church. Ed. Philip Schaff. Vol. 8. Grand Rapids, Mich.: W. B. Eerdmans, 1974. *St. Augustine on the Psalms*. Trans. Dame Scholastica Hebgin and Dame Felicitas Corrigan. ACW. Vol. 29 [I]: Psalms 1–29. Westminster, Md.: The Newman Press; London: Longmans, Green and Co., 1960. Vol. 30 [2]: Psalms 30–37: 1961.

———. *In epistolam Johannis*. PL 35:1982. *Homilies on the Gospel According to St. John and His First Epistle by S. Augustine, Bishop of Hippo*. Trans. with notes and indexes. Vol. 2. A Library of Fathers of the Holy Catholic Church Anterior to the Division of East and West. Translated by Members of the English Church. Oxford: John Henry Parker, 1849.

———. *Sermones in Vigiliis Paschae* in *Sermones de tempore*. PL 38. Sermons "For the Vigil of Easter." In *Sermons*. Trans. Sister Mary Sarah Muldowney, R.S.M. The Fathers of the Church, vol. 38. Washington, D.C.: Catholic University of America Press, 1959.

Bartholomaeus Anglicus. *On the Properties of Things: John Treviso's Translation of Bartholomaeus Anglicus Proprietatibus Rerum (1495), A Critical Text*. Ed. M. C. Seymour et al. 2 vols. Oxford: Clarendon Press, 1975.

Bauerreiss, Romuald. "*Arbor vitae*. Der 'Lebensbaum' und seine Verwendung in Liturgie, Kunst und Brauchtum des Abendlandes." *Abhandlungen der Bayerischen Benediktiner-Akademie* 3 (Munich, 1938); publ. simultaneously as separate vol. Munich: Neuer Filserverlag, 1938.

Bergin, Thomas Godard. "Diana's Hunt." In his *Boccaccio*. Pp. 66–71. New York: The Viking Press, 1981.

[Bernard, Saint, Abbot of Clairvaux.] *Sermones super Cantica Canticorum*. S. Bernardi Opera, vols. 1–2. Ed. J. Leclerq, C. H. Talbot, H. M. Rochais. Rome: Editiones Cisterciensis, 1957. *Cantica Canticorum: Eighty-Six Sermons on the Song of Solomon by Saint Bernard*. Trans. and ed. Samuel J. Eales. London: Elliot Stock, 1895.

*Le Bestiaire d'amour rimé: Poème inédit du XIII<sup>e</sup> siècle*. Ed. Arvid Thordstein. Etudes Romanes de Lund 2. Lund: C.W.K. Gleerup; Ejnar Munksgaard: Copenhagen, 1941.

*Le Bestiaire divin.* See Guillaume, Clerc de Normandie.
*Bestiario d'amore.* See Richard de Fournival.
*Il Bestiario moralizzato.* In *Testi e Interpretazioni.* Ed. Maria Romano. Pp. 721–888. Studi del Seminario di Filologia Romanza dell'Università di Firenze. Milan-Naples: Ricciardi, 1978.
*Il Bestiario toscano secondo la lezione dei codici di Parigi e di Roma.* Ed. M[ilton] S. Garver, K[enneth] McKenzie. Rome: Società Filologica Romana, 1912. Extract from *Studi romanzi* 8 (1912).
[*Il Bestiario tosco-veneziano.*] *Ein Tosco-Venezianischer Bestiarius.* Ed. Max[imilian] Goldstaub and Richard Wendriner. Halle a. S.: Max Niemeyer, 1892.
[Bianciotto, Gabriel, ed. and trans.] Pierre de Beauvais, Guillaume le Clerc, Richard de Fournival, Brunetto Latini, Corbechon. *Bestiaires du Moyen Age.* Paris: Stock, 1980.
Billanovich, Giuseppe. *Petrarca letterato,* vol. 1. *Lo scrittoio del Petrarca.* Rome: Edizioni di "Storia e Letteratura," 1947.
———. "Nella biblioteca del Petrarca, I: Il Petrarca, il Boccaccio e le *Enarrationes in Psalmos* di s. Agostino." *Italia medioevale e umanistica* 3 (1960): 1–27.
Boccaccio, Giovanni. *Ameto.* Trans. Judith Serafini-Sauli. Garland Library of Medieval Literature 33. Series B. New York and London: Garland, 1985.
———. *Amorosa visione.* Ed. Girolamo Claricio. Milan, 1521. (Contains Claricio's appendix, *Apologia contro i detrattori della poesia di messer Gio. Boccaccio.*) *Amorosa visione.* Bilingual edition. Trans. Robert Hollander, Timothy Hampton, Margherita Frankel, intro. Vittore Branca. Hanover, N.H., and London: University Press of New England, 1986.
———. *La Caccia di Diana.* Ed. Ignazio Moutier. Florence: Magheri, 1832. *La Caccia di Diana.* Ed. S. Morpurgo and A. and O. Zenatti. Nozze Casini-Polsinelli. Florence: Carnesecchi, 1884. *La Caccia di Diana e le Rime.* Ed. Aldo Francesco Massèra. Collezione di Classici Italiani 16, Num. 1. Città di Castello: S. Lapi, 1914; rprt. Turin: Unione Tipografico-Editrice Torinese, 1919. *La Caccia di Diana.* In *Opere Minori.* [Ed. Enrico Bianchi.] Florence: Salani Editore, 1964. *Rime, Caccia di Diana.* Ed. Vittore Branca. Padua: Liviani, 1958. [Partial edition] "*Dalla 'Caccia di Diana.'*" Ed. Pier Giorgio Ricci. La Letteratura Italiana: Storia e Testi 9. Milan-Naples: Ricciardi, 1965. *Caccia di Diana.* Ed. Vittore Branca. Milan: Mondadori, 1967. *Caccia di Diana.* In *Opere minori in volgare.* Ed. Mario Marti. Vol. 4. Milan: Rizzoli, 1972.
———. *De casibus virorum illustrium.* Ed. Pier Giorgio Ricci and Vittorio Zaccaria. In Giovanni Boccaccio, *Tutte le opere,* vol. 9. Milan: Mondadori, 1981; rprt. 1983.
———. *Comedìa delle ninfe fiorentine.* Ed. Antonio Enzo Quaglio. In Giovanni Boccaccio, *Tutte le opere,* vol. 2. Milan: Mondadori, 1964.
———. *Il Corbaccio.* In *Opere minori in volgare.* Ed. Mario Marti. Vol. 4. Milan: Rizzoli, 1972 [essentially reproduces the text ed. Tauno Nurmela. Suomalaisen Tiedeakatemian Toimituksia: Annales Academiae Scientiarum Fennicae, ser. B., vol. 146. Helsinki: Suomalainen Tiedeakatemia, 1968]. *The Corbaccio.* Trans. and ed. Anthony K. Cassell. Urbana and London: University of Illinois Press, 1975.

———. *Decameron*. Ed. Vittore Branca. In Giovanni Boccaccio, *Tutte le opere*, vol. 4. Milan: Mondadori, 1976.

———. *Eclogues*. Latin text and trans. Janet Levarie Smarr. New York: Garland Publishing, 1987.

———. *Elegia di madonna Fiammetta*. Ed. Carlo Salinari and Natalino Sapegno. In Giovanni Boccaccio, *Decameron, Filocolo, Ameto, Fiammetta*. Ed. Enrico Bianchi, Carlo Salinari, and Natalino Sapegno. Milan-Naples: Ricciardi, 1952.

———. *Esposizioni sopra la Comedìa di Dante*. Ed. Giorgio Padoan. In Giovanni Boccaccio, *Tutte le opere*, vol. 6. Milan: Mondadori, 1965.

———. *Filocolo*. Ed. Antonio Enzo Quaglio. In Giovanni Boccaccio, *Tutte le opere*, vol. 1. Milan: Mondadori, 1967. *Filocolo*. Trans. David Cheney with Thomas G. Bergin. New York: Garland, 1985.

———. *Filostrato*. Ed. Vittore Branca. In Giovanni Boccaccio, *Tutte le opere*, vol. 2. Milan: Mondadori, 1964.

———. *Genealogie deorum gentilium libri XV*. Ed. Vincenzo Romano. 2 vols. Scrittori d'Italia. Bari: Laterza, 1951.

———. [*Genealogie*] *Boccaccio on Poetry: Being the Preface and the Fourteenth and Fifteenth Books of Boccaccio's Genealogia Deorum Gentilium*. Ed., intro., and trans. Charles G. Osgood. Princeton, N.J.: Princeton University Press, 1930; rprt. Library of Liberal Arts: Indianapolis: Bobbs-Merrill, 1956.

———. *De mulieribus claris*. Ed. Vittorio Zaccaria. In Giovanni Boccaccio, *Tutte le opere*, vol. 10. Milan: Mondadori, 1967. *Concerning Famous Women*. Trans. Guido A. Guarino. Rutgers, N.J.: Rutgers University Press, 1963; rprt. London: Allen and Unwin, 1964.

———. *Ninfale fiesolano*. Ed. Armando Balduino. In Giovanni Boccaccio, *Tutte le opere*, vol. 3. Milan: Mondadori, 1974.

———. *Opere di Giovanni Boccaccio*. Ed. Cesare Segre, comment. Maria Segre Consigli and Antonia Benvenuti. Milan: Mursia, 1963; rprt. 1978.

———. *Opere minori in volgare*. Ed. Mario Marti. 4 vols. Milan: Rizzoli, 1969–1972.

———. *Rime, Caccia di Diana*. Ed. Vittore Branca. Padua: Liviana Editrice, 1958.

———. *Teseida delle nozze d'Emilia*. Ed. Alberto Limentani. In Giovanni Boccaccio, *Tutte le opere*, vol. 2. Milan: Mondadori, 1964.

———. *Trattatello in laude di Dante*. Ed. Pier Giorgio Ricci. In Giovanni Boccaccio, *Tutte le opere*, vol. 3. Milan: Mondadori, 1974.

———. *Tutte le opere*. Ed. Vittore Branca. Vols. 1, 2, 3, 4, 6, 9, and 10 (of prospectus of 12). Milan: Mondadori, 1964–.

[Boethius. *De consolatione Philosophiae.*] *The Consolation of Philosophy*. [Latin text and] Trans. H. F. Stewart. LCL. London: William Heinemann, 1918.

Bologna, Ferdinando. *I pittori alla corte angioina di Napoli (1266–1414) e un riesame dell'arte nell'età fridericiana*. Rome: Ugo Bozzi Editore, 1969.

Branca, Vittore. *Il cantare trecentesco e il Boccaccio del "Filostrato" e del "Teseida."* Florence: Sansoni, 1936.

———. "Per l'attribuzione della *Caccia di Diana*" and "Nuove note sulla *Caccia di Diana*," both in *Tradizione delle opere di Giovanni Boccaccio*.

———. *Tradizione delle opere di Giovanni Boccaccio*, vol. 1. *Un primo elenco dei codici e tre studi*. Rome: Edizioni di Storia e Letteratura, 1956; rprt. 1958.

———. *Profilo biografico.* In Giovanni Boccaccio, *Tutte le opere*, vol. 1. Pp. 3–203. Milan: Mondadori, 1967; rprt. Florence: Sansoni, 1976.

———. *Giovanni Boccaccio: The Man and His Works.* Trans. Richard Monges, co-trans. Dennis J. McAuliffe. Foreword by Robert C. Clements. New York: New York University Press, 1976.

———. *Poliziano e l'umanesimo della parola.* Turin: Einaudi, 1983.

Branca, Vittore, Paul Watson, and Victoria Kirkham. "Boccaccio visualizzato." *Studi sul Boccaccio* 15 (1985–1986): 85–188.

Brunetto Latini. *Li Livres dou trésor de Brunetto Latini.* Ed. Francis J. Carmody. University of California Publications in Modern Philology 22. Berkeley and Los Angeles: University of California Press, 1948.

Cahiers, Charles, and A. Martin. *Mélanges d'archéologie, d'histoire et de littérature.* Paris, 1847–1856.

———. *Nouveaux mélanges d'archéologie, d'histoire et de littérature.* Vol. 1. Paris, 1847.

Callmann, Ellen. "The Growing Threat to Matrimonial Bliss as Seen in Fifteenth-Century Florentine Poets." *Studies in Iconography* 5 (1979): 73–92.

Callu, Florence, François Avril, and Michel Brunet. *Boccace en France: De l'humanisme à l'érotisme.* Paris: Bibliothèque Nationale, 1975.

Cantarelli, Giuseppe. *Il Museo Stibbert a Firenze.* 4 vols. Florence: Cassa di Risparmio, 1974.

Carlill, James, trans. *Physiologus.* In *The Epic of the Beast, Consisting of English Translations of the History of Reynard the Fox and Physiologus.* Trans. William Caxton, modernized by William Swan Stallybrass (*Reynard*) and James Carlill (*Physiologus*). Introd. William Rose. Broadway Translations. London: George Routledge; New York: E. P. Dutton, 1924.

Carmody, Francis James. "*De bestiis et aliis rebus* and the Latin Physiologus." *Speculum* 13 (April 1938): 153–159.

———. *Physiologus: The Very Ancient Book of Beasts, Plants and Stones, Translated from Greek and Other Languages.* San Francisco: The Book Club of California, 1953.

———. "Bestiary." *New Catholic Encyclopedia.* Vol. 2. New York: McGraw-Hill, 1967.

———, ed. *Physiologus latinus: Editions préliminaires versio B.* Paris: Librairie E. Droz, 1939.

———, ed. *Physiologus Latinus Versio Y.* University of California Publications in Classical Philology 12, no. 7. Pp. 95–134. Berkeley and Los Angeles: University of California Press, 1941.

Cassell, Anthony K. *Dante's Fearful Art of Justice.* Toronto: University of Toronto Press, 1984.

———. *Lectura Dantis Americana: Inferno I.* Foreword by Robert Hollander; with a new trans. of canto by Patrick Creagh and Robert Hollander. Lectura Dantis Americana, vol. 1. Philadelphia: University of Pennsylvania Press, 1989.

———, trans. See Giovanni Boccaccio, *The Corbaccio.*

Cecchi, Emilio, and Natalino Sapegno. *Il Trecento.* Storia della letteratura italiana 2. Milan: Garzanti, 1965.

Chaucer, Geoffrey. *The Works of Geoffrey Chaucer.* Ed. Fred N. Robinson. Boston: Houghton Mifflin, 1957.

Chiaro Davanzati. *Rime*. Ed. A. Menichetti. Collezione delle Opere inedite o rare, vol. 26. Bologna: Commissione per i Testi di Lingua, 1965.

Cicero. *Cicero in Twenty-Eight Volumes*. Vol. 12. *Pro Caelio, De Provinciis consularibus, Pro Balbo*. Trans. R. Gardner. Cambridge, Mass.: Harvard University Press; London: William Heinemann, 1970.

Claricio, Girolamo, ed. See Giovanni Boccaccio, *Amorosa visione*.

Claudian. *On Stilicho's Consulship*. Trans. Maurice Platnauer. LCL. London: William Heinemann, 1922; rprt. 1963.

[*Clavis Melitonis*.] *S. Melitonis Clavis. Analecta sacra spicilegio solemensi*. Ed. Jean-Baptiste Pitra. Vol. 3. Paris: Firmin Didot Frères, 1855.

Comparetti, Domenico. *Virgilio nel medioevo*. 2 vols. Florence: Seeber, 1872; 2nd ed. 1895; new ed. Giorgio Pasquali. Florence: "La Nuova Italia," 1937; rprt. 1981. *Vergil in the Middle Ages*. Trans. E.F.M. Benecke. Intro. Robinson Ellis. London: Swan Sonnenschein; New York: Macmillan, 1895; rprt. Hamden, Conn.: Archon Books, 1960.

Contini, Gianfranco, ed. *Poeti del Duecento*. 2 vols. Milan: Ricciardi, 1960.

Cronin, Grover, Jr. "The Bestiary and the Medieval Mind—Some Complexities." *Modern Language Quarterly* 2 (1941): 191–198.

Cropper, Elizabeth. "The Beauty of Woman: Problems in the Rhetoric of Renaissance Portraiture." In *Re-writing the Renaissance: The Discourses of Sexual Difference in Early Modern Europe*. Ed. Margaret W. Ferguson, Maureen Quilligan, and Nancy J. Vickers. Chicago: University of Chicago Press, 1986.

Curato, Baldo. *Introduzione al Boccaccio*. Cremona: Editrice "Padus," 1961.

Curley, Michael J., trans. *Physiologus*. Austin and London: University of Texas Press, 1979.

Curtius, Ernst Robert. *European Literature and the Latin Middle Ages*. Trans. Willard Trask. Princeton, N.J.: Princeton University Press, 1973.

Daniélou, Jean. *The Bible and the Liturgy*. Ed. and trans. Michael A. Mathis. Liturgical Studies. Notre Dame, Ind.: University of Notre Dame Press, 1956.

Dante Alighieri. *La Commedia secondo l'antica vulgata*. Ed. Giorgio Petrocchi. 4 vols. Milan: Mondadori, 1966–1967.

———. [*La Commedia*] *The Divine Comedy*. Trans. with comment. Charles S. Singleton. Bollingen Series. 6 vols. Princeton, N.J.: Princeton University Press, 1970–1975.

———. *Dante's Lyric Poetry*. Ed. and trans. K. Foster and P. Boyde. Vol. 1: The Poems: Text and Translation; Vol. 2: Commentary. Oxford: Clarendon Press, 1967.

———. *Vita nuova*. Ed. Domenico De Robertis. In *Opere minori di Dante Alighieri*. Vol. 1, pt. 1. Milan and Naples: Ricciardi, 1984.

———. [*Vita nuova*] *Dante's Vita Nuova*. New edition. Trans. and an essay by M. Musa. Bloomington and London: Indiana University Press, 1973.

*Dictionnaire d'archéologie et de liturgie*. 15 vols. in 30. Ed. Fernand Cabrol. Paris: Létouzey et Ané, 1907–1953.

di Pino, Guido. *La polemica del Boccaccio*. Florence: Vallecchi, 1953.

Donaldson-Evans, Lance K. *Love's Fatal Glance: A Study of Eye Imagery in the Poets of the Ecole Lyonnaise*. Romance Monographs 38. University, Miss.: Romance Monographs, 1980.

Druce, George Claridge. "The Elephant in Medieval Legend and Art." *Archaeological Journal* 76 (1919): 1–73.

———. "The Mediaeval Bestiaries and Their Influence on Ecclesiastical Decorative Art." *Journal of the British Archaeological Association* 25, n. s. (1919): 41–82; 26 (1920): 35–79.

———. "The Lion and Cubs in the Cloisters." *Canterbury Cathedral Chronicle* 23 (April 1936): 18–22.

———, trans. *The Bestiary of Guillaume le Clerc Originally Written in 1210–11*. Printed for private circulation by Headley Brothers. Ashford, Kent: Invicta Press, 1936.

Duchesne, L. *Origines du culte chrétien*. 2nd ed. Paris: A. Fontemoing, 1898.

Durling, Robert M. *The Figure of the Poet in Renaissance Epic*. Cambridge, Mass.: Harvard University Press, 1965.

———, trans. *Petrarch's Lyric Poems*. Cambridge, Mass.: Harvard University Press, 1976.

Eco, Umberto. *Art and Beauty in the Middle Ages*. Trans. Hugh Bredin. New Haven: Yale University Press, 1986.

Eden, P. T., ed. and trans. *Theobaldi "Physiologus."* Leiden: E. J. Brill, 1972.

Edgerton, Samuel J., Jr. *Pictures and Punishment: Art and Criminal Prosecution During the Florentine Renaissance*. Ithaca, N.Y.: Cornell University Press, 1985.

Edsman, Carl-Martin. *Le Baptême de feu*. Acta Seminarii Neotestamentici Upsaliensis 9. Leipzig: Alfred Lorenz; Uppsala: Lundquist, Almquist, and Wiksell, 1940.

Elliott, T[homas] J., trans. *A Medieval Bestiary*. With wood engravings by Gillian Tyler. Boston: David R. Godine, 1971. (Trans. of Middle English bestiary MS. B.M. Arundel 292, F4; contains a useful general bibliography.)

*Encyclopedia Britannica*. 11th ed., 1910–1911.

Esmeijer, Anna Catharina. *Divina quaternitas: een onderzoek naar methode en toepassing der visuele exegese (A Study of Methods and Applications of Visual Exegesis [with a Summary in English])*. Published dissertation. Rijksuniversiteit te Utrecht. Amsterdam, 1973.

Ferrières, Henri de. [fl. 1370.] *Livre du roy Modus: Li Livres du roy Modus et de la royne Ratio*. Ed. Gunnar Tilander. Paris: Société des Anciens Textes Français, 1932.

Feuille, G. L. "Une mosaïque chrétienne de l'henchir Messaouda (Tunisie, région d'Agareb)." *Cahiers archéologiques fin de l'antiquité et Moyen Age* 4 (1949): 9–15.

Fido, Franco. "Le due Veneri di Robert Hollander (A Proposito del libro: *Boccaccio's Two Venuses*. New York, 1977)." In *Il regime delle simmetrie imperfette. Studi sul Decameron*. Milan: Franco Angeli, 1988.

Fournival, Richard de. *Le Bestiaire d'amour suivi de la Réponse de la Dame*. Ed. C. Hippeau. Collection des Poètes Français du Moyen Age 4. Caen and Paris, 1852–1877; rprt. Geneva: Slatkine Reprints, 1969.

———. *Li Bestiaires d'amours di Maistre Richart de Fornival e li Response du Bestiaire*. Ed. Cesare Segre. Milan and Naples: Ricciardi, 1957.

———. *Il Bestiario d'Amore di Riccardo di Fornival*. Volgarizzamento del sec.

XIII. Ed. G. Grion. In *Propugnatore* 2, pt. 1 (1869): 147–179 and 273–306.
Freccero, John. *Dante: The Poetics of Conversion.* Ed. and intro. Rachel Jacoff. Cambridge, Mass.: Harvard University Press, 1986.
Frederick II of Hohenstaufen. *De arte venandi cum avibus.* Ed. Karl Willemsen. Leipzig: Insula, 1942. *The Art of Falconry Being the* De Arte Venandi cum Avibus *of Frederick II of Hohenstaufen.* Trans. and ed. Casey A. Wood and Marjory Fyfe. Stanford, Cal.: Stanford University Press, 1943.
[Fulgentius.] *Fulgentius the Mythographer.* Trans. and intro. Leslie George Whitbread. Columbus, Ohio: Ohio State University Press, 1971.
Galletti, Salvatore. *Patologia al Decameron.* Palermo: S. F. Flaccovio, 1969.
Garnier de Rochefort [attr.], pseudo-Rabanus Maurus. *Allegoriae in universam Sanctam Scriptorem.* PL 112, cols. 850–1088.
Garver, M[ilton] S. "Sources of the Beast Similes in the Italian Lyric of the Thirteenth Century." *Romanische Forschungen* 21 (1908): 276–320.
[Gaston Phoebus] Gaston Phébus, Count of Foix. *Livre de Chasse édité avec introduction, glossaire et reproduction des 87 miniatures du manuscrit 616 de la Bibliothèque Nationale de Paris.* Ed. Gunnar Tilander. *Cynegetica* 18. Karlshamn [Sweden]: Johanssons Boktryckeri, 1971. *Illuminated Manuscripts: Medieval Hunting Scenes ("The Hunting Book" by Gaston Phoebus).* Text by Gabriel Bise after Gaston Phoebus. Trans. J. Peter Tallon. Fribourg-Geneva: Miller Graphics, n.d. [but 1978].
Gervaise. "Le Bestiaire de Gervaise." Ed. Paul Meyer. *Romania* 1 (1872): 420–443.
Giacalone, Giuseppe. *Boccaccio minore e maggiore.* Rome: Avio, 1959.
Goldstaub-Wendriner. See *Il Bestiario tosco-veneziano.*
Grabher, Carlo. *Boccaccio.* Turin: Unione Tipografico-Editrice Torinese, 1945.
Gratian. *Decretum magistri Gratiani.* Ed. Emil Ludwig Richter, 1879; rprt. Graz: Akademisch Druck- u. Verlagsanstalt, 1959.
Gregory the Great. [*Moralia*] *Moralium libri sive expositio in librum Job.* PL 75, cols. 509–1162; *PL* 76, cols. 9–782. *Morals on the Book of Job. A Library of Fathers of the Holy Catholic Church Anterior to the Division of East and West.* Translated by Members of the English Church. 4 vols. Oxford: John Henry Parker, 1844–1850.
Gregory of Nyssa. *In baptismum Christi. PG* 46.
Guarino, Guido A., trans. Giovanni Boccaccio, *Concerning Famous Women.* Rutgers, N.J.: Rutgers University Press, 1963; rprt. London: Allen and Unwin, 1964.
Guillaume, Clerc de Normandie. *Le Bestiaire divin de Guillaume clerc de Normandie, Trouvère du XIII*ᵉ *siècle.* Ed. C. Hippeau. Collection des Poètes du Moyen Age, 1. Caen and Paris: 1852–1877; rprt. Geneva: Slatkine Reprints, 1970.
———. *Der Bestiaire divin des Guillaume le Clerc.* Ed. Max Friedrich Mann. Französische Studien 6, no. 2. Heilbronn: Henninger, 1888.
———. *Le Bestiaire: Das Thierbuch des normannischen Dichters Guillaume le clerc.* Ed. Robert Reinsch. Altfranzösischer Bibliothek 14. Leipzig: O. R. Reisland, 1892.
———. *Le Bestiaire de Guillaume.* Ed. C. Cahier and A. Martin. In *Mélanges d'archéologie, d'histoire et de littérature.* Paris, vol. 2 (1851): 106–232; vol. 3 (1853): 203–288; vol. 4 (1856): 55–87.

―――. *The Bestiary of Guillaume le Clerc Originally Written in 1210–11.* Trans. George Claridge Druce. Printed for private circulation by Headley Brothers. Ashford, Kent: Invicta Press, 1936.
Ham, Edward B. "The Cambrai Bestiary." *Modern Philology* 36 (1939): 225–237.
Henkel, Nikolaus. *Studien zum Physiologus im Mittelalter.* Tübingen: Max Niemeyer Verlag, 1976.
Henri de Ferrières. See Ferrières, Henri de.
Hoepffner, Ernst, ed. *La prise amoureuse von Jehan Acart de Hesdin.* Dresden: Gedruckt für die Gesellschaft für romanische Literatur, 1910.
Hollander, Robert. *Boccaccio's Two Venuses.* New York: Columbia University Press, 1977.
―――. *Boccaccio's Last Fiction: "Il Corbaccio."* Philadelphia: University of Pennsylvania Press, 1988.
[Hugh of Saint Victor, attributed.] *De Bestiis et aliis rebus. PL* 177, cols. 14–154.
[Hugh of Saint Victor.] Hugonis de Sancto Victore. *De sacramentis. PL* 176, cols. 173–618. *On the Sacraments of the Christian Faith (De Sacramentis).* Trans. Roy J. Deferrari. Cambridge, Mass.: The Mediaeval Academy of America, 1951.
Hulme, Edward F. *Natural History, Lore, and Legend.* London: Bernard Quaritch, 1895.
Illiano, Antonio. "Per una rilettura della *Caccia di Diana.*" *Italica* 61 (1984): 312–334.
[Isidore of Seville in] *Liturgia mozarabica. PL* 85.
[Isidore of Seville.] Isidori Hispalensis Episcopi *Etymologiarum sive Originum libri XX.* Ed. Wallace M. Lindsay. Oxford: Scriptorum Classicorum Bibliotheca Oxoniensis. Oxonii, 1911; rprt. 1957.
―――. *Liber numerorum. PL* 83.
―――. *Quaestiones in Vetus Testamentum. PL* 83.
James, Montague Rhodes. "The Bestiary." *History* 16 n. s., no. 61 (April 1931): 1–11.
―――, ed. *The Peterborough Psalter and Bestiary of the Fourteenth Century.* Roxburghe Club Publications 178. Oxford: F. Hall, at the University Press, 1921.
―――, ed. *The Bestiary, Being a Reproduction in Full of the Manuscript Ii.4.26 in the University Library, Cambridge, with Supplementary Plates from Other Manuscripts of English Origin, and a Preliminary Study of the Latin Bestiary as Current in England.* Roxburghe Club Publications 190. Oxford: J. Johnson, at the University Press, 1928.
Jean Acars [or Acart] de Hesdin. *La prise amoureuse.* See Acars, Jean de Hesdin.
Jean de Meung and Guillaume de Lorris. *Le Roman de la Rose.* Ed. Ernest Langlois. 5 vols. Paris: Société des Anciens Textes Français, 1914–1924.
[Jerome, Saint.] S. Eusebii Hieronimi, *Breviarum in Psalmos. PL* 26, cols. 821–1278.
Justin. *Dialogus cum Tryphone Judaeo. PG* 6.
Karpp, Heinrich. *Die frühchristlichen und mittelalterlichen Mosaiken in Santa Maria Maggiore.* Baden-Baden: Bruno Grimm, 1966.

Kaske, Robert A., in coll. with Arthur Groos and Michael W. Twomey. *Medieval Christian Literary Imagery: A Guide to Interpretation.* Toronto Medieval Bibliographies 11. Toronto and London: University of Toronto Press, 1989.

Katzenellenbogen, Adolf. *Allegories of the Virtues and Vices in Medieval Art from Early Christian Times to the Thirteenth Century.* London: The Warburg Institute, The University of London, 1939; rprt. New York: W. W. Norton, 1964.

Kelly, Henry Ansgar. *The Devil, Demonology, and Witchcraft: Christian Beliefs in Evil Spirits.* Garden City, N.Y.: Doubleday, 1968; rev. 1974.

Kirkham, Victoria. "Reckoning With Boccaccio's *Questioni d'amore*." *MLN* 89.1 (1974): 47–59.

———. "Numerology and Allegory in Boccaccio's *Caccia di Diana*." *Traditio* 34 (1978): 303–329.

———. "'Chiuso parlare' in Boccaccio's *Teseida*." In *Dante, Petrarch, Boccaccio. Studies in the Italian Trecento in Honor of Charles S. Singleton.* Ed. Aldo S. Bernardo and Anthony L. Pellegrini. Pp. 305–351. Binghamton, N.Y.: Medieval and Renaissance Texts and Studies, 1983.

———. "An Allegorically Tempered *Decameron*." *Italica* 62.1 (1985a): 1–23.

———. "Boccaccio's Dedication to Women in Love." In *Renaissance Studies in Honor of Craig Hugh Smyth.* Ed. Andrew Morrogh, Fiorella Superbi Gioffredi, Piero Morselli, Eve Borsook. Vol. 1, pp. 333–343. 2 vols. Villa I Tatti, The Harvard University Center for Italian Renaissance Studies 7. Florence: Giunti Barbèra, 1985b.

———. "Eleven is for Evil. Measured Trespass in Dante's *Commedia*." *Allegorica* 10 (1989): 27–50.

Klingender, Francis Donald. *Animals in Art and Thought to the End of the Middle Ages.* Ed. Evelyn Antal and John Harthan. Cambridge, Mass.: MIT Press, 1971.

Kren, Thomas. *Renaissance Painting in Manuscripts: Treasures from the British Library.* New York: Hudson Hills Press, 1983.

Latini, Brunetto. See Brunetto Latini.

Lauchert, Friedrich. *Geschichte des Physiologus.* Strasbourg: K. J. Trübner, 1889.

Léonard, Emile G. *Un poète à la recherche d'une place et d'un ami: Boccace à Naples.* Paris: Droz, 1944.

———. *Les Angevins de Naples.* Paris: Presses Universitaires de la France, 1954. Ital. trans. R. Liguori. *Gli Angioini di Napoli.* Varese: dall'Oglio, 1967.

Lewis, C. S. *The Discarded Image: An Introduction to Medieval and Renaissance Literature.* Cambridge: Cambridge University Press, 1964; rprt. 1967.

*Liturgia mozarabica.* PL 85.

Livy. [*Ab urbe condita: History*] *Livy with an English Translation in Fourteen Volumes.* Ed. and trans. B. O. Foster et al. LCL. London: William Heinemann; Cambridge, Mass.: Harvard University Press, 1919–1951.

Lundberg, Per. *La typologie baptismale dans l'ancienne église.* Acta Seminarii Neotestamentici Upsaliensis 10. Leipzig: Alfred Lorenz; Uppsala: Lundquist, Almquist, and Wiksell, 1942.

Macrobius. *Commentarii in somnium Scipionis.* Ed. James Willis. Leipzig: Teubner, 1970. *Macrobio: Commento al Somnium Scipionis.* Ed. Mario Regali. Biblioteca di Studi Antichi 38. Pisa: Giardini Editori, 1983. *Commentary on the Dream of*

Scipio. Trans. William Harris Stahl. New York and London: Columbia University Press, 1952.
Maier, Jean-Louis. *Le Baptistère de Naples et ses mosaïques: Etude historique et iconographique.* Fribourg, Switzerland: Editions Universitaires, 1964.
Mâle, Emile. *Religious Art in France of the Thirteenth Century: A Study in Medieval Iconography and Its Sources of Inspiration.* Trans. Dora Nussey. New York: E. P. Dutton, 1913; rprt. *The Gothic Image: Religious Art in France of the Thirteenth Century.* New York: Harper and Row, 1958.
Mann, Max Friedrich. "Zur Bibliographie des Physiologus." *Anglia Beiblatt* 10 (1900): 274–287; 12 (1901): 13–23; 13 (1902): 18–19.
———, ed. *Der Bestiaire divin des Guillaume le Clerc.* Französische Studien 6, no. 2. Heilbronn: Henninger, 1888.
Marcus, Millicent. "The Sweet New Style Reconsidered. A Gloss on the Tale of Cimone (*Decameron* 5, 1)." *Italian Quarterly* 81 (1980): 5–16.
———. "Misogyny as Misreading: A Gloss on *Decameron* 8, 7." *Stanford Italian Review* 4, no. 1 (1984): 23–40.
*Il Mare amoroso.* Ed. Emilio Vuolo. Rome: Istituto di Filologia Moderna, Università di Roma, 1962. See also partial ed. in *Poeti del Duecento.* Ed. Gianfranco Contini. La letteratura Italiana: Storia e Testi, vol. 2, pt. 1. Pp. 483–500. Milan-Naples: Ricciardi, 1960.
Mayer, Alfons, ed. *Der waldensische Physiologus. Romanische Forschungen* 5 (1890): 392–418.
Mazza, Antonia. "L'inventario della 'parva libreria' di Santo Spirito e la biblioteca del Boccaccio." *Italia medioevale e umanistica* 9 (1966): 1–71.
[Mazzatinti, G. ed.] *Un bestiario moralizzato tratto da un manoscritto eugubino del sec. XIV.* Ed. G. Mazzatinti, with notes by E. Monaci. Rome: Accademia dei Lincei, 1889.
McCulloch, Florence. *Medieval Latin and French Bestiaries.* University of North Carolina Studies in Romance Languages and Literatures, no. 33. Chapel Hill, N.C.: University of North Carolina Press, 1960.
McKenzie, K[enneth]. "Per la storia dei bestiari italiani." *GSLI* 64 (1914): 358–371.
Menichetti, A., ed. See Chiaro Davanzati, *Rime.*
Mermier, Guy. "De Pierre de Beauvais et particulièrement de son Bestiaire." *Romanische Forschungen* 78 (1967): 338–371.
Meyer, Paul. "Les bestiaires." *Histoire littéraire de la France* 34 (1915): 362–390.
Migiel, Marilyn. "Between Art and Theology: Dante's Representation of Humility." *Stanford Italian Review* 5, no. 2 (1985): 141–159.
Migne, Jacques Paul, ed. *Patrologiae cursus completus . . . Series Prima Latina.* 221 vols. Paris: Sirou-Vrayet, 1841–1879. Cited as *PL.*
*Missale Romanum.* Ratisbon: Pustet, 1963.
Monges, Richard, trans. See Vittore Branca, *Giovanni Boccaccio: The Man and His Works.*
Monson, Don A. "Andreas Capellanus and the Problem of Irony." *Speculum* 63.3 (1988): 539–572.
Moore, Edward. *Studies in Dante.* 2nd series. Oxford: Clarendon Press, 1899.
Morris, Richard. *An Old English Miscellany.* Early English Text Society. London, 1872. (Theobaldus, pp. 201–209.)
Musa, Mark, trans. *Dante's Vita Nuova.* New edition. Trans. and an essay by M.

Musa. Bloomington and London: Indiana University Press, 1973. (Contains a long introductory essay by translator.)

Muscetta, Carlo. "Giovanni Boccaccio e i novellieri." In *Il Trecento*. Ed. Emilio Cecchi and Natalino Sapegno. Storia della letteratura italiana 2. Pp. 315–558. Milan: Garzanti, 1965.

———. *Giovanni Boccaccio*. Bari: Laterza, 1972.

[Neckham, Alexander.] *De naturis rerum libri duo*. . . . Ed. Thomas Wright. Great Britain, Public Record Office. Rerum britannicarum medii aevi Scriptores: or, Chronicles and Memorials of Great Britain and Ireland During the Middle Ages. [Rolls Series, 34.] London: Longman, Green, 1863; rprt. Nendeln/Liechtenstein: Kraus Reprint, 1967.

*Il Novellino*. Ed. C. Alvaro. Milan: Garzanti, 1945.

*Il Novellino*. Ed. Guido Favati. Genoa: Fratelli Bozzi, 1970.

Nurmela, Tauno, ed. See Boccaccio, *Il Corbaccio*.

Osgood, Charles G., ed., intro., and trans. *Boccaccio on Poetry: Being the Preface and the Fourteenth and Fifteenth Books of Boccaccio's Genealogia Deorum Gentilium*. Princeton, N.J.: Princeton University Press, 1930; rprt. Library of Liberal Arts. Indianapolis: Bobbs-Merrill, 1956.

Ovid. *Ars amatoria. Remedia amoris*. In *Ovid, The Art of Love and Other Poems*. Trans. J. H. Mozley. LCL. Cambridge, Mass.: Harvard University Press; London: William Heinemann, 1962.

———. *Metamorphoses*. Ed. and trans. Frank Justus Miller. 2 vols. LCL. Cambridge, Mass.: Harvard University Press; London: William Heinemann, 1916.

"*Ovide moralisé*": *Poème du commencement du quattorzième siècle*. Ed. C. De Boer et al. Verhandelingen der Koninlijke Nederlandse Akademie van Wetenschappen, Afdeeling Letterkunde, N. R., 15, 21, 30 no. 3, 37, 43. Amsterdam: North-Holland Publishing Company, 1915, 1920, 1931, 1936, 1938.

*Ovide moralisé en prose*. Ed. C. De Boer. Verhandelingen der Koninlijke Nederlandse Akademie van Wetenschappen, Afdeeling Letterkunde, N. R., 61 no. 2. Amsterdam: North-Holland Publishing Company, 1954.

Pace, Antonio, ed. See Antonio Pucci, *Il contrasto delle donne*.

Perry, Ben Edwin. "Physiologus." *Real-Encyclopädia der Classischen Altertumswissenschaft*. Ed. Pauly-Wissowa. Vol. 39, pt. 1 (1941): 1074–1129.

Peter of Beauvais. See Pierre de Beauvais.

Peter Lombard. *Commentarium in Psalmos*. PL 191.

Petrarca, Francesco. [*Canzoniere; Rime sparse*.] *Petrarch's Lyric Poems*. Trans. and ed. Robert M. Durling. (Facing Italian text and English trans.) Cambridge, Mass.: Harvard University Press, 1976.

———. *Familiarum rerum libri*. Ed. V. Rossi (vols. 1–3); ed. V. Rossi and U. Bosco (vol. 4). Florence: Sansoni, 1933–1942. *Letters on Familiar Matters: Rerum familiarum libri*. Trans. Aldo S. Bernardo. *Libri* I–VIII. Albany, N.Y.: State University of New York Press, 1975. *Libri* IX–XVI. Baltimore and London: The Johns Hopkins University Press, 1982. *Libri* XVII–XXIV, Baltimore and London: The Johns Hopkins University Press, 1985.

———. [*De remediis utriusque fortunae*.] *Four Dialogues for Scholars*. Ed. and trans. Conrad Rawski. Cleveland, Ohio: Press of Western Reserve University, 1966.

Petri Damiani. *De bono religiosi status*. PL 145, cols. 763–792.

[Philippe de Thaon] Philippe de Thaün. *Le Bestiaire: Texte Critique*. Ed. Emmanuel Walberg. Paris and Lund: H. Möller, 1900; rprt. Geneva: Slatkine Reprints, 1970.

*Physiologus.* [Physiologus.] See versions, studies, and editions under J. Carlill, F. J. Carmody, M. J. Curley, P. T. Eden, N. Henkel, F. Lauchert, M. F. Mann, A. Meyer, R. Morris, B. E. Perry, Philippe de Thaon, J. H. Pitman, A. W. Rendell, F. Sbordone, Theobaldus, and M. Wellmann.

Picot, Emile. "Le cerf allégorique dans les tapisseries et les miniatures." *Bulletin de la Société française de reproduction de manuscrits à peintures* 3, no. 2 (1913): 57–67.

Pierre de Beauvais. "Bestiaire en prose de Pierre le Picard." *Mélanges d'archéologie, d'histoire et de littérature.* Charles Cahier and Arthur Martin, eds. Paris. Vol. 2 (1851): 85–100, 106–232; vol. 3 (1853): 203–288; vol. 4 (1856): 55–87.

Pierre de Beauvais, Guillaume le Clerc, Richard de Fournival, Brunetto Latini, Corbechon. *Bestiaires du Moyen Age.* Ed. and trans. Gabriel Bianciotto. Paris: Stock, 1980.

Pitman, J. H., ed. and trans. *Physiologus.* New Haven, Conn.: Yale University Press, 1924.

Pitra, Jean-Baptiste, ed. See *Clavis Melitonis.*

[Plato.] *Timaeus a Calcidio translatus.* Ed. J. H. Waszink (with P. G. Jensen). In Raymond Klibansky, ed. *Plato Latinus.* Vol. 4. London: Warburg Institute; Leiden: E. J. Brill, 1962.

Plato. *The Dialogues of Plato.* Trans. B. Jowett. 4th ed. rev. Oxford: Clarendon Press, 1953.

———. *Timaeus and Critias.* Trans. and intro. Desmond Lee. Harmondsworth, U.K.: Penguin Books, 1965; rprt. 1971.

Pliny. *Natural History,* VIII–IX; vol. 3. Ed. H. Rackham. LCL. London: William Heinemann; Cambridge, Mass.: Harvard University Press, 1947.

[Plutarch.] *Plutarch's Moralia in Sixteen Volumes.* Ed. and trans. Bernard Ott Perrin, Harold Cherniss, William C. Helmbold, Paul A. Clement, Herbert B. Hoffleit et al. 16 vols. LCL. London: William Heinemann; Cambridge, Mass.: Harvard University Press, 1915+ (many reprints).

———. [*De sollertia animalium.*] *Whether Land or Sea Animals are Cleverer.* In *Plutarch's Moralia.* Trans. Harold Cherniss and William C. Helmbold. Vol. 12. LCL. London: William Heinemann; Cambridge, Mass.: Harvard University Press, 1957.

*Poeti del Duecento.* Ed. Gianfranco Contini. 2 vols. Milan: Ricciardi, 1960.

Poliziano, Angelo [*Stanze per la giostra.*] *The Stanze of Angelo Poliziano.* Trans. David Quint. Amherst, Mass.: University of Massachusetts Press, 1979. (Contains both Italian text and English trans.)

Poole, Gordon. "Boccaccio's *Caccia di Diana.*" *Canadian Journal of Italian Studies* 5, no. 3 (Spring 1982): 149–156.

Potter, Joy Hambuechen. "Woman in the *Decameron.*" In *Studies in the Italian Renaissance: Essays in Memory of Arnolfo B. Ferruolo.* Pp. 87–103. Ed. Gian Paolo Biasin, Albert N. Mancini, and Nicolas J. Perella. Naples: Società Editrice Napoletana, 1985.

*The Princeton Encyclopedia of Classical Sites.* Ed. Richard Sitwell et al. Princeton, N.J.: Princeton University Press, 1976.

Pucci, Antonio. *Il contrasto delle donne.* Ed. Antonio Pace. Menasha, Wis.: George Banta Publishing Company, 1944.

Puech, Henri-Charles. "Le Cerf et le serpent. Note sur le symbolisme de la mosaïque découverte au baptistère de l'henchir Messaouda." *Cahiers archéologiques fin de l'antiquité et Moyen Age* 4 (1949): 17–60.
Pugh, Ellen. "*De Proprietatibus Rerum* by Bartholomaeus Anglicus." In *Renaissance Papers*. Ed. Allan H. Gilbert. Durham, N.C.: University of North Carolina Press, 1954.
[Rabanus Maurus, attributed.] *Allegoriae in Sacram Scripturam.* See Garnier de Rochefort.
Rabanus Maurus. *De universo.* PL 111, cols. 9–614.
Rendell, Alan Wood, trans. *Physiologus: A Metrical Bestiary of Twelve Chapters by Bishop Theobald Printed at Cologne in 1492.* London: J. and E. Bumpus, 1928.
*Re-writing the Renaissance: The Discourses of Sexual Difference in Early Modern Europe.* Ed. Margaret W. Ferguson, Maureen Quilligan, and Nancy J. Vickers. Chicago: University of Chicago Press, 1986.
Ricci, Pier Giorgio. "Una lacuna nella *Caccia di Diana?*" In *Studi sulla vita e le opere del Boccaccio.* Pp. 308–310. Milan: Ricciardi, 1985.
Robertson, D. W. *A Preface to Chaucer: Studies in Medieval Perspectives.* Princeton, N.J.: Princeton University Press, 1962; rprt. 1970.
Roche, Thomas P. "The Calendrical Structure of Petrarch's *Canzoniere.*" *Studies in Philology* 71 (1974): 152–172.
*Le Roman de la Rose.* See Jean de Meung.
Rotili, Mario. *I codici danteschi miniati a Napoli.* Naples: Libreria Scientifica Editrice, 1972.
Sabatini, Francesco. *Napoli angioina: Cultura e società.* Naples: Edizioni Scientifiche Italiane, 1975.
Sbordone, Francesco. *Ricerche sulle fonti e sulla composizione del Physiologus greco.* Naples: G. Torella, 1936a.
———. "La tradizione manoscritta del *Physiologus latino.*" *Athenaeum*, n. s., 27 (1949): 246–280.
———, ed. *Physiologi graeci singulas variarum aetatum recensiones . . . in lucem protulit F. Sbordone.* Milan: In Aedibus Societatis "Dante Alighieri"; Albrighi, Segati & C., 1936b.
Schrader, J. L. "A Medieval Bestiary." *The Metropolitan Museum of Art Bulletin* 44, no. 1 (Summer 1986): 3–56.
Scolari, A. "*Inferno* I, 49–54." *Studi Danteschi* 54 (1982): 1–14.
Se Boyar, Gerald E. "Bartholomaeus Anglicus and His Encyclopaedia." *Journal of English and Germanic Philology* 19 (1920): 168–189.
Shepard, Odell. *The Lore of the Unicorn.* London: George Allen and Unwin, 1930; rprt. New York: The Metropolitan Museum of Art, Avenel Books, 1982.
Singleton, Charles S. "Rivers, Nymphs, and Stars." In *Journey to Beatrice, Dante Studies 2.* Pp. 159–183. Cambridge, Mass.: Harvard University Press, 1958.
———. "The Poet's Number at the Center." *MLN* 80 (1965): 1–10.
———, trans. Dante Alighieri. *The Divine Comedy.* Trans., with comment., Charles S. Singleton. Bollingen Series. 6 vols. Princeton, N.J.: Princeton University Press, 1970–1975.
Sitwell, Richard, ed. See *The Princeton Encyclopedia of Classical Sites.*
Smarr, Janet Levarie. "The *Teseida,* Boccaccio's Allegorical Epic." *NEMLA Italian Studies* 1 (1977): 29–35.

———. *Boccaccio and Fiammetta. The Narrator as Lover.* Urbana, Ill.: University of Illinois Press, 1986.
———, trans. Giovanni Boccaccio, *Eclogues.* New York: Garland Publishing, 1987.
Steele, Robert R. *Mediaeval Lore from Bartholomew Anglicus.* Pref. William Morris. London: Alexander Moring, The De La More Press, 1893; rprt. 1905.
Stern, H. "Le Décor des pavements et des cuves dans les baptistères paléochrétiens." *Actes du V<sup>e</sup> Congrès International d'Archéologie Chrétienne. Aix-en-Provence. 13–19 Septembre 1954.* Pp. 381–390. Vatican City: Pontificio Istituto di Archeologia Cristiana, 1957.
*Storia di Napoli.* 10 vols. Naples: Società Editrice Storia di Napoli, 1967–1971.
Swarzenski, Hanns. *Die lateinischen illuminierten Handschriften des XIII. Jahrhunderts in den Ländern an Rhein, Main und Donau.* Berlin: Deutscher Verein für Kunstwissenschaft, 1936.
Tertullian. *De baptismo. PL* 1. *On Baptism.* In The Ante-Nicene Fathers. Ed. Alexander Roberts and James Donaldson. Vol. 3. Grand Rapids, Mich.: William Eerdmans, 1957.
Terverant, Guy de. "Cerf." In *Attributs et symboles dans l'art profane, 1450–1600.* Travaux d'Humanisme et Renaissance 29. Cols. 65–67. Geneva: Droz, 1958. Supplément, vol. 34, 1964.
[Thaün, or Than, Philippe de.] See Philippe de Thaon, *Le Bestiaire.*
[Theobaldus, Abbot of Monte Cassino.] Theobaldus Episcopus. *Theobaldi "Physiologus."* Ed and trans. P. T. Eden. Leiden: E. J. Brill, 1972.
[Theobaldus Episcopus.] *Physiologus: A Metrical Bestiary of Twelve Chapters by Bishop Theobald Printed at Cologne in 1492.* Trans. Alan Wood Rendell. London: J. and E. Bumpus, 1928.
[Theobaldus] [Pseudo-Hildebert of Tours of Le Mans.] Hildeberti Cenomanensis Episcopi. *Physiologus. PL* 171. Cols. 1217–1224.
[Theobaldus] Richard Morris. *An Old English Miscellany.* Pp. 201–209. Early English Text Society. London, 1872.
Thiébaux, Marcelle. "An Unpublished Allegory of the Hunt of Love: *Lis dis dou cerf amoreus.*" *Studies in Philology* 62 (1965): 531–545.
———. "The Medieval Chase." *Speculum* 42 (1967): 260–274.
———. *The Stag of Love.* Ithaca, N.Y.: Cornell University Press, 1974.
Thomas Aquinas, Saint. [*Summa contra gentiles.*] *On the Truth of the Catholic Faith: Summa contra gentiles.* Trans. Anton C. Pegis, J. F. Anderson, Vernon J. Bourke et al. Garden City, N.Y.: Doubleday, 1955–1957. Rprt. as *Summa contra gentiles.* Notre Dame Press, 1975.
———. *Summa Theologiae.* Ed. Ottawa Institute of Medieval Studies. 4 vols. Ottawa: Impensis Studii Generalis Ordinis Praedicatorum, 1941–1944. *Summa Theologica.* Trans. Fathers of the English Dominican Province. 3 vols. New York: Benziger Brothers, 1947–1948.
[Thomas of Cantimpré.] Thomas Cantimpratensis. *Liber de natura rerum.* Ed. H[elmut] Boese. Vol. 1: Text (vol. 2 has not appeared). Berlin and New York: Walter de Gruyter, 1973.
Thorndike, Lynn. *History of Magic and Experimental Science.* 8 vols. History of Science Society Publications 40 n.s. New York: Columbia University Press, 1923–1958.

Tilander, Gunnar, ed. See Gaston Phébus; Ferrières, Henri de.
Torraca, Francesco. *Per la biografia di Giovanni Boccaccio.* Rome: Dante Alighieri, 1912.
———. "Giovanni Boccaccio a Napoli." *Rassegna Critica della Letteratura Italiana* 20 (1915): 145–245; 21 (1916a): 1–80; rprt. *Giovanni Boccaccio a Napoli, (1326–1339).* Rome: Società Tipografica Arpinate, 1916b.
Treu, Ursula Ilse Pauline. "Bestiary." *Encyclopedia Britannica,* vol. 3, 1970.
Underwood, Paul A. "The Fountain of Life in Manuscripts of the Gospels." *Dunbarton Oaks Papers* 5 (1950): 41–138.
Vasari, Giorgio. *Le vite dei più eccellenti pittori, scultori e architetti.* Ed. Carlo L. Ragghiante. 4 vols. Milan-Rome: Rizzoli, 1945–1949.
Villani, Filippo. *Le vite d'uomini illustri fiorentini.* Ed. Giammaria Mazzuchelli. Florence: Sansone Coen, 1847.
Villani, Giovanni. *Cronica di Giovanni Villani a miglior lezione ridotta.* 3 vols. Florence, 1823; rprt. Rome: Multigrafica Editrice, 1980.
[Vincent of Beauvais.] Vincentius Bellovacensis. *Speculum naturale.* Strasbourg: Printer of the 1481 *Legenda Aurea,* ca. 1483. (In the University of Illinois Library, Urbana.)
Virgil. *Aeneid.* In *Virgil with an English Translation.* 2 vols. Trans. H. Rushton Fairclough. LCL. Cambridge, Mass.: Harvard University Press; vol. 1, 1916, rprt. 1967; vol. 2, 1918, rprt. 1969.
———. *Georgics.* In *Virgil with an English Translation,* vol. 1.
Waddell, Helen Jane, trans. *Beasts and Saints.* With woodcuts by Robert Gibbings. London: Constable and Co., 1934 (many reprints).
*Der waldensische Physiologus.* Ed. A. Mayer. In *Romanische Forschungen* 5 (1890): 392–418.
Wasselynck, René. "Les compilations des *Moralia in Job* du VII$^e$ au XII$^e$ siècle." *Recherches de théologie ancienne et médiévale* 29 (1962): 5–32.
———. "Les *Moralia in Job* dans les ouvrages de morale du haut moyen âge latin." *Recherches de théologie ancienne et médiévale* 31 (1964): 5–31.
———. "L'influence de l'exégèse de S. Grégoire le Grand sur les commentaires bibliques médiévaux (VII$^e$–XII$^e$ s.)." *Recherches de théologie ancienne et médiévale* 32 (1965): 157–204.
Watson, Paul F. *The Garden of Love in Tuscan Art of the Early Renaissance.* Philadelphia: The Art Alliance Press, 1979.
———. "A Preliminary List of Subjects from Boccaccio in Italian Painting, 1400–1550." In Vittore Branca, Paul Watson, Victoria Kirkham, "Boccaccio visualizzato," *Studi sul Boccaccio* 15 (1985–1986): 149–166.
Watson, Paul F., and Victoria Kirkham. "Amore e virtù: Two Salvers Depicting Boccaccio's *Comedìa delle ninfe fiorentine* in the Metropolitan Museum." *Metropolitan Museum Journal* 10 (1975): 35–50.
Wellmann, Max. "Der Physiologus: Eine Religions-Geschichtlich-Naturwissenschaftliche Untersuchung." *Philologus.* Supplementband 22 (1930): 1–116.
Whitbread, Leslie George, trans. and ed. *Fulgentius the Mythographer.* Columbus, Ohio: Ohio State University Press, 1971.
White, Beatrice. "Medieval Animal Lore." *Anglia* 72 (1954): 21–30.
White, Lynn, Jr. "Natural Science and Naturalistic Art in the Middle Ages." *American Historical Review* 52 (1947): 421–435.

White, T[erence] H[anbury], trans. *The Bestiary, A Book of Beasts, Being a Translation from a Latin Bestiary of the Twelfth Century.* New York: G. P. Putnam's Sons, 1954; rprt. Capricorn Books, 1960. [A trans. of *De bestiis* attr. to Hugh of Saint Victor. White's translation is from the same manuscript in the Cambridge University Library Ii.4.26 reproduced by M. R. James, q.v.]

Williamson, John. *The Oak King, The Holly King, and the Unicorn: The Myths and Symbolism of the Unicorn Tapestries.* New York: Harper and Row, 1986.

Wilpert, Josef. *Die römischen Mosaiken und Malereien der kirchlichen Bauten vom IV. bis XIII. Jahrhundert.* Freiburg im Breisgau: Herder, 1924.

Wittkower, Rudolf and Margot. *Born Under Saturn. The Character and Conduct of Artists: A Documented History from Antiquity to the French Revolution.* New York: Random House, 1963.

# INDEX

The names of the women protagonists may be consulted in the Glossary of the Huntresses (pp. 196–218). Only those singled out for discussion in the Introduction or Commentary are listed in the following Index.

Abraham, Claude K., 74n.31
Abrotonia, 164
Acars (or Acart) de Hesdin, Jean, 21; *La prise amoureuse (Love's Capture)*, 20–21, 39, 76n.43, 76n.44
Actaeon, 11, 21, 51, 61, 67, 94n.48, 158, 180, 185. *See also* Ovid; stag(s)
Adam and Eve, 63, 65
Adam de la Halle, 69n.3
Aeneas, 20. *See also* Virgil, *Aeneid*
*Aeneid. See* Virgil
Aesop, 67
Africo, 82n.24, 154, 159
Agapes, in *Comedìa delle ninfe fiorentine,* 42
Agostino d'Ancona, 6
Albertus Magnus, Saint, 14; *De animalibus,* 14, 16, et passim in Commentary
Alcibiades, and wind instruments, 189
*Allegoriae in Sacram Scripturam* (attr. falsely to Rabanus Maurus, tentatively to Garnier de Rochefort), 7, 16, 80n.17, et passim in Commentary
allegory, 67–68; óf stag, 44–68
Alps, 12
*altercatio*, Hunt as, 27
Ambrose, Saint, 52, 195; *Hexameron,* passim in Commentary
Ameto, 30–32, 80n.15, 154, 191, 193–194; he thanks Venus, 191; transformation of, 193–194. *See also* Boccaccio, Giovanni, *Ameto*
Amore. *See* Cupid
Anderson, David, 69n.3
Andrea Acciaiuoli, 9–11; meaning of her name, 71n.14
Andreas Capellanus, 8, 20, 95n.53; *De amore (The Art of Courtly Love),* 8, 20, 159, 164
Andreuccio da Perugia, 156
Angevins, 5, 10, 14, 40, 44, 69n.2, 69n.3
animals, as beastly appetites, 34–38, 53, 62, 82nn.28–30
Anonymous Lady. *See* Mystery Lady
Antichrist, leopard as, 166
Apennines, 12

Apollo, 154, 189–190
appetites, 31; concupiscible and irascible, 184–185. *See also* animals
Apuleius, 7, 37, 39, 50, 61; *Metamorphoses (The Golden Ass),* 37–38, 50, 61, 83n.31
Aquinas, Thomas. *See* Thomas Aquinas, Saint
Arcita, in *Teseida,* 40
Aristotle, 13; *Historia Animalium,* 13
*Art of Courtly Love. See* Andreas Capellanus
Augustine, Saint, Bishop of Hippo, 5, 6, 18, 26, 29, 53, 85; *Enarrationes in Psalmos (Expositions on the Psalms),* 43–44, 50, 53, 85n.7, 85n.8; *Sermones in Vigiliis Paschae (Sermons on the Easter Vigil),* 56–57, 91n.29, 91n.30
avarice, daughters of. *See* filiation, of sins; pride, daughters of
"Ave Maria" (in Boccaccio's *Rime*), 79n.6
Averroës, 5
Avignon, 5

backsliding. *See* recidivism
Baia, 63, 93n.42, 155
Baldassare Castiglione. *See* Castiglione, Baldassare
baptism, 7, 21, 31–32, 43–61, 67, 86n.9, 87n.10, 88n.11, 88n.12, 89n.18, 90n.22, 94n.49, 163; in *Filocolo,* 57–61; by fire, 52–53, 89n.19, 193; Old Testament prefigurations of, 90n.23; as renewal, 51; semantics of, 51–55. *See also* "Benedictio aquae"; hart; liturgy; stag(s)
baptistries, 44. *See also* San Gennaro; San Giovanni in Fonte; San Giovanni in Laterano
Barbato da Sulmona, 5
Bardi, Franceschino de'. *See* Franceschino de' Bardi
Bardi Bank, 4
Barrile, Giovanni, 10–11, 72n.17
Barrile (or Barrili) family, 10

Bartholomaeus Anglicus, 63; *De natura rerum (On the Nature of Things, Des Proprietez des choses)*, 63, et passim in Commentary
Baths of Venus. *See* Terme di Venere
Bauerreiss, Romuald, 87n.10
bear(s) *(Hunt* 5.28), 168, 199, 214; as deceit, 169; as Devil, 169; vulnerable heads of, 168–169
Beatrice, 7, 8, 23–25, 27, 154
beaver, 14; *(Hunt* 10.29), 178; *(Hunt* 10.30), 178–179, 212, 215; testicles of, 178
Bede, the Venerable, 29
"Benedictio aquae," "Benedictio fontis" (Benediction of the Waters), 49, 56, 89n.17, 90n.27
Berarda Gattoli, 15
Berita Brancazzi *(Hunt* 6.1), 171
Bernard, Saint, 5; *Sermones in Cantica Canticorum*, 167–168, 194. *See also* fox, foxes
bestiaries, 7, 13–19, 67, et passim in Commentary
*Bestiario moralizzato*, 14, et passim in Commentary
*Bestiario toscano, Il*, 14, et passim in Commentary
Biancifiore, in *Filocolo*, 58, 191
Bible, 7, 40;
 Genesis (2), 62; (3), 182; (3:14), 29; (3:15), 30; Exodus (17), 90n.23; Leviticus (11:6), 16; Numbers (21:6), 29; 1 Kings (Vulg. 3 Kings) (18:38), 89n.19; Job (39:13–14), 16; Psalms, 85n.8; individual Psalms: (29 [Vulg. 28]), 85n.7, (42:1 [Vulg. 41:1]), 40, 43, 49, 50, 53, 61, 67, 87n.10, (56:5), 170, (102:5), 167; Cantica Canticorum (Canticle of Canticles, Song of Solomon, Song of Songs), 167; Isaiah (13:14), 182, (32:2–15), 17, (63:1–3), 54, (65:25), 29; Wisdom (11:21), 26

 Matthew (3:16), 52, (8:20), 168, (17:1–8), 89n.18; Mark (1:10), 52, (17:1–3), 89n.18; Luke (3:22), 52, (9:28–36), 89n.18, (13:22), 167; John (1:32), 52, (3:5), 50; Romans (6:3–6), 50; 1 Corinthians (7:9), 53; Galatians (6:3), 85n.6; Ephesians (4:22–24), 32, 53; Colossians (3:9–10), 54; 2 Peter (1:16–18), 89n.18
Billanovich, Giuseppe, 78n.3, 86n.8
boar(s) *(porco)*, *(Hunt* 3.36–40), 162, 200; wild boar(s) *(cinghiar, cinghiali)*, 172; *(Hunt* 6.28), 172, 204; *(Hunt* 11.28–36), 206, 208, 216; Isidore on derivation of name *(aper)*, 172. *See also* pigs

Boccaccio, Giovanni, 3–4, 13, 22, 23, 30, 40, 44, 62, 67–68, 69n.2, 71n.14, 76n.1, 78n.3, 81n.21, 83n.31, 86n.8, 88n.12, 92n.37, 93n.42, 153, 173, 189, 191, 192, 194; *Ameto*, 9, 27, 30, 33, 42, 59, 80n.15, 84n.5, 154, 155, 157, 158, 165, 172, 191; *Amorosa visione (Amorous vision)*, 23–25, 77n.1, 92n.38, 157, 159, 164, 165; "Ave Maria" *(Rime* XLI), 79n.6; *Bucolicum carmen (Eclogues)*, 27, 69n.3, 80n.15; *Caccia di Diana*, see *Hunt*; *Comedìa delle ninfe fiorentine*, see above *Ameto*; *Corbaccio*, 9, 61–62, 80n.12, 81n.24, 92n.39, 92n.40, 93n.41; *Decameron* (5.1), 9, (7.2), 69n.3, 157, 159, 163, (6.4), 175, 189, 192; *Elegia di madonna Fiammetta (Amorous Fiammetta)*, 9, 159; *Esposizioni sopra la Comedìa di Dante (Expositions on the Comedy)*, 36, 82n.29, 82n.30, 88n.12, 94n.44, 94n.45, 164, 184, 192–193; *Filocolo*, 8, 57–61, 82n.24, 91n.32, 91n.33, 91–92n.35, 156, 157, 158, 192; *Filostrato*, 190; *Genealogie deorum gentilium (Genealogies of the Gentile Gods)*, 6, 11, 36, 63–66, 69n.3, 69n.5, 78n.3, 88n.13, 93n.43, 94n.46, 156; *De mulieribus claris (Concerning Famous Women)*, 9–11, 36, 71n.14, 82n.28; *Ninfale fiesolano (Nymphs of Fiesole)*, 82n.24, 154; *Rime*, 155, 159; *Teseida delle nozze d'Emilia (Theseiad of Emilia's Nuptials)*, 40, 59, 92n.37, 158, 159, 162, 190; *Trattatello in laude di Dante (Short Treatise in Praise of Dante)*, 18, 75n.35
Boethius, 5, 6, 7, 26, 35, 37, 67; Boethian tradition of men-as-animals, 33–38; *Consolation of Philosophy*, 35, 82n.26
Bologna, Ferdinando, 73n.25
Branca, Vittore, 22, 69n.1, 71n.15, 72n.17, 77n.2, 78n.3, 78n.4, 80n.14, 83–84n.2, 89n.14, 152–153, 156, 161, 164, 178, 186, 187, 197
brook, 157; as symbol of baptism, 43, 86–87n.10, 157. *See also* baptism; Bible, Psalm 42 (Vulg. 41); Jordan river; stag(s)
Brunetto Latini, 14; *Li Livres dou Tresor*, passim in Commentary
buffalo. *See* bull(s)
bull(s), 34; raging bull *(Hunt* 13.56), 184–185; *(Hunt* 14.18), 186, 214; symbol of violence and lust, 184–185. *See also* Minotaur

*caccia, cacce*, as literary form, 80n.14
Callisto, 11, 158–159

Callmann, Ellen, 92n.38
Campidoglio, 10
canon law, 3, 23, 54, 56
cantari, tradition of, 89n.14, 153, 161
cardinal points of compass, 62
cardinal virtues, 62
Cassell, Anthony K., 74n.27, 80n.12, 90n.24, 93n.41, 166, 170, 192
Cassiodorus, 5
*cassone, cassoni,* 59–61, 84n.3, 92n.38
Castiglione, Baldassare (*Il Cortegiano [The Book of the Courtier]*), on wind instruments, 189
catalog, as literary form, 6, 10, 12, 23, 153. See also *sirventese*
Catella (Caterina) Fellapane, (*Hunt* 3.47), 163; (*Hunt* 11.9–10), 180, 201
Catella Sighinolfi (Caterina-Catrina Sighinolfi), in *Decameron* 3.6, 156
Cavalcanti, Guido, 8, 165
Chalcidius, 34, 81n.24, 165. See also Plato, *Timaeus*
Chariot of Time, stags pulling, 42
charity, 31, 58; Charity (Agapes), 42, 191
Charming Lady. See Mystery Lady
chastity, 22, 26, 30. See also Diana
Chiaro Davanzati, 174
Chichibio, 175
Christ, 43, 59, 170; baptism of, 52, 88n.11; beasts likened to, 15; Crucifixion of, 44, 54; divinity of, 15, 170; lion as, 15, 170; as panther, 183–184; Pantocrator, 44; Resurrection of, 54; Transfiguration of, 54, 89n.18, 92n.36, 191
Christopher, J. P., 90n.26
Cicero, 5, 93n.42
Cimone, 9, 71n.13, 191
Cino da Pistoia, 5, 78n.3
Circe, 36, 62, 94n.48
Claricio, Girolamo, 22, 76n.1
Claudian, 7, 11–12, 72n.18, 88n.13; as a Florentine, 72n.18; *On Stilicho's Consulship,* 11–12, 72n.18, 169; as possible source for *Hunt,* 11–12
*Collectiones.* See Paolo da Perugia
*Comedìa* (Dante Alighieri). See Dante Alighieri
*Comedìa delle ninfe fiorentine.* See Boccaccio, Giovanni, *Ameto*
Comparetti, Domenico, 70n.7
*conflictus, Hunt* as, 27
*Consolation of Philosophy* (Boethius), 7
Constantine, Emperor, 49
*contaminatio,* 7
*contrasto, Hunt* as, 27, 57
*Contrasto delle donne.* See Pucci, Antonio
conversion, 54, 57, 59. See also metamorphosis; transfiguration

cormorant (*marangon, Hunt* 8.52), 207
cortex ("rough bark of the words"), 66, 85n.7
cosmos, theories of, 26; number and, 26
Covella d'Anna, 15, 198
crane (*Hunt* 8.5), 175, 200
*Credo,* 58
crowns. See garland(s)
Crucifixion, 44
Cupid (Amore, Love), 3, 20, 38, 39, 99, 154; in *Hunt* 1.5–6, 154; in *Ternario e Ballata* (*Ternario* and Ballad), 224–227
Curato, Baldo, 77n.2
Curley, Michael, 73n.22, et passim in Commentary
*Cynegetica,* 41

d'Ancona, Agostino, 6
Dante Alighieri, 5, 6, 8, 11, 12, 13, 23–24, 25, 26, 27, 29, 35, 36–37, 54, 62, 67–68, 79n.8, 154, 161, 181, 185; manuscripts of, 70n.6; *Comedìa (Divina Commedia, Divine Comedy),* 6, 7, 12, 13, 23, 34, 54, 161, 192; *Inferno (Hell),* 16, 30, 34–37, 61, 66, 158, 162, 164, 167, 192, 194; *Purgatorio (Purgatory),* 12, 27, 33, 35, 62, 80n.13, 154, 157, 158, 166, 184, 185, 189, 190, 192; *Paradiso (Paradise),* 61, 157, 161, 164; *Rime petrose,* 164; *Vita nuova,* 7, 8, 12, 24, 26, 39, 67, 70n.8, 70n.11, 71n.12, 79n.12, 157, 164, 165, 181, 194; cited in *Hunt* 18.29–30, 49ff.
"dark wood" of sin (*selva oscura,* forest), 37, 57, 61, 85n.7. See also Dante Alighieri, *Inferno*
Davanzati, Chiaro, 174
*Decretum.* See Gratian
deer. See doe; hart; hind; stag(s)
Devil (Satan), 15, 56–57, 73n.21, 170; as fallow deer, 182; as fox, 168; as leopard (pard), 166. See also lion; serpent(s)
Diana, 3, 4, 7, 8, 11–12, 22, 24–26, 27, 28, 30, 32, 50, 52, 57, 66, 67, 77n.2, 79n.11, 80n.14, 89n.14, 92n.38, 94n.48, 99, 101, 169, 194, 197; (*Hunt* 1.13), 156; (*Hunt* 2.23), 157–158; (*Hunt* 2.40), 159; (*Hunt* 3.1–3), 160; on *cassone,* 59–61, 92n.38; in Claudian, 88n.13; in *Filocolo,* 59–61. See also Venus
*Diatessaron.* See Tatian
Dido, 20, 39, 177
di Pino, Guido, 77n.2
*Dis dou cerf amoreus, Li (The Tale of the Amorous Stag),* 20, 39
*disputatio, Hunt* as, 27

*Divina Commedia (Divine Comedy)*. *See* Dante Alighieri
doe, 57, 82n.24, 86n.10; in Poliziano, 39, 83n.2; in *Filocolo,* 57–58. *See also* hind; stag(s)
dogs, as symbol of fidelity and wisdom, 186
*dolce stil nuovo,* 7, 12
Dominic, Saint, birth of, 157
Donaldson-Evans, Lance, 71n.12
dove, 44; as attribute of Venus, 89n.15; as symbol of Holy Spirit, 52
Dragone (*Hunt* 14.5–6), 185–186
Durling, Robert, 79n.10, 83n.1

eagle, 34; (*Hunt* 4.2), 164; (*Hunt* 4.19–23), 166–167
Earthly Paradise. *See* Eden
Easter, 49, 56; vigil of, 56, 91n.29, 91n.30
Eden, 12, 33, 50, 62, 63, 67, 157
Edgerton, Samuel, 82n.27
Egidius Romanus, 5
elephant, 14; (*Hunt* 10.42–48), 179–180, 212, 214; jointless legs of, 179–180; as sinner, 180
*elephos* (deer), 61. *See also* doe; hart; hind; stag(s)
eleven, numerological meaning as sin and evil, 29–30, 81n.19, 81n.20. *See also* numbers
Elijah (Elias), 52, 89n.19
Emilia, 40
*epiclesis,* doctrine of, 52, 89n.16. *See also* baptism
epithalamium, 55, 57, 72n.16. *See also* marriage
*Etymologiae (Etymologies)*. *See* Isidore of Seville
Eustace, Saint, 20
Eve, 30; daughters of, 9. *See also* Bible, Genesis; Fall; serpent(s)
exorcism, 56, 91n.28
*exsufflatio,* 56, 91n.28

Fair Lady. *See* Mystery Lady
falcon (*Hunt* 8.30), 175–176, 216
Fall, of man, 53; serpent at, 182
fallow deer (*daino, Hunt* 13.14), 182–183, 200; as Devil, 182; Isidore on derivation of name (*damnula*), 182–183
Felice, 57–58
Fiammetta in *Ameto,* 155, 164; in *Ternario e Ballata (Ternario* and Ballad), 222–223. *See also* Boccaccio, Giovanni, *Elegia di Madonna Fiammetta*
Fido, Franco, 94n.48
fierce plague (*Hunt* 12.30), 181. *See also* serpent(s)

filiation, of sins, 29, 81n.18, 182. *See also* pride, daughters of
Filocolo. *See* Florio
Filostrato, 190
Fiore Canovara, and unicorn (*Hunt* 7.17, 7.23), 174
fire, 52–53; fiery coals and serpent (*Hunt* 12.22), 181, 208; fiery combat (*Hunt* 18.9), 193; of love (*Hunt* 4.12, 9.39), 177, 193. *See also* baptism; flames
flames (*Hunt* 13.29–30), 183, 214. *See also* garland(s); roses
Florence, 4. *See also* lion, lions as mascots
Florentines, in Naples, 6, 69n.3
Florio (Filocolo), 57–59, 191. *See also* Boccaccio, Giovanni, *Filocolo*
Folco Portinari, 154
forest. *See* "dark wood" of sin; Eden; Purgatory
Fountain of Life, 63. *See also* Paradise, rivers of
four, symbolism of. *See* numbers
fox, foxes, 15, 35; as Devil, 168; Isidore on derivation of name (*vulpes*), 167; Saint Bernard on, 167–168; Saint Gregory on, 167; two foxes (*Hunt* 4.53), 167, 217
France, 5
Franceschino de' Bardi, 10
Francesco di Giorgio Martini, 59–61
fraud, 18; hedgehog and ostrich as, 17–19; wings of, 16
Frederick II of Hohenstaufen, Emperor, 5, 14, 19, 164, 166; *De arte venandi cum avibus (The Art of Falconry),* 14, 19, 73n.24, 164, 167, 175
French language, 5
fronds. *See* garland(s)
Fulgentius, 76n.39

Galletti, Salvatore, 77n.2
garland(s), 184; (*Hunt* 2.30), 159; (*Hunt* 11.1), 180; (*Hunt* 13.29–30), 183, 200, 207, 214; in the *Ternario e Ballata (Ternario* and Ballad), 220–221
Garnier de Rochefort. *See Allegoriae in Sacram Scripturam;* Rabanus Maurus
Gaston Phébus (or Phoebus), count of Foix, 19; *Livre de Chasse (Book of the Hunt),* 19, 169
Gawain, Sir, 20
Gelasian sacramentary, 49
*Genealogie, Genealogies*. *See* Boccaccio, Giovanni
Gentle Lady (*Hunt* 5.52), 171. *See also* Mystery Lady
Giacalone, Giuseppe, 77n.2
Giottino, 36

Giovanna, mistress of Guido Cavalcanti, 165
Giovanna I, Queen of Naples, 9, et passim in Glossary of the Huntresses
gittern, 40
*Golden Ass.* See Apuleius, *Metamorphoses*
goshawk(s), 164; (*Hunt* 15.19), 188, 213; Isidore on derivation of name (*accipiter*), 188
Gospel books, illustrated, 63
*Gospel of the Nazarenes,* 52
Gospel of Saint-Médard de Soissons, 64
Grabher, Carlo, 77n.2
grace, 32, 51, 52, 191, 192–193. *See also* Venus
Graffiacane (*Hunt* 14.5–6), 185–186
Gratian, 7, 52, 89n.17, 90n.22, 91n.28
Graziolo de' Bambaglioli, 6
Gregory the Great, 16, 17–19, 29, 73n.26, 74n.26, 75n.32, 75n.34; *Moralia in Job (Morals on the Book of Job)*, 5, 7, 18–19, 74n.32, 75n.34, 75n.35
Gregory of Nyssa, 52, 98n.20
griffins, 14, 61, 92n.38
Guido Cavalcanti, 8, 165
Guido del Duca, 35
gyrfalcon(s), 164; (*Hunt* 8.7), 175, 200

Hankins, James, 81n.24
hare(s), 15, 16, 17, 74nn.28–31, 172; (*Hunt* 3.26–27), 162, 201, 205; (*Hunt* 6.38), 172, 209, 213, 216. *See also* rabbit(s)
harp, 188, 198
hart, 40; in Psalm 42 (Vulg. 41), 40, 49, 50. *See also* doe; hind; stag(s)
hawking, 19
hedgehog(s), 15, 17–18, 74n.32, 75n.33; (*Hunt* 5.55–58), 171, 198
Hell. *See* Dante Alighieri, *Inferno*
Henri de Ferrières, 19; *Livres du roy Modus et de la royne Ratio (Book of King Modus and Queen Ratio)*, 19, 76n.37
hind, Dido as, 20, 39. *See also* doe; stag(s)
Hollander, Robert, 78n.2, 79n.5, 92n.40, 94n.48, 95n.51
Holy Ghost. *See* Holy Spirit
Holy Spirit (Holy Ghost), 49, 52. *See also* dove; *epiclesis;* Trinity
Honorable Lady (*Hunt* 4.56), 168. *See also* Mystery Lady
horn, as symbol of pride, 163
hound, 58, 81n.24. *See also* dogs
Hugh of Saint Victor, 29, 72n.20, 162; *De bestiis,* falsely attributed to, passim in Commentary
Hunt (*Caccia di Diana, Diana's Hunt*): analogs in hunt literature, 19–21; attribution of, 72n.17, 76–77n.1; as a *contrasto,* 27–28, 57; dating of, 3, 21,

69n.1; as diptych, 153; as epithalamium, 72n.16; and *Filocolo,* 57–61; as lacunous, 77n.2 (*see also* Ricci, Pier Giorgio); literary background of, 3–21; manuscripts of, 152–153; poetic structure of, 22–38, 63–68; textual integrity of, 22–27; title of, 152–153; Wellesley manuscript of, 152, 155, 156, 178
hunter, sagacity of, 160; as symbol, 72n.21
hunting, 8, 19–21; as amorous chase, 39; literature on, 19–21, 75n.36; religious hunt, 87n.10. *See also* Thiébaux, Marcelle
huntresses, 155; Glossary of the, 196–218
hydra (*Hunt* 14.54–56), 14, 187, 202
hysteron proteron, 161

iconology, 7
Ilario, 58
Illiano, Antonio, 164, 167
Isidore of Seville, *Etymologiae (Etymologies)*, 5, 7, 13, 29, 162, 163, 167, 172, 182, 187, 188, et passim in Commentary
Iulio, in Poliziano, 39

Jacopo Torriti, 44
Jean de Meung, 74n.31
Jerome, Saint, 5, 29, 85n.7
Jesus. *See* Christ
*jeu parti,* 28
*Jeu de Robin et Marion,* 69n.3
Joan, Queen of Naples. *See* Giovanna I
John of Salisbury, 20, 76n.39
Jordan river, 52
Justinian Code, 5

Kaske, Robert E., 75n.34
Kirkham, Victoria, 70n.10, 71n.14, 79n.7, 79n.11, 81n.21, 91n.31, 92n.37, 160, 172, 192, 194

labyrinth, 61–62, 67
lambs, 44
Lateran, 49, 51, 57, 63, 86n.9. *See also* San Giovanni in Laterano
Latini, Brunetto. *See* Brunetto Latini
Lauchert, Friedrich, 73n.22
Laura, in Petrarch, 39
laurel, 80n.15, 191
Leo the Great, 49
Léonard, E. G., 69n.3
Leonardo da Vinci, 36
leopard (*leopardo, Hunt* 12.57), 15, 182, 218; (*Hunt* 13.3), 218; leopard as heretic, 182; leopard as a hybrid, 182; as mascots in Florence, 166

leopardess *(lonza)*, 15, 33–34, 164, 166; (*Hunt* 4.14–15), 166; as lust, 166. *See also* leopard
leporine symbolism. *See* rabbit(s)
Lewis, C. S., 81n.24
Lia, 31, 154, 158
lily, as symbol of purity, chastity, 90n.23
lion, 14, 15, 34; as Devil, 57, 170; imitated from Dante, 170; lion cub, 34; lion cub in *Caccia* (*Hunt* 5.34–48), 169, 213; lion cub in *Filocolo*, 57–58; lions as mascots, 166. *See also* Christ
liturgy, 56. *See also* baptism
Livy, 5; *Ab urbe condita*, 155
*locus amoenus*, 11, 63; (*Hunt* 2.1–15), 157
*lonza*. *See* leopardess
love, Love. *See* Cupid
Luca da Penne, 5
Lucius, in Apuleius, 37–38, 50, 61, 94n.48

Macrobius, *Commentary on the Dream of Scipio*, 35, 82n.25
Maier, Jean-Louis, 87n.11
Malacoda, 189
Mâle, Emile, 94n.49
Malebranche, devils in Dante's *Commedia*, 185
mallards (*Hunt* 8.56), 207, 213, 216; (*Hunt* 15.26), 217
Marcus, Millicent, 71n.13
Mariotto di Nardo, 40
marriage, 57, 59–61, 63, 193. *See also* epithalamium
Mars, 27, 190
Marti, Mario, 197
Martianus Capella, 79n.11
Martini, Francesco di Giorgio. *See* Francesco di Giorgio Martini
Massèra, A. F., 164, 174, 197
"Master of the *Sentences*." *See* Peter Lombard
matrimony. *See* marriage
Mazza, A., 81n.24
McCulloch, Florence, 73n.23; *Medieval Latin and French Bestiaries*, passim in Commentary
Medusa, Medusan, 9
Mensola, 154, 159
messenger (*messo*), of Diana (*Hunt* 1.8, 1.13), 99, 154, 156
*Metamorphoses*. *See* Ovid
metamorphosis, 4, 59, 67; meaning Transfiguration of Christ, 92n.36
Minerva, and wind instruments, 189
Minotaur, 34, 184–186
missal, Roman, 49, 90n.27
*Moamin et Ghatrif*, 19
monoceros. *See* unicorn
*Mons Virgilianus*, 70n.7

Monson, Don A., 95n.53
Monte Vergine, 70n.7
*Moralia in Job (Morals on the Book of Job)*. *See* Gregory the Great
mosaics, 40, 44–49, 63
mountain(s), 62
Moutier, Ignazio, 22, 76n.1
Muscetta, Carlo, 24, 77n.2, 79n.9
Mystery Lady, 3–4, 8, 10, 23–25, 27, 33, 54, 55, 67, 71n.12, 72n.20, 99, 101, 166, 194, 197; as Beatrice, 23–25, 27; (in *Hunt* 1.46, 1.53, 1.54–55), 157, 164; (*Hunt* 4.3), 165; (*Hunt* 4.12), 165; (*Hunt* 5.52), 171; (*Hunt* 16.46), 190; (*Hunt* 18.16–58), 194–195

naker (*naccaro, nacchero, Hunt* 15.24), 188–189, 217; as drum or trumpet, 188–189
Naples, 6, 8, 9, 14, 15, 21, 33, 37, 63, 155; bay of, 12, 159; court of, 63; cultural milieu of, 4–6, 21, 63, 69n.3; Kingdom of, 3, 5, 10; University of, 3, 5; use of name "Napoli" in Boccaccio's works, 156. *See also* Parthenope
narrator, of *Hunt*, 3, 4, 37, 157, 176–177. *See also* stag-narrator
Nastagio degli Onesti, 163
*natura, naturae* (characteristics of animals), 14; of beavers, 179; of stags, 41, 85n.6
Neoplatonism, 25
nets (*Hunt* 2.51), 160
"new life." *See* baptism
New Testament. *See* Bible
Niccolò Acciaiuoli, 10–11, 71n.15
nine, numerological meaning of. *See* numbers
nudity, nude bathers, 159
numbers, symbolism of: three, 25–27, 79n.11, 80n.12, 192; four, 44, 62, 86–87n.10; seven, 3, 25–27, 29–31, 37, 79n.11, 81n.21, 86n.9, 86n.11, 172; eight, 49; nine, 7, 24–27, 80n.12, 193; ten, 25, 81n.19; eleven, 28–30, 81n.19, 81n.20; thirty, 32; thirty-three, 23–25, 27; fifty-eight, 8, 24–25; fifty-nine, 7; sixty, 7, 23–24, 70n.8
numerology, 23–27
Nurmela, Tauno, 92n.39
nymphs, as virtues, 27, 30, 31, 55, 61

*Odyssey*, 27
offspring. *See* filiation, of sins; pride, daughters of; serpent(s); wolf
"old man," symbolism in baptism, 51, 53, 67
Old Testament. *See* Bible
olive leaves (*Hunt* 2.30), 159, 191
Oppian, 19

ostrich, 15, 16, 198; wings of, 73n.26, 74n.27; (*Hunt* 15.38), 189, 205. *See also* fraud
Ovid, 7, 11, 19, 20, 21, 28, 35, 50, 61, 67, 94n.48, 158; *Ars amatoria (Art of Love)*, 20, 160; *Metamorphoses*, 7, 11, 27, 37, 154, 158–159, 180, 185; *Remedia amoris (Remedies of Love)*, 19

Pace, Antonio, 80n.16
Palemone, in *Teseida*, 40; prayer to Venus, 190
Palermo, 14; royal palace at, 87n.10
panther, 14; (*Hunt* 13.38), 183–184; sweet fragrance of, 183–184; symbol of Christ, 183–184
*paolin*, 13; *paolino* (*Hunt* 8.55), 176, 207
Paolo da Perugia, *Collectiones*, 6, 70n.5
Papias, 5
Paradise, 44, 61; rivers of, 44, 62. *See also* Dante Alighieri, *Paradiso*
Parthenope (*Hunt* 1.12), 3, 7, 10, 33, 34, 52, 61–63, 67, 99, 155–156, 164, 194; source of name, 70n.7, 156
*partimen*, 28
Paschal Vigil. *See* Easter, vigil of
Paul, Saint, 32, 53, 168, 193
Peronella (Peronelle), origin of name, 69n.3
Peter of Beauvais, 13
Peter Lombard, 29, 89–90n.21; "Master of the *Sentences*," 193
Petrarca, Francesco (Petrarch), 5, 7, 10, 39, 67, 72n.18, 72n.19, 81n.24, 83n.1, 85n.8, 94n.48, 153–154; as Boccaccio's "first guiding light," 12, 72n.19; *Canzoniere, Rime sparse*, 67, 83n.1, 153–154; *Trionfi (Triumphs)*, 42, 92n.38
Pezzuolo (*Hunt* 14.5–6), 185–186
Phébus (or Phoebus), Gaston, count of Foix. *See* Gaston Phébus
Phoenix, 44
"Physiologus," *Physiologus*, 13–15, 42, 167, 168; date of composition, 73n.22
"pia fraus," 170
pigs (*porco, porci*), (*Hunt* 3.36–40, 7.39), 162, 200. *See also* boar(s)
Plato, 34, 81n.24; *Phaedo*, 81n.24; *Timaeus*, 34, 35, 81n.24, 165
Platonic tradition, 33–38
Plautus, 5
Pliny, 5, 13; *Natural History*, 13
Plutarch, 84n.4
poetry, 63, 93n.43; as allegory, 63–67; as Boccaccio's calling, 23, 78n.3; in praise of women, 9–11
Poliziano, 39; *Stanze per la giostra (Stanzas for the Joust)*, 39, 83n.2

Poole, Gordon, 94n.47
porcupine (*Hunt* 14.37–38), 187, 215; Isidore on derivation of its name (*histrix*), 187
Portinari, Folco, 154
Potter, Joy Hambuechen, 71n.14
pride, 33; daughters of, 29, 81n.18
Principessella, her name, 169
Provençal, 28
Prudentius, *Psychomachia*, 55. *See also* psychomachia
psychomachia, 28, 31–32, 55, 67, 74n.31
Pucci, Antonio, 80n.16
Puech, Henri-Charles, 84n.4, 86n.9, 87n.10, 87n.11
Purgatory, 27, 61; Purgatory, Mount, 27, 61, 62; gate of, 166. *See also* Dante Alighieri, *Purgatorio*
purple, significance of color (*Hunt* 2.29), 159. *See also* red; vermilion
Pythagoras, 37
Pythagorean theory, thought, 25, 26

Quaglio, Antonio Enzo, 90n.25
*quinario*, 153
Quint, David, 83n.2
Quintilian, 5

Rabanus Maurus, 7, 13, 80n.17; *De universo*, 86n.10, 94n.49. *See also Allegoriae in Sacram Scripturam*
rabbit(s), 15, 17, 74nn.28–31, 84n.3, 209, 213, 216. *See also* hare(s)
recidivism, 54, 90n.24
red, symbolism of, 54, 58, 90n.23, 191, 207, 214. *See also* purple; vermilion
rhinoceros. *See* unicorn
Ricci, Pier Giorgio, 23, 77n.2, 197
Richard of St. Victor, 16, 74n.27; *De eruditione*, 16
Robert the Wise, of Anjou, King of Naples, 3, 4, 5, 10, 69n.3, 70n.3; et passim in Glossary of the Huntresses
Robertson, D. W., 95n.52
Rochefort, Garnier de. *See Allegoriae in Sacram Scripturam*, attributed falsely to Rabanus Maurus
roebuck(s), derivation of name (*caper*), 161; as emblem of Christ, 161; (*Hunt* 3.8), 161, 203; (*Hunt* 11.17), 203, 213, 218; (*Hunt* 14.44), 201
*Roman de la Rose*, 74n.31
roses (*Hunt* 13.28–30), 183, 184, 214. *See also* garland(s)
Rotili, Mario, 70n.6

Sabatini, F., 69n.2, 69n.3, 70n.4
Sallust, 5

*salute* (*Hunt* 18.58, "salvation," "safety"), 4, 8, 13, 38, 94n.47, 181; used by Dante in *Vita nuova* as "greeting" and "salvation," 181; in *Ternario e Ballata* (*Ternario* and Ballad), 224–225
*salvamente* (*Hunt* 12.15), 181, 195. See also *salute*
salvation. See *salute*
San Clemente in Rome, mosaics in, 44, 45 (*Fig. 3*), 46 (*Fig. 4*), 63, 87n.10, 87n.11
San Gennaro, 44
San Giovanni in Fonte, mosaics in, 40, 44, 48 (*Fig. 6*), 63, 87n.11
San Giovanni in Laterano, mosaics in, 47 (*Fig. 5*), 87n.10. See also Lateran
Santa Maria Maggiore, 86n.10
Santa Restituta, 44
Satan. See Devil
Saul, 33
Sbordone, Francesco, 73n.22
Scholasticism, 5
Scholari, A., 166
secrecy, in love, 164
*selva oscura*. See "dark wood" of sin
Seneca, 5
*senhal*, 8, 164
*senno*, 102; (*Hunt* 2.58), 160; (*Hunt* 8.58), 176
serpent(s), (snake[s]), 3, 28, 29, 33, 43, 44, 50, 53, 61, 80–81n.17; head as vulnerable (*Hunt* 12.41–42), 181–182, 208, 212; offspring of, 28; (*Hunt* 11.57), 181, 208. See also Eve; Fall; stag(s)
seven, numerological meaning of. See numbers
"Sicut cervus." See Bible, Psalm 42:1 (Vulg. 41:1)
Siegfried, 20
Simonetta, in Poliziano, 39–40, 83n.2
sin(s), "dark wood" of (*selva oscura*, forest), 37, 57, 61, 85n.7 (*see also* Dante Alighieri, *Inferno*); animals as, 34–38; filiation of, 29, 81n.18, 182; powers of darkness, 56–57. See also eleven; numbers; pride, daughters of; serpent(s)
Singleton, Charles S., 79n.10, 80n.13
*sirventese*, 6, 7, 12–13, 23–24, 29, 70n.8, 70n.9, 79n.6, 153. See also *ternario*, *Ternario e ballata*
Smarr, Janet Levarie, 69n.2, 72n.15, 80n.15, 81n.24, 92n.37, 94n.50
snake. See serpent(s)
*sonetti caudati*, 23–25
south (*Hunt* 2.33, 4.3), symbolic meaning of, 159, 165, 208
spring, season of love and renewal (*Hunt* 1.1–3), 153–154
*sputatio*, 56
stag(s), 20, 44, 50, 84n.6, 86n.9, 88n.13; in allegory and art, 39–68, 89n.13; as Christian man, 40–51; drawing Diana's chariot, 89n.13; renewed by eating or breathing snakes, 41, 44, 53, 61, 84n.4, 84n.5, 85n.7, 163; sanguinary stag, 20; of sensual love, 39–40; as symbol of baptism, 40–57, 67; as symbol of pride, 163; at water brook, 43, 86–87n.10; three horned stags (*Hunt* 3.49–52), 163, 199, 212; white stag (*Hunt* 4.36), 167, 204, 217. See also Actaeon; doe; hind
stag-narrator, of *Hunt*, 3, 4, 8, 37, 156, 157, 176–177; (*Hunt* 11.30), 180; metamorphosis of (*Hunt* 18.11–12), 193–194
Stibbert Museum, 59, 92n.38
storks, 30–32, 55
stream (*Hunt* 2.9), 157, (*Hunt* 2.25–27), 158–159. See also brook
Suetonius, 5
*Summa contra Gentiles*. See Thomas Aquinas, Saint
Swabian house, 14. See also Frederick II
swan(s), 14, 30–32, 55; on *cassoni*, 60–61, 92n.38; (*Hunt* 15.8), 187–188, 199, 205; as pride, 188; singing along in time to harp, 187–188

Tatian, *Diatessaron*, 52
ten, rule of, 25. See also numbers
*tenso*, 28
Terence, 5
Terme di Venere, Roman Baths at Baia, 63, 93n.42, 155
*ternario*, *Ternario e ballata* (*Ternario* and Ballad), 23, 153, 165; text of, 220–227
Tertullian, 54, 90n.22
*terza rima*, 23, 153
Thiébaux, Marcelle, 20, 75n.36, 76nn.37–40, 76n.42, 76n.44, 88n.13, 160
Thomas Aquinas, Saint, 5, 6, 29; *Summa contra Gentiles*, 6
Thomas Cantimpratensis (Thomas of Cantimpré), 13; on bears, 168–169; et passim in Commentary
three, numerological meaning of. See numbers
tiger(s) (*Hunt* 6.4–5), 171, 198, 200
*Timaeus*. See Plato; see also Chalcidius
Torraca, Francesco, 10, 72n.17, 165
Torriti, Jacopo. See Jacopo Torriti
transfiguration, 4, 38, 52, 59, 89n.18; of Ameto, 193–194; of Christ, 54, 89n.18, 92n.36; of stag-narrator (*Hunt* 17.40), 191; (*Hunt* 18.11–12), 193–194
transformation. See transfiguration; metamorphosis
Trinity, 27, 49, 80n.12; trinitarian symbolism, 31. See also Holy Spirit; numbers
*Tusco-Venetian Bestiary*, 14

Ulysses, 36
Underwood, Paul A., 86n.9, 87n.10, 88n.12, 91n.34
unicorn, 14, 33; (*Hunt* 7.9–12), 173, 206, 210, 211; ferocity of, 173, 175; as the proud, 174
Unnamed Lady. *See* Mystery Lady

Valerius Maximus, 5
"Valley of the Ladies" ("Valle delle Donne," *Decameron*, Concl., Day 6), 157, 159
Vanna, 165, 222–223
*variatio*, as poetic technique, 153
Vasari, Giorgio, 36
Vatican, 87n. 10
venery, 8, 20; love as, 20. *See also* hunting
Venus, 3, 4, 7, 12, 22, 25–28, 30–32, 38, 39, 51–52, 56, 57, 61, 66, 77n.2, 79n.11, 80n.14, 158, 165, 190–192, 194; appears in a cloud (*Hunt* 17.29–30), 191; in Apuleius, 37; depicted in art and literature, 40, 61, 84n.3, 89n.15, 92n.38; in *Filocolo*, 59–61; in *Filostrato*, 190; Filostrato's prayer to, 190; as grace, 32, 52, 67, 158; (*Hunt* 17.34), 191; Isis as, 37; as Luxuria, 89n.15; prayer to (*Hunt* 17.16), 190–191. *See also* Baia; Diana; Terme di Venere
vermilion, as blood (*Hunt* 4.46), 167; vermilion cloaks, 32. *See also* purple; red
vices: anger, 35, 82, 85; avarice, 35, 82, 164, 194; cowardice, 35, 82; deceit, 169; fraud, 15–16, 18, 35, 82, 172; greed, 194; heresy, 15, 166, 167, 187; hypocrisy, 16, 74n.27, 166; inconstancy, 35, 82; lust, 17, 31, 35, 36, 53, 82, 85, 166, 184, 192; pride, 15, 16, 29, 33, 73n.26, 81n.17, 85, 162, 163, 173, 186, 188, 194; rapaciousness, 36; self-exculpation, 18; sloth, 31, 35, 194; violence, 170, 172, 173, 184

Villani, Filippo, 22
Villani, Giovanni, 5, 69n.3
Virgil, 27, 39, 40, 70n.7; *Aeneid*, 20, 40, 76n.41; *Eclogues*, 27; ( = Virgilio) as character in Dante Alighieri's *Divina Commedia*, 30, 36
virtues: cardinal and theological, 27; charity, 31, 33, 191; chastity, 180; faith, 31; fortitude, 31, 180; humility, 16, 195; *pietas*, 85; seven virtues, 31; temperance, 31; wisdom, 33, 160, 186, 194. *See also* nymphs
*Vita nuova*. *See* Dante Alighieri
Vulcan, 27, 190

Walter of Brienne, 36
Wasselynck, René, 75n.34
Watson, Paul F., 84n.3, 89n.13, 92n.38, 157, 172, 192
Wellesley manuscript of *Caccia di Diana*. *See Hunt*
west, symbolic meaning of, 159
Wilpert, Josef, 87n.11
wolf, wolves, 34, 35, 81n.24; in *Filocolo*, 57–58; (*Hunt* 3.58), 163–164, 202; (*Hunt* 6.41–44), 172, 197, 209; she-wolf (*lupa*), 164; as symbol of the Devil, 163, 172; weak in flanks, 164; wolfcubs (*Hunt* 6.41–44), 172, 210. *See also* pride, daughters of
women, as authorities on love, 8; ennobling power of, 9; and literary patronage, 10–11, 71n.14; preponderance of in Boccaccio's works, 9–10

Xenophon, 19

Zizzola Barrile, 72n.17, 99, 217
Zizzola d'Anna, 24; (*Hunt* 16.26), 190, 198, 218
zoology, 5, 14

University of Pennsylvania Press
MIDDLE AGES SERIES
Edward Peters, General Editor

Edward Peters, ed. *Christian Society and the Crusades, 1198–1229*. Sources in Translation, including The Capture of Damietta by Oliver of Paderborn. 1971

Edward Peters, ed. *The First Crusade: The Chronicle of Fulcher of Chartres and Other Source Materials*. 1971

Katherine Fischer Drew, trans. *The Burgundian Code: The Book of Constitutions or Law of Gundobad and Additional Enactments*. 1972

G. G. Coulton. *From St. Francis to Dante: Translations from the Chronicle of the Franciscan Salimbene (1221–1288)*. 1972

Alan C. Kors and Edward Peters, eds. *Witchcraft in Europe, 1110–1700: A Documentary History*. 1972

Richard C. Dales. *The Scientific Achievement of the Middle Ages*. 1973

Katherine Fischer Drew, trans. *The Lombard Laws*. 1973

Edward Peters, ed. *Monks, Bishops, and Pagans: Christian Culture in Gaul and Italy, 500–700*. 1975

Jeanne Krochalis and Edward Peters, ed. and trans. *The World of Piers Plowman*. 1975

Julius Goebel, Jr. *Felony and Misdemeanor: A Study in the History of Criminal Law*. 1976

Susan Mosher Stuard, ed. *Women in Medieval Society*. 1976

Clifford Peterson. *Saint Erkenwald*. 1977

Robert Somerville and Kenneth Pennington, eds. *Law, Church, and Society: Essays in Honor of Stephan Kuttner*. 1977

Donald E. Queller. *The Fourth Crusade: The Conquest of Constantinople, 1201–1204*. 1977.

Pierre Riché (Jo Ann McNamara, trans.). *Daily Life in the World of Charlemagne*. 1978

Edward Peters, ed. *Heresy and Authority in Medieval Europe*. 1980

Suzanne Fonay Wemple. *Women in Frankish Society: Marriage and the Cloister, 500–900*. 1981

Edward Peters. *The Magician, the Witch, and the Law*. 1982

Barbara H. Rosenwein. *Rhinoceros Bound: Cluny in the Tenth Century*. 1982

Steven D. Sargent, ed. and trans. *On the Threshold of Exact Science: Selected Writings of Anneliese Maier on Late Medieval Natural Philosophy*. 1982

Benedicta Ward. *Miracles and the Medieval Mind: Theory, Record, and Event, 1000–1215*. 1982

Harry Turtledove, trans. *The Chronicle of Theophanes: An English Translation of anni mundi 6095–6305 (A.D. 602–813)*. 1982

Leonard Cantor, ed. *The English Medieval Landscape*. 1982

Charles T. Davis. *Dante's Italy and Other Essays*. 1984

George T. Dennis, trans. *Maurice's Strategikon: Handbook of Byzantine Military Strategy.* 1984

Thomas F. X. Noble. *The Republic of St. Peter: The Birth of the Papal State, 680–825.* 1984

Kenneth Pennington. *Pope and Bishops: The Papal Monarchy in the Twelfth and Thirteenth Centuries.* 1984

Patrick J. Geary. *Aristocracy in Provence: The Rhône Basin at the Dawn of the Carolingian Age.* 1985

C. Stephen Jaeger. *The Origins of Courtliness: Civilizing Trends and the Formation of Courtly Ideals, 939–1210.* 1985

J. N. Hillgarth, ed. *Christianity and Paganism, 350–750: The Conversion of Western Europe.* 1986

William Chester Jordan. *From Servitude to Freedom: Manumission in the Sénonais in the Thirteenth Century.* 1986

James William Brodman. *Ransoming Captives in Crusader Spain: The Order of Merced on the Christian-Islamic Frontier.* 1986

Frank Tobin. *Meister Eckhart: Thought and Language.* 1986

Daniel Bornstein, trans. *Dino Compagni's Chronicle of Florence.* 1986

James M. Powell. *Anatomy of a Crusade, 1213–1221.* 1986

Jonathan Riley-Smith. *The First Crusade and the Idea of Crusading.* 1986

Susan Mosher Stuard, ed. *Women in Medieval History and Historiography.* 1987

Avril Henry, ed. *The Mirour of Mans Saluacioune.* 1987

María Rosa Menocal. *The Arabic Role in Medieval Literary History.* 1987

Margaret J. Ehrhart. *The Judgment of the Trojan Prince Paris in Medieval Literature.* 1987

Betsy Bowden. *Chaucer Aloud: The Varieties of Textual Interpretation.* 1987

Michael Resler, trans. *EREC by Hartmann von Aue.* 1987

A. J. Minnis. *Medieval Theory of Authorship.* 1988

Uta-Renate Blumenthal. *The Investiture Controversy: Church and Monarchy from the Ninth to the Twelfth Century.* 1988

Robert Hollander. *Boccaccio's Last Fiction: "Il Corbaccio."* 1988

Ralph Turner. *Men Raised from the Dust: Administrative Service and Upward Mobility in Angevin England.* 1988

David Anderson. *Before the Knight's Tale: Imitation of Classical Epic in Boccaccio's Teseida.* 1988

Charlotte A. Newman. *The Anglo-Norman Nobility in the Reign of Henry I: The Second Generation.* 1988

Joseph F. O'Callaghan. *The Cortes of Castile-León, 1188–1350.* 1989

William D. Paden, ed. *The Voice of the Trobairitz: Essays on the Women Troubadors.* 1989

William Chester Jordan. *The French Monarchy and the Jews: From Philip Augustus to the Last Capetians.* 1989

Edward B. Irving, Jr. *Rereading* Beowulf. 1989

David Burr. *Olivi and Franciscan Poverty: The Origins of the* Usus Pauper *Controversy.* 1989

Willene B. Clark and Meradith T. McMunn, eds. *Beasts and Birds of the Middle Ages: The Bestiary and Its Legacy.* 1989

Richard C. Hoffmann. *Land, Liberties, and Lordship in a Late Medieval Countryside: Agrarian Structures and Change in the Duchy of Wrocław.* 1990

J. M. W. Bean. *From Lord to Patron: Lordship in Late Medieval England.* 1990

Mary F. Wack. *Lovesickness in the Middle Ages: The* Viaticum *and Its Commentaries.* 1990

Robert I. Burns, S. J., ed. *Emperor of Culture: Alfonso X the Learned of Castile and His Thirteenth-Century Renaissance.* 1990

E. Ann Matter. *The Voice of My Beloved: The Song of Songs in Western Medieval Christianity.* 1990

Patricia Terry, trans. *Poems of the Elder Edda.* 1990

Ronald E. Surtz. *The Guitar of God: Gender, Power, and Authority in the Visionary World of Mother Juana de la Cruz (1481–1534).* 1990

Lawrence Nees. *A Tainted Mantle: Hercules and the Classical Tradition at the Carolingian Court.* 1991

Anthony K. Cassell and Victoria Kirkham, eds. and trans. *Diana's Hunt. Caccia di Diana. Boccaccio's First Fiction.* 1991

Ellen E. Kittell. *From* Ad Hoc *to Routine: A Case Study in Medieval Bureaucracy.* 1991

Katherine Fischer Drew, trans. *Laws of the Salian Franks.* 1991

This book was set in Linotron Bembo. A copy of a typeface first used in 1495 for Cardinal Bembo's *De Aetna*, Bembo was first issued by the Monotype Corporation in 1929. Bembo is one of many classic typefaces revived under the direction of Stanley Morison.

Printed on acid-free paper.